Configurations of Comparative Poetics

*Published with the support of the School
of Hawaiian, Asian, and Pacific Studies, University of Hawaiʻi*

Configurations

of Comparative Poetics

Three Perspectives on Western
and Chinese Literary Criticism

ZONG-QI CAI

 UNIVERSITY OF HAWAI'I PRESS • HONOLULU

©2002 UNIVERSITY OF HAWAI'I PRESS
All rights reserved
Printed in the United States of America
07 06 05 04 03 02   6 5 4 3 2 1

Library of Congress Cataloging-in-Publication Data
Cai, Zongqi.
    Configurations of comparative poetics : three perspectives on Western and Chinese literary criticism / Zong-qi Cai.
        p.   cm.
    Includes bibliographical references and index.
    ISBN 0-8248-2338-9 (alk. paper)
    1. Poetics.   2. Literature, Comparative—Chinese and Western.
    3. Literature, Comparative—Western and Chinese.   I. Title.

    PN1042 .C17   2001
    809.1—dc21

                                                            2001041522

University of Hawai'i Press books are printed
on acid-free paper and meet the guidelines for
permanence and durability of the Council on
Library Resources.

Designed by Integrated Composition Systems
Printed by The Maple-Vail Book Manufacturing Group

For Jing Liao

Contents

Acknowledgments

T his book is the fruit of more than one and a half decades of my studies and teaching in comparative and Chinese literature. I wish to thank all my teachers who taught me and guided my work in these two fields, especially Professors Lucien Miller and Cheng Ch'ing-mao of the University of Massachusetts at Amherst and Professors Yu-kung Kao, Earl Miner, Andrew Plaks, and David Quint of Princeton University.

An immediate reason for the birth of this book is the abiding enthusiasm shown for it by Sharon F. Yamamoto, editor at the University of Hawai'i Press. As early as 1992, when I was fresh from graduate school and had only a few published articles to my credit, she expressed an intense interest in the project and worked hard to secure for me an advance contract from the University of Hawai'i Press. In subsequent years, she continued to reaffirm her support at our yearly encounters at the Association for Asian Studies meetings, even though I failed to deliver the manuscript by the due date. Without her unfailing faith and extraordinary patience, I certainly would not have embarked on and struggled my way through this difficult project. After Ms. Yamamoto left for her new position at the East-West Center, Patricia Crosby, executive editor at the University of Hawai'i Press, took over the editing of this book. She gave me just as much support and encouragement. I am particularly grateful to her for allowing me to include an unusually large number of Chinese characters in both the text and the back matter. In addition to Chinese characters for names, terms, and titles, all major citations of Chinese works, except for two extremely long passages, are accompanied by original texts.

I would like to acknowledge a fellowship grant from the Institute of Advanced Study, University of Illinois, in 1997, which gave me valuable uninterrupted time to resume work on this much delayed project. Later the Research Board of the University of Illinois provided me with the funds to enlist the help of Ms. Pi-hsia Hsu, a graduate assistant, in the preparation of the final manuscript.

My special thanks to my two colleagues and friends at Illinois: Leon Chai, for his illuminating comments on the manuscript, and Alexander L. Mayer, for his useful suggestions about the translations of some Buddhist texts. Two anonymous reviewers read through the manuscript very carefully and offered many insightful comments and suggestions; to them both I am greatly indebted.

Part of chapter 2 appeared in "The Making of a Critical System," from Zong-qi Cai, ed., *A Chinese Literary Mind: Culture, Creativity, and Rhetoric in Wenxin diaolong* copyright © 2001 by The Board of Trustees of the Leland Stanford Jr. University, reprinted by permission of Stanford University Press. An earlier version of chapter 5 appeared in "In Quest of Harmony," in *Philosophy East & West* 49, no. 3 (1999): 317–345. Sections of chapter 7 are from "Poundian and Chinese Aesthetics of Dynamic Force," in *Comparative Literature Studies* 30, no. 2: 56–74, copyright © 1993 by The Pennsylvania State University. Portions of chapter 8 appeared in "Derrida and the Madhyamika Buddhism," in *International Philosophical Quarterly* 33, no. 2: 183–195, copyright © 1993 by Fordham University; and in "Derrida and Seng-Zhao," in *Philosophy East & West* 43, no. 3 (1993): 389–404. I am grateful to the editors and publishers for their permission to reprint my work.

Finally, the deepest of my thanks goes to my wife, Jing Liao, to whom the book is dedicated.

Major Chinese Dynasties

Shang	ca. 1600–ca. 1028 B.C.
Zhou	ca. 1027–ca. 256 B.C.
Western Zhou	ca. 1027–771 B.C.
Eastern Zhou	770–256 B.C.
Spring and Autumn period	770–403 B.C.
Warring States period	403–221 B.C.
Qin	221–206 B.C.
Han	206 B.C.–A.D. 220
Former Han	206 B.C.–A.D. 8
Xin (Wang Mang)	A.D. 9–23
Later Han	25–220
Three Kingdoms	220–265
Wei	220–265
Shu	221–263
Wu	222–280
Jin	265–420
Southern and Northern Dynasties	
Southern	420–589
(Liu) Song	420–479
Southern Qi	479–502
Southern Liang	502–557
Southern Chen	557–589
Northern	386–581
Northern Wei	386–534
Eastern Wei	534–550

Northern Dynasties *(continued)*

Western Wei	535–556
Northern Qi	550–577
Northern Zhou	557–581

Sui 581–618

Tang 618–907

Five Dynasties 907–960

Song 960–1279

  Northern Song 960–1127

  Southern Song 1127–1279

Liao 907–1125

Jin 1115–1234

Yuan 1206–1368

Ming 1368–1644

Qing 1616–1911

Prologue

THIS BOOK IS A COMPREHENSIVE COMPARATIVE STUDY OF Western and Chinese poetics, two of the world's major traditions of literary thought that have existed well over two thousand years. The greatest challenge I face in this project is to achieve an optimal balance of scope and depth. The scope must be broad enough to allow me to review the historical development of these long traditions and to formulate my general views about their overriding concerns, their distinctive orientations, and their culture-specific systematics. To gain such a panoramic view, I begin with broad parallel surveys. Promising and indispensable though they are, such surveys are extremely hazardous. The danger of overgeneralization is particularly high as I need to spread my attention over a vast area of inquiry. To minimize this danger, I try my utmost to ensure that the limited amount of material that can be included in my surveys is representative. I focus on the important statements, tenets, or manifestos that are generally considered to define Western and Chinese literary thought at different historical periods. Moreover, I pursue detailed studies of particular subjects and issues central to Western and Chinese poetics at different periods. These thematically focused studies will yield ample concrete illustrations of my general views on Western and Chinese poetics. By combining the broad surveys with these in-depth studies, I believe that a proper balance of scope and depth can be achieved.

The first part of the book, made up of the first four chapters, focuses on the macrocosmic structures of Western and Chinese poetics.[1] The macrocosmic structures of a critical tradition may be understood as constituted by its foundational concepts of literature. The first two chapters provide an overview of major Western and Chinese concepts of literature. Chapter 1 begins with Plato and Aristotle, continues through Wordsworth and Romantic criticism, then moves on to the New Criticism, phenomenological criticism, structuralism, and deconstruction of recent times. Chapter 2 begins with the *Book of Documents,* a Zhou chronicle of legendary and historical events from high antiquity to seventh century B.C., proceeds to the *Spring and Autumn Annals* of sixth century B.C. and the "Great Preface to the *Book of Poetry*" of the Han, and moves on to *Literary Mind and the Carving of Dragons* by Liu Xie of the fifth century. The detailed discussion of these texts is followed by summary accounts of the influential concepts of literature developed from the Six Dynasties to the Qing. In both Western and Chinese traditions, new concepts of literature often arise in response to the broader paradigmatic shifts of cosmological thinking. To better acquaint general English readers with Chinese philosophical traditions, chapter 3 reviews the highlights of several major Chinese cosmological theories that have fostered various early concepts of literature. Synthesizing the findings of the first three chapters, chapter 4 sets forth the systematics of Western and Chinese poetics. Western critics demonstrate an overriding concern with literature's relationship with truth. They constantly reconceptualize literature in relation to truth and develop corresponding conceptual models for investigating particular literary subjects and issues. By contrast, Chinese critics share an overriding concern with literature's role in harmonizing various processes affecting human life. They continuously reconceptualize literature in relation to cosmic and sociopolitical processes and establish various critical tenets centered upon the Dao. By furnishing new centers of reference for critical judgment, Western and Chinese concepts of literature give rise to particular literary theories and movements and therefore set Western and Chinese poetics on their distinctive paths of development.

The second part of the book, chapters 5 to 8, examines microcosmic textures of Western and Chinese poetics. Microcosmic textures may be conceived as a host of particular literary theories crucial to the development of a critical tradition. I shall compare Plato's and Confucius' theories of harmony in chapter 5, the Romantic and Chinese theories of literary creation in chapter 6, the modernist and Chinese theories of the Chinese written character in chapter 7, and the postmodernist and Buddhist theories of deconstruction in chapter 8. These chapters provide in-depth discussions of many critical issues of pivotal importance. Among these issues are mimesis and praxis, intellectual and ethical pursuits, sensory perception and suprasensory imagination, emotion and image, the forces of nature and of subjectivity, metaphor and allegory, graphs and representation or nonrepresentation, the nature and modes of linguistic signification, and so forth. Special effort will be made to show how Western and Chinese critics explore these critical issues within their own conceptual models and therefore yield different yet equally valuable theoretical insights.

Most of these issues lie at the heart of four major movements of Western literature—the classical, the Romantic, the modernist, and the postmodernist. So my discussion of Plato, Wordsworth, Pound, and Derrida can help flesh out what I have said about the constant shifts of critical locus in Western poetics. Many of these issues also are of great importance to the development of Chinese poetics at different periods. Although the Chinese texts discussed in chapters 5 to 8 do not fall into a neat chronological order, they demonstrate the shaping influence of three major schools of Chinese thought—Confucianism, Daoism, and Buddhism—on Chinese poetics. My analysis of these texts serves to testify, reverberate, and amplify my general observations on the shifting loci of Chinese cosmological and literary thought. In short, by discussing the divergences within each tradition as well as between them, I strive to shed light on the inner dynamics of Western and Chinese poetics, sustained by their own evolving differentiae.

The epilogue is devoted to theoretical reflections on the three critical perspectives introduced in this book—the intracultural, the crosscultural, and the transcultural. Each of these perspectives is devised to steer this project clear of particular kinds of flawed approaches and prejudiced views. The intracultural perspective stresses the investigation of the roots and patterns of development of a tradition without explicit comparisons with another tradition. This perspective serves to counter the questionable practice of taking critical issues out of their own cultural contexts and comparing them as if they were universals in a cultural vacuum. The cross-cultural approach emphasizes the need to cross the barriers of cultural biases, especially the polemics of similitude and the polemics of difference that have long plagued West-China comparative studies.[2] The transcultural perspective represents a search for a new, all-embracing interpretive horizon in which we can assess our findings of similarities and differences in ways that enable us to transcend cultural biases and better appreciate our common humanity. These three perspectives help me to explore the dynamic relationship of cultural specificity and commonality in Western and Chinese poetics.

In studies of Western and Chinese poetics, cultural specificity is neglected or misconstrued for different reasons. In the case of Western poetics, it is largely neglected due to the dominant role of Western poetics in the current literary scholarship. Since Western poetics has long been in the powerful position of setting trends of literary scholarship around the world, it is only natural that scholars of Western literature seldom feel the need to reflect upon the cultural specificity of Western poetics. Consequently, some scholars are tempted to take Western critical terms, concepts, and paradigms as universally valid and apply them to studies involving non-Western traditions. For instance, this tendency is quite obvious in some projects of postcolonial cultural studies. Although these projects aim to expose the Western cultural domination over non-Western traditions, they, ironically, are conceived on strictly Western postmodernist paradigms. As shown in chapters 1 and 4, Western poetics is in large measure a product of thinking about literature within truth-based cosmological paradigms. By developing an awareness of this cultural specificity of Western poetics, scholars of Western literature will clearly see the need to go beyond the confines of Western poetics and draw theoretical insights from non-Western critical traditions.

In the case of Chinese poetics, cultural specificity is often misconstrued due to the entrenched practice of evaluating Chinese poetics in terms of its conformity to the Western critical system. Much of the twentieth-century scholarship on Chinese literary criticism is oriented toward a modernization, or rather Westernization, of Chinese literary thought. Modern literary theoreticians not only develop new literary theories modeled on different Western critical schools, they also seek to present traditional Chinese literary thought within the framework of Western poetics. When forced into this framework, however, Chinese critical terms, concepts, and modes do not exhibit the kind of internal coherence demanded of a critical system. This gives rise to a widely held belief that Chinese critical writings are mostly random, impressionistic, and woefully unsystematic. This alleged lack of systematic coherence has been perceived as a prominent, culture-specific feature of Chinese poetics. This is obviously a gross mistake. The cultural specificity of any critical tradition should not be defined negatively in terms of the deficiency, alleged or otherwise, of certain elements valued by other traditions. Rather, cultural specificity should be defined in terms of a tradition's foundational concepts of literature, its pattern of historical development, and its underlying cosmological paradigms. Seen in this light, the cultural specificity of Chinese poetics is anything but lacking in systematic coherence. Rather, it possesses a process-based systematics as opposed to the truth-based systematics of Western poetics. In chapters 2, 3, and 4, we perceive clear patterns of internal coherence on various levels of Chinese critical discourse. We may even reconstruct a nomenclature of Chinese critical terms that are often considered hopelessly elusive. Hopefully, by reflecting upon the cultural specificity of Chinese poetics, scholars of Chinese literature can do a better job systematically introducing it to Western readers.

As long as we treat Western and Chinese poetics on equal footing, we are able to appreciate the cultural specificity of each as evidence of the rich diversity and resourcefulness in our common endeavor to understand literature. To ensure that it will help deepen our sense of commonality, I place my discussion of cultural specificity within a broader field of common critical concerns. As indicated by the titles of chapters 5 to 8, the subjects of my inquiry are not confined by geographical and cultural boundaries. Literature's nature and functions, poetic harmony, and the creative process are obviously subjects of common interest to most, if not all, critical traditions. In comparing Western and Chinese approaches to these subjects, we shall be able to understand them in more diverse ways than known to the Western or Chinese tradition alone.

Indeed, a balanced, constructive dialogue between Western and Chinese poetics can yield enormous benefits of mutual illumination. Whether or not this book succeeds in demonstrating such benefits, I hope it will stimulate scholars of Western and Chinese literature to intensely engage with each other and work together to integrate Chinese and other non-Western poetics into the mainstream of literary scholarship. Such a common endeavor will help us transcend geographical and cultural boundaries and broaden immeasurably the horizon of our critical inquiry in the twenty-first century.

PART I

Macrocosmic Structures
of Western and Chinese Poetics

CHAPTER I

The Orientation of Western Poetics

Conceptualizing Literature as Truth,
Untruth, or Antitruth

To examine the orientation of western poetics, a good place to begin is the grand scheme drawn up by M. H. Abrams to delineate the development of Western critical traditions. In his classic book, *The Mirror and the Lamp,* Abrams conceives of four coordinates of criticism (universe, artist, work, and audience) and arranges them in a triangular diagram (see figure 1), with "work" in the center.

This analytical scheme, Abrams believes, is applicable to all critical theories because "a critic tends to derive from one of these terms his principal categories for defining, classifying, and analyzing a work of art, as well as major criteria by which he judges its value."[1] As he situates diverse critical theories inside this scheme, Abrams finds that they fall into four broad categories under the four terms mimetic, pragmatic, expressive, and formal theories. For Abrams, the successive rise of these four categories signifies the shift of critical attention from the universe in classical and neoclassical times, to the reader in the writings of Horace, Cicero, Sir Philip Sidney, and Dryden, to the author in the Romantic era, and to the text in post-Romantic periods.[2] If we view this historical development within Abrams' diagram, we may claim that a continual shift of critical locus among the four terms represents the fundamental orientation of Western poetics.

Abrams' analytical diagram, though somewhat dated and challenged by a number of critics, is still the most serviceable one for our comprehensive survey of Western poetics.[3] In this diagram, we can not

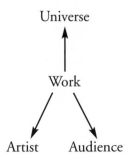

Figure 1. Four Coordinates
of Criticism

only perceive the shifting loci of Western poetics but also trace the inherent relationship between Western poetics and Western philosophical thinking. In noting that each of the four terms is an integral part of an "explicit or implicit 'worldview,'"[4] Abrams invites us to contemplate the broader intellectual developments that have given rise to the four categories of critical theory. In my opinion, the shaping influence of Western philosophical thinking on Western critics is most clearly reflected in their continual practice of making truth-, untruth-, or antitruth-claims about literature. The question of truth, the central issue of Western philosophy, has dominated Western critical discourse from Plato to our time. Literature has always been conceptualized as a form of truth or untruth in relation to the ultimate reality (truth or antitruth) as defined by a given philosophical tradition. Influenced by ever emerging philosophical concepts of the ultimate truth or antitruth, Western critics have variously conceptualized literature as mimetic truth, expressive truth, ontic truth, phenomenological truth, deconstructive antitruth, and so forth during different historical periods. As shown below, some of these concepts of literature are, as in the case of Plato and Aristotle, nothing but variants of philosophical truth-claims made by the same thinkers. Others, though not made by philosopher-critics, nevertheless reveal the influence of certain truth-claims made in philosophical realms. These concepts of literature provide changing criteria "for defining, classifying, and analyzing a work of art," and bring about continual shifts of critical locus among the four terms. As these concepts of literature undergird the development of major Western critical theories, we should carefully examine them and seek insight into the inner dynamics of the development of Western poetics.

LITERATURE AS MIMETIC TRUTH OR UNTRUTH

It is generally believed that there are three basic meanings of the word "truth" in the English language. As summarized by Eliot Deutsch, they are (1) "truth as reality, truth as being—*truth as opposed to nonbeing or the purely fictional*"; (2) "truth as the conformity of the thing to our idea, definition, or conception of the thing—*truth as opposed to the counterfeit, the fake*"; and (3) truth "as a property of a statement, proposition, or belief, usually as the linguistic or mental entity is thought to correspond to or with what is in fact the case—*truth as opposed to the erroneous, the false.*"[5] In conceptualizing the nature of literature, Western critics employ the word "truth" primarily with the first two of these meanings. Their conceptualization of literature normally involves an evaluation of the "truthfulness" (second meaning) of literature to the ultimate truth (the first meaning) or its contemporary metamorphosis, the ultimate antitruth. When commenting on specific qualities of a given literary work, however, Western critics tend to avail themselves of the third meaning as well. The following discussion of truth-claims pertains mainly to the first two meanings of "truth."

The concept of literature as truth (or untruth) is as old as Western literature itself. It can be traced to Hesiod, who believes "the end of poetry is to impart truth" and who repudiates the concept expressed in Homer that "poetry charms and delights."[6] In making their truth-claim about poetry, Hesiod and his followers stir up what Plato calls the "ancient quarrel between philosophy and poetry" involving, among others, Solon, Parmenides, Pindar, Aristophanes, and Plato himself.[7] In this ancient quarrel, it is Plato who turns the tide against poetry and establishes the philosophical question of truth as the central issue in Western discussions of literature. As William C. Greene judiciously points out, "The first and most persistent question that Plato set himself with regard to poetry was the question of truth: how is the truth of poetry related to the truth of ordinary everyday life, or to scientific truth, and from what source does the poet gain his knowledge and his authority?"[8]

Whitehead's famous remark that "all Western philosophies are footnotes to Plato" is perhaps the most emphatic, most frequently quoted statement made on the enduring legacy of Plato. If Plato deserves this tribute, he does so for his conception of a dualistic ontological paradigm more than for anything else. His ontological paradigm consists in a separation of a permanent, determining existence from a changing, determined existence. In designing this dualistic ontological paradigm, Plato seeks not only to make intelligible the ultimate reality but also to create a cosmic order that unifies all things, from the heavenly gods down to minuscule phenomena here on earth, through a laborious hierarchization of their gradually diminishing likeness or truthfulness to the Divine Maker.[9]

Plato conceptualizes literature in the same way as he does any other phenomena within the dualistic, truth-based paradigm. In *Ion* and book 10 of the *Republic,* Plato rejects poetry outright on account of its appeal to imagination, the base part of the mind, and its inability to convey, the absolute truth. In the earlier books of the *Republic* and in *Timaeus* and the *Laws,* he gives his conditional acceptance of Homeric tales and the like because they are capable of representing the truth of everyday life. His less known praise of the muse in his early works like *Phaedrus* and the *Symposium* is a tacit admission of the possibility of direct cognition of the absolute truth through artistic intuition. As all these views are discussed in detail in chapter 4, I shall limit my present discussion to the best known and most influential of these views—Plato's relentless denunciation of poetry in the tenth book of the *Republic:*

> [H]e [the poet] is like him [the painter] in two ways: first, inasmuch as his creations have an inferior degree of truth—in this, I say, he is like him: and he is also like him in being concerned with an inferior part of the soul; and therefore we shall be right in refusing to admit him into a well-ordered State, because he awakens and nourishes and strengthens the feelings and impairs the reason. . . . The imitative poet implants an evil constitution, for he indulges the irrational nature which has no discernment of greater and less, but thinks the same thing at one time great and at another small—he is a manufacturer of images and is very far removed from the truth.[10]

Here Plato explains the two related reasons for his banishment of poetry from his ideal Republic. First, poetic imitations are, like paintings, "thrice removed from the truth, and could easily be made without any knowledge of the truth."[11] Second, they not only manufacture false images of the truth, but also impair the reason, the very faculty for the cognition of truth, through an indulgence in feelings or the irrational part of the soul. This definition of poetry as an inferior imitation is hardly accepted by later critics, but it sets up a relational paradigm in which they conceptualize the nature of poetry. Indeed, his definition of poetry in relation to truth constitutes what we may call the originating Western conception of literature. All subsequent Western conceptions of literature are in great measure explanations, modifications, or reformulations of this originating conception.

Such a profound, determinative effect of Plato's conception of literature is immediately conspicuous in the writings of his pupil Aristotle. Like Plato, Aristotle investigates the nature of literature in relation to truth. In using this relational scheme of Plato, however, Aristotle redefines both of its terms. While Plato sees truth as the universal (ideas) of which the phenomenal world is a mere reflection, Aristotle conceives truth to be the pure form and pure actuality, toward which the matter (potentiality) of the phenomenal world evolves. According to him, the matter is merely a potentiality that becomes actualized by the inner necessity, and through the acquisition, of form. In *Metaphysics* Aristotle criticizes Plato's notion of universals and seeks to differentiate his forms from them. He stresses that his forms are substantial as Plato's universals are not. However, as Bertrand Russell points out, "The view that forms are substances, which exist independently of the matter in which they are exemplified, seems to expose Aristotle to his own argument against Platonic ideas. A form is intended by Aristotle to be something quite different from a universal, but it has many of the same characteristics."[12] In *Poetics,* Aristotle obviously slips into Plato's notion of universals when he talks about poetry's relationship to the universal vis-à-vis history's relationship to the particular:

> It is also evident from what has been said that it is not the poet's function to relate actual events, but the *kinds* of things that might occur and are possible in terms of probability of necessity. The difference between the historian and the poet is not that between using verse or prose; Herodotus' work could be versified and would be just as much a kind of history in verse as in prose. No, the difference is this: that the one relates actual events, the other the kinds of things that might occur. Consequently, poetry is more philosophical and more elevated than history, since poetry relates more of the universal, while history relates particulars. "Universal" means the kinds of things which it suits a certain kind of person to say or do, in terms of probability or necessity: poetry aims for this, even though attaching names to the agents. A "particular" means, say, what Alcibiades did or experienced.[13]

Although he follows Plato in evaluating literature in relation to the universals, Aristotle reaches a conclusion directly opposite to his teacher's. Whereas Plato regards literature as a more remote and hence inferior imitation of the truth than the external world, Aristotle takes literature to be a closer and hence superior imitation of the ultimate truth than the external world. He explains that poetry represents a higher order of truth than actual life because it does not tell of what has happened but what may happen according to the law of necessity or probability. According to him, what has happened belongs to the realm of particulars; what may happen or ought to happen pertains to the workings of the universal. Insofar as poetry tells of what may or ought to happen by means of its free arrangement of events, historical or fictional, it must of necessity stand closer to the universal than actual life and hence should be seen as a higher mimetic truth. Given this, Aristotle sees fit to claim that "poetry is more philosophical and more elevated than history." In light of this new conception of literature, Aristotle attaches supreme importance to plot, which is for him the primary artistic means of transcending the actuality of life and revealing its inner necessity or truth. Moreover, he confers an all-important status on tragedy, a genre that excels in revealing the universal truth of human life through plot arrangement.

LITERATURE AS EXPRESSIVE TRUTH

If Aristotle elevates poetry to a status higher than the external world and redefines it as a superior mimetic truth, Wordsworth, the standard-bearer of the Romantic movement in the nineteenth century, raises poetry to a still higher place or, in fact, the highest possible place in the scale of human knowledge: He identifies poetry with the truth itself. In his "Preface to *Lyrical Ballads*," a manifesto against the dominant classical and neoclassical ideas, he gives an eloquent elucidation of his new conception of literature as expressive truth:

> Aristotle, I have been told, hath said, that poetry is the most philosophic of all writing; it is so: its object is truth, not individual and local, but general, and operative; not standing upon external testimony, but carried alive into the heart by passion; truth which is its own testimony, which gives strength and divinity to the tribunal to which it appeals, and receives them from the same tribunal . . . Poetry is the breath and finer spirit of all knowledge; it is the impassioned expression which is in the countenance of all Science. . . . Poetry is the first and last of all knowledge.[14]

It is interesting to note that here Wordsworth first aligns himself with Aristotle, the arch exponent of the mimetic theories he rebels against, and cites his well-known claim of poetry's superiority over history. This invocation of Aristotle seems to be at once sincere and ironic—sincere because Wordsworth does want to line up Aristotle as a major defender of poetry against Plato's accusation and thereby gain more authority for his own theory, and ironic because he cites Aristotle's conception of literature only for the purpose of demolishing it. There are three notable evidences of his surreptitious cannibalization of Aristotle's conception in this passage.

First, Wordsworth misquotes Aristotle as saying "poetry is the most philosophic of all writing," whereas Aristotle only says "poetry is more philosophical and more elevated than history." This seemingly innocent change from "more philosophical" to "the most philosophical" marks a quantum leap from an apology for poetry in Aristotle to a glorification of it by Wordsworth and other Romantics. Second, he pays lip service to Aristotle's idea of truth as "not local and individual, but general and operative," for he endeavors in *Lyrical Ballads* to reveal truth through "local and individual" situations in humble rustic life, not by building a plot on the generalized rules of conduct laid down by Aristotle. This relocation of the universal in the particular signifies a radical departure from the classical and neoclassical concern with the universal in and of itself to the Romantic preoccupation with the universal in the particular—a shift that has already been evident in Blake's visionary poetry and is to culminate in Coleridge's theory of the symbol. Third, Wordsworth goes on to repudiate the conception of mimetic truth held by Aristotle as well as all other classical and neoclassical theorists—and he does so as if he were elaborating on an idea of Aristotle's. Indeed, when Wordsworth says that poetry conveys the truth that is its own testimony "carried alive into the heart," an uninformed reader may very well mistake his remarks as a paraphrase of Aristotle's view. For a reader familiar with Western critical tradition, however, it is not difficult to tell that they represent a revolutionary claim for poetry made by Wordsworth himself. Before this time few Western critics dared to make so complete a break with the mimetic tradition and regard poetry as a revelation of the truth in the heart of a poet.[15] Nor would they entertain so vehemently the notion of a union of human feeling and the truth as did Wordsworth. As pointed out earlier, Plato denounces feeling as something that belongs to the irrational part of the soul and holds it responsible for the distortion of the truth in poetry. Even though Aristotle establishes the legitimacy of feelings for tragedy, he leaves no doubt that feelings, pity and fear in particular, are useful only to the extent that the audience may be purged of them through watching them played out on the stage. Such a distrust of feeling is entrenched in classical and neoclassical criticism and persists to the time of Wordsworth.

Viewed against the dominance of mimetic theories for more than two millennia, Wordsworth's declarations that poetry is "the spontaneous overflow of powerful emotions" and is "the first and last of knowledge" amount to nothing less than a revolutionary breakthrough in Western critical thinking. His new conception of literature as expressive truth has far-reaching practical and theoretical ramifications for the reorientation of Western criticism toward the poet or the author during the nineteenth century. In practical criticism, this conception leads to the revitalization and privileging of the long neglected genre of lyric that deals chiefly with inward feelings. Theoretically, this conception lays the ground for the emergence and dominance of four closely related constants in high Romantic criticism: (1) a worship of the poet as a genius or a divine being who delivers truth to mankind through creative imagination,[16] (2) an ardent celebration of feeling, (3) a glorification of poetry as the abode of the truth, and (4) an espousal of the ideal of the universal in the particular.

Of these four constants of Romantic criticism, the first lost its appeal rather quickly. An unfavorable reaction to the excessive worship of the poet is already evident in the critical writings of late Romantics. While the high Romantics most often foreground their worship of poets—whom Shelley, for instance, calls "the institutors of laws, and the founders of civil society, and the inventors of the arts of life . . . legislator and prophets"[17]—some late Romantics tend to leave out such an idealization of poets in their glorification of poetry. This shift away from the poet becomes very conspicuous in the famous essay "The Study of Poetry" by the Victorian critic Matthew Arnold:

> Only one thing we may add as to the substance and matter of poetry, guiding ourselves by Aristotle's profound observation that the superiority of poetry over history consists in its possessing a higher truth and a higher seriousness (φιλοσοφώτερον χαὶ σπουδαιότεροι). Let us add, therefore, to what we have said, this: that the substance and matter of the best poetry acquire their special character from possessing, in an eminent degree, truth and seriousness.[18]

Here Arnold seems to praise poetry in the vein of the high Romantics. Upon close examination, however, we can see an important difference. Most high Romantics enshrine poetry mainly on the grounds that it is the brainchild of a poet as a cultural hero or even world-soul and captures the transcendental flight of the poet's divine imagination.[19] But for Arnold, poetry deserves to be accorded the highest possible status because it constitutes the artistic truth of our real life, a truth that surpasses the sum total of all practical truths. It is poetry in and of itself, not the poet's "egotistical sublime," that possesses "in an eminent degree, truth and seriousness." So, in place of the deified poet, Arnold seeks to enshrine poetry as a substitute for religion and philosophy. "We should conceive of poetry worthily," he writes, "and more highly than it has been the custom to conceive of it. We should conceive of it as capable of higher uses, and called to higher destinies, than those which in general men have assigned to it hitherto. More and more mankind will discover that we have to turn to poetry to interpret life for us, to console us, to sustain us. Without poetry, our science will appear incomplete; and most of what now passes with us for religion and philosophy will be replaced by poetry."[20]

This foregrounding of poetry at the expense of the poet is aptly reflected in Arnold's exercise of practical criticism. In discussing Wordsworth's works, for instance, he rebukes those who mistook Wordsworth's idiosyncratic philosophy for poetic excellence[21] and calls our attention to the artistic qualities of his poetry. To Arnold, what makes Wordsworth's poetry great is not the poet's emotional and intellectual life, but "the successful balance, in Wordsworth, of profound truth of subject with profound truth of execution."[22] It is to bring out such intrinsic artistic qualities that Arnold develops his touchstone method of criticism. If we compare Arnold's studies of Wordsworth and other poets with, say, the studies of Shakespeare by pre-Romantic and Romantic critics,[23] we see that Arnold decidedly weaned himself away from the long tradition of Romantic poet-worship and redirected his attention toward the work itself. Seen in a broader historical perspective, Arnold's critical reorientation sets the stage for new concepts of literature as ontic truth to emerge in the twentieth century.

LITERATURE AS ONTIC TRUTH

The first half of the twentieth century witnesses the rise of numerous concepts of literature as ontic truth.[24] These new concepts of literature coincide with a continued reaction against the tenets of Romantic criticism and undergird the development of text-oriented theories ranging from Anglo-Saxon practical criticism to Russian formalism and American New Criticism. In launching their own concepts of literature, the exponents of these text-oriented theories usually mark their points of departure by denouncing the Romantic concepts of the author. T. S. Eliot is among the first to practice this rite of "author-bashing." In his pioneering essay, "Tradition and Individual Talent," Eliot launches a full-scale attack on the Romantic notion of the poet's emotion as the essence of poetry.

> Poetry is not a turning loose of emotion, but an escape from emotion; it is not the expression of personality, but an escape from personality. . . . To divert interest from the poet to the poetry is a laudable aim: for it would conduce to a juster estimation of actual poetry, good or bad . . . emotion which has its life in the poem and not in the history of the poet. The emotion of art is impersonal.[25]

If Arnold merely deplored excessive poet-worship, Eliot issues an open call for the banishment of the poet, or at least the poet's emotion, from the center of criticism. While granting the Romantic emphasis on emotion, Eliot nevertheless seeks to separate it from the poet and redefine it as an artistic crystallization of "numberless feelings, phrases, images" in what he calls "the mind of Europe."[26] While Eliot locates the meaning and value of a literary work in its dynamic relationship with European literary and intellectual traditions as a whole, I. A. Richards and William Empson look for the same exclusively in the text itself (in the emotive use of language for Richards and the exploitation of ambiguities for Empson) and develop new techniques of close reading. This expulsion of the poet from the critical center poses this question to all critics: After the departure of the poet as the purported conveyor of truth, is there still truth in literature? Probably out of a natural apathy to high-flown Romantic ontological claims, these British critics do not deal with this question and refrain from conceptualizing literature as a new kind of truth. They seem quite content to address, without any ontological pretensions, the practical issue of meaning and value in individual works.

The philosophical question of truth returns to center stage in the writings of the first generation of American New Critics, led by Allen Tate and John Crowe Ransom. Associated with the agrarian revival in the southern United States, these New Critics seek to accomplish what Matthew Arnold attempted to do—to enshrine poetry as ontic truth that can, in Arnold's words, "console us" and "sustain us" against the onslaught of science and industrialization. Where Arnold depended on his impressionistic or intuitive "touchstone" method to locate the ontic truth of poetry, Ransom avails himself of analytical close reading to achieve the same goal. For Ransom, it is only in concrete poetic images (as opposed to abstract ideas of science and philosophy) that a critic can find the truth of life or "the object which is real, individual and qualitatively infinite."[27] When a critic undertakes a close reading of an individual poem, Ransom argues that the critic "should regard the poem as nothing short of a desperate ontological and metaphysical manoeuvre."[28] The primary aim of formal study, Ransom maintains, is not to find the meaning and value of a text in question but to discover the truth for human life in general. Ransom's conception of literature as ontic truth provides a much needed theoretical grounding for the more sophisticated studies of poetic language and form to be undertaken by the second generation of American New Critics, including Cleanth Brooks, Robert Penn Warren, W. K. Wimsatt, and Monroe Beardsley.

> Literature gives us a picture of life—not the picture that science gives and not a picture that is actually (historically) true, but a picture that has its own kind of truth—a "truth" that includes important elements that science, from its very nature, is forced to leave out. The "truth" of literature takes the form, not of abstract statement, but of a concrete and dramatic presentation; which may allow us to experience imaginatively the "lived" meanings of a piece of life. . . . We shall be constantly concerned with the implications of this fact. We shall be concerned not only because questions of form are in themselves important, but because without an understanding of, and feeling for, form, we can never grasp the human significance of literature.[29]

This long passage by Brooks, Purser, and Warren spells out the significance of New Critical investigation of literary form as an "ontological and metaphysical manoeuvre." In their common search for the ontic truth in literary form, Brooks, Purser, and Warren tend to focus on examining the unifying principle of form in a literary text. However, they have different ideas as to what constitutes such a principle. Cleanth Brooks holds that "the truth which the poet utters can be approached only in terms of paradox," ambiguity, and irony.[30] These structuring devices effect a disruption of commonplace conceptual frames and bring about a new organic unity of heterogeneous meanings on an artistic plane. This new organic structure of meanings is none other than what he and Purser and Warren call the truth of life crystallized in "the vivid and moving form" of literature.[31] Instead of paradox and irony, W. K. Wimsatt adopts the nineteenth-century concept of a "concrete universal" to indicate the organic unity of diverse and often conflicting parts in a poetic text.[32]

For René Wellek and Austin Warren, the unifying principle of form does not function merely on a single plane, as do Brooks' "paradox" and Wimsatt's "concrete universal." Rather, it is "gestalt," or what they call a system of "norms" that governs the workings of various strata of a text (sound stratum, rhetorical stratum, and so forth) and meanwhile brings all these strata into an organic whole. Having discerned such a stratified structure, these two critics feel confident enough to declare that the work of art "is an object of *knowledge sui generis* which has a special ontological status. It is neither real (physical, like a statue) nor mental (psychological, like the experience of light or pain) nor ideal (like a triangle). It is a system of norms of ideal concepts which are intersubjective."[33] Believing that they alone are capable of providing a taxonomic description of the ontological essence of literary form, Wellek and Austin Warren claim superiority for their own critical orientation. They label all other critical schools as "extrinsic studies" that reveal merely relative, historically confined truths such as "psychological truth," "social truth," and others.[34] In contrast, they describe their own critical pursuit as "intrinsic study" that sheds light on the absolute, ontological truth.

Wellek and Austin Warren's taxonomic description of form represents the most sophisticated analysis of the ontic truth of literature ever made by the New Critics. Their sweeping attack on all extrinsic studies of literature betokens a broad triumph of New Criticism over other existing theories of literature in the mid-twentieth century. However, Wellek and Austin Warren, in their zealous efforts to make New Criticism less polemic and more systematic and scientific, unwittingly venture beyond the boundaries of New Criticism and embrace two structuralist or quasi-structuralist concepts—the "generality" and the "intersubjectivity" of the ontic truth of literature. Indeed, their theory presages the structuralists' effort to formulate even more radical conceptions of ontic truth than those developed by New Critics.

LITERATURE AS PHENOMENOLOGICAL TRUTH

The rise of phenomenological criticism may be seen as a reaction against the formalist trends like New Criticism. Whereas New Critics regard literary form and language as the abode of ontic truth, phenomenological critics relate the reading process to an engagement with phenomenological truth or the pure Cogito.

Husserl considers both psychical experience and spatiotemporal objects to exist only relatively, and assigns ultimate existence to the pure

Cogito, which emerges from a phenomenological engagement (that is, what he calls eidetic and transcendental reductions) of subject and object. Maurice Merleau-Ponty gives an exposition of this phenomenological belief in the interaction or even fusion of subjective and objective horizons:

> We have the experience of a world, not understood as a system of relations which wholly determine each event, but as an open totality the synthesis of which is inexhaustible. . . . From the moment that experience—that is, the opening on to our *de facto* world—is recognized as the beginning of knowledge, there is no longer any way of distinguishing a level of *a priori* truths and one of factual ones, what the world must necessarily be and what it actually is.[35]

Inspired by the Husserlian worldview, phenomenological critics direct serious critical attention to the reading process. These critics believe that the ultimate reality, the pure Cogito, emerges through a realization of the intentionality of objects in a mental state untainted by rational concepts and categories. In their opinion, the reading of a literary text approximates such a phenomenological process because it effectively dissolves the barrier between subject and object. In the course of reading, the object of print, the authorial consciousness, and the reading subject merge into a new, transpersonal consciousness. Although Georges Poulet generally is known to be more interested in the *"critique de conscience"* than the analysis of reader's response, he offers some illuminating comments on the phenomenological implications of reading:

> And so I ought not to hesitate to recognize that so long as it is animated by this vital inbreathing inspired by the act of reading, a work of literature becomes (at the expense of the reader whose own life it suspends) a sort of human being, that is a mind conscious of itself and constituting itself in me as the subject of its own objects.[36]

While adopting the phenomenological paradigm of subject-object relationship for their examination of reading, phenomenological critics hold different views about the dynamics and consequence of reading. For Roman Ingarden, the dynamics of reading should be understood in terms of an aesthetic concretization of the structural gestalt of a literary text. In his writings he provides a highly schematic anatomy of literary structure and aesthetic concretization.

Ingarden contends that every literary work is a stratified structure composed of four interrelated strata: sound-formations, meaning-units, schematized aspects, and presented world. The first three strata each possess aesthetic as well as material qualities. The aesthetic value qualities of these three strata are called, respectively, sound-configuration, sense-correlate, and ready aspects. Abstracted or bracketed from the material qualities of their respective strata, these value qualities each provide the material base for abstracting the value quality at a higher stratum. For instance, the function of sound-configuration is, as Eugene H. Falk says, "to provide a material base for all other layers, and most immediately for the layer of meaning-units."[37] Then, the confluence of the first three strata results in the highest stratum, the presented world. According to Ingarden, "This presented world has its own life, its own truth, and its own idea, governed by 'organic' structural functions and aesthetic interdependencies that can indeed endow the presented world with the semblance of autonomy that is all its own."[38] This autonomy is none other than what Ingarden calls the view of life or metaphysical qualities, perhaps identifiable with the phenomenological truth. Describing how metaphysical qualities emerge from our intuition of the successive strata of aesthetic value qualities in the course of reading, Ingarden writes:

> These 'metaphysical' qualities—as we would like to call them—which reveal themselves from time to time are what makes life worth living, and, whether we wish it or not, a secret longing for their concrete revelation lives in us and drives us in all our affairs and days. Their revelation constitutes the summit and the very depths of existence. . . . If the manifestation of a metaphysical quality is effected by the cooperation, not only of the object stratum, but also indirectly of all the remaining strata of a literary work of art, this again shows that, despite the stratified structure, the literary work of art forms an *organic* unity. And obversely: if the manifestation of a metaphysical quality is to occur, the strata must cooperate harmoniously in a determinate way and fulfill specific conditions. In particular, the polyphony of value qualities must not merely show a harmony that permits the appearance of a metaphysical quality; instead, it must be harmoniously compatible with it, so that the given metaphysical quality is *required* by the harmony as a complementing element.[39]

Ingarden's gestalt of four interrelated strata is in all likelihood the model of the stratified structure conceived by Wellek and Austin Warren, as his notion of an "organic unity" of literary strata lies at the heart of their theory of literature. The first German edition of Ingarden's

The Literary Work of Art was published in 1931 and his *Cognition of the Literary Work* first appeared in Polish in 1937. These two books pre-date Wellek and Warren's *Theory of Literature* by many years. Wellek and Warren were quite familiar with Ingarden's works, as they mentioned his name twice in *Theory of Literature*. It is very easy for us to overlook Wellek and Warren's debt to Ingarden because his works did not become widely known until they were extensively translated into English in the 1960s and 1970s. According to Ingarden himself, this oversight is at least in part due to Wellek and Warren's failure to fully acknowledge their debt to him. In the preface to the third German edition of *The Literary Work of Art*, Ingarden writes, "The title of my work is mentioned several times in the notes and in the bibliography, but a reader unacquainted with it cannot gather from that the degree to which René Wellek's book relies on my arguments."[40]

In any case, there is some resemblance between Ingarden's gestalt and Wellek and Warren's paradigm as both involve an extensive use of noninterpretive, linguistic terms and exhibit a strong schematic feature. However, Ingarden's gestalt is essentially different from the New Critical as well as the structuralist models of literary structure that were developed later. It does not entail the operation of an overarching rhetorical principle such as paradox or irony, nor the proliferation of structuralist binarisms predicated on the *langue/parole* dichotomy. Rather, it involves successive intentional acts of consciousness, or a process of phenomenological reduction, leading to the cognition of what Ingarden calls simple qualities or essences (sound-configuration, sentence-correlate, ready-aspect) and derived essences (metaphysical quality) that emerges from the interface of these simple essences.

If Ingarden's reinstitution of the subject is evident in his anatomy of the structural gestalt, it is even more conspicuous in his analysis of what he calls the aesthetic concretization of the structural gestalt. New Critics seldom explicitly acknowledge the fact that the structure of a literary work is to a great extent a mental construct of an interpretive reader, although they themselves always play such a readerly role in their practical criticism. Later, structuralists are to dismiss the relevance of interpretation to literary study and hence it is out of the question for them to talk about the role of the reader in conjunction with their study of literary structure. By contrast, Ingarden attaches great importance to the reader's role. According to Ingarden, the reconstruction of a structural gestalt only completes the pre-aesthetic investigation of a work. The critic must next cast himself in the role of a perceptive reader and bring the work to life through a series of aesthetically significant concretizations of its structural gestalt. After this the critic must "move from the aesthetic attitude, in which his concretizations are carried out, to the aesthetic-reflective cognition of the results of his aesthetic concretizations."[41] By so doing, the critic can not only draw attention "to the richness of potentialities contained in the schema of a work,"[42] but also show how to realize those rich potentialities by properly filling gaps and points of indeterminacy on all levels of cognitive, concretizing acts.[43]

If Ingarden divides his attention between the pre-aesthetic analysis and the aesthetic concretization of literature, many later phenomenological critics focus their attention on the latter issue of aesthetic concretization. Poulet, for instance, devotes himself to a study of aesthetic concretization as intentional acts of consciousness. He argues that, by filling the gaps and indeterminacies within a schematic structure, one not only derives intense aesthetic pleasure but actually reenacts the intentional acts of consciousness:

> As soon as I replace my direct perception of reality by the words of a book, I deliver myself, bound hand and foot, to the omnipotence of fiction. I say farewell to what is, in order to feign belief in what is not. I surround myself with fictitious beings; I become the prey of language. There is no escaping this take-over. Language surrounds me with its unreality. On the other hand, the transmutation through language of reality into a fictional equivalent, has undeniable advantages. The universe of fiction is infinitely more elastic than the world of objective reality. It lends itself to any use: It yields with little resistance to the importunities of the mind. Moreover—and of all its benefits I find this the most appealing—this interior universe constituted by language does not seem radically opposed to the me who thinks it. Doubtless what I glimpse through the words, are mental forms not divested of an appearance of objectivity. But they do not seem to be of another nature than my mind which thinks them. They are objects, but subjectified objects. In short, since every thing has become part of my mind thanks to the intervention of language, the opposition between the subject and its objects has been considerably attenuated. And thus the greatest advantage of literature is that I am persuaded by it that I am free from my usual sense of incompatibility between my consciousness and its objects.[44]

Here Poulet redefines reading as an experience identical to the phenomenological process described by Merleau-Ponty. For Poulet the reading of literature does not merely afford emotional and aesthetic experiences, moral lessons, and intellectual ideas. In the process of reading, Poulet seems to suggest, we can experience a new consciousness emerging in the virtual space of our own thought, the objects of print, and the authorial consciousness. Since this new consciousness transcends the separation between subject and object, between the fictional and the actual, it approximates to the pure Cogito or the ultimate truth as envisioned by phenomenologists like Husserl and Merleau-Ponty. In a broader sense, such an idea of reading represents a significant reconceptualization of literature as phenomenological truth. Indeed, the phenomenological conception of literature is distinguished by its departure from the long tradition of presenting truth as the alien other for us to perceive—that is, as an absolute entity existing out there in the universe, in the author's mind, or in the workings of a particular text or language as a whole. Phenomenological critics like Poulet seem to believe that truth co-arises and is inseparably bound up with our perceptual experience exemplified by the reading of literature. In other words, literature, or to be exact the reading of it, approximates to the coming-into-being of phenomenological truth.

In examining the reading process, Wolfgang Iser largely shies away from the issue of phenomenological consciousness and focuses instead on examining the dynamics of reading. According to him, reading is not a process of surrendering one's consciousness to a new consciousness almost identifiable with the pure Cogito (as Poulet would have it). Nor is it a process of achieving "aesthetic concretizations" of the schema of a work, as Ingarden argues. Rather, it is a dynamic process of recreation:

> The production of the meaning of literary texts—which we discussed in connection with forming the "gestalt" of the text—does not merely entail the discovery of the unformulated, which can then be taken over by the active imagination of the reader; it also entails the possibility that we may formulate ourselves and so discover what had previously seemed to elude our consciousness. These are the ways in which reading literature gives us the chance to formulate the unformulated.[45]

In explaining the "unformulated," Iser utilizes Ingarden's ideas of gaps and indeterminacies within the "gestalt" of a text. However, his view on the realization of the unformulated is different from Ingarden's. For Ingarden, gaps and indeterminacies are to be filled in an orderly, well-structured manner as determined by the work's gestalt itself. Thus there is not much need for re-creation on the part of the reader. But for Iser, reading is anything but a rigidly structured cognitive process. "The act of recreation," he argues, "is not a smooth or continuous process, but one which, in its essence, relies on *interruptions* of the flow to render it efficacious. We look forward, we look back, we decide, we change our decisions, we form expectations, we are shocked by their non-fulfillment, we question, we muse, we accept, we reject."[46] Probably because of his emphasis on the reader's dynamic recreative role, Iser becomes better known as an archexponent of the reader-response theory than as a practitioner of phenomenological criticism.

LITERATURE AS SEMIOTIC TRUTH

The advent of structuralist criticism marks the culmination of the development of text-oriented theories in the twentieth century. Structuralist criticism constitutes formalism in its pure, extreme form. It is characterized by its singular inquiry into the system of linguistic signification and by its sweeping exclusion of practically all issues hitherto central to literary criticism. It does not merely lay aside any consideration of authorial experience and the outside world as do earlier formalist theories. It also dismisses as irrelevant the issue of aesthetic structure and interpretation, the main object of investigation by New Critics.

Seen from a broader historical perspective, structuralist criticism represents a continued rebellion against the legacy of Romantic criticism. However, their rebellion is much more radical than the New Critics'. As shown above, most New Critics still adhere to two constants of Romantic Criticism—"particularity" and "subjectivity." They, like the Romantics, champion the idea of concrete universal and search for the truth of the world in a particular text. For them, this truth is subjective in the sense that it is realized in the mind of an individual, even though they now take that individual to be not a creative Romantic poet but an analytical-minded interpreter of literary form. However, these two constants of Romantic criticism are to disappear when structuralist criticism arrives on the scene.

Structuralist criticism is founded on Ferdinand de Saussure's theory of *parole* and *langue.* Structuralist critics believe that the ontic truth is to be found not in the matrix of a particular text (*parole,*) but in a semiotic system (*langue*) governing all texts. For them, the cognition of this ontic truth entails not the making of subjective aesthetic judgments about a particular text but an investigation of intersubjective conventions of signification that govern the functioning of all texts. Commenting on this structuralist transcendence of "particularity" and "subjectivity," Jonathan Culler writes:

> The type of literary study which structuralism helps one to envisage would not be primarily interpretive; it would not offer a method which, when applied to literary works, produced new and hitherto unexpected meanings. Rather than a criticism which discovers or assigns meanings, it would be a poetics which strives to define the conditions of meanings. . . . The study of literature, as opposed to the perusal and discussion of individual works, would become an attempt to understand the conventions which make literature possible.[47]

Interestingly, structuralist critics, in relocating the ontic truth from a particular aesthetic structure to a general semiotic system, seem to have retraced the paths of New Critics and Romantics and returned to the classical ideal of an objective, universal truth. As Roland Barthes observes, the goal of all structuralist activity is to reconstruct an "object" (a semiotic system) by making manifest its rules of functioning:

> Structure is therefore actually a *simulacrum* of the object, but a directed, interested *simulacrum,* since the imitated object makes something appear which remained invisible, or if one prefers, unintelligible in the natural object. Structural man takes the real, decomposes it, then recomposes it; . . . the simulacrum is intellect added to object, and this addition has an anthropological value, in that it is man himself, his history, his situation, his freedom and the very resistance nature offers to his mind.[48]

Here Roland Barthes uses "imitation," a term debunked by Romantics and New Critics alike, to characterize the structuralist activity. He calls the structuralist reconstruction of a semiotic system "a simulacrum of the object" and describes the reconstructive process as "an activity of imitation."[49] In choosing the term "imitation," Barthes probably wishes to underscore the structuralist departure from Romantic and New Critical emphasis on "particularity" and "subjectivity" and the structuralist return to Aristotelian concerns with the universal, operative truth. Whereas Aristotle seeks to reveal the universal truth through an analysis of the surface, local structure of a dramatic plot, structuralists endeavor to unveil the same through an analysis of the deep, global system of signifying conventions that makes possible language and literature as well as all other cultural phenomena.

Yet, despite this common concern with the general and operative truth, it would be ill advised to call the structuralist practice "an activity of imitation." This is because the term "imitation" presupposes an ontological gap and contradicts the structuralist belief in the immanence of one and the same semiotic system at work in all cultural phenomena.

LITERATURE AS DECONSTRUCTIVE ANTITRUTH

With the exception of Plato, all the major critics examined so far conceptualize literature as a truth of one kind or another, and derive from their truth-claims the basic criterion for evaluating literary works. Emerging in the 1970s, deconstructive criticism turns this long tradition on its head and makes the deconstruction of truth-claims the sole purpose of its own existence. The first generation of deconstructive critics, led by Paul de Man, Geoffrey Hartman, and J. Hillis Miller, formulates a concept of literature grounded in the deconstructive philosophy of the French thinker Jacques Derrida.

Derrida derives his tenets of deconstruction from Saussurean linguistics—the same source of theoretical insights for structuralism, the predecessor of deconstructive textualism.[50] To the structuralists, the Saussurean binary opposition of *parole* and *langue* provides the basis for claiming absolute truth in the semiotics of language. But for Derrida, the Saussurean idea of the insubstantial, arbitrary nature of linguistic signs lays the theoretic ground for deconstructing all claims of truth in and through language. Derrida contends that the operation of *parole* does not presuppose the existence of a self-present *langue,* the semiotic truth, as the structuralists would have us believe. On the contrary, it precludes any possibility of a self-present truth in language—be it *langue* or any other truth-claims (eidos, God, Matter, essence, origin [*archè*], end [*telos*]) made in the history of Western metaphysics. Insofar as all these truth-claims are in and of themselves arbitrary linguistic signs, they are subjected to the rules of *différance*—a coinage by Derrida to denote the unavoidable gap between a signifier and its signified(s) in terms of spatial distance and temporal deferment. Owing to this gap, any truth-claim inevitably falls short of being a transcendental self-presence.

The existence and dominance of all truth-claims in Western metaphysics, argues Derrida, depend upon the suppression of *différance* inherent in these truth-claims. This suppression of *différance* is achieved through an exercise of what Derrida calls "phonocentrism" and "logocentrism." Phonocentrism denotes the practice of privileging spoken words over writing on the ground of its proximity to a transcendental signified called the logos. Logocentrism refers to a belief in the fusion of human speech, consciousness, and God in the logos. According to Derrida, phonocentrism and logocentrism furnish the dualistic paradigm in which Western thinkers, beginning with Plato, have conceptualized the ultimate reality in the form of truth. Typically, they seek to reify their truth-claims by aligning truth with the *phoné* or the transcendental logos. Meanwhile they denigrate the opposites of truth by associating them with the *gram* or corporeal sign of writing. Moreover, from this phonocentric-logocentric paradigm, Western thinkers derive all the essential hierarchical binarisms as principal categories of Western thinking. Those hierarchical binarisms include spirit / body, subject / object, mind / matter, and inside / outside.

To Derrida, Western metaphysics is like a castle built on sand. It is grounded on the false assumption of the self-presence of the *phoné* or the logos. To undermine the foundation of Western metaphysics, Derrida chooses to "implode" the *phoné,* the logos, and reified truth-claims by calling forth the infinite play of signifiers inside them. By analyzing this play of *différance,* he shows that the transcendental self-presence invested in all those terms is nothing but illusion. In deconstructing these terms, Derrida also seeks to overturn the hierarchy of all binary oppositions that arise from them. In overturning the hierarchical binary oppositions, Derrida focuses on the *aporias,* the so-called undecidable or contradictory points that reveal the play of *différance* inside the privileged term of a given binary opposition and hence invalidate any attempt to reify the term as a self-presence aligned with the logos.

Inspired by Derrida's philosophy, deconstructive critics have applied the Derridean textual analysis to many literary classics. As a rule, they seek to undermine authoritative interpretations of major literary works, to emphasize the rhetoricity of any thematic referents, to demonstrate the figural textualization of both authorial and readerly consciousness, to reveal the open-ended intertextuality of a "work of organic unity," and to elucidate the free-floating, open-ended process of linguistic signification. On the theoretical plane, they focus on exposing and dismantling logocentric assumptions that undergird all concepts of literature as truth.

According to deconstructive critics, each and every Western concept of literature belies a logocentric assumption of its own. For instance, various concepts of literature as mimetic truth embraced by classical and neoclassical critics as well as other universe-oriented critics are founded on the assumed existence of a self-present referent out there in the universe. The Romantic concept of literature as expressive truth rests on the assumption of an unmediated divine presence in a poet's imagination or in his poetic symbols. The New Critical concept of literature as ontic truth is grounded on the assumption that a self-contained, unified meaning can emerge from the reconciliation of opposing forces of language by irony, paradox, and other rhetorical constructions. The structuralist concept of literature as semiotic truth is predicated on the existence of an overarching structuring code or system (*langue*) that makes possible the generation of all speeches (*parole*). The concept of literature as phenomenological truth operates on the assumption that a pure consciousness or Cogito emerges from the interaction between text, authorial consciousness, and reader's consciousness. Because they hold all logocentric assumptions to be false and deceptive, deconstructive critics show no hesitation whatsoever about annulling all existing concepts of literature built upon them.

In nullifying the truth-claims in Western poetics as well as metaphysics, deconstructionists inevitably set up a new hierarchical binary opposition between privileged "truth-disclaiming" terms like *différance* and the now denigrated truth-claims.[51] Keenly aware that this hierarchical opposition will lead to the reification of his own deconstructive stance as a new self-present signified or truth, Derrida seeks to prevent this by his witty deconstructions of his own deconstructive terms. Among his students in literary criticism, however, many cannot care less about this paradox of "truth-disclaiming" terms becoming truth-claims in and of themselves. For instance, Paul de Man unhesitatingly stakes a truth-claim for literature on the ground that literature distinguishes itself by its embodiment and often self-conscious celebration of *différance,* a truth that inscribes or displaces all truth-claims. He declares that "literature turns out to be the main topic of philosophy and the model for the kind of truth to which it aspires."[52]

De Man's valorization of *différance* as an all-unifying truth reveals two important points of divergence from Derrida's deconstruction. The first point concerns *archi-écriture* or deconstructive textual analysis. Derrida pursues an infinite play of *différance* to demolish not only truth-claims in philosophical and literary writings but also his own truth-disclaiming stance. As he intends *archi-écriture* to go on and on without a destination, he may be assumed to regard it as an end in itself even though he may object to this assumption. De Man, however, does not share Derrida's enthusiasm for this kind of self-perpetuating *archi-écriture*. For him, the play of *différance* serves the practical purposes of invalidating the presumptions of fixed, self-present meanings in literature and breaking any closure in human thought and action at large. Thus he may be seen to take deconstructive textual analysis as a means rather than an end in itself. The second point concerns philosophical argument. Whereas Derrida's self-perpetuating *archi-écriture* disallows the adoption of any fixed position, positive or negative, de Man's limited use of *archi-écriture* leads to a new totalizing argument for taking *différance*-laden literature as the truth to which philosophy should aspire. In a way, his claim for literature as a higher truth than philosophy harks back to Aristotle's favorable comparison of literature with history.

These two points of divergence become all the more prominent in the later generation of deconstructive critics active from the mid-1980s to the present day. As compared with de Man and other early deconstructionists, they are far less interested in the pursuit of pure *archi-écriture* for the sake of deconstructing truth-claims in the rarefied realms of philosophical and critical abstraction. Instead, they self-consciously take up *archi-écriture* as a useful method for their psychoanalytical, Marxist, feminist, and other post-structuralist analyses of literary texts. Typically they use this deconstructive method to open up literary language, in order to see its inherent connections with strategies of power for perpetuating the hierarchies of sexual, ethnic, racial, and class relationships. By exposing the underlying *aporias* or contradictions, they aim to challenge authority, to shake up institutions, and to overturn certain social values, norms, and hierarchies. For sure, they are more concerned with achieving these practical goals than staking out grand truth-claims as does de Man. Nonetheless, they follow the same dualistic mode of thinking as do their truth-claiming and truth-disclaiming predecessors, because they too often set up, consciously or not, a new hierarchical binary opposition in which one set of values, norms, and principles is valorized explicitly or implicitly as truth over the other. In this sense, they remain heirs to the tradition of conceptualizing literature as truth in Western poetics.

Within the space of a chapter, it is impossible to survey all the major Western critical theories, nor examine any of them in an exhaustive fashion. Even though I have limited my discussion to one single issue, what I have examined constitutes only a fraction of the wealth of material worthy of our careful investigation. Nonetheless, I believe that the array of truth-claims discussed is broad and representative enough to demonstrate the paramount importance of truth as a defining issue in all major periods of Western poetics. It is true that many critics do not explicitly address the issue of truth. Among those who do, some may not explore it on the same level of critical abstraction as others. But since the time of Plato, the issue of truth has always loomed large in Western critical consciousness. It has not only dictated the ways Western critics conceptualize literature but also guided all other critical endeavors, theoretical and practical. To a great extent, it is new ideas of truth in Western thought that help foster new concepts of literature. By the same token, the changing locus of truth initiates a corresponding shift of critical locus among the four coordinates of criticism. In short, we may say that a continual reorientation toward new loci of truth constitutes the fundamental orientation of Western poetics.

CHAPTER 2

The Orientation
of Chinese Poetics
Conceptualizing Literature
as a Harmonizing Process

IN EXAMINING THE ORIENTATION OF CHINESE POETICS, I shall begin with a critique of James J. Y. Liu's adaptation of Abram's analytical diagram to reconstruct the system of Chinese poetics. In his influential book *Chinese Theories of Literature*, Liu conceives of five major Chinese theories of literature on the basis of Abrams' diagram: (1) metaphysical theories, (2) deterministic and expressive theories, (3) technical theories, (4) aesthetic theories, and (5) pragmatic theories.[1] These theories are reconstructed on essentially the same principles used by Abrams to distinguish mimetic, expressive, formal, and pragmatic theories. In so adapting Abrams' analytical diagram, Liu aims to accomplish two broad goals. The first is to go beyond the traditional practice of impressionistic criticism and introduce a systematic approach to studies of Chinese poetics. The second is to make the heritage of Chinese poetics accessible to general Western readers by presenting it in a critical scheme familiar to them. Liu's efforts to achieve these two goals deserve our sincere admiration. They have been and will long remain a source of inspiration for us. While we acknowledge our debt to Liu's luminous accomplishments in the study of Chinese poetics, we must honestly confront the faults in his adaptation of Abrams' diagram.

Reading his *Chinese Theories of Literature*, one gets a strong impression that he is trying to force the entire Chinese critical tradition into Abrams' diagram. The writings of individual critics are divided up into many parts in order to fit Abrams' analytical diagram. The result of such a reconstruction of Chinese poetics is not very satisfactory. Often we cannot get a complete picture of a critic's views as they are scattered throughout the book. As we go through the five theories, we find a mass of scattered remarks by different critics rather than a picture of Chinese poetics as a coherent whole. From these faults, we can see that the system of Chinese poetics cannot be properly reconstructed on the model of Abrams' diagram.

Why does an analytical diagram that works so well for Western poetics fare so badly when applied to Chinese poetics? To answer this question, we must understand the profound ramifications of Abrams' four artistic coordinates: universe, artist, work, and audience. Abrams uses these four terms as the organizing coordinates of Western poetics not just because they deal with the major factors involved in the creation and reception of literature. More importantly, it is because these four terms each have been at different historical periods the center of reference from which a critic derives "his principal categories for defining, classifying, and analyzing a work of art, as well as major criteria by which he judges its value."[2] As suggested by Abrams, each of these four terms can serve as the center of reference in Western poetics because each is an integral part of an "explicit or implicit 'worldview'."[3] Apparently, Liu fails to understand these culture-specific ramifications and assumes that the four terms are universal coordinates of criticism readily applicable to Chinese poetics. Of course, this assumption is wrong. None of the four terms have been regarded as the center of reference in Chinese poetics, nor has there been an "explicit or implicit 'worldview'" in China that allows any of the four terms to be so privileged. For traditional Chinese critics, these four terms only mark different phases of a cyclical artistic process just as Liu himself observes.[4] So, although it is worth our while to investigate the evolving Chinese views on the four terms, we should not reconstruct the system of Chinese poetics based on Abrams' diagram.

From Liu's faulty adaptation of Abrams' diagram we can learn an important lesson. We cannot map out the orientation of Chinese poetics simply by taking it apart and putting its component parts into an analytical scheme borrowed from the Western tradition. A more appropriate approach is to examine a sizable body of texts about literature written over different times and seek to find the distinctive orientation of Chinese poetics.

Following this inductive approach, I next closely examine some of the most important early texts on literature and identify four distinctive concepts of literature during the formative eras of Chinese poetics. Although there exist other ideas about literature, these four concepts represent the major developments in early Chinese critical thinking. While I focus on the four concepts, I must stress that they do not present a clear-cut pattern of unilinear evolution. The emergence of a new concept does not mean an abrupt disappearance of the old ones. Many critics cling to old concepts even when a new one is the vogue of the day. Other critics espouse old and new concepts alike and integrate them with varying degrees of success. Therefore, a new concept is often born of a successful synthesis of diverse existing concepts. In fact, the last of the four concepts to be examined below is such a case.

After my detailed discussion of the four concepts, I review the highlights of the major concepts of literature developed after Liu Xie. As we reflect upon the continuity between the four concepts and these later ones, we shall discern what brings them all together as an interrelated whole and what distinguishes each of them from the others. Our discovery of their common denominator(s) and differentiae will help shed light on the distinctive orientation of Chinese poetics.

THE RELIGIOUS CONCEPT OF LITERATURE IN THE *BOOK OF DOCUMENTS*

"Shi yan zhi" 詩言志 (Poetry expresses the heart's intent) is the earliest known statement on literature, allegedly made by the legendary emperor Shun 舜 during a conversation with his music official Kui 夔. This statement is recorded in "Canon of Yao" ("Yao dian" 堯典), chapter 1 of the *Book of Documents* (*Shu jing* 書經, *Shang shu* 尚書), one of the six Confucian classics.[5] Although few believe that this statement actually came from the mouth of the legendary emperor, most scholars agree that it conveys the earliest known concept of literature.

> I bid you, Kui, the emperor said, to preside over music and educate our sons, [so that they will be] straightforward yet gentle, congenial yet dignified, strong but not ruthless, and simple but not arrogant. Poetry expresses the heart's intent (*zhi*);[6] singing prolongs the utterance of that expression. The notes accord with the prolonged utterance, and are harmonized by the pitch tubes. The eight kinds of musical intruments attain to harmony and do not interfere with one another. Spirits and man are thereby brought into harmony.
>
> Oh! yes, replied Kui, I will strike and tap the stones, and a hundred beasts will follow one another to dance.[7]

帝曰。夔。命女典樂。教胄子。直而溫。寬而栗。剛而無
虐。簡而無傲。詩言志。歌永言。聲依永。律和聲。八音克
諧。無相奪倫。神人以和。夔曰。於。予擊石拊石。百獸
率舞。

Brief as they are, these remarks cover the entire cycle of the literary process: its origins in the human heart, its external manifestations, and its effects on the outside world. Poetry is seen as the initial part of a performance that aims to harmonize internal and external processes. During this performance, the performers seek to convey *zhi* or the movement of the heart's intent through poetic utterances, chanting, singing, music-playing, and dancing.[8] One desired result of this performance is the achievement of inner equilibrium, a mental state deemed conducive to the moral education of the young. By watching or participating in such a performative process, the young can acquire a balanced, harmonious character. The more important goal of this performance, however, is to bring the affairs of men into accord with the spirits. Through an intensifying series of rhythmic, bodily movements that culminate in the "dance of one hundred beasts," the performers seek to please the spirits and achieve harmony with them. The "dance of one hundred animals" ordered by Kui is generally believed to represent a form of totemic dance that involves the wearing of animal hides.[9] However, scholars such as Kong Yingda 孔穎達 (574–648) prefer to take "the dance of one hundred animals" as a realistic description. According to Kong, this description of animals being moved to dance in unison is intended to manifest the miraculous effects of harmony between the spirits and men. He writes, "It is easy to move the spirits and men, but not birds and beasts. When even a hundred beasts follow one another to dance, one can see that the harmony between the spirits and men has been achieved."[10]

This dance, totemic or not, marks the center of the entire performance, and it is deemed most instrumental to the achievement of harmony between the spirits and men.[11] Poetry, songs, and music are subordinated to dance because they mainly serve to intensify rhythmic bodily movements to the point of dancing. The crescendo of the performing acts represents an ascending scale of value based largely on the physical force of performance. Poetry, the least dynamic physically, is placed at the bottom. Dance, the most dynamic physically, constitutes the culminating point of the entire performance.

The primacy of religious dance shown in the *"Shi yan zhi"* statement may be corroborated by several well-known accounts of high antiquity. In many descriptions of the earliest music, for instance, we take note of the dominance of dance. In *Spring and Autumn Annals of Master Lü* (*Lüshi chunqiu* 呂氏春秋), we are told that "the music of Ge Tianshi 葛天氏 (legendary emperor of high antiquity) of old times is such:

three people held ox-tails, and stomped their feet to sing the eight songs."[12] In *Rituals of Zhou,* there is a description of six ancient sacrificial performances that survived to Zhou times. They all begin with certain fix-pitched music and culminate in special sacrificial dances to honor the heavenly god, the spirit of the earth, the deities of mountains and rivers, and royal ancestresses and ancestors.[13] Again, in *Rituals of Zhou* we catch a glimpse of the all-important status of dance in the description of the duties of a music master (*yueshi* 樂 師). The foremost of his duties is the teaching of various dances, and only after it comes the teaching of music itself.[14]

However, if we look through the chronicles and ritual texts about high antiquity, including the "Canon of Yao" itself, we note that accounts of ancient religious dance are outweighed, in both quantities and assigned importance, by accounts of music. Does this indicate that in high antiquity religious dance was not quite as important as revealed in the *"Shi yan zhi"* statement? Or does this merely reflect the emphasis on music in the much later time of the Zhou, when most accounts of high antiquity were recorded in various chronicles and ritual texts? To ascertain the primacy of religious dance in the *"Shi yan zhi"* statement, a number of eminent scholars have decided to go beyond the extant historical and ritual texts and make use of the oracle bone writings discovered at the turn of the 20th century.

To find vestiges of religious dance in oracle bone writings, these scholars focus on the graphs 𡳿 and 𡳿, whose later combined form 止 appears in *"shi"* and *"zhi"*—two of the three characters that make up the *"Shi yan zhi"* statement. The first graph, 𡳿, is glossed as "to go" because it conveys the image of a foot stepping forward on the ground and thus suggests the idea of "going".[15] According to Chow Tse-tsung, this idea of "going" becomes the core meaning of 之 in the clerical script developed in the third century B.C., which is in turn "the direct antecedent of the modern 之."[16] The second graph, 𡳿, is glossed as "to stop" because it merely represents the shape of a human foot and does not have the ground (represented by a horizontal stroke) underneath it. So, without the ground to walk on, the foot in this graph properly suggests the idea "to stop."[17] These two graphs later merged into 止, which appears both in 𡳿, the ancient simplified form of (*shi*) 詩 , and in 𡳿, the small seal form of *zhi*.

Wen Yiduo 聞 一 多 (1899–1946) traces 止 in the character *zhi* (heart's intent) to 止 ("stop") and takes 心 as the graph for human heart, the home of all inward activities of man. Based on this combination of 𐤷 and 𐤷, he contends that what poetry expresses, *zhi* or the heart's intent, is "what stops and stays in the heart" or more specifically, "what one remembers, records and cherishes in the heart."[18] For his part, Ch'en Shih-hsiang, tracing the graph 𐤷 in the character *shi* to both 𐤷 (human feet that "go") and 𐤷 (human feet that "stop"), argues that the character *shi* (poetry) means not only "what goes and stops in the heart," as Wen Yiduo says, but also actually "going and stopping"—that is, rhythmic dancing that accompanies the movement in the heart.[19] Ater an exhaustive study of 𐤷 and other related graphs, Chow Tse-tsung affirms the intimation of religious dance at the etymological root of the character *shi*. He argues that, "Poetry probably begins with man's spontaneous expression of emotions. The primitive men's strong emotions and desires are expressed through magic and ceremony-making. When they stamp in a strange rhythmical dance around a camp fire and mark the beat with cries and grunts, they are making a spell, in the hope that their prayer, their imitation of animals, or nature's sounds and gestures will provide them power over animals or nature and fulfill their wish."[20] Of course, a reading of oracle bone writings is always conjectural to some degree and hence one may very well find reason to disagree with the views of these scholars. Still, their basic arguments about the primacy of religious dance in the earliest poetry are quite convincing.

Taking into consideration the textual and inscriptional evidence just mentioned and the immediate context in which the statement was made, it seems safe to say that the *"Shi yan zhi"* statement presents a distinctive religious concept of literature. It is marked by a subordination of poetry to music and dance, by a recognition of poetry's auxiliary role in invoking the numinous spirits, and by an overriding concern with the harmony between the numinous spirits and man. Although the importance of dance-centered religious performance disappeared in later times, this statement remains, as Zhu Ziqing 朱自清 (1898–1948) says, "the pioneering outline"(*kai shan gangling* 開山綱領) of Chinese literary criticism.[21] It was to wield an enduring influence on the development of traditional Chinese literary criticism for one simple reason. It set forth the core belief of literature as a process—one that arises from inward responses to the outer realms, manifests itself in different artistic forms, and in turn harmonizes various processes in the realms of heaven, earth, and man.[22] This core belief was to become the basic conceptual model for understanding literature for centuries to come.

THE HUMANISTIC CONCEPT OF LITERATURE IN THE *ZUO COMMENTARY* AND *SPEECHES OF THE STATES*

In developing the *"Shi yan zhi"* statement into their own concepts of literature, later critics tend to reconceptualize the origins and formation of literature and reassess literature's functions in terms of its impact on different external phenomena. This long, continual process of reappropriating the *"Shi yan zhi"* statement was already well under way in the Spring and Autumn period or even earlier.

The statement occurs many times in the *Zuo Commentary* (*Zuo zhuan* 左傳) and *Speeches of the States* (*Guo yu* 國語), two primary historical texts about the Spring and Autumn period. In repeating this statement, however, the authors of the two texts seek to express a concept of literature quite different from the one presented in the "Canon of Yao." First of all, when talking about the expression of *zhi*, they seldom mention dance and focus instead on exploring the nature of *zhi*. The following passage from *Zuo Commentary*, Duke Zhao 25th year, is a good example:

> [Zhao] Jianzi asked, "May I ask you what the *li* (ritual) is?" [Zi Dashu] replied, "I heard the late Grand Master Zichan saying '*li* is the law of heaven, the righteous manifestation of earth, and the conduct of the people.' As it is the law of heaven and earth, and people abide by it. . . . People have the emotions of fondness, dislike, happiness, anger, sorrow, and joy; they arise from the six *qi* or ethers. Therefore, we must cautiously apply rules and set up appropriate norms in order to regulate the six *zhi*. [23]

> 簡子曰。敢問何為禮。對曰。吉也聞諸先大夫子產曰。夫
> 禮。天之經也。地之義也。民之行也。天地之經。而民實則
> 之。……民有好惡喜怒哀樂。生于六氣。是故審則宜類。以
> 制六志。

Judging by the context, the "six *zhi*" apparently refers to the six types of emotion. As a matter of fact, Kong Yingda explicitly glosses *zhi* as *qing* 情 (emotion). He writes; "This 'six *zhi*' is what is called 'six *qing*' in the *Book of Rites* (*Li ji* 禮記). What lies inside oneself is *qing* or emotion. When this *qing* is stirred up, it is then *zhi*. So, *qing* and *zhi* are one and the same thing." [24] It is important to stress that here *zhi* as emotion should not be confused with the type of emotion referred to in the Six Dynasties critical tenet "Poetry traces emotion" (*shi yuan qing* 詩緣情). While the latter is emotion devoid of explicit social and moral meanings and appreciated solely for its aesthetic value, the former, as Zhu Ziqing points out, "cannot be separated from the '*li*,' nor from the political affairs and moral education."[25] To demonstrate this conception of *zhi* as moral sentiment, Zhu Ziqing examines examples of its use in *Analects* in the sense of a "moral choice," and its use in the *Book of Poetry* (*Shi jing* 詩經) in connection with moral remonstration (*feng* 諷) and moral praise *(song).*[26]

What is the primary expressive form of this moral *zhi?* For the authors of *Zou Commentary* and *Speeches of the States,* it is music that includes songs and poetry.[27] As Zhu Ziqing points out, people at the time "expressed *zhi* with music, expressed *zhi* with songs, and expressed *zhi* with poems. . . . To communicate with one another through music and songs was for them a way of life."[28] Considering this dominance of music, it is little wonder that "music-words" (*yueyu* 樂語) became an all-important subject of education. Of the six types of music-words (*xing* 興, *dao* 道, *feng* 諷, *song* 誦, *yan* 言, *yu* 語) mentioned in *Rituals of Zhou,*[29] Zhu explains, the first and second seem to be the music of multiple instruments, the third and fourth solo music, and the fifth and sixth verbal citations of words of songs in daily life.[30] The dominance of music and the subordination of poetry are also reflected in the fact that the two major types of poetry of the time, *xianshi* 獻詩 (or *caishi* 采詩) and *fushi* 賦詩, are both sung aloud to music on courtly occasions.[31] The first type consists of poems originally composed and sung by ordinary people and later collected and set to music by musicians for submission to the sovereign. The second type includes poems, mostly those of the *Book of Poetry,* selected by feudal lords or officials to be presented with music on diplomatic occasions for the purpose of expressing their own *zhi* as well as those of their states.[32]

The primary goal of the music-centered courtly performances depicted in the *Zuo Commentary* and *Speeches of the States* is to harmonize sociopolitical and natural processes, not to please the numinous spirits as in the "Canon of Yao." In this regard, three specific functions are discussed in those two texts. The first function is to enable the ruler to gauge the popular sentiment and the state of governance.[33] In the *Zuo Commentary,* Duke Xiang 29th year (512 B.C.), Ji Zha 季札 (fl. 512 B.C.) comments on the musical performance of all the major groups of poems in the *Book of Poetry,* correlating their aesthetic qualities with the conditions of governance and popular sentiment in their provenance:

[Duke Zha] requested to listen to the music of Zhou. So, the performers were ordered to sing for him the airs of Zhounan and Shaonan. Zha said, "Beautiful! They mark the beginning of a [kingly] foundation, and are still incomplete. Yet it is aspiring but not resentful."

They sang the airs of Bei, Yong, and Wei for him. Zha said, "Beautiful! Profound! They are grave but not despondent. I heard that the virtues of Kangshu of Wei and Duke Wei are like these airs of Wei."

They sang the airs of Wang for him. Zha said, "Beautiful! They are pensive, but not timid. This was the Zhou that had moved to the east."

They sang the airs of Zheng for him. Zha said, "Beautiful! They have gone too far in elaboration. The people cannot endure, and the state of Zheng will be the first to perish."

They sang the airs of Qi for him. Zha said, "Beautiful! How broad and wide! They are great airs! It was their great ruler who was the exemplary figure of the Eastern Sea. Their state was beyond measure."

They sang the airs of Bin for him. Zha said, "Beautiful! A grand sweep! They are joyful but not excessive. This was [the time of] the Duke of Zhou who had moved to the east."

They sang the airs of Qin for him. Zha said, "These are called the sounds of the Xia. Being such, they are great, eminently great. This was the good old way of Zhou."

They sang the airs of Wei for him. Zha said, "Beautiful! What a flow of sounds! They are vast and yet subtle. They are out of the ordinary, and yet move with ease. Aided with these virtues, the lords of Wei were illustrious."

They sang the airs of Tang for him. Zha said, "The thought is so profound! Among these people weren't there the remnants of lines of Tao and Tang? If not so, how could their somber concern be so far-reaching? Except the descendants of Tao and Tang, who could display such [a deep concern]?"

They sang the airs of Chen for him. Zha said, "When a state is without a ruler, can it last long?" From the airs of Kuai to the end of the airs [in the *Book of Poetry*], he offered no critical comments.

Then they sang the lesser odes (*xiaoya*) for him. "Beautiful!" Zha said, "They are wistful but not faithless. They are plaintive, but do not air grievances outright. Is the virtue of Zhou on the decline? There are still remnants of the people of the late kings."

They sang the great odes (*daya*) for him. Zha said, "How vast! So joyful! They are dexterous and yet display a quality of straightforwardness. This is the virtue of King Wen, isn't it?"

They sang the hymns (*song*) for him. Zha said, "Completely perfect! They are straightforward but not overbearing. They are dexterous but unbending. Coming close, they are not overcrowded. Going afar, they do not become adrift. They move around but do not go beyond bounds. They repeat but do not border on monotony. They are mournful, but do not render one distraught. They are joyful, but not in an excessive degree. They are useful, but not exhaustible. They are vast, but not grandiose. When giving, they do not waste. When taking, they do not covet. Staying put, they do not get stranded. When moving, they do not go astray. The five sounds harmonize and the eight winds are in accord. The rhythm is well controlled and follows the proper order. It is the like of the fullest and the most complete virtue."[34]

For Ji Zha, excess in music and poetry, as shown in the airs of Zheng, signifies moral decay and sociopolitical disorder. Conversely, the character of the mean betokens the moral virtues of the people and the proper governance by the rulers. This character is best shown in various virtues not taken to excess: "grave but not despondent," "pensive but not timid," "straightforward but not overbearing," and so on. He considers the hymns of Zhou to embody the ideal of abiding by the mean (*zhizhong* 制中) and praises these hymns for properly keeping thirteen different virtues to the mean. In addition to his comments on the poems, he observes the general correlates between music ("five sounds") and ethical and sociopolitical realities ("eight winds").[35] In his opinion, it is by virtue of these correlates that music and poetry serve the function of revealing public sentiment and the state of governance.

The second function of the music-centered courtly performances is to help shape the moral character of the members of the ruling class. If the "Canon of Yao" passage already touched upon the edifying effect of music and poetry, Yan Zi 晏子 (?–500 B.C.)[36] offers an explanation of music's power to transform man in the *Zuo Commentary*, Duke Zhao 22nd year (519 B.C.). Like Ji Zha, he pursues a correlative argument. He argues that elements of music arise from the myriad categories of things and naturally become their symbolic correlates. "There are the breath," says he, "the two types of dance, the three subjects, the four objects, the five notes, the six pitch tubes, the seven sounds, the eight winds, and the nine songs—together they form [the substance for music]" 一 氣，二體，三類，四物，五聲，六律，七音，八風，九歌，以相 成也.[37] So intricately bound up with the inherent order of things, he contends, music can bring into play the multifarious opposites and harmonize them in the course of performance. Moreover, such a harmonious music performance can induce a corresponding mental equilibrium in the mind of the listener and render him or her virtuous and harmonious. "There are the qualities of clear and turbid," he continues, "big and small, long and short, fast and unhurried, plaintive and joyful, hard and soft, slow and speedy, high and low, outgoing and incoming, comprehensive and scattered—all these qualities complement one another. A gentleman listens to such music and thereby attains peace of mind. When he has peace of mind, his virtues become harmonious" 清濁大小，短長疾徐，哀樂剛柔，遲速高下，出入周疏，以相濟也。君子聽之，以平其心，心平德和.[38]

The third and most important function is to bring about harmony between nature and man. For the people of the Spring and Autumn period, the harmonization of human affairs is often merely part of broader endeavors to achieve the all-important harmony with natural processes and forces that decisively impact the survival and well-being of man. In "Speeches of Zhou," the entertainer Zhoujiu 州鳩 in 522 B.C. gave an excellent exposition of how music, songs, and poetry bring about such harmony. In an attempt to dissuade him from violating the rules for making musical instruments, Zhoujiu explained to King Jing 景王 (r. 544–520 B.C.) the inherent relationship between music and natural processes. Zhoujiu, too, pursues a correlative argument. He begins by reaffirming the relationship between governance and music through their common principles of harmony and peacefulness: "Governance manifests itself in music. Music arises from harmony. Harmony arises from peaceful accord. Pitches are to harmonize music. Musical scales are to bring pitches in accord" 夫政象樂，樂從和，和從平。聲以和樂，律以平聲.[39] To demonstrate the correlation between music and natural processes, he first shows how harmonious music serves to regulate the "eight winds."[40] Thanks to such music, he says, "the cosmic breath (*qi*) hence does not impede the *yin*, nor dispel the *yang*. Yin and yang follow each other in order, wind and rain arrive with the season, living things grow well and flourish, people are benefited and brought into harmony. All things are in place and music is brought to completion. Neither those above nor those below are worn out. This is called the rectification of music" 於是乎氣無滯陰，亦無散陽，陰陽序次，風雨時至，嘉生繁祉，人民龢利，物備而樂成，上下不罷，故曰樂正.[41] Moreover, Zhoujiu believes that through harmonious music man can achieve harmony with not only natural processes but also the numinous spirits. "Therefore," he concludes, "we chant with the virtue of the mean, and we sing with the notes of the mean. The virtue and notes are not violated and therefore they bring harmony between the spirits and man. Thus the spirits are put at ease and the commoners are made to listen"於是乎道之以中德，詠之以中音，德音不愆，以合神人，神是以寧，民是以聽.[42]

In sum, the reformulation of the *"Shi yan zhi"* statement in the *Zuo Commentary* and *Speeches of the States* gives birth to a new, humanistic concept of literature. In elevating the status of music and in rethinking the functions of music and poetry, the speakers in those two texts consistently display an overriding concern with sociopolitical and natural processes that immediately affect the conditions of human existence. These humanistic concerns form a striking contrast to the overriding concern with the numinous spirits in earlier times. It is true that the people of the Spring and Autumn period continue to discuss harmony between the spirits and men. But as shown in Zhoujiu's remarks on music, this harmony is usually not the direct result of the magical invocation of divinities through powerful rhythmical dance, chanting, and singing. Rather, it is an indirect consequence arising from the harmonization of natural and sociopolitical processes through rituals and music. In view of this ascendancy of humanistic concerns over religious ones, it seems appropriate to use the term "humanistic" to characterize the new concept of literature expressed in the *Zuo Commentary* and *Speeches of the States*.

THE DIDACTIC CONCEPT OF LITERATURE IN THE "GREAT PREFACE"

The *"Shi yan zhi"* statement goes through yet another significant reformulation in Han times, developing into a full-fledged didactic concept of literature in the "[Great] Preface to the Mao Text of the *Book of Poetry*" ("Mao *Shi* xu" 毛詩序).[43] The "Great Preface" is, as Stephen Owen says, "the most authoritative statement on the nature and function of poetry in traditional China."[44] What distinguishes it from earlier discussions of poetry is its elevation of poetic verbalization over music and songs and its reassessment of poetry's functions in purely didactic terms.

To begin with, let us see how poetry is redefined in relation to music and songs in the "Great Preface." Elaborating on the *"Shi yan zhi"* statement, the author goes to great lengths to stress the central importance of *yan* 言 or words. "Poetry is where the heart's intent goes," he writes, "What is still in the heart is 'intent'; what is expressed in words is 'poetry.' Emotions are stirred inside and manifest themselves in words" 詩者，志之所之也，在心為志，發言為詩. The author apparently believes that what lies in the heart, be it called *zhi* or *qing*,

manifests itself primarily in poetic verbalization. To support his eleva-
tion of words, he simply cites a passage from the "Record of Music"
("Yue ji" 樂記):

> Emotions move within and take form in words. If words cannot express
> them adequately, we sigh them out. If sighing is not adequate, we sing
> them out. If singing is not adequate, we unconsciously move our hands
> to gesticulate, and stamp our feet to dance.[45]

情動於中而形於言，言之不足故嗟嘆之，嗟嘆之不足故
永歌之，永歌之不足，不知手之舞之，足之蹈之也。

Whereas in the "Record of Music" this passage occurs at the very end
and strikes us as an unimportant afterthought,[46] here it constitutes the
cornerstone of his argument for the elevation of poetic verbalization
over music and dance.

A comparison of this passage with the "Canon of Yao" and "Speeches
of Zhou" passages shows how it in effect reverses the conventional aux-
iliary role accorded to poetry. In the "Canon of Yao" passage, poetry is
placed at the head of a continuum of other ritualistic activities: chant-
ing, singing, music-playing, and dancing. This placement gives the il-
lusion that poetry initiates those activities and thus is of central impor-
tance. However, upon close examination, one finds that poetry only
prepares the audience for what is to come. Verbal utterances are but the
raw material to be transformed successively into chanting, singing,
music-playing, and dancing. Thus, the succession of these activities in-
dicates a process of the intensification of bodily movements—the nor-
mal exhalation in speaking, the prolonged exhalation in chanting and
singing, music-playing, and finally to the movement of the whole body
in dancing. This process seems to imply an ascending scale of impor-
tance in proportion to the intensification of bodily movement. Poetic
verbalization lies at the very bottom of this scale as it entails the least
bodily movement and is farthest away from the point of culmination.
The "Speeches of Zhou" passage deals primarily with music and leaves
out the discussion of dance. Nonetheless, it adopts a similar scale of value
that sets music performance over verbalization and considers poetry-
chanting to be merely a component of music. In the "Great Preface,"
poetry is also placed before chanting, singing, and dancing. However,
this same sequence of activities indicates a descending scale of impor-
tance. Now, what is at the center of these activities is poetry, the least
physically prominent. All other activities are presented as complements

to poetic verbalization. Chanting, singing, and dancing become necessary in a graduated manner when poetic verbalization cannot adequately express emotions.[47] This marginalization of music and dance is evident throughout the "Great Preface." Dance is mentioned only in the passage cited above. Nor is music being discussed for its own sake. Indeed, even when the author cites another passage from the "Record of Music" about *sheng* 聲 (sounds) and *yin* 音 (tones), he seems to refer to the emotive tonality of poetic verbalization only.

> Emotions are discharged in sounds. As those sounds assume a pattern, they are called "tones." The tones of a well-governed time are peaceful and joyful; the governance is marked by harmony. The tones of a time of chaos are woeful and filled with anger; the governance is deviant. The tones of a fallen state are sorrowful and contemplative; the people are in dire straits.[48]

> 情發於聲，聲成文謂之音。治世之音安以樂，其政和。亂世之音怨以怒，其政乖。亡國之音哀以思，其民困。

In "Record of Music," these remarks are immediately followed by a lengthy, exclusive discussion of music's relationship to the ethico-sociopolitical order. By contrast, here the remarks lead to praise of the transforming power of poetry in complete disassociation with music. It is quite clear that the words "sounds" and "tones" are now used in reference to the tonality of poetic verbalization rather than actual sounds and notes of music. For the first time in Chinese criticism, the author has established the importance of poetic verbalization over dance, music, and songs.[49]

In my opinion, this redefinition of literature as a verbalization-centered form of social intercourse arises in response to two profound changes taking place during the Warring States period and Han times: the gradual divorce of poetry from music, and the gradual shift of man's overriding concern from natural processes to human relationships. Toward the end of the Spring and Autumn period, these two changes were already underway. For instance, in Confucius' discussion of poetry *(shi)*, or rather the *Poetry* (the *Book of Poetry*) in *Analects*, we find plenty of evidence of these two changes.[50] In *Analects*, Confucius makes nineteen references to the *Poetry*.[51] In all but two of these references, he discusses the *Poetry* separately from music. Not only does he recognize the independence of poetry from music and examines it in its own right, but he also puts it on a par with music. He declares, "Let a man be inspired by the *Poetry*, set straight by the rituals, and perfected by music."[52] The shift of his overriding concern to human relationships is no less prominent. In discussing the *Poetry,* he completely leaves out any consideration of its impact on natural forces, and focuses exclusively on its ethical, social, and political functions. For example, in his summary statement on the *Poetry,* he explains how it can help regulate human relationships in the spirit of the mean and provide the norm of human interaction among equals, between fathers and sons, and between the ruler and his subjects. He says, "How come you, little ones, do not study the *Poetry?* The *Poetry* may help to inspire, to observe, to keep company, and to express grievances. It may be used in the service of one's father at home and in the service of one's lord abroad" 小子何莫學夫詩？詩可以興，可以觀，可以群，可以怨，邇之事父，遠之事君.[53]

In later texts written during the Warring States period, we can observe the continuation of these two changes. In *Mencius* (*Meng Zi* 孟子) and *Strategies of the States* (*Zhanguo ce* 戰國策), for instance, the discussions of the *Poetry* no longer occur in the immediate context of the music performance of the *Poetry,* nor do they entail any serious consideration of the issue of music.[54] In contrast to the foregrounding of the nature-man relationship in the *Zuo Commentary* and *Speeches of the States,* these two later texts display an overriding concern with human relationships in the tradition of *Analects.* By the first century A.D., when the "Great Preface" was supposedly written, poetry had become independent of music and the Confucian doctrine had been established as the state ideology. Under such circumstances, it is only too natural that the author of the "Great Preface" would redefine poetry as the verbalization-centered form of social intercourse and stress its ethical, social, and political functions.

The "Great Preface" offers a comprehensive examination of four specific harmonizing functions of poetry. The first function is to harmonize an individual's inner and outer lives. By transforming emotions into words, the author contends that one can restore inward equilibrium and maintain outward moral decorum. In this regard, he writes that poetry "arises from emotion and ends in conformity to rituals" 發乎情，止乎禮儀.[55] The second function is to foster harmony among the people of a given state. According to the author, one's emotional utterances resonate with those of other people in his state and therefore register the "tones of a well-governed time" or the "tones of a time of chaos." Thanks to this moral empathy, the words of a person denote the air (*feng*) of an entire state. The third function is to bring about harmony between the subjects and the ruler. In the author's opinion, the airs are a particularly desirable mode of communication with the rulers and his subjects. This is because they are "concerned mainly with patterning [of expressions] and allow for subtle remonstrance" 主文而 諷諫.⁵⁶ Through highly suggestive airs, "those who express [their grievances] are not held culpable, and those who hear it find enough to warn themselves" 言之者無罪，聞之者足以戒.⁵⁷ This subtle form of communication enhances harmony between those above and those below without impairing the social hierarchy that separates them. The fourth function is to exert moral influence over the populace. By using the airs as a means of moral instruction, the ruler can show his people examples of good and bad government, and moral and immoral conduct. Through these four functions, the author believes, poetry can not only rectify ethical and sociopolitical processes but also bring about harmony between the numinous spirits and men. For this reason, he declares, "to move heaven and earth, and to win the sympathy of ghost and spirits, nothing is nearly comparable to poetry" 動天地，感鬼神，莫近於詩.⁵⁸

The author of the "Great Preface" also touches upon the origin of poetry. He believes that poetic verbalizations arise in response to sociopolitical realities and therefore embody the pattern of orderliness or chaos of the outer world. Based on this belief, he identifies the four known genres in the *Book of Poetry*—airs (*feng* 風), great odes (*daya* 大雅), lesser odes (*xiaoya* 小雅), and hymns (*song* 頌)—with responses to different ethical and sociopolitical realities. According to him, an air is born of a single person's responses to the conditions of his own state. "Therefore," writes he, "that which concerns the affairs of one state and is tied to the fundamental existence of one single person is called an air" 是以一國之事，繫一人之本，謂之風.⁵⁹ An ode "recounts the events of the world and observes the customs within the four corners" 言天下之事，形四方之風.⁶⁰ A hymn arises in response to grand virtues and accomplishments of a ruler, and it serves to "report his accomplishments to the divinities" 以其成功告於神明者也.⁶¹ In addition to these four genres, he mentions "changed airs" (*bianfeng* 變風) and "changed odes" (*bianya* 變雅) as responses to the times of moral decay and sociopolitical chaos.

By elevating poetry over music, by realigning it with ethical and sociopolitical processes, and by reconceptualizing its functions in terms of the harmonization of those processes, the author has transformed the *"Shi yan zhi"* statement into a full-fledged didactic concept of literature. In my view, the rise of this didactic concept has as much to do with the changing contexts of discussing the *Poetry* as with the broad sociopolitical changes noted above. In the *Zuo Commentary* and *Speeches of the States,* remarks on the *Poetry* are mostly made by the dukes and their close attendants when commenting on ongoing courtly ceremonies. In such contexts, the speaker and the listener are in the presence of each other, and neither assumes a detached moralizing position. Thus, their remarks on poetry often strike us as descriptive rather than prescriptive. Most speakers seek to understand the impact of music and poetry on sociopolitical and natural processes by means of correlative reasoning. By contrast, the author of the "Great Preface" casts himself in the role of an invisible, implied speaker, addressing a broad audience ranging from the monarch to commoners. The inherent detachment of a preface writer enables him to go beyond the confines of ongoing courtly ceremonies and to reconceive the *Poetry* as the verbalization-centered form of social intercourse as it is used in his own time. Moreover, this detachment allows him to stand on the high ground of Confucian morality and prescribe how the *Poetry* should be used by the ruler and his subjects alike. As this didacticism permeates and unifies his entire argument, it seems fitting to characterize his concept of literature as a didactic one.

THE COMPREHENSIVE CONCEPT OF LITERATURE IN *WENXIN DIAOLONG*

If the author of the "Great Preface" developed the *"Shi yan zhi"* statement into a full-fledged didactic concept of literature, Liu Xie transforms this "pioneering outline" of Chinese literary criticism into a comprehensive concept of literature. His magnum opus, *Wenxin diaolong* 文心雕龍 (The Literary Mind and the Carving of Dragons) is ordinarily not placed in the lineage of the *"Shi yan zhi"* traditions as we know them today.[62] This is probably because of its lack of strong didacticism for which the *"Shi yan zhi"* traditions became known after the Han. Here, in linking *Wenxin diaolong* with the *"Shi yan zhi"* traditions, I do not intend to associate it with the latter's didacticism but to show how Liu Xie inherited from the latter the basic framework of understanding literature as a harmonizing process. As we shall see, through this model Liu reconceptualizes all the major aspects of literature: its nature, its origins, its formation in the mind and language, and its functions.

In redefining literature as a process, Liu Xie takes the elevation of poetry over music as his point of departure, as does the author of the "Great Preface." While the latter surreptitiously reverses the dominance of music over poetry, Liu openly places poetry above music and expounds on the rationale of this elevation of poetry in explicit terms:

> The body of music is sounds, and blind music masters must tune their instruments. The mind of music is poetry, and gentlemen should rectify their literary expressions. . . . Therefore we know that Ji Zha observed the language of songs, not merely listened to their sounds.[63]

樂禮在聲，鼓師務調其器；樂心在詩，君子宜正其文⋯故知季札觀辭，不直聽聲而已。(*WXDL* 7 / 99–101, 107–108)

Here Liu establishes the importance of poetry over music in a rather clever way. He accepts the traditional praise of music but adds that the miraculous power of music comes from words of poetry rather than its sounds. This seemingly insignificant qualification amounts to nothing less than a negation of the traditional view of music. As sounds are traditionally considered the essence of music, his comparison of sounds to the body means a relegation of music itself to a secondary status. Moreover, by calling poetry the mind of music, he tactfully transfers the traditional praise of music to poetry. To underscore this elevation of poetry over music, he compares literary-minded gentlemen (*junzi* 君子) favorably with illiterate blind musicians working with instruments. In addition, he reinterprets the story of Ji Zha's observation of the Zhou music, suggesting that Ji Zha cared more about the words than sounds of songs and music.

Unlike the author of the "Great Preface," however, Liu Xie does not consider poetry to be superior to music on the grounds of the efficacy of verbalization for rectifying intraclass and interclass relationships. In his opinion, poetry or, broadly speaking, literature, is primarily "patterns" (*wen* 文) of written words and secondarily "tones" (*yin* 音) of verbalization. What makes literature superior to music is the visual impact of its written words, not the auditory effects of its verbalization that are not dissimilar to those of music. In chapter 48 ("Zhi yin" 知音 [An Understanding Critic]), he seeks to establish the paramount importance of written words by comparing them favorably with sounds of music. "In reading a work of literature," writes he, "one opens a text and penetrates the feelings [of the author]. . . . Although we cannot see the faces of writers of a remote age, we may look into their works and immediately see their minds" 觀文者披文以入情⋯世遠莫見其面，覘文輒見其心 (*WXDL* 48 / 97, 100–101). To Liu, it is written words, not fleeting sounds of verbalization or music, that enable us to see the minds of writers of yore. Moreover, writing has the power of making manifest what lies hidden in nature. "If one's mind is set on the mountains and rivers," he continues, "a zither can express his feelings. What is more, when the tip of a writing brush brings things into form, how can the basic principles remain hidden?" 夫志在山水，琴表其情，況形之筆端，理將焉匿? (*WXDL* 48 / 104–107)[64] In the dynamic process of writing and reading alike, Liu believes, one can penetrate the basic principles of things through a creative patterning of written words.

In light of this conception of literature as primarily the "patterning" of written words, Liu Xie reconceptualizes the origins of literature in a way unknown to earlier critics. Whereas earlier critics traced the origins of literature to *zhi* or the movement of the heart's intent in response to specific external processes, Liu Xie attributes the birth of literature to the natural manifestation of the Dao (the Ultimate Process), as well as to conscious human endeavors to transform their inward experiences into "patterns" of written words. Liu sets forth this view of the dual origins of literature in the opening paragraph of the first chapter of *Wenxin diaolong*, "Yuan Dao" 原道 (The Dao as the Source):

> The pattern *(wen)* as a power is very great. It is born together with heaven and earth, and why is it so? With the black [of heaven] and the yellow [of the earth], the myriad colors are compounded. With the squareness [of earth] and the roundness [of heaven], all forms are distinguished. The sun and the moon overlap each other like two jade disks, manifesting to those below the magnificent image of heaven. Rivers and mountains are brilliantly adorned to display the orderly configurations of the earth. These are the patterns of the Dao. As man looked up to see the radiance above and looked down to observe the inner loveliness below, the positions of high and low were determined and the two primary forms [heaven and earth] came into being. Only human beings, endowed with intelligence, can integrate with them. Together they are called the Triad. Human beings are the efflorescence of the Five Agents and are, in fact, the mind of heaven and earth. When mind came into being, language was formed. When language was formed, the pattern became manifest. This is the Dao, the natural course of things. (*WXDL* 1 / 1–21)

文之為德也大矣，與天地並生者何哉？夫玄黃色雜，方圓體分，日月疊璧，以垂麗天之象；山川煥綺，以鋪理地之形：此蓋道之文也。仰觀吐曜，俯察含章，高卑定位，故兩儀既生矣。惟人參之，性靈所鍾，是謂三才；為五行之秀，實天地之心。心生而言立，言立而文明，自然之道也。

If the origins of literature are only marginally discussed in earlier texts, Liu makes this issue the sole focus of the first three foundational chapter of *Wenxin diaolong*. He argues that literature shares with heaven and earth the same origin in the Dao, the Ultimate Process, and hence is an autonomous process that runs parallel to heaven and earth. This argument is based on his identification of literature's graphic form with the spatiovisual configurations of heaven and earth as analogous patterns *(wen)* of the Dao. He believes that heaven, earth, and humans all manifest the Dao through spatiovisual forms proper to themselves—for heaven, the sun and moon and other celestial images; for earth, mountains and rivers and other topographical shapes; and for humans, the graphic patterns of words. Of these three analogous forms, he holds that the last is more efficacious than the other two. It yields the most subtle secrets of the Dao because it is the brainchild of humans who are "the efflorescence of the Five Agents" and "the mind of heaven and earth."

Liu Xie is apparently aware that these claims are potentially contradictory. To say that the pattern of literature is identical with those of heaven and earth is to suggest it is formed as unconsciously as they are. To say that it is more refined because of human participation is to presume that it is *not* unconsciously formed as they are. To resolve this contradiction, Liu Xie ingeniously uses the traditional myths about the origins of written characters. By recounting these myths, Liu Xie points to the dual sources of writing: the markings on the "Yellow River Diagram" and the "Luo River Writing" presented to humans by the tortoise and dragons, and the trigrams and hexagrams invented and elucidated by the ancient sages. The first source signifies the ultimate nonhuman origin of literature in the Great Primordium. "The origins of human pattern began in the Great Primordium. So it goes that the 'Yellow River Diagram' gave birth to the eight trigrams, and that the 'Luo River Writing' contained the nine divisions. In addition, there were the fruit of jade tablets inscribed with gold, and the flower of green strips with red words. For all these was anyone responsible? No. They also came from the principle of the spirit" 人文之元，肇自太極…若乃《河圖》孕乎八卦，《洛書》韞乎九疇，玉版金鏤之寶，丹文綠牒之華，誰其尸之，亦神理而已 (*WXDL* 1 / 42–43, 52–57). In saying that the "Yellow River Diagram" and the "Luo River Writing" gave birth to the eight trigrams and the nine divisions, Liu Xie makes clear that the latter are a human elucidation of the former and that in the final analysis they should be regarded as a natural manifestation of the Dao analogous to the outer configurations of heaven and earth. The second source reveals the penultimate human origin of writing in the cosmological diagrams drawn by the ancient sages. "The Images of the *Book of Changes* were first to illuminate the numinous spirits that lie obscurely hidden. Fu Xi began [the *Book of Changes*] by marking [its eight trigrams] and Confucius completed it by adding the Wings [Commentaries]. For the two trigrams of Qian and Ku, Confucius composed the 'Patterned Words.' The pattern of words is indeed the 'mind of heaven and earth'" 幽贊神明，《易》象惟先。庖犧畫其始，仲尼翼其終。而《乾坤》兩位，獨制《文言》，言之文也，天地之心哉！ (*WXDL* 1 / 44–51). In Liu's opinion, the Images of the *Changes* are superior to the "Yellow River Diagram" because they do far more than provide a rough sketch of cosmic forces. They make known the innermost secrets of the Dao, establish the warp and woof of the universe, and perfect the laws of the human world (*WXDL* 1 / 96–109). It is on this ground that Liu Xie sees fit to claim the superiority of these "human patterns" to all naturally formed patterns in heaven and earth (*WXDL* 1 / 14–41). By explaining the ultimate and penultimate origins of literature in this light, Liu Xie forestalls the potential contradiction arising from his view that the "patterns" of man's writing are at once analogous with and superior to the patterns of heaven and earth. In exploring the origins of writing, Liu Xie seeks to exhibit the inherent links between the Dao and the human world and between the trigrams and hexagrams and the writings of subsequent ages. Because the ancient sages were endowed with plentiful intelligence, they could comprehend the workings of the Dao and give the most subtle revelation of them in their writings. By the same token, the writings of subsequent ages could continue to manifest the Dao largely because they were derived from the luminous writings of the ancient sages. To set forth the crucial role of the sages' writings in the manifestation and transmission of the Dao, Liu writes: "Therefore we know that the Dao passed down its *wen* (patterns) through the sages and that the sages illuminated the Dao through their own *wen* (writings). It penetrates everywhere unimpeded, and is applied day after day without being exhausted. The *Book of Changes* says, 'That which can make the world move lies in language.' That by which language can make the world move is the patterning *(wen)* of the Dao" 故知道沿聖以垂文，聖因文而明道，旁通而無滯，日用而不匱。《易》曰：鼓天下之動者存乎辭，辭之所以能鼓天下者，乃道之文也 (*WXDL* 1 / 110–117).

Liu Xie devotes much of the first chapter and the entirety of the second chapter "Zhengsheng" 徵聖 (Applying the Sages ['writings'] as the Touchstone) and the third chapter "Zongjing" 宗經 (Adopting the Classics as the Models) to tracing the transmission of the Dao from the *Book of Changes* down to different literary genres of his own time. First, he establishes an order among the Confucian classics themselves, extending from the *Book of Changes,* to the *Book of Documents,* to the *Book of Poetry,* to the *Book of Rites,* and to the *Spring and Autumn Annals* (*WXDL* 1 / 74–95; 3 / 12–25). Then, he sets forth the different modes of observation and expression (*WXDL* 2 / 42–59; 2 / 64–67; 3 / 35–74) and the resulting stylistic characteristics (*WXDL* 3 / 103–110) in these five classics. On the basis of their stylistic characteristics, he takes each of the five classics to be the source of given genres of writing (*WXDL* 3 / 85–102). In this manner, he establishes an elaborate genealogy of literary genres, beginning with the five classics and ending with the multitude of belletristic and nonbelletristic genres of his own time.

Liu Xie's view on literary creation is no less radically different from those of Han and pre-Han critics.[65] If literature is to them part of a public, expressive-performative process centered on dance, music, or verbalization, it means to Liu Xie a process of composing a written, belletristic work, a process that is largely private, contemplative, and creative. In discussing the expressive-performative processes, earlier critics tended to focus on the interaction with the processes of a given realm—the numinous, the natural, or the human. When Liu Xie looks into the contemplative-creative process, however, he carefully analyzes the interaction with external processes on *multiple* levels at different compositional stages.

Liu Xie devotes chapters 26 ("Shensi" 神思 [Spirit and Thought]), and chapter 46 ("Wuse"物色 [The Colors of Nature]), exclusively to the examination of the entire creative process. The opening passage of the latter chapter describes the arousal of emotion at the initial stage of literary composition. "Springs and autumns revolve around in succession. The *yin* force brings bleakness and the *yang* force brightness. As the colors of nature are stirred into movement, the mind, too, is swayed. . . . When the colors of nature greet him, how can man remain unmoved?" 春秋代序，陰陽慘舒，物色之動，心亦搖焉⋯物色相召，人誰獲安？ (*WXDL* 46 / 1–4; 11–12) Liu contends that the writer responds to the physical processes on a simple psychological level. The cycle of seasons, along with the changing appearances of the myriad things, engenders delight, pensiveness, melancholy, or sorrow in the heart of the writer. These responses awaken the writer's desire to write about what is inside his heart. "Thus when the poets feel moved by physical things," writes Liu Xie, "their categorical associations are endless. They linger around in the sphere of the myriad images, and meditate and chant gently in the domain of what they have seen and heard" 是以詩人感物，聯類無窮，流連萬象之際，沈吟視聽之區 (*WXDL* 46 / 29–32).

In chapter 26 ("Shensi"), Liu Xie begins by examining how such a categorical association leads to the flight of the poet's spirit at the next stage. Now the writer is no longer responding to concrete physical things. Instead he is quietly contemplative, and his innermost spirit wanders off to meet things or objects (*wu* 物), defying the restrictions of time and space.

> An ancient said, "while one's body is on the rivers and lakes, his mind remains at the foot of the high palace tower." This is what is called "spirit and thought." In the process of literary thinking, the spirit goes afar. As one silently reaches the state of mental concentration, his thought may trace back one thousand years. As one shows the slightest movement in countenance, his vision may go through ten thousand *li*.
>
> 古人云：形在江海之上，心存魏闕之下。神思之謂也。文之思也，其神遠矣。故寂然凝慮，思接千載；悄焉動容，視通萬里。(*WXDL* 26 / 1–10)

This outbound flight is often taken as the sole meaning of "spirit and thought." However, if we examine what immediately follows, we see that it is only the initial part of a reciprocal process. Having traced the spirit's outbound flight, Liu proceeds to show how it courses along with things and eventually returns with them toward one's ears and eyes:

> In the midst of his chanting and singing, the sounds of pearls and jade issue forth. Right before his brows and lashes, the spectacle of wind-blown clouds spreads out. All this is made possible by the principle of thought. When the principle of thought is at its most miraculous, the spirit wanders with external things.
>
> 吟詠之間，吐納珠玉之聲；眉睫之前，卷舒風雲之色：其思理之致乎！故思理為妙，神與物游。(*WXDL* 26 / 11–17)

Liu reaffirms the notion of *shensi* as a "double journey" as he examines various factors controlling the outbound and inbound flights. He notes that the outbound flight is controlled by the psychological-moral process (*zhi*) and the physiological-moral process (*qi*). "The spirit dwells in the bosom, intent (*zhi*) and vital breath (*qi*) control the pivot of its outlet" 神居胸臆，而志氣統其關鍵 (*WXDL* 26 / 18–19). Then he identifies the perceptual processes (aural and visual) and the intellectual processes (the conscious use of language) as crucial to mediating the influx of external things from afar. "External things come in through the ear and the eye, with language controlling the hinge and trigger [for their influx]" 物沿耳目，而辭令管其樞機 (*WXDL* 26 / 20–21). To Liu, the success of *shensi* depends on a well-coordinated operation of all these processes controlling the "double journey." "When the hinge and trigger allow passage, no external things can hide appearances. When the pivot of its outlet is closed, the spirit is impeded" 樞機方通，則物無隱貌；關鍵將塞，則神有遁心 (*WXDL* 26 / 22–25). The final result of *shensi*, Liu believes, is mutual transformation of the inner (*shen* 神, *yi* 意, and *qing* 情) and the outer (*wu* 物 and *xiang* 象) into *yixiang* 意象 or "idea-image" and a perfect embodiment of this idea-image in the medium of *yan* 言 or language (*WXDL* 26 / 48–64).

To achieve this ideal result of *shensi*, Liu maintains, a writer must cultivate various qualities essential to the smooth operation of these processes. He must learn to obtain the state of "the emptiness and still-ness," a necessary condition for the outbound flight of his spirit. "There-fore in shaping and developing literary thought," Liu writes, "what is the most important is 'emptiness and stillness'" 是以陶鈞文思，貴在虛靜 (*WXDL* 26 / 26–27). To ensure a smooth passage of his spirit, the writer must "remove obstructions in the five viscera and cleanse the spirit" 疏瀹五藏，澡雪精神 (*WXDL* 26 / 28–29) or, in other words, he must build up his vital energy and his moral character. To improve his intellectual capability, he must "accumulate learning and thus store up treasures" 積學以儲寶 (*WXDL* 26 / 30) and "contemplate the prin-ciples [of things] and thus enrich his talent" 酌理以富才 (*WXDL* 26 / 31). To sharpen his perceptual power, he must "examine and observe things to bring them to the fullest light" 研閱以窮照 (*WXDL* 26 / 32). Finally, in order to put forth his "idea-image" in language, he must "fol-low the flow of ideas and feelings to search for felicitous expressions" 馴致以懌辭 (*WXDL* 26 / 33). After a writer has cultivated all these qual-ities, Liu believes, he will be able to effectively engage with external processes on the intuitive, physiological, moral, psychological, and in-tellectual levels. What emerges from this well-coordinated operation of *shensi* will be a great work of literature.

Liu Xie's view on the functions of literature also stand in sharp con-trast to those held by earlier critics. If the discussion of the functions of literature is the most important part of Han and pre-Han critical texts, it is the least important part of Liu's concept of literature. None of the fifty chapters of *Wenxin diaolong* is devoted to this issue, whereas a great many chapters are written solely to discuss the origins and formation of literature. Unlike the author of the "Great Preface," Liu Xie does not expatiate on how literature can and should be used to rectify human relationships, enhance ethical and sociopolitical order, and bring man in accord with the spirits. Instead, he merely acknowledges that "using poetry to eulogize good and correct evil deeds is a long-standing practice" 順美匡惡，其來久矣 (*WXDL* 6 / 32–33) and perfunctorily mentions these two edifying functions in a number of chapters.[66] On the theoretical level, Liu regards literature as an autonomous process whose value should be judged, not by how it harmonizes certain specific processes, but by how it embodies the Dao within its *wen* or beautiful configurations and thereby "sets forth the warp and woof of the cosmos, perfects and unifies the lasting laws" 經緯區宇，彌綸彝憲 (*WXDL* 1 / 106–107).

Liu Xie's concept of literature is by any measure a remarkably comprehensive one.[67] In formulating it, Liu has deftly assimilated and transformed earlier critical concerns with various external and internal processes. Let us first consider his treatment of external processes.[68] On the stratum of the ultimate cosmological process, we observe his transformation of the early religious obsession with *shen* (the numinous spirits) into an artistic engagement with *shen* (the mysterious operation of the Dao) in the mind as well as the outer world.[69] On the stratum of natural processes, he keenly observes the relationship of literature with the *yin* and *yang,* the Five Agents, and concrete natural processes as do different speakers in the *Zuo Commentary* and *Speeches of the States.* However, he wants to explore the relevance of those natural processes to artistic creation, not the usefulness of literature in regulating those natural processes for the sake of growth and prosperity.[70] On the stratum of ethical and sociopolitical processes, we notice his shift of attention from practical didactic concerns of the "Great Preface" to a "metaphysical" task of embodying the ideal moral and social order in a belletristic work.

Turning our attention to internal processes, we note that, on the stratum of suprasensory experience, Liu substitutes contemplative intuition for invocation as the means of contact with the ultimate reality. On the stratum of physiological experience, we observe his sublimation of magico-ritualistic bodily movements, prominent in the "Canon of Yao" passage, into an endeavor to cultivate and exercise *qi* or inward vital breath for literary creation.[71] On the stratum of psychological experience, we see that he shifts his interest from the expression of *zhi,* the central concern of the "Great Preface," to the "artistic configurations of emotion" (*qingwen* 情 文). On the stratum of moral experience,

he relegates moral remonstration and teaching to peripheral signifi-
cance, even though he acknowledges the relevance of the author's moral
character to literary creation.

Liu has made it possible for us to perceive different aspects of liter-
ature in terms of a complex, multilevel interaction of internal and ex-
ternal processes. Most modern critics agree that Liu's grand scheme of
these interacting processes is centered upon the Dao, but they hold
vastly different views about the nature of the Dao. They variously iden-
tify Liu's Dao with the human Dao in *Analects,* the naturalistic Dao in
Lao Zi and *Zhuang Zi,* the Buddhist Dao, and the synthesis of the Con-
fucian and the Daoist Dao in *Commentaries to the Book of Changes* (*Yi
zhuan* 易傳).[72] Following the last and most prevailing of these views,
I would argue that the Dao in *Wenxin diaolong* is identical to the Dao
depicted in the *Commentaries to the Book of Changes,* especially the
"Commentary on the Appended Phrases" ("Xici zhuan" 系辭傳). Liu's
great indebtedness to this particular commentary is fully discussed in
the next chapter.

TWO PURE AESTHETIC CONCEPTS OF LITERATURE IN THE SIX DYNASTIES

In tracing literature to the Dao, Liu Xie establishes a conceptual model
much broader than the *"Shi yan zhi"* statement for understanding lit-
erature. It is true that later critics will repeat that statement again and
again to indicate the immediate causes for poetic creation and to in-
voke the long didactic tradition associated with the statement. In ex-
amining the origin and nature of *wen* or refined literature, however,
they almost invariably adopt the *wen*-Dao model established by Liu
Xie. Of course, the adoption of this model does not mean that Chi-
nese concepts of literature are to become monolithic thereafter. Quite
the contrary, as later critics embrace new philosophical notions of the
Dao and accordingly reconceptualize the *wen*-Dao relationship, they
bring forth many new concepts of literature. Here let us review the high-
lights of these concepts.

The shift from the *"Shi yan zhi"* to the *wen*-Dao model is already
quite noticeable in two important critical texts written shortly after Liu
Xie's *Literary Mind.* Both texts are prefaces to literary anthologies, one
written by Zhong Hong 鍾嶸 (ca. 468–518) for his *Grading of Poets* (*Shi
pin* 詩品) and the other by Xiao Tong 蕭統 (501–531) for his *Anthol-
ogy of Refined Literature* (*Wenxuan* 文選). Zhong's is an anthology de-
voted exclusively to pentasyllabic poetry from the Han to his own time.

Contrary to what one may expect, he does not repeat the *"Shi yan zhi"* statement nor does he dwell upon the notion of *zhi* or moral sentiment in his preface. Although he cites a remark by Confucius on poetry and appropriates a few phrases from the "Great Preface," he gives little more than passing attention to the didactic tradition. His interest is focused instead on the aesthetic significance of *qing* 情 (emotion). He examines how the change of four seasons stirs one's emotion,[73] how poets "gallop forward with their emotions" 騁 其 情,[74] and how pentasyllabic poems afford inexhaustible aesthetic pleasures through their descriptive and expressive efficacy.[75] In the opening paragraph, he traces the ultimate origin of poetry to the cosmic *qi* (ether) and comments on the illuminating effects of poetry on the 三 才 or the Triad (heaven, earth, and man).[76] His comments are reminiscent of Liu Xie's opening remarks in the *Literary Mind.*

The echoes of Liu Xie's remarks can be even more clearly heard in the opening paragraph of Xiao Tong's preface. Xiao, too, begins with a broad reflection on the ultimate origin and nature of literature. Like Liu Xie, he traces the development of *wenji* 文 籍 (writings) to the Eight Trigrams and maintains that these protographs are coeval with both *tianwen* 天 文 (the heavenly pattern) and *renwen* 人 文 (the human pattern).[77] However, he does not consider the Confucian classics to be crucial to the development from these protographs to the refined literature of his own time. While Liu Xie holds up Confucian classics as the ideal models for refined literature, he not only leaves them out in his discussion of the history of writing, but excludes them altogether from his anthology itself. The convenient excuse he gives for this exclusion is that these sagely works allow no cutting and selecting required of an anthology.[78] In explaining his exclusion of non-Confucian philosophical texts, he is more honest and forthright: "The writings of Lao [Lao Zi] and Zhuang [Zhuang Zi] and the likes of Guan [Guang Zi] and Mencius have the primary goal of establishing their philosophical ideas, and literary competence is not essential to them. Therefore, from the present anthology they are also omitted" 老 、 莊 之 作 ， 管 孟 之 流 ， 蓋 以 立 意 為 宗 不 以 能 文 為 本 ； 今 之 所 撰 ， 又 以 略 諸.[79] This seems to be the real reason for his exclusion of Confucian classics as well. At the end of the preface, he identifies two distinguishing traits of refined literature: "The depiction of events is born of deep contemplation, and the locus of principles lies in the domain of refined phrases" 事 出 於 沉 思 ， 義 歸 乎 翰 藻.[80] Apparently, neither the Confucian classics nor non-Confucian philosophical texts exhibit these two traits and hence their exclusion from his anthology.

It is apparent that Zhong's and Xiao's concepts of literature are for-mulated on the *wen*-Dao model, even though the Dao is not explic-itly described in their prefaces. The cosmic *qi* and the Eight Trigrams, to which they respectively trace the origin of literature, are none other than the modus operandi of the Dao as depicted by Liu Xie in the first chapter of the *Literary Mind*. In adopting the *wen*-Dao model, however, both Zhong and Xiao leave the Confucian sages out of con-sideration completely. Liu Xie considers the sages to be the indispen-sable intermediary between *wen* and the cosmological Dao. He main-tains that "the Dao passed down its *wen* (pattern) through the sages and that the sages illuminated the Dao through their own *wen* (writ-ings)" 道沿聖以垂文，聖因文而明道 (*WXDL* 1 / 111–112). By con-trast, Zhong and Xiao quietly banish the sages from the illustrious his-tory of writing. This banishment is obviously intended to facilitate their common critical agenda—to introduce pure aesthetic standards for grading individual poets and for establishing the literary canon. The implementation of these standards results in the exclusion of Con-fucian classics in their anthologies. Considering their radical depar-ture from Liu's emphasis on the Confucian classics, we can distinguish Zhong's and Xiao's concepts of literature as pure aesthetic ones.

NEO-CONFUCIAN CONCEPTS
OF LITERATURE IN THE TANG AND THE SONG

In the Tang and Song, the *wen*-Dao model dominates the theoretical thinking about literature and is emblazoned in two new critical tenets. The first is *"wen yi guan Dao"* 文以貫道 (*"Wen* is for transmitting the Dao"), first presented by Wang Tong 王通 (ca. 584–618)[81] and later expounded by Liu Zongyuan 柳宗元 (773–819), Han Yu 韓愈 (768–824), Li Han 李漢 (fl. 806–821), and other exponents of the Ancient Prose Movement (*Guwen yundong* 古文運動).[82] The second tenet is *"Wen yi zai Dao"* 文以載道 (*"Wen* is for carrying the Dao"), put for-ward by Zhou Dunyi 周敦頤 (1017–1073) and embraced by Shi Jie 石介 (1005–1045), Wang Anshi 王安石 (1021–1086), Cheng Yi 程頤 (1032–1085), Wang Bai 王柏 (1197–1274), and other Song exponents of the *Dao xue* 道學 ("learning of the Dao").[83] These two groups of crit-ics will hereafter be referred to as the *guan Dao* and the *zai Dao* advo-cates. The two tenets seem identical in the original as much as in En-glish translation. For instance, *"guan* Dao" 貫道 is glossed as "like '*zai* Dao'" 猶載道 in *Hanyu da cidian* 漢語大詞典 (A Comprehensive Dic-tionary of Chinese).[84] If understood in terms of a reaction against

Zhong Hong's and Xiao Tong's aesthetic concepts of literature, the two tenets indeed can be regarded as very similar to each other. In developing their aesthetic concepts of literature, we have noted, Zhong Hong and Xiao Tong exclude ancient Confucian classics and canonize literati compositions strictly on the grounds of their literary merits. Of these merits, the most prized are descriptive verisimilitude, expressive eloquence, metrical virtuosity, flights of imagination, and above all the artistry of parallelism. In reconceptualizing *wen* and the Dao, the *guan Dao* and the *zai Dao* advocates do just the opposite. They restore Confucian classics as the core of *wen* and exclude from *wen*'s rightful lineage all literati compositions that strive for literary refinement for its own sake. However, if we carefully compare the statements on the *wen*-Dao relationship by the *guan Dao* and the *zai Dao* advocates, we can easily perceive subtle yet essential divergences between them.

In discussing the *wen*-Dao relationship, many *guan Dao* advocates give due attention to the cosmological Dao even though they stress the transmission of the Confucian Dao through their time by a long lineage of preeminent Confucians. Consider, for instance, Han Yu's, Su Xun's 蘇洵 (1009–1066), and Bai Jiuyi's 白居易 (772–846) famous and highly original discussions on the cosmological Dao.[85] In their discussions we take note of a convergence with Liu Xie's view on the *wen*-Dao relationship. Like Liu Xie, they believe that contemporary literary writings are capable of revealing or even embodying the cosmological Dao as did the ancient Confucian classics. In discussing this continued dynamic relationship between *wen* and the cosmological Dao, they present an impressive array of evidence of resonance and correspondence between cosmological and literary processes. Thanks to their belief in this dynamic *wen*-Dao relationship, they maintain a highly positive attitude toward literature despite their allegiance to the moralistic neo-Confucian traditions. Their strong affirmation of literature's value is expressed eloquently by Liu Zongyuan's claims that "*wen* is for illuminating the Dao" 文者以明道 and that his literary writings are "not far from the Dao" 於道不遠 and enable him to "add wings to the Dao" 羽翼夫道也.[86] Guided by this positive attitude toward literature, they show considerable restraints in their criticism of the Six Dynasties literature. While they denounce the pursuit of metrical virtuosity and ornate parallelism for their own sake, they have no inclination whatsoever to dismiss the merit of literary refinement. In fact, what they try to accomplish is to realign literary refinement with the high moral purpose of "illuminating the Dao." It is to achieve this goal that they launch the famous Ancient Prose Movement, an endeavor to reinvent the ancient prose through innovative diction and the powerful cadence of utterance.

In reconceptualizing the *wen*-Dao relationship, the *zai Dao* advocates follow a very different tact. Many of them seek to disassociate *wen* from the cosmological Dao and identify it exclusively with the Confucian ethico-sociopolitical order. For instance, Shi Jie ambitiously attempts to codify all major aspects of *wen* within the rubric of the Confucian ethico-sociopolitical order:

> Thus the Two Forms are the quintessence of *wen*, the Three Bonds the manifestation of *wen*, the Five Constant Virtues the substance of *wen*, the Nine Categories the numbers of *wen*, moral virtues the basis of *wen*, rituals and music the adornments of *wen*, filial piety and the deference for elder brothers the beauty of *wen*, accomplishments of enterprises the appearance of *wen*, moral education the luminosity of *wen*, justice and governance the principles of *wen*, and orders and commands the sounds of *wen*.[87]

> 故兩儀，文之體也；三綱，文之象也；五常，文之質也；九疇，文之數也；道德，文之本也；禮樂，文之飾也；孝悌，文之美也；功業，文之容也；教化，文之明也；刑政，文之綱也；號令，文之聲也。

Exhaustive though it seems, this long list conspicuously excludes literary refinement, which has been treated as the most important attribute of *wen* in the majority of critical texts written since Cao Pi 曹丕 (187–226). Shi's radical banishment of literary refinement results from a rethinking of the *wen*-Dao relationship guided by the *zai Dao* tenet.

Explaining this tenet, Zhou Dunyi writes, "*Wen* is that which carries the Dao. Wheels and shafts of a cart are decorated, but we find no use for them. They are nothing but decorations. What more can we say about an empty vehicle? Refined expressions are artistry, and moral virtues are inner substance" 文所以載道也，輪轅飾而人弗庸，徒飾也。況虛車乎？文辭，藝也；道德，實也。[88] This explanation aptly sets the *zai Dao* apart from the *guan Dao* tenet. The verb *guan* 貫 in the phrase *guan Dao* means "going through and linking up." So, the tenet "*Wen yi guan Dao*" literally means that *wen* is that through which the Dao passes and transmits itself. In such a circumstance, *wen* is certainly not extraneous to the Dao and in fact it becomes an inseparable part or even an embodiment of it as it passes through. By contrast, the verb *zai* 載 in the phrase *zai Dao* merely means "carrying" without the slightest intimation of bonds between a vehicle and what it carries. So, the phrase *zai Dao* denotes a *wen*-Dao relationship radically different from the one indicated by the phrase *guan Dao*. In fact, by comparing *wen* to an empty vehicle, Zhou stresses the separation of *wen* from the Dao and hence its insubstantiality and meaninglessness in and of itself. Just as those who regard *wen* as the embodiment of the Dao would avidly engage in literary pursuits, those who see *wen* in the same light as Zhou does would naturally disparage literary pursuits.

Guided by such a rethinking of the *wen*-Dao relationship, the *zai Dao* advocates launch a concerted endeavor to denigrate literary refinement. The strategies employed for this end vary considerably. Some seek to underscore the expendability of literary refinement by comparing it to empty vehicles, fish traps, landing crafts, and similar metaphors of insubstantiality borrowed from Daoist and Buddhist sources. Some attempt to explain away the literary refinement in Confucian classics by arguing that it is a spontaneous manifestation of the sages' luminosity, not the result of conscious literary endeavor on their part.[89] Some like Shi Jie simply redefine *wen* entirely in moralistic terms and thereby dispose of literary refinement once and for all. Some are even more vocal and unabashed in denouncing literary refinement. For instance, Cheng Yi goes so far as to argue that literature is a frivolous pursuit that ruins the learning of the Dao. "Indulgence in playthings saps one's will," Cheng declares. "To pursue literature is also a plaything" 玩物喪志，為文亦玩物也.[90]

Seen in a broad historical perspective, both the *guan Dao* and the *zai Dao* tenets have inherited the didactic tradition of the "Great Preface." However, while the author of the "Great Preface" relates poetry to concrete sociopolitical events and processes, the *guan Dao* and the *zai Dao* advocates are more inclined to discuss literature in relation to their neo-Confucian notions of the Dao. Considering their different attitudes toward literary refinement, they can be seen to have respectively developed positive and negative neo-Confucian concepts of literature. "Negative" seems to be a particularly suitable label for what the *zai Dao* advocates have said about literature. As shown above, their views of literature can be differentiated best in terms of the degree of negativity shown toward it.

MAJOR MING AND QING CONCEPTS OF LITERATURE

Ming and Qing critics are not nearly as preoccupied as their Tang and Song predecessors with abstract, theoretical questions about literature. They do not show much interest in debating the usefulness of *wen*, nor do they aim to put forward new grand critical tenets. Instead they turn their attention to much more practical questions concerning *zhiwen* 至文 (perfect literary works). Literary excellence is an issue lying at the heart of Ming and Qing literary thought. When Ming critics debate about imitation and creativity or about the canonization of certain historical periods, they usually proceed from their preconceived criteria of *zhiwen*. Qing critics tend to do the same when they engage one another in three major literary debates of their times—focused respectively on the merits of ancient prose and parallel prose, on the relationship between literature and philological scholarship, and on the compositional rules for poetry and prose (*shi fa* 詩法, *wenfa* 文法). More often than not, Ming and Qing critics formulate their own criteria of *zhiwen* by modifying or challenging various existing concepts of literature constructed on the *wen*-Dao model.

The overall direction of the Ming literary criticism is heavily influenced by the Seven Former and the Seven Latter Masters (*Qianhou qizi* 前後七子). Particularly influential are Li Mengyang 李夢陽 (1473–1530) and He Jingming 何景明 (1483–1521) of the former group, and Li Panlong 李攀龍 (1514–1570), Wang Shizhen 王世貞 (1526–1590), and Xie Zhen 謝榛 (1495–1575) of the latter group. These critics vie with one another in devising theories and methods of imitation and schemes of literary periodization and canonization. Engrossed in these highly practical issues, they have not developed any particularly noteworthy concepts of literature. For fresh, original ideas about *wen* and the Dao, we must turn to those who denounce their imitative practices and embrace the ideal of spontaneous creativity.

Li Zhi 李贄 (1527–1602), an iconoclastic thinker in the late Ming, launches the most relentless and sweeping of attacks on imitative practices and the underlying neo-Confucian concepts of literature. According to him, the neo-Confucian notions of *wen* and the Dao are nothing but impediments to the creation of *zhiwen*. The neo-Confucian *daoxue* only defiles one's childlike heart and renders one's words insincere and hypocritical. According to him, the ancient sages produced *zhiwen* not because they harped on the Dao and strove for literary refinement. Rather, it is simply because they had a childlike heart and spoke with complete spontaneity. If one can free oneself from the shackles of the *daoxue* and restore one's childlike heart, Li believes, *zhiwen* can flow out from one's mouth spontaneously. Li's theory of the childlike heart (*tongxin shuo* 童心說) represents a totalistic negation of the neo-Confucian concepts of literature.[91]

Jiao Hong 焦竑 (1541–1620), another late Ming critic, also stresses the expression of spontaneous emotion as a way to counter the pernicious influence of the *daoxue*. Instead of explicitly pitting the dogmatic *daoxue* against spontaneous emotional expression, however, he ingeniously redefines the *daoxue* as an intuitive comprehension of the inner principles of all things rather than the monolithic neo-Confucian Dao alone. Simply by depicting one's inward perception of these principles, he argues, one can produce the *zhiwen* of the world. According to him, these inner principles were compellingly revealed not only in Confucian classics but also in *Lao Zi, Zhuang Zi, Hanfei Zi,* and other philosophical, political, and historical texts. As a result, these texts all became the models of *zhiwen* for different prose genres in later times. For Jiao, the six Confucian classics are no longer the exclusive model for all types of *wen* as argued by Liu Xie, nor even the sole model for ancient prose as claimed by the *guan Dao* advocates. The Confucian classics are merely the model for a particular kind of sociopolitical tract written by Dong Zhongshu 董仲舒 (ca. 179 B.C.–ca. 104 B.C.), Yang Xiong 揚雄 (53 B.C.–A.D. 18), Liu Xiang 劉向 (ca. 77 B.C.–ca. 6 B.C.), and other Confucian scholars. Although Jiao's views of the *daoxue* and *zhiwen* are not openly iconoclastic as Li Zhi's, they certainly amount to a revolt against the neo-Confucian concepts of literature.[92]

The Qing critics seem far less inclined to take on the neo-Confucian concepts of literature in an explicit manner. Instead, they tend to quietly challenge particular neo-Confucian notions of *wen* for the purpose of advancing their own literary agendas. For instance, Yuan Mei 袁枚 (1716–1798) and Ruan Yuan 阮元 (1764–1849) take issue with the overly narrow identification of the sages' *wen* with the ancient prose by the *guan Dao* advocates. By arguing that parallel prose is an inherent part of the sages' *wen,* they seek to revive a literary tradition long suppressed by neo-Confucian critics.[93] With the rise of philological scholarship during the Qian-Jia reigns, Weng Fanggang 翁方綱 (1733–1818) and Jiao Xun 焦循 (1763–1820) target the *zai Dao* advocates for criticism. Guided by their mistaken notion of an antithesis between *wen* and the Dao, they hold, the Song *zai Dao* advocates badly neglected literary refinement and turned their prose and poetical works into a hodgepodge of philosophical quotations (*yulu* 語錄). To redress this neglect of *wen,* Weng and Jiao advocate an integration of philosophical scholarship into prose and poetical works. Some critics like Duan Yucai 段玉裁 (1735–1815) go so far as to regard philological scholarship as the core of *wen.*[94] To other critics, this redefinition of *wen* has gone to another extreme. To correct this overreaction to the Song *zai Dao* advocates, Zhang Xuecheng 章學誠 (1738–1801) argues for an integration of philosophical principles, philological investigations, and literary diction.[95]

None of the Ming and Qing critics examined so far are particularly fruitful and innovative in their reconceptualizations of literature. Audacious and extraordinary though they are, Li Zhi's remarks on *zhiwen* are more of an iconoclastic statement than a serious effort to discuss *zhiwen* as a literary ideal. In discussing *zhiwen,* Weng Fanggang, Jiao Xun, and others do little more than broaden the scope of *wen* set by the earlier *guang Dao* and the *zai Dao* advocates. For more innovative efforts to reconceptualize literature, we need to turn our attention to two new aesthetic concepts of literature developed on the *wen*-Dao model by Ye Xie 葉燮 (1627–1703) and Yao Nai 姚鼐 (1732–1815).

In "Origins of Poetry" ("Yuan shi" 原詩), Ye Xie offers a rigorously analytical study of the dynamic interplay between *wen* and the cosmological Dao. Like Xiao Tong, he does not explicitly talk about the Dao even though he focuses his attention on the writer's engagement with cosmic processes. This seems to be Ye's conscious choice, probably aimed at disassociating himself from the neo-Confucian *daoxue.* Indeed, throughout the essay he does not address any didactic concerns nor does he use any terms and concepts that would remind us of neo-Confucian views on *wen* and the Dao. Unlike Xiao Tong and Liu Xie, however, Ye does not examine the cosmic processes for the purpose of demonstrating the sacred origin of literature. His primary aim is to explore the dynamics of literary creation—to investigate how *zhiwen* results from the writer's intense engagement with cosmic processes.

Following an unusually analytical approach in his investigation, he conceives of three phases in the development of all occurrences: *li* 理, the inner principles that determine what can occur; *shi* 事, actual occurrences in the worlds of nature and man; and *qing* 情, external forms manifested by those occurrences. According to Ye, the development through these three phases depends on the cosmic *qi* or ethers. If *qi* fills and pulsates through them, the three phases will develop with a great momentum. To Ye, this natural, wondrous course of development is what produces the *zhiwen* of heaven and earth.[96]

To produce comparable *zhiwen* in a work of literature, Ye maintains, a writer must enact the dynamic interplay of *li, shi,* and *qing* in his imaginative world. Whether he can succeed depends on his exercise of four internal powers: *cai* 才 (talent), *dan* 膽 (courage), *shi* 識 (judgment), and *li* 力 (strength). If the writer can effectively exercise these four internal powers to engage the external *li, shi,* and *qing,* he can produce *zhiwen* comparable to that of heaven and earth.[97] In fact, like Liu Xie,

Ye believes that such *zhiwen* is even superior to the *zhiwen* of heaven and earth. If Liu Xie bolsters this claim merely by repeating the legends about the making of the *Book of Changes,* Ye offers a rational explanation based on the nonpareil aesthetic efficacy of literary *zhiwen*. Because the *li, shi,* and *qing* of a poetic work are fictitious rather than real, a poet cannot possibly depict them realistically with referential language. Only when he lets his imagination roam in the nebulous, suprasensory realm can he hope to capture the indefinite, ineffable state of *li, shi,* and *qing* and create literary *zhiwen* capable of generating inexhaustible aesthetic pleasure.[98] In short, by reexamining the *wen*-Dao interplay from the point of literary creation and by substantiating the superiority of human *wen* in terms of its aesthetic efficacy, Ye Xie presents us with a highly original aesthetic concept of literature.

Yao Nai is an eminent leader of the Tongcheng school known for its espousal of the neo-Confucian orthodoxy and its imitation of the Tang and Song ancient prose. A dedicated neo-Confucian scholar and writer, he avidly advocates an integration of philosophical principles, philological scholarship, and literary refinement.[99] However, when he theorizes about literature, he is able to set aside his neo-Confucian beliefs and discuss its origin and nature in relation to the cosmological Dao. Echoing the views of Liu Xie, he writes:

> I hear that the Dao of heaven and earth is nothing but yin and yang, hard and soft. *Wen* is the essence of heaven and earth and is the manifestation of yin and yang, hard and soft. Only the words of the sages can embrace the two ethers (*qi*) together without being partial to any of the two. Nonetheless, with regard to the contents of the *Book of Changes,* the *Book of Poetry,* the *Book of Documents,* and *Analects,* there are also places where [the qualities of] hard and soft can be distinguished.[100]

> 鼐聞天地之道，陰陽剛柔而已。文者，天地之精英，而陰陽剛柔之發也。惟聖人之言，統二氣之會而弗偏，然而《易》、《詩》、《書》、《論語》所載，亦間有可以剛柔分矣。

In tracing *wen* to the Dao, he aims to accomplish a goal quite different from those of Xiao Tong, Liu Xie, and Ye Xie. If Xiao and Liu aim to demonstrate *wen*'s sacred origin, and if Ye seeks to reveal the dynamics of literary creation, Yao strives to construct broad aesthetic categories based on the Dao. Insofar as "the Dao of heaven and earth are nothing but yin and yang, hard and soft," he argues that all forms of *wen,* born of the Dao, must possess the "beauty of yang and hard" (*yang yu gang zhi mei* 陽 與 剛 之 美) and the "beauty of yin and soft" (*yin yu rou zhi mei* 陰 與 柔 之 美), whether they are ancient Confucian classics or contemporary belletristic writings.[101] If richly endowed with "beauty of yang and hard," he continues, a written composition exhibits a dynamic pattern (*wen*) like that of thunder and lightning, or strong gusts of wind, or a raging river. If richly endowed with the "beauty of yin and soft," it displays a gentle pattern (*wen*) like that of a breeze, wafting smoke, or a meandering brook in the deep woods. By devising these two broad categories, Yao provides a simple and effective solution to the unchecked proliferation of aesthetic categories and subcategories since the Tang. The multitudinous appearances and qualities of writing, he believes, can all be subsumed under the two broad aesthetic categories. By grounding the two categories in the Dao, he establishes a new overarching principle of aesthetic judgment. Because the "one yang and one yin constitute Dao," he reasons that a fine literary work must contain elements of both categories. Like yin and yang interaction, he explains, one category may gain ascendance over the other, but never can one category exist without the other.[102] If the interplay of these two categories in a literary work is nearly as miraculous as the yin-yang interplay of the Dao, he contends that the work is the *zhiwen* that "communes with the numinous spirits" 通 乎 神 明.[103] Unlike Ye Xie, Yao Nai explores the *wen*-Dao relationship mainly from the point of literary reception. Nonetheless, his aesthetic concept of literature is by and large as original and sophisticated as Ye Xie's. As Ye and Yao reexamine the *wen*-Dao relationship from the opposite perspectives of literary creation and reception, their concepts of *wen* seem to complement each other very well.

Our discussion of the major concepts of literature has shed light on some of the unique features of Chinese thinking about literature. Traditional Chinese critics share a core belief in literature as a harmonizing process. This process arises in the heart (*xin*) of a composer or author when he responds to various external processes on physiological, psychological, moral, intellectual, or intuitive levels. As he makes known his responses by dancing, music-playing, singing, speaking, or writing, this process moves from the inner to the outer world and thus brings the two into harmony.

In describing literature as a harmonizing process, traditional Chinese critics variously stress its subordination to or independence from religious, ritualistic, ethical, sociopolitical, or other artistic activities. In the "Canon of Yao," poetry is depicted as an auxiliary part of a dance-centered, religious performance. In the *Zuo Commentary* and *Speeches of the States,* poetry is seen as a relatively more important but nonetheless auxiliary part of a music-centered, courtly ceremony. In the "Great Preface," poetry is described as the central part of verbalized social intercourse. In *Wenxin diaolong, wen* or refined literature is explored as a text-centered, largely belletristic pursuit. In the two famous prefaces by Zhong Hong and Xiao Tong, *wen* is even more unequivocally endorsed as an autonomous belletristic pursuit. The development of Chinese literary thinking up to this time aptly reflects a pattern of literary evolution similar to the tri-stage development of Western literature and arts sketched by Elliot Deutsch: "In sum, art emerges from religion, first from its identification with religion by way of its centering in magical or holy power, and second from its subservient role in communicating an independently formulated meaning. It then becomes autonomous by virtue of its own quality and strives, when autonomous, to be at once aesthetically forceful, meaningful, and beautiful."[104] Unlike its Western counterpart, however, Chinese belletristic writing cannot maintain for long its predominance and its autonomy eminently achieved during the Six Dynasties. With the rise of neo-Confucianism in Tang and Song times, pure belletristic pursuit is condemned as decadent and *wen* is once again subordinated by many to ethical and sociopolitical enterprises. Indeed, *wen* is reconceptualized by most neo-Confucians as part of broader ethical and sociopolitical efforts to illuminate and transmit the Confucian Dao. Meanwhile, the dominant status of writing is continuously challenged by the emergence of orally based or derived genres: first, lyric songs (*ci* 詞) in Tang and Song times, then drama in Yuan and Ming times, and finally vernacular fiction in Ming-Qing times.[105] In fact, to elevate the status of these new, marginalized genres, many critics see fit to reestablish music or verbalization as the center of *wen.*

Traditional Chinese critics explain the origin, creation, and function of literature in terms of interaction between different internal and external processes. They trace the origin of literature to inward responses to external processes. Over time they have identified different external processes as pivotal to the rise of literature. These processes include the numinous spirits in the "Canon of Yao"; the natural forces in the *Zuo Commentary* and *Speeches of the States;* the ethico-sociopolitical processes in the "Great Preface"; both the cosmological and Confucian Dao in *Wenxin diaolong;* the cosmological processes in the writings of Zhong Hong, Xiao Tong, Ye Xie, and Yao Nai; and the neo-Confucian Dao in the writings of both the *guan Dao* and the *zai Dao* advocates from

Tang to Qing times. In examining the process of literary creation, traditional Chinese critics stress the interaction with these processes on different levels of human experience—especially the physiological, the psychological, the moral, the intellectual, and the intuitive. In describing the functions of literature, they emphasize harmony with numinous spirits, the attunement with natural forces, the rectification of human relationships, the revelation of the cosmological Dao, and the illumination and transmission of the neo-Confucian Dao.

In sum, traditional Chinese critics conceptualize the major aspects of literature within particular resonantial schemes of internal and external processes. Influenced by both literary trends and paradigmatic shifts of cosmological thinking, they continuously modify existing resonantial schemes or develop new ones for their reconceptualization of literature. Looking at literature anew through their newly honed or developed schemes, they redirect the focus of critical attention from one set of internal and external processes to another. This continuous shift of critical locus signifies the overall orientation of Chinese poetics.

CHAPTER 3

Early Chinese Worldviews
and Concepts of Literature

L IKE THEIR WESTERN COUNTERPARTS IN CHAPTER I, THE
Chinese concepts of literature discussed in chapter 2 are, in
Abrams' words, expressive of "explicit or implicit 'worldviews'" preva-
lent at different historical periods. Not only do they bear the imprints
of thinking about literature through particular worldviews, they often
constitute part of the exposition of the worldviews in question. For in-
stance, as I demonstrate below, many statements about literature in the
Book of Documents, the *Zuo Commentary,* and *Speeches of the States*
occur in the course of discussing certain worldviews. My study of Chi-
nese concepts of literature would be woefully incomplete without in-
vestigating the influence of Chinese worldviews on them. In launch-
ing this investigation, I limit my discussion to early Chinese worldviews
and concepts of literature.[1] By sacrificing some breadth of coverage,
I hope to gain a greater depth in my analysis of the inherent relation-
ship between Chinese cosmological and literary thought.

THE GHOSTS- AND SPIRITS-CENTERED WORLDVIEW
AND THE RELIGIOUS CONCEPT OF LITERATURE

The worldview that emerges from accounts of high antiquity in pre-
Han and Han texts is one centered upon numinous "ghosts and spir-
its" (*guishen* 鬼神). Similar to many supernatural beings of the West,
these ghosts and spirits are conscious, anthropomorphic rulers of the
universe. But unlike their Western counterparts, they are bound up in-
separably with the ongoing processes in the worlds of nature and man.

Some of them are the spirits of tribe ancestors and ancestresses who departed from the human realm but continue to wield a decisive influence over the course of its social and political development. Others are nature divinities, indwelling masters of natural forces and processes.

This merging of ghosts and spirits with ongoing natural and human processes is aptly reflected in the glosses of the words "ghosts" and "spirits" given in various texts. Zheng Xuan defines "heavenly spirit" simply as the combination of "the five emperors and the sun, the moon, and stars" 五帝與日月星辰也.[2] In glossing the two words used in "Annals of the Five Emperors" (*Wudi benji* 五帝本紀), the first chapter of Sima Qian 司馬遷's (145 B.C. or 135 B.C.?), *Records of the Historian* (*Shiji* 史記), Zhang Shoujie 張守節 (fl. 720) writes, "What is numinous in a ghost is called spirit. Ghosts and spirits are the spirits of mountains and rivers. They can bring up clouds and call down rains, and nourish the growth of ten thousand things' 鬼之靈者曰神也。鬼神謂山川之神也。能興雲致雨，潤養萬物.[3] Commenting on a different passage, Zhang glosses the two words in a similar fashion, saying that, "The spirit of the heaven is called spirit; the spirit of humans is called ghost. It is also said that the fine ether of a sage is called spirit; the fine ether of a worthy man is called ghost" 天神曰神，人神曰鬼。又云聖人之精氣謂之神，賢人之精氣謂之鬼.[4]

The merging of conscious beings and impersonal processes betokens a religious worldview characterized by the absence of any absolute division between the other and this world, between what is nature and what is human.[5] Guided by such a worldview, the earliest peoples organized all aspects of their life around various sacrificial rites dedicated to the ghosts and spirits who controlled all natural and human processes.[6] The centrality of religious rites in the life of earliest peoples may be clearly observed in "Annals of the Five Emperors." What we find there are almost exclusively accounts of how the five legendary emperors brought all processes, natural and human, into harmony by piously performing sacrificial rites for ghosts and spirits. Among the religious rites described are the "Three Rites" (*sanli* 三禮), which, as Ma Rong 馬融 (79–166) notes, are "dedicated to the heaven's spirit (*tianshen* 天神), the earth's god (*diqi* 地祇), and the ghosts of humans (*rengui* 人鬼)."[7]

Since this trinity of ghosts and spirits is at once conscious beings and impersonal processes, it is natural for ritual performers to communicate and interact with them in corresponding ways. They would speak personally and directly to ghosts and spirits as conscious beings—reporting human activities to them and calling earnestly upon them for blessings.[8] The performers would also seek to interact with them as impersonal processes through physical movements, culminating in a ritualistic or totemic dance. This emphasis on the velocity of physical movements is generally considered to be a salient feature of religious performances intended to "control over the mysterious forces that are everywhere present in nature and life and that are potentially active in the affairs of man."[9] In a remark from the "Great Commentary" ("Da zhuan" 大傳) or the "Commentary on the Appended Phrases" ("Xici zhuan" 系辭傳), one of the Ten Commentaries on the *Book of Changes,* we can find a vestige of such an ancient belief in a correlation between ritualistic dance and the mysterious processes of nature:

> They [the sages] made a drum of it [the *Book of Changes*], made a dance of it, and so exhausted the potential of its numinous power.[10]

鼓 之 舞 之 以 盡 神 。

In this passage, as well as most other places in the "Great Commentary," the authors speaks of *shen* 神 as the mysterious operation of impersonal processes of nature with little suggestion of the presence of conscious divinities therein. Noting this disappearance of divinities, Willard J. Peterson maintains that the term *shen* is used adjectivally in the "Great Commentary," referring to "a certain quality, state or condition which cannot be fully apprehended and which some of us today might acknowledge as present more in an abstract and depersonalized manner than was perhaps characteristic of the divinities, spirits, demons, and *numen* (and *shen*) which some of our ancestors recognized."[11] Corresponding to this new meaning of *shen,* Richard John Lynn renders *shen* as an abstract "numinous power." In the passage just cited, we note a similar disassociation of *gu* 鼓 (drum) and *wu* 舞 (dance) with conscious divinities. Indeed, the *shen* brought into full play by *wu* and *gu* is no longer the kind of living divinities invoked in the "Canon of Yao," but the numinous power of the Dao. Similarly, *wu* and *gu* themselves are no longer an actual sacrificial dance and its principal instrument, but metaphorical expressions for the act of "bringing [a numinous power] into full play." Nevertheless, the way *gu, wu,* and *shen* are used here unmistakably harks back to what we see in the "Canon of Yao"—the use of drums and dance to move ghosts and spirits. Such a use of drums and dance reveals an entrenched ancient belief in a magical mutual response between the powerful performative rhythm and ghosts and spirits as impersonal processes.

According to some scholars, the centrality of magico-religious dance in the earliest religious rites is even embedded in the etymologies of two homophonic Chinese characters—*wu* 舞 (dance) and *wu* 巫 (a shaman who communes with the spirits through dance, songs, and chants). From very early on, these two characters have been considered to be closely related to, if not completely cognate with, each other. One character is often defined in terms of the other. For instance, in *Explanations of Simple and Compound Characters* (*Shuowen jiezi* 説文解字), Xu Shen 許慎 (ca. 58–ca.147) glosses *wu* 巫 (small seal script) as follows: "*Wu* 巫 is *zhu* 祝, a priest who invokes the spirits. It is a female capable of performing invisible acts and calling down the spirits. [The graph] is a pictorial presentation of the profile of a person dancing with two sleeves."[12] Xu's gloss of *wu* is certainly open to question by modern scholars on the ground that 巫 analyzed by him is in the small seal script, a form of writing developed as late as the Qin. Nonetheless, when turning to the oracle bone script, the oldest extant form of writing, Xu Zhongshu 徐中舒, a modern scholar, finds that *wu* (dance) in oracle bone script is nothing but a pictorial confirmation of Xu's gloss: 𣏟 , a shamanlike figure dancing to pray for rain.[13]

Xu Shen's and Xu Zhongshu's inscriptional explanations may be conjectural in one way or another,[14] but they seem to corroborate numerous accounts by eminent scholars about dance's magico-religious function and its subjugation of poetry in early primitive traditions. In his "Preface to the 'Nine Songs,'" ("Jiuge xu" 九歌序) in *Songs of the Chu* (*Chuci* 楚辭), Wang Yi 王逸 (ca. 89–158) writes, "In the city of Ying in the southern Chu of the old days, which lies in the area between the Ruan and Xiang rivers, the populace believed in ghosts and were fond of sacrificial services. In performing sacrificial services, they invariably sang songs and performed drum dances in order to please various spirits."[15] Later, Ruan Yuan 阮元 (1764–1849), in explaining the meaning of *song* 頌 (hymns), probably the most ancient part of the *Book of Poetry*, writes that "*song* is none other than appearance (*rong* 容)" and that "various segments of the three *song* or hymns are all appearances of dance, and are therefore called *song*. Like musical plays after the Yuan, its songs, its dance, and its [playing of] musical instruments are all actions and gestures."[16] With this explanation, Ruan intends to stress poetry's complete integration with, or rather subordination to, dance in those religious hymns of high antiquity. Over the centuries, many Chinese scholars have accepted and further developed Ruan Yuan's view on *song*'s relationship to dance. Liang Qichao 梁啓超 (1873–1929) contends that "*song* is dance music or drama script."[17] Chow Tse-tsung 周策縱 traces *song* to a particular ritualistic *weng* 甕 dance.[18] In discussing the origins of Chinese poetry and drama, Zhang Binglin 章炳麟 (1869–1936), Chen Mengjia 陳夢家 (1911–1966), Wang Guowei 王國維 (1877–1927), and Liu Shipei 劉師培 (1884–1919) also stress the pivotal importance of religious dance for the birth of these two literary forms.[19] Most recently, Ye Shuxian 葉舒憲 boldly and maybe a bit too imaginatively identifies *song* with various types of primitive dance, including those associated with fertility, burial, and even head-hunting.[20]

The "Canon of Yao" passage is one of the earliest extant accounts of the magico-religious use of dance in remote antiquity. The poetry-chanting, music-playing, and dancing depicted in the passage is actually part of the "Three Rites" being performed by the order of Shun himself. In commenting on this sacrificial performance, Shun and Kui made no mention of the words of poetic invocation and focus exclusively on how the act of poetry-chanting leads to a powerful dance capable of bringing the spirits and man into harmony. Their emphasis on the velocity of performing acts reveals a keen awareness that ghosts and spirits, as impersonal processes, are most responsive to the powerful rhythm of a ritualistic performance. In other words, they seemed to believe that the physical force built up by poetry-chanting, music-playing, and dancing can produce a magical impact on the heaven's spirit, the earth's god, and the ghosts of humans. Considering its nonpareil power to touch ghosts and spirits, they would naturally regard dance as the culmination of a ritualistic performance. In stressing this magical power of dance in their *"Shi yan zhi"* statement, they clearly articulated a religious concept of literature deeply rooted in a ghosts-and spirits-centered worldview.

THE *LI*-CENTERED WORLDVIEW
AND THE HUMANISTIC CONCEPT OF LITERATURE

The humanistic concept of literature bears the imprint of the *li*-centered worldview predominant in the Spring and Autumn period. In the *Book of Rites,* there is a summary account of the gradual transition from the concern with ghosts and spirits in Shang times to the concerns with *li* or rites that govern human affairs:

> The people of the Yin revered spirits, and [its rulers] led the people in performing services to spirits. They put the services to ghosts before the

observance of *li,* and punishment before reward. They stressed awesome authority and displayed little affection. . . . The people of the Zhou revered *li,* and were fond of acts of benefaction. They served ghosts and honored spirits, but kept a distance from them. They demonstrated an understanding of human sentiments and were dedicated [to state affairs]. They measured rewards and punishments according to hierarchical ranks. Therefore, they were affectionate but lacked awesome authority.[21]

殷人尊神率民以事神。先鬼而後禮。先罰而後賞。尊而不親……周人尊禮尚施。事鬼敬神而遠之。近人而忠焉。其賞罰用爵列。親而不尊。

This passages offers a very perceptive observation on the transition from Shang and Zhou worldviews. It shows us that the transition does not register an abrupt replacement of one set of values, beliefs, and practices centered on ghosts and spirits by another centered upon the *li* of human society. We are told that the Shang rulers "led the people in performing services to spirits and put the services to ghosts before the observance of *li.*" This shows that the Shang people's obsession with ghosts and spirits did not prevent them from developing and observing rites for the governance of human affairs. On the other hand, we learn that "the people of Zhou revered *li* and were fond of acts of benefaction. They served ghosts and honored spirits, but kept a distance from them." Devoted though they were to human affairs, the Zhou people obviously continued to piously honor ghosts and spirits. So we must understand the transition from the Shang to the Zhou *weltanschauung* in terms of a gradual reversal of the two competing sets of values, beliefs, and practices.

The fading of the ghosts- and spirits-centered worldview was already evident toward the end of the Shang period. Based on his careful analysis of oracle bone inscriptions, Dong Zuobin divides the late Shang into five periods, suggesting, as Benjamin I. Schwartz says, "an evolution from an outlook which stressed a heavy reliance on divination, an enormous emphasis on sacrifices to nature deities and the mythic or semimythic predynastic ancestors, irregularity and 'ad hoc arrangements' in the performance of ancestral sacrifices, and the reliance on a vast group of diviners to an outlook in which the volume of divination is markedly diminished, sacrifices to nature deities and remote ancestors are regularized in an annual five-phase cycle of sacrifices."[22] The diminished importance of ghosts and spirits is also reflected in the waning of the notion of the high god or *Shangdi* 上帝 developed in what Dong calls the "Period V" of the Late Shang. The emergence of the high god, as Chang Kwang-chih says, "coincides with the supremacy of Shang and its ruling clan"[23] and may be attributed to late Shang kings' efforts to legitimize their claims of universal supremacy. By creating a transcendent god who rules over "the indwelling spirits of earth, mountains, rivers, heavenly bodies, and other divine beings"[24] and by claiming a special relationship of their lineage of ancestors to the high god, late Shang kings aimed to establish an absolute religious dominion over all local cults of ancestral spirits or nature deities, and thereby extend their sociopolitical hegemony over all those who practiced them. As Schwartz points out, "It is precisely the last two kings Ti Yi [Di Yi 帝乙] and Ti Hsin [Di Xin 帝辛] who came to have the title Ti [Di 帝 prefixed to their temple names, as if to assert that they ascribe to themselves the powers of the high god himself."[25]

The notion of *shangdi* began to be eclipsed by the notion of *tian* 天 (Heaven) in the early Zhou. *Tian* is essentially a reconceptualization of the high god as an adjudicator of the absolute moral will by the early Zhou rulers. To counter the late Shang kings' claims to *shangdi's* powers by means of their royal lineage, the early Zhou kings claimed a special relationship with *tian* in terms of their fulfillment of its moral will and their consequent procurement of the mandate to rule the world. For early Zhou kings, the notion of *tian* or Heaven serves not only to invalidate the Shang kings' lineage-based claims of absolute authority, but also to sanctify their own morality-based claims to the divine right of universal supremacy. In parts of the *Book of Documents* and the *Book of Poetry* dating back to the early Zhou, we can find numerous occurrences of the word *tian* expressing this new moralistic notion of the high god.[26] While the words *di* and *shangdi* continue to be used in those texts, they more often than not take on the moralistic ramifications of *tian*. The rise of the notion of *tian* has important humanistic implications. It heralds an eventual "deanthromorphization" of the high god into the abstract moral will that does not interfere in concrete actions and behaviors but wields "the ultimate powers of judgment for the ethical and ritual performance" of an entire dynastic line.[27] Still denoting the presence of abstract conscious divinity, *tian* itself would come under challenge upon the surge of humanistic spirit in the late Western Zhou.

Beset by the rapid disintegration of moral and social order, the people of the late Western Zhou began to doubt and even reject the existence of an absolute moral authority high above who was supposed to guide the human society and ensure justice, peace, and prosperity. In the folk songs of the *Book of Poetry* dating from different periods of the Western Zhou, we can perceive gradually changing attitudes toward Heaven and the high god. If the Zhou hymns and other earlier parts of the *Book of Poetry* are filled with solemn praise of Heaven,[28] we encounter many expressions of doubt about Heaven in poems dating from the reign of King Li 厲王 (857–842 B.C.).[29] Next, in poems dating from the reign of King You 幽王 (781–771 B.C.), we see an intensification of doubts and grievances into unmitigated outcries against Heaven.[30] Such doubts and protests against Heaven turned out to be catalysts for the advent of the humanistic age. With their faith in Heaven and other divinities shaken thoroughly, the ruling elites on their own began to seriously address the practical tasks of regulating human relationships and the processes of the physical heaven and earth. In so doing, they helped bring about a transformation of ghosts- and spirits-centered rites into elaborate systems of court-presided rites, ceremonies, and rules that govern various aspects of human life.[31] Even though many ghosts- and spirits-centered rites continued to be performed during and after the late Western Zhou, they gradually lost their magico-religious significance and became codified into the new systems of human-centered rites and ceremonies. In the *Zuo Commentary,* we can already find remarks on the secularization of the old religious rites. "People are the hosts of spirits. The sage kings therefore first secured the welfare of the people, and after that put forth their strength in serving the spirits" 夫民。神之主也。是以聖王先成民。而後致力於神.[32] "Sacrifices are offered for the benefits of men. People are the hosts of the spirits" 祭祀以為人也。民神之主也.[33] "The Meanings of Sacrifice" (*Ji yi* 祭義), chapter 24 of the *Book of Rites,* explains the rationale of this secularization of the old religious rites. It first identifies "spirit" as the finest of a man's ether (*qi* 氣) and "ghost" as the finest of a man's *po* 魄 (soul that enters the earth after death). Since after death "spirit" arises from the body and becomes the essence (*jing* 精) of the myriad things, it follows that "ghosts and spirits were named reverently and presented as the [arbiters of] law of the commoners, so that the masses would feel awe and the multitude would obey willingly" 明命鬼神。以為黔首則。百眾以畏。萬民以服.[34] Moreover, as ghosts and spirits originally came from men themselves, sacrificial services to them would "teach people to return to antiquity, trace the primal beginning, and not forget those by whom he was given birth" 教民反古復始。不忘其所由生也.[35] Judging by this explanation, ghosts- and spirits-centered rites were then given the new meaning of ethical and social practices that aim to inculcate civic obedience and filial piety in the minds of common people.

Confronting the emergence of human-centered rites and ceremonies, many began to reconceptualize *li* as an abstract ethico-sociopolitical order or even an all-embracing cosmic principle during the Spring and Autumn period. In the *Zuo Commentary*, we can find numerous instances where speakers sought to conceptualize *li* as the abstract principle underlying concrete rites, ceremonies, and other regulatory practices. In the *Zuo Commentary*, Duke Zhao 26 (515 B.C.), for example, Yan Zi conceives of *li* as a broadly inclusive moral principle:

> That the ruler order and the subject obey, the father be kind and the son dutiful, the elder brother loving and the younger respectful, the husband be harmonious and the wife gentle, the mother-in-law be kind and the daughter-in-law obedient—these are *li*. That the ruler in ordering order nothing against the right, and the subject obey without duplicity; that the father be kind and at the same time reverent, and the son be dutiful and at the same time able to remonstrate; that the elder brother, while loving, be friendly, and the younger docile, while respectful; that the husband be righteous, while harmonious, and wife correct, while gentle; that the mother-in-law be condescending, while kind, and the daughter-in-law be pleasant, while obedient—these are fine things of *li*.[36]

> 君令臣共。父慈子孝。兄愛弟敬。夫和妻柔。姑慈婦听。
> 禮也。君令不違。臣共而不貳。父慈而教。子孝而箴。兄
> 愛而友。弟敬而順。夫和而義。妻柔而正。姑慈而從。婦
> 听而婉。禮之善物也。

In describing *li*, Yan Zi turns his attention from concrete ritualistic and ceremonial practices to what they aim to bring about—a broad array of ideal reciprocal relationships in a hierarchical society. By using *li* to encompass all those ideal human relationships, he effectively enshrines *li* as the cardinal moral principle. Insofar as people abide by this moral principle, he contends, they will carry themselves and treat one another in manners most appropriate to their positions in a hierarchical society. Such proper attitudes and behaviors inspired by *li* are what he called the "fine things of *li*."

About two centuries earlier, *li* was already conceived to be a normative sociopolitical order that guarantees peace, order and harmony in a hierarchical society. In the *Zuo Commentary*, Duke Yin 11 (711 B.C.), we see an exposition of this notion of *li*:

Li is that which governs states and clans, establishes the country, institutes an order among the commoners, and produces benefits for posterity.³⁷

禮經國家。定社稷。序民人。利後嗣者也。

Here, *li* is seen to possess the absolute authority that ghosts and spirits, the high god, or Heaven used to exercise over human affairs. To justify this displacement of divinities by an impersonal sociopolitical order as the basis of governing human affairs, many sought to elevate *li* to an ultimate cosmic principle. We find such a cosmological valorization of *li* by Zi Dashu 子大叔 (?–507 B.C.), a minister of the state of Zheng, in the *Zuo Commentary*, Duke Zhao 25 (516 B.C.):

> Zi Dashu met with Zhao Jianzi. Jianzi asked him about the ceremonies of bowing, yielding, and moving around. "These," he replied, "are matters of ceremony and demeanor, not *li*." "Allow me to ask," said Jian Zi, "What is *li?*" He replied, "I have heard our late grand minister Zi Chan say '*Li* is the principle of heaven, the righteousness of the earth, and [the norm of] people's conduct.' As it is the principle of the heaven, people abide by it. They abide by the luminosity of the heaven and follow the nature of the earth. They nourish their lives with [heaven's] six vital forces and make use of the five phases. The vital forces form five tastes, manifest themselves in five colors, and assume the pattern of five sounds. If things become excessive, there will arise obscurity and chaos, and people will lose their nature. Therefore, people observe *li* in order to preserve their nature."³⁸

子大叔見趙簡子。簡子問揖讓周旋之禮焉。對曰。是儀
也。非禮也。簡子曰。敢問何為禮。對曰。吉也聞諸先大
夫子產曰。夫禮。天之經也。地之義也。民之行也。天地
之經。而民實則之。則天之明。因地之性。生其六氣。用
其五行。氣為五味。發為五色。章為五聲。淫則昏亂。民
失其性。是故為禮以奉之。

In answering Jianzi's question about *li*, Zi Dashu takes special care to distinguish *li* as an abstract principle from concrete ceremonial practices which he identifies as *yi* 儀. In explaining *li* as the ultimate cosmic principle, he emphasizes its supreme power in regulating the elemental forces and processes of nature represented by the "six vital forces" (*liuqi* 六氣) and the five phases (*wuxing* 五行). He indicates that *li* is capable of regulating and harmonizing those forces and processes mainly because it can keep them from becoming "excessive" and make them adhere to the mean. For him and many of his contemporaries, *li* should be regarded as the ultimate cosmic principle precisely because it could most effectively make all processes, natural or human, "adhere to the mean" (*zhizhong* 制中) and ensure harmony in all realms. This elevation of *li* to be the ultimate cosmic principle signifies the birth of a new, humanistic worldview that has its origins in the actual social practices of man.[39]

The humanistic concept of literature bears indelible traces of re-thinking literature through the *li*-centered worldview. First, we can observe the result of a corresponding process of "secularization." Ghosts and spirits have ceased to be the focus of attention. Even when the word *shen* (spirits) is mentioned, it usually denotes an impersonal cosmic authority lurking in the background rather than live conscious beings who directly control all natural and human processes. Poetry and music are no longer discussed in the context of the performance of ghost- and spirits-centered rites. With this retreat of ghosts and spirits, magico-religious dance foregoes its erstwhile dominant status. In fact, it becomes so insignificant that it practically disappears from the discussion of poetry and music. Second, we can see a similar shift of man's overriding concern to the regulation of human relationships and natural processes. It is in connection with this new humanist concern that music rises to occupy the center of court-presided ceremonies, with poetry as its useful aid. If dance was once favored for its power-ful rhythm capable of affecting ghosts and spirits, music is now priv-ileged for its power to favorably influence natural and human processes through its intricate system of correlation and resonance with them. Third, we can take note of a valorization of music in close associa-tion with *li* itself. Music's power to "bring unity and harmony" (*tong-tong* 統同)[40] is often perceived as complementary to *li*'s role in es-tablishing sociopolitical hierarchy. On account of this complementary relationship with *li,* music is not infrequently elevated to a status al-most identical with that of *li,* and spoken of together with *li* as *liyu* 禮樂 (ritual and music).[41] In such cases, the discussion of music and poetry often constitutes an inseparable part of an exposition of the *li*-centered worldview.

THE CONFUCIAN WORLDVIEW
AND THE DIDACTIC CONCEPT OF LITERATURE

The worldview underlying the didactic concept of literature is the one presented in *Analects* (*Lunyu* 論語), a collection of dialogues between

Confucius and his disciples. As this Confucian worldview is in many ways developed from the *li*-centered worldview, we can best observe its distinguishing features through comparisons with the latter, especially with regard to the understanding of the functions of *li.*

If the primary function of *li* is considered to be the regulation of natural processes in the *Zuo Commentary* and *Speeches of the States,* this function is completely ignored in *Analects.* The word *li* occurs a total of 73 times in *Analects.* But not even once is it used in connection with natural processes.[42] In *Analects* Confucius does not mention natural processes such as "six vital forces" and "five phases," let alone discuss the regulation of them by means of *li.* For Confucius, *li*'s primary function is to help establish a normative ethico-sociopolitical order. As clearly shown in the *Zuo Commentary, li* itself is commonly regarded as the normative ethico-sociopolitical order by people living shortly before or during the time of Confucius. But for Confucius, *li* is only an instrument for achieving the Dao, the name he prefers to use for the normative ethico-sociopolitical order. Confucius defines *li* mainly as a system of prescriptions of proper behavior governing human transactions in a hierarchical society. In order to achieve the Dao, Confucius holds that all members of the broadly defined educated class must conscientiously observe the rules of "behavior of persons related to each other in terms of role, status, rank, and position within a structured society."[43]

> Master K'ung [Confucius] replied saying, "A ruler in employing his ministers should be guided solely by the prescriptions of ritual. Ministers in serving their ruler, solely by devotion to his cause."[44]

> 孔子對曰。君使臣以禮。臣事君以忠。

> If a gentleman attends to business and does not idle away his time, if he behaves with courtesy to others and observes the rules of ritual, then all within the Four Seas are his brothers.[45]

> 君子敬而無失。與人恭而有禮。四海之內、皆兄弟也。

> If those above love ritual, then among the common people none will dare to be disrespectful.[46]

> 上好禮、則民不莫敢不敬。

In these passages, Confucius stresses that prescriptions of proper behavior should guide the social intercourse between the ruler and his ministers, and among all the functionaries or *shi* 士. To Confucius, the observation of the prescriptions of *li* is anything but a small gesture of courtesy in human interaction. Rather, it is a profoundly significant moral act. It can help transform the external behavior and inward life of those involved. Moreover, the transforming influence of *li* can spread from the top to the bottom of the society and bring about peace and order in the world. For this reason Confucius contends that the best form of government is one that governs by *li*. "The Master said, if it is possible to govern countries by ritual and yielding, there is no more to be said [about other forms of government]. But if it is not really possible, of what use is ritual?" 子曰。能以禮讓為國乎。何有。不能以禮讓為國。如禮何.[47] This statement aptly sums up Confucius' view of the pivotal importance of *li* in establishing a good government.

In expounding the moral significance of *li* for the life of an individual, Confucius does not merely set forth attitudes and sentiments appropriate for different human relationships in a hierarchical society, as did Yan Zi in the *Zuo Commentary*, Duke Zhao 26. He goes to great lengths to demonstrate the interaction and interdependence between the external prescriptions of behavior and the inner moral life of an individual. He stresses that it is the presence of one's genuine moral sentiment that makes the observation of *li* meaningful:

> The Master said, High office filled by men of narrow views, ritual performed without reverence, the forms of mourning observed without grief—these are things I cannot bear to see![48]
>
> 子曰。居上不寬。為禮不敬。臨喪不哀。吾何以觀之哉。
>
> The Master said, Ritual, ritual! Does it mean no more than presents of jade and silk? Music, music! Does it mean no more than bells and drums?[49]
>
> 子曰。禮云禮云。玉帛云乎哉。樂云樂云。鍾鼓云乎哉。

In observing the prescriptions of behavior in a genuine, moral spirit, Confucius believes, one does not just achieve rapport with other people and contribute to the harmony of the society at large. In the process one also brings to realization one's inner moral virtues. Without external acts of observing *li*, one's innate moral qualities will not be brought to life. Moreover, through its power of "adhering to the mean," *li* can prevent moral virtues from becoming excessive to a fault:

"The Master said, Courtesy not bounded by the prescriptions of ritual becomes tiresome. Caution not bounded by the prescriptions of ritual becomes timidity. Daring not bounded by the prescriptions of ritual becomes turbulence. Straightforwardness not bounded by the prescriptions of ritual becomes harshness" 子曰。恭而無禮、則勞。慎而無禮、則葸。勇而無禮、則亂。直而無禮、則絞.[50] While *li* brings one's moral virtues into an ideal, perfect balance, one will internalize *li* in the deepest of his consciousness, and demonstrate the spirit of *li* in every single action spontaneously. Through this moral spontaneity one can attain the ideal of *ren* 仁, the highest possible moral excellence. It is because of this supreme spiritual value of *li* that Confucius said, "He who can himself submit to ritual [*li*] is Good [*ren*]" 克己復禮為仁.[51]

Unlike Zi Dashu and other earlier or contemporary thinkers, Confucius does not seek to elevate the *li* to the status of a normative ethico-sociopolitical order or a cosmic principle. Instead, he codifies *li, ren,* and other key concepts within the broader framework of the Dao. As Benjamin I. Schwartz points out, *Analects* is "one of the earliest texts available to us in which the term tao [dao] or way or road takes on its extended abstract and encompassing meaning."[52]

The term "Dao" occurs sixty times in *Analects,* and refers mostly to the normative ethico-sociopolitical order rather than a cosmic principle. In *Analects,* there is only one reference to the Dao in the nonhuman universe, when the term "Dao" appears in the expression of *tiandao* 天道 (the way of Heaven): "Our Master's views concerning culture and the outward insignia of goodness, we are permitted to hear; but about Man's nature and the ways of Heaven he will not tell us anything at all" 夫子之文章。可得而聞也。夫子之言性與天道。不可得而聞也.[53] This passage shows that Confucius acknowledges the presence of the Dao in the nonhuman universe but refrains from talking about it. This noncommittal attitude toward the Dao of Heaven is consistent with his reluctance to talk about four kinds of preternatural phenomena: "prodigies, feats of strength, disorders, or spirits" 怪、力、亂、神.[54] There seem to be two main reasons for Confucius to avoid talking about the Dao of Heaven. First, he believes that it is beyond the ken of human knowledge. Second, he sees no need to talk about the Dao of Heaven itself because it has already been made manifest in the history of Xia, Shang, and early Zhou Dynasties.

Schwartz gives an excellent exposition of the meaning of the Confucian Dao: "It refers to nothing less than the total normative sociopolitical order with its networks of proper familial and proper so-

ciopolitical roles, statuses, and ranks, as well as to the 'objective' pre-
scriptions of proper behavior—ritual, ceremonial, and ethical—that
govern the relationships among these roles. On the other side, it obvi-
ously and emphatically also embraces the 'inner' moral life of the liv-
ing individual."[55] For Confucius, the Dao is not a utopia, but what
was already realized in human history—in the legendary Xia and the
relatively recent Shang and Zhou dynasties. He was convinced that the
Dao could be realized again in his own time, so long as the elite class
could submit themselves to *li* outside and strive for the attainment of
ren, the ultimate good inside. This "rerealization" of the Dao is the sa-
cred mission he sought to accomplish by teaching and political per-
suasion throughout his life.

To sum up, the worldview in *Analects* is distinguished from the *li*-
centered worldview by its disassociation of *li* from natural processes,
by its redirection of attention from court-presided rites and ceremonies
to the interpersonal intercourse across various classes of a hierarchical
society, by its emphasis on the interaction and interdependence of *li*
(outer prescriptions of behavior) and *ren* (a "transcendental" total of
inner moral virtues), and by its codification of *li* and *ren* within the
broader scheme of the Dao realized in human history.

The trajectory from the *li*-centered to the Confucian worldview is
aptly reflected in the transition from the humanistic to the didactic con-
cept of literature. In the "Great Preface," we see a corresponding dis-
association of literature from natural processes. We cannot find any
mention there of yin and yang, nor "five phases," nor "six vital forces,"
to say nothing of concrete natural processes. We observe also a similar
shift of attention from ceremonial performances to the interpersonal
interaction across all social strata, an interaction intended to rectify
human relationships in a hierarchical society. Furthermore, we notice
a similar emphasis on the dynamic reciprocity between the outer so-
ciopolitical conditions and the inner moral sentiment. Judging by these
correspondences and similarities, we can say that the didactic concept
of literature is born of rethinking literature within the framework of
the Confucian worldview.

THE "ORGANISMIC" WORLDVIEW AND LIU XIE'S
COMPREHENSIVE CONCEPT OF LITERATURE

Liu Xie's comprehensive concept of literature is in many ways the prod-
uct of rethinking literature through the "organismic" worldview set
forth in the "Great Commentary," the two parts of which constitute

two of the so-called Ten Wings (*Shiyi* 十翼) or the Ten Commentaries to the *Book of Changes*. For more than two millennia, the Ten Commentaries were attributed to Confucius, but this view is jettisoned by most modern scholars on the grounds of the lack of reliable evidence of Confucius' involvement with the compilation of the Ten Wings. Now there is a consensus view that the Ten Wings are post-Confucian works composed by Confucian scholars living in the Warring States and early Han times.

The worldview developed in the "Great Commentary" is often called an "organismic" worldview on account of its revelation of the dynamic links of ongoing processes in all realms as a constantly changing totality.[56] The development of this "organismic" worldview is one of the several competing endeavors since the Warring States period to construct an all-inclusive cosmological scheme to accommodate divergent notions about correspondence, correlation, and interdependence among all phenomena and processes.[57] Zou Yan 騶衍 (305–240 B.C.), the authors of the treatise "Great Plan" ("Hong fan" 洪範) in the *Book of Documents,* the compilers of the "Monthly Ordinances" ("Yueling" 月令) section of the *Record of Rites,* and Dong Zhongshu 董仲舒 (179–104 B.C.) all seek to build such cosmological schemes based on the cycle of the Five Phases (*wuxing* 五行).[58] With varying degrees of sophistication, they attempt an exhaustive cataloguing of natural and human phenomena under the five phases locked in a perpetual cycle of mutual generation and overcoming. By so doing, they bring forth various cosmological schemes in which all things are not only determinably linked but follow a predestined course of development. Their cosmological schemes have arisen out of man's desire for a well-ordered universe and a mastery of the destiny of all things. Elaborate and impeccable though they seem in theory, these schemes often can hardly work in reality. The static identification of things with the Five Phases is not workable because the intrinsic qualities of things are too complex to be reduced to a single characteristic associated with wood, fire, earth, metal, or water. Equally problematic is the coordination of ongoing processes with the cycle of the Five Phases. There are far more factors than the Five Phases that influence the course of development of things. Thus, no one can actually predict the outcome of ongoing processes based on their predetermined cycle.

Unlike the *wuxing* cosmologists, the authors of the "Great Commentary" do not seek to conceive a comprehensive cosmological scheme in a fixed cycle. Instead they discover a scheme underlying the

Changes' dynamic, open system of divination symbols and texts. In its early form, the *Changes* consists of two main strata of materials: a sequence of sixty-four hexagrams and oracle texts. As divination symbols, the sixty-four hexagrams are each composed of six broken or unbroken lines. The six lines of a hexagram are derived from the combination of two of the Eight Trigrams (*bagua* 八卦), which represent eight alternative combinations of undivided and divided lines (i.e., —, - -). The first of the sixty-four hexagrams ䷀, named *Qian* 乾, is composed of two of the first trigram ☰, also named *Qian* 乾. The oracle texts fall into three types. The first type is *guaming* 卦名 (hexagram names), which are each made up of one or two written characters often taken from *yaoci,* the third type. The second type is *tuan* 彖 (judgments) or *guaci* 卦辭 (hexagram statements), which are phrases made up of prognosticating terms such as "well-fortuned" (ji 吉), "ill-fortuned" (*xiong* 凶), "prevalence" (*heng* 亨), and "remorse" (*lin* 吝). The third type is *yaoci* 爻辭 (line statements), which explain the prognosticating implications of each individual line of a hexagram.

The origins of trigrams, hexagrams, and the accompanying oracle texts are all shrouded in myths and legends. Tradition has it that the legendary sage Fu Xi 伏羲 of high antiquity invented the Eight Trigrams, King Wen of the Zhou (r. 1171–1122 B.C.) developed the sixty-four hexagrams and composed the *guaci* or Judgments, and Duke of Zhou (d. 1094 B.C.) supplied the *yaoci* or line statements. Most twentieth-century scholars express doubt about these traditional views, but they themselves cannot establish the authorship and dates of these two strata of the *Changes* on a factual basis. Nonetheless, they generally agree that the trigrams appeared in remote antiquity and that the oracle texts were "added by adepts in divination who were still familiar with the technique of the tortoise oracle."[59] Now it is also generally believed that these two strata each came from many different hands and merged into a dynamic system of divination in the early Zhou.

In explaining this system of symbols and texts as an intricate all-inclusive cosmological scheme, the authors of the "Great Commentary" focus on addressing three fundamental questions: What is the ultimate cosmological principle embodied in the *Changes*? What are the archetypal patterns of change and transformation set up in the *Changes*? What use can we make of the *Changes*?

In the opening paragraph of the "Great Commentary," the authors seek to answer the first question by looking into the primal cosmic forces that are coextensive with the first two hexagrams:

As Heaven is high and noble and Earth is low and humble, so it is that *Qian* [Pure Yang, hexagram 1] and *Kun* [Pure Yin, hexagram 2] are defined. The high and the low being thereby set out, the exalted and the mean have their places accordingly. There are norms for action and repose, which are determined by whether hardness or softness is involved. Those with regular tendencies gather according to kind, and things divide up according to group; so it is that good fortune and misfortune occur. In Heaven this [process] creates images, and on Earth it creates physical forms; this is how change and transformation manifest themselves. In consequence of all this, as hard and soft stroke each other, the eight trigrams activate each other. It [the Dao] arouses things with claps of thunder, moistens them with wind and rain. Sun and moon go through their cycles, so now it is cold, now hot. The Dao of *Qian* forms the male; and the Dao of *Kun* forms the female. *Qian* has mastery over the great beginning of things, and *Kun* acts to bring things to completion.[60]

天尊地卑。乾坤定矣。卑高以陳。貴賤位矣。動靜有常。
剛柔斷矣。方以類聚。物以群分。吉凶生矣。在天成象。
在地成形。變化見矣。是故剛柔相摩。八卦相蕩。鼓之以
雷霆。潤之以風雨。日月運行。一寒一暑。乾道成男。坤
道成女。乾知大始。坤作成物。

Here the authors set forth a cosmological order with a set of archetypal bipolar phenomena: high and low, *Qian* and *Kun,* the exalted and the mean, action and repose, and hardness and softness. It is by virtue of an association with these bipolar phenomena that the myriad things gather in groups and give rise to the orderliness of the world. All these archetypal bipolar phenomena are not static dichotomous entities irrevocably separated from and opposed to each other. Rather, they are opposite yet complementary dyads that perpetually interact with and transform each other. According to the authors, what generates, sustains, and unifies all phenomena is an ultimate bipolar principle of change and transformation. It is this bipolar principle that creates images in Heaven and physical forms on Earth, and sets in motion the cycles of sun and moon, cold and heat. Of the several pairs of archetypal bipolar phenomena mentioned, the authors choose to use *Qian* and *Kun,* the titles of the first two of the sixty-four hexagrams as well as the Eight Trigrams, to name this cosmological principle. Of this bipolar cosmological principle, Qian is the creative, male force which initiates things, and Kun is the receptive, female force which brings things to completion.[61]

Probably aware that the terms "the Dao of Qian" and "the Dao of Kun" do not yet enjoy a wide currency, the authors make a special effort to identify them with yang and yin, two terms commonly used to denote a bipolar principle. "The Master said: '*Qian* and *Kun,* do they not constitute the two-leaved gate in the *Changes*? Qian is a purely yang thing, and Kun a purely yin thing. The hard and the soft exist as hexagrams only after yin and yang combine their virtues, for it is in this way the numbers of Heaven and Earth become embodied in them and so perfectly realize their luminous, bright virtues'" 子曰。乾坤。其易之門邪。乾。陽物也。坤。陰物也。陰陽合德而剛柔有體。以體天地之撰。以通神明之德.[62] Then, by further arguing that "the reciprocal process of yin and yang is called the Dao," 一陰一陽之謂道,[63] the authors identify the operation of Qian and Kun with that of the all-encompassing Dao itself. Based on this identification, they make a broad claim for the *Changes* as an embodiment of the three ultimates—the Dao of Heaven, the Dao of Earth, and the Dao of Man:

> As a book, the *Changes* is something which is broad and great, complete in every way. There is the Dao of Heaven in it, the Dao of Man in it, and the Dao of Earth in it. It brings these three powers together and doubles them. This is the reason for there being six lines. What these six lines embody are nothing other than the Dao of the three powers.[64]

> 易之為書也。廣大悉備。有天道焉。有人道焉。有地道焉。兼三才而兩之。故六。六者。非它也。三才之道也。

Since the *Changes* is one of six Confucian classics, few would doubt that the Dao of Man in it is largely identical with Confucius' Dao as the ideal ethico-sociopolitical order once realized in human history. Meanwhile, the Dao of Heaven and the Dao of Earth remind us of Lao Zi's Dao that generates, sustains, and guides all natural processes. The affinity of the *Changes* with the Daoist worldview may be understood in terms of a common abiding concern with cosmogonic and cosmological processes. In *Dao de jing* 道德經 (the Classic of the Way and its Power), Lao Zi adumbrates the bipolar principle of yin-yang transformation with a highly symbolic statement: "The way [Dao] begets one; one begets two; two begets three; and three generates the myriad creatures" 道生一，一生二，二生三，三生萬物.[65] According to Richard Wilhelm, this fundamental view of Lao Zi is reflected in the basic structure of a trigram. "In the *Book of Changes*," Wilhelm notes, "T'ai Chi - - - is represented as the basis of all existence. . . . The establishment of this line results, furthermore, in the appearance of polar duality, which is the primary positive pole designated by an undivided (yang) line and the secondary negative pole designated by a divided (yin) line. Together with the originally established line, we obtain a triad as a basis of reality. Therefore we read in *Tao Te Ching,* 'One produced two; two produced three; and the three produced the ten thousand things.'"[66] This blending of Daoist ideas into the Confucian classic lies at the heart of a debate that has continued unabated for centuries about the character of the "Great Commentary." While many Confucian scholars chose to ignore the Daoist elements in the "Great Commentary," some did acknowledge and complain about the presence of Daoist ideas. They even went so far as to chastise fellow Confucians for paying undue attention to metaphysical and divinatory issues and turning the Confucian classic into the Daoists' *Changes* (*Daojia zhi Yi* 道家之易) and the diviners' *Changes* (*Fangshu zhi Yi* 方術之易). But for scholars who were not intellectually committed to the Confucian tradition, the "Great Commentary" is far more Daoist and Confucian.[67] No matter what labels we wish to apply to the "Great Commentary," we must come to terms with the fact that its authors, self-consciously or not, synthesized the Confucian and Daoist notions of the Dao. The broad claims they made for the Dao of the *Changes* strike us as encompassing as those made by Confucians and Daoists about their respective Dao. As the ultimate cosmic principle, the Dao of the *Changes* unifies all phenomena and processes, in *both* the nonhuman and human worlds, not just in one of them.

After their exposition of the ultimate cosmological principle, the authors proceed to address the second question about the archetypal patterns of change and transformation. Again in the divination system of the *Changes* they find a ready answer to this second question. Whereas they discern the bipolar cosmological principle in hexagram 1 (of purely yang lines) and hexagram 2 (of purely yin lines), they perceive the archetypal patterns of change in varied combinations of yin and yang lines in the Eight Trigrams and all other hexagrams:

> Since the Dao consists of change and action, we refer to it in terms of the "moving lines" [*yao*]. Since the moving lines consist of different classes, we refer to them as "things." Since things mix in together, we refer to these as "patterns." When these patterns involve discrepancies, fortune is at issue there.[68]

道有變動。故曰爻。爻有等。故曰物。物相雜。故曰文。
文不當。故凶生焉。

Here the authors trace step by step the formation of *wen* or the archetypal patterns of change—from the individual lines to the clustering of lines as a "thing" and finally to the combination of miscellaneous "things" into an archetypal pattern (*wen* 文).

According to them, the moving lines (*yao*), the most basic component, symbolize the primary forces of change: "The lines as such reproduce every action that takes place in the world" 爻也者效天下之動者也.[69] Moreover, they identify the movement of the lines with that of the Dao itself. "The movement of the six hexagram lines embodies the Dao of the three ultimates" 六爻之動。三極之道也.[70] According to them, the movement of yin and yang forces does not follow a single fixed, predetermined path such as the Five Phase cycle, but charts its own course depending on their configurations in a given situation. This dynamic movement of yin and yang forces gives rise to eight basic trigrams: "This is what generates the two modes [the yin and yang]. The two basic modes [– and - -] generate the four basic images [☰, ☷, ☱, ☶], and the four basic images generate the eight trigrams [by adding first one unbroken (yang) line — to each, then one broken (yin) line - -]. The eight trigrams determine good fortune and misfortune and good fortune and misfortune generate great enterprise" 是生兩儀。兩儀生四象。四象生八卦。八卦定吉凶。吉凶生大業.[71]

What emerge from the Eight Trigrams, the authors believe, are the "things" (*wu*). Elsewhere in the "Great Commentary," such "things" are referred to as an "image" (*xiang* 象): "When the eight trigrams formed ranks, the basic images were present there within them" 八卦成列。象在其中矣.[72] As Willard Peterson rightly points out, the word "Image" used in the "Great Commentary" "connotes resemblance and implies an act of perception."[73] In its explicit sense of resemblance or likeness, "Images" refers to the physical shapes as well as the names of trigrams or hexagrams. The names of most trigrams and hexagrams are "words or terms referring to particular objects and activities which are involved in 'figuring' (*hsiang* [*xiang*]) the situation revealed by the act of divination."[74] Explaining this sense of resemblance, the authors write, "The term *image* means 'the making of resemblance'" 象也者像也.[75] The authors also offer an explanation of Image's sense of observation: "The sages had the means to perceive the mysteries of the world and, drawing comparisons to them with analogous things, made images out of those things that seemed appropriate. This is why these are called 'Images'" 聖人有以見天下之賾。而擬諸其形容。象其物宜。是故謂之象.[76] Here the authors make it clear that the Images are records of the sages' perception of "the mysteries of the world." To reiterate this point, they write, "What one sees of this [the inexhaustible alternation of yin and yang][77] is called the 'Images.' As these take physical shapes, we may say that they are *concrete things*" 見乃謂象。形乃謂之器.[78]

To the authors, it is not a single Image, but multiple Images in their haphazard, irregular, or illogical relation to each other (*xiangza* 相雜) that reveal the incipient trends of events and hence foretell good or bad fortune. Why can this combination of disparate, enigmatic Images constitute an archetypal pattern of change and transformation, a pattern that serves "both to ascertain man's position in the structure of the world and to provide him with a guide to conduct within his unique historical situation"?[79] To this question that is truly puzzling to a modern logical mind, Hellmut Wilhelm gives an eloquent answer: "The authors of the *Book of Changes* did not limit themselves to setting up single images, they went way beyond that and made a system of such images. In this system the images represent fixed values. Definite situations are isolated (abstracted) from chaos, definite values are allotted to them, and thereby they are endowed with duration. In chaos (i.e., in the real world) a given situation, sometimes an historical one, will be perceived as an image; it will be formulated (imagined), and a fixed value inherent in it will be established (adjudged), whereby it is confirmed as a pillar of order. This system of images linked to values lacks hierarchy, to be sure. No order of ranking the values is set up here, but rather a distribution of values is made to the various situations portrayed, which in themselves are equal to one another. In this way the system preserves a freedom and lack of bias despite its logical self-containedness."[80]

Even for the ancients, to perceive what is embodied in the "pattern" of Images—the incipient good or bad fortune in a given situation and the comprehension of the "mysteries of the world" at large—is no easy task. To render the import of Images intelligible to the people, the sages attached oracle texts, made up of elliptic and often enigmatic references, to particular objects or historical events, to the trigrams and hexagrams, and also to individual component lines: "They [the sages] have attached phrases to it, and it is by means of these that it makes its pronouncements. It determines things to involve either good fortune or misfortune, and this is how it renders decisions" 系辭焉。所以告也。定之以吉凶。所以斷也.[81] To further explain the relationship between the Images and the texts, the authors write, "The eight trigrams make their pronouncements in terms of images, and the line texts and Judgments address themselves to us in terms of the innate tendencies of things. The hard and soft lines intermingle and take up positions, thus allow-

ing good fortune and bad to be seen" 八卦以象告。爻象以情言。剛
柔雜居。而吉凶可見.[82]

In discussing the significance of the trigrams and hexagrams as archetypal patterns of change, the authors not only clearly define the functions of their three components ("moving lines," "Images," and "attached phrases"), but set forth their inherent hierarchical relationship:

> The Master said: "Writing does not exhaust words, and words do not
> exhaust ideas. If this is so, does this mean that the ideas of the sages cannot be discerned?" The Master said: "The sages established images in
> order to express their ideas exhaustively. They established the hexagrams
> in order to treat exhaustively the true innate tendency of things and their
> countertendencies to spuriousness. They attached phrases to the hexagrams in order to exhaust what they had to say. They let change occur
> and achieve free flow in order to exhaust the potential of the benefit involved. They made a drum of it, made a dance of it, and so exhausted
> the potential of its numinous power."[83]

子曰。書不盡言。言不盡意。然則聖人之意。其不可見
乎。子曰。聖人立象以盡意。設卦以盡情偽。系辭焉以盡
其言。變而通之以盡利。鼓之舞之以盡神。

The hierarchy of ideas (*yi* 意), Images (*xiang* 象), and words (言) represent a descending order of abstraction. The ideas are the "mysteries
of the world" imaged in the minds of the sages. The Images are the resemblances of the "mysteries of the world" made by the sages through
trigrams and hexagrams. Attached phrases are the enigmatic mentions
of particular objects or historical situations by the sages to make manifest the Images' luminous import.[84] In explaining this tripartite hierarchy, however, the authors offer no clues as to how this mosaic of abstract graphic forms and concrete words should be processed and
interpreted in one's mind. Using music as an analogy, Hellmut Wilhelm explains how this mosaic allows us to imagine what is beyond
our senses: "To continue the comparison [with music]: the structure
of the hexagram, and its relation to the system, determine the musical
form, so to speak, while the image of the situation furnishes the theme.
No absolute limitation is imposed upon the freedom of the musical
imagination in developing the theme within the frame of a definite
form. But we can enjoy the music only when we follow this imagination; the closest possible union between theme and form furthers
the perfection of expression in a natural way."[85] Judging by the way
graphic symbols and attached phrases are organized, we are apparently

intended to respond to them in such a mode of "musical" imagination and conjure up an "organismic" cosmological scheme, one that "mirrors and correlates all the processes and forms of the natural world as well as with the infinitely varied circumstances of human life."[86]

In addressing the third question about the usefulness of the *Changes,* the authors spare no efforts to convince us of the paramount importance of consulting and studying it:

> The *Changes* is a paradigm of Heaven and Earth, and so it shows how one can fill in and pull together the Dao of Heaven and Earth. Looking up, we use it [the *Changes*] to observe the configurations of Heaven, and looking down, we use it to examine the patterns of Earth. Thus we understand the reasons underlying what is hidden and what is clear. We trace things back to their origins and turn back to their ends. Thus we understand the axiom of life and death.[87]

易 與 天 地 准 。 故 能 彌 綸 天 地 之 道 。 仰 以 觀 於 天 文 。 俯 以 察 於 地 理 。 是 故 知 幽 明 之 故 。 原 始 反 終 。 故 知 死 生 之 説 。

According to the authors, the *Changes* not only yields all these secrets of Heaven and Earth but also provides the very basis for the building of civilization as a whole. Speaking of the development of material culture, they go so far as to assert that a number of hexagrams "were themselves the source of inspiration for the invention by sages of nets and baskets (B2.8), plows (B2.11), periodic markets (B2.15), clothing (B2.25), boats and oars (B2.27), domestication of beasts of burden (B2.30), gates and watches (B2.32), pestles and mortars (B2.35), bows and arrows (B2.38), buildings and houses (B2.42–43), funeral paraphernalia and rites (B2.46), and writing and systems of governance (B2.49)."[88] Moreover, they regard the *Changes* as the source of inspiration for the establishment of the earliest ethico-sociopolitical order in the human world. It was in the course of making the *Changes* that the sages perceived the nexus of all the movements and activities in the world and "thus enacted statutes and rituals accordingly" 以 行 其 典 禮.[89] Since we can observe and grasp the Dao of Heaven, the Dao of Earth, and the Dao of Man in the *Changes* and hence pursue the most propitious course of action, the authors urge, all ordinary men should emulate gentlemen (*junzi* 君 子) and devote themselves to the contemplation of the *Changes.*

In reifying the Dao of Heaven and Earth and the Dao of Man in a set of graphic symbols and the written records of verbalizations, the authors depart from traditional Daoist and Confucian views on signs, language, and cosmology. Lao Zi, Zhuang Zi, and other Daoist thinkers repeatedly stress the impossibility of language, verbalizations or written words, to convey the ultimate reality, let alone be an embodiment of it. Although Confucius holds a more sympathetic view of language, in *Analects* he falls far short of identifying his Dao of human history with the patterns (*wen*) of the graphic symbols and oracle texts. The closest Confucius comes to discussing the pattern (*wen*) of the Dao is his remarks on the Zhou dynasty: "Chou could survey the two dynasties. How great a wealth of culture [wen]!" 周監於二代。郁郁乎 文哉.[90] "When King Wen died, did that mean that culture (*wen*) ceased to exist?" 文王既沒。文不在茲乎.[91] This *wen* of the Dao is unquestionably a lofty abstract notion cherished in the mind of Confucius, not patterns of divination symbols and texts.

Considering this long-standing distrust of graphic symbols and language as the means of conveying the ultimate Dao, the authors must present a cogent argument to support their claim that the *Changes* is an embodiment of the Dao of Heaven, Earth, and Man. In making this argument, they find good use for the traditional tales about the origins of the *Changes*. Retelling the tale about the origin of the eight trigrams, the oldest stratum of the *Changes,* they identify the ultimate nonhuman origin of the *Changes*. The tale has it that the eight trigrams were made by Fu Xi, a semihuman creature, based on the Diagram of the Yellow River and the Writing of the Luo River, which had been brought forth by nature itself.[92] Then, by repeating the tale about King Wen's and the Duke of Zhou's making of the hexagrams and oracle texts, the authors affirm the penultimate human origin of the *Changes*.[93] By pointing up the dual origins of the *Changes,* the authors intend to convince us that the *Changes* is something that transcends the boundaries between what is nature and what is manmade. As such, it is not a "representation" of the Dao of Heaven, Earth, and Man, but a participatory agent in the Dao of these three realms. Thus, they hail the *Changes* as the "spirit thing" (*shenwu* 神物),[94] and assert that "the *Changes* is without consciousness and is without deliberate action" 易。無思也。 無為也.[95] Meanwhile, in rendering the Dao intelligible in an organismic scheme of human design, the *Changes* blends nature's laws with the elements of human creation and thus becomes something of a "second nature." As such, it possesses the supreme power of regulating heaven and earth and determining the ethico-sociopolitical order of the human world.

Having reviewed the highlights of the "Great Commentary," we can clearly see how extensively Liu Xie has drawn from it to formulate his views about the nature, origins, and functions of literature. His elevation of writing over speech and his notion of literature as "patterns" (*wen*) of the Dao are apparently inspired by the valorization of the trigrams and hexagrams as cosmic symbols in the "Great Commentary." His claim that literature is at once parallel and superior to the *wen* of Heaven and Earth falls in line with the assertion that the *Changes* is derived from and yet regulates Heaven and Earth. His examination of the ultimate and penultimate origins of literature is taken straight from the discussion of dual origins of the eight trigrams, which he explicitly identifies as a prototype of writing and literature. His praise of the sages' transmission of the Dao and their launch of the literary tradition is also adapted from the "Great Commentary," where the sages are lauded for their pivotal roles in making manifest the Dao and initiating the project of civilization. His discussion of the creative process is an innovative endeavor to examine the complex interaction of internal and external processes within the tripartite structure of ideas, Images, and words set up in the "Great Commentary." His view of literature's all-regulating function is borrowed from the description of the *Changes'* role in establishing the warp and woof of the universe.[96]

What is even more noteworthy is Liu's self-professed desire to construct a grand system of literary criticism modeled on the all-embracing cosmological scheme of the *Changes*.[97] In chapter 50 ("Xu zhi" 序志 [Exposition of My Intentions]), the epilogue to the entire book, he tells us that to be such a "systematizer" of literary criticism is the only way left for him to realize his childhood dream of "holding red-lacquer ritual vessels and following Confucius in a southbound journey" (*WXDL* 50 / 34–35). He regrets that it is no longer possible to establish himself as a great Confucian exegete because "Ma Rong 馬融 (79–166), Zheng Xuan, and other Confucian scholars have already thoroughly expounded the Confucian classics" (*WXDL* 50 / 44–45). But thanks to the deficiencies of earlier literary critics, he sees the opportunity of achieving immortality through a systematic codification of the principles of literature. To him, not being rigorously systematic is the greatest deficiency of his predecessors. He finds their writings to be "not comprehensive" (*buzhou* 不周), "careless and inadequate" (*shulue* 疏略), "fragmented and disorderly" (*suiluan* 碎亂), or "insufficient in the treatment of essentials" (*guayao* 寡要).[98] Thus, the best way for Liu Xie to surpass his predecessors is to set down the principles of literature in as systematic a fashion as possible. For this purpose, he models "his principles of organizing chapters and naming chapters" on the symbolic numerology of fifty, or "the numerology of great evolution" (*da yan zhi shu* 大衍之數) in the *Changes* (*WXDL* 50 / 129– 132).[99] In the *Book of Changes,* this numerology serves to signify the "organismic" totality of the universe: the Great Primordium, Heaven and Earth, the sun and the moon, five phases, four seasons, twelve months, and twenty-four *qi* or ethers.[100] In adopting this numerology as the organizing matrix for *Wenxin diaolong,* Liu Xie doubtless wishes to construct a grand literary system to encompass the "organismic" totality of literary experience— from its ultimate cosmological origin to minute rhetorical details, from the entire literary tradition to individual talents, from nonbelletristic to belletristic genres and subgenres, from the creative to the receptive process, from the author's character to the reader's qualities, and so forth.[101] In view of all this, all the correspondences with the "Great Commentary" noted above should not be explained in terms of an unself-conscious influence by that philosophical text. Rather, they should be seen as the result of Liu's consistent, self-conscious thinking about literature through the "organismic" cosmological scheme set forth in the "Great Commentary."

This survey shows that early Chinese thinkers consistently conceive of the ultimate reality as an all-unifying process. They tend to identify numinous conscious beings with the controlling processes of nature or, conversely, to elevate given processes operating in nature or the human world to an absolute cosmic principle. Examples of the former case are the ancestral spirits worshipped by the earliest people, the high god of the late Shang royal lineage, and the moral Heaven revered by early Zhou rulers. Examples of the latter case are the *li* principle of the Spring and Autumn period, Confucius' Dao of human history, the Dao of the *Changes,* and the neo-Confucian Dao of Tang and Song times. These evolving worldviews do not feature rigid dualistic divisions between the ultimate and the relative, the above and the below, the divine and the human. Placing these dyads in a relationship of mutual correspondence, mutual influence, or even mutual transformation, these worldviews each engineer a reordering of natural and human processes within a different and often more elaborate cosmological scheme.[102] What emerges from each is therefore a new kind of "anthropocosmic vision of the unity of man and heaven."[103]

Early Chinese worldviews have exerted a great influence on the development of early concepts of literature discussed in chapter 2. First, they have fostered a common belief that literature is a process arising from human interaction with external processes and in turn harmonizing both internal and external processes. Second, they have furnished early Chinese critics with ever more complex cosmological schemes, in which they continuously reconceptualize the nature of literature, its origins, its formation, and its functions. As a result, these worldviews have left indelible imprints on the early concepts of literature.

As shown above, the prominent features of these concepts can indeed be traced, with varying degrees of certainty, to the early worldviews examined above. The centrality of magico-religious dance and music in the earliest *"Shi yan zhi"* statement befits the immediate context of the performance of the Three Rites to honor the most important ghosts and spirits. Moreover, it agrees with the paramount role of such dance and music depicted in various accounts of religious life in high antiquity and in the oracle bone graph (*shi*) for poetry. Of course, whatever one may say about high antiquity is unavoidably speculative to a great degree, as our knowledge of it comes mainly from legendary accounts collected in much later times and from conjectural explanations of oracle bone graphs. There is no exception to my discussion on the ghosts- and spirits-centered worldview and the religious concept of literature. Thanks to the general accuracy of the historical records in the *Zuo Commentry* and *Speeches of the States,* we can affirm an inherent relationship between the *li*-centered worldview and the humanistic concept of literature on a more reliable basis. In these two Zhou chronicles, many remarks on music and poetry are often an integral part of a broader cosmological inquiry. So it is hardly surprising that both realms of inquiry are marked by corresponding shifts of emphasis from ghosts and spirits to natural and human processes. Similarly, by investigating corresponding shifts of emphasis from the man-nature harmony to the ethico-sociopolitical harmony alone in *Analects* and the "Great Preface," we can establish a close relationship between the Confucian worldview and the didactic concept of literature. The development of this didactic concept was completely in sync with the momentous rise of Confucian thought in the Han. By examining Liu Xie's extensive borrowing of essential ideas, terms, and even passages from the "Great Commentary," we can ascertain that Liu Xie has consciously and consistently formulated his comprehensive concept of literature within its "organismic" scheme.

My investigation of early Chinese cosmological and literary thought has revealed a complex, multifaceted relationship between the two. Sometimes, we can trace a fairly clear line of influence from a particular mode of cosmological thinking prevalent at a given time, say the *li*-centered worldview in the Spring and Autumn period or the Confucian worldview in the Han. However, even when a concept of literature is bound up with a currently dominant worldview, it can and in fact often does contain many important elements associated with the older worldviews. For instance, we can find an abundance of references to ghosts and spirits in various concepts of literature developed long after the waning of the ghosts- and sprits-centered worldview. This eclectic tendency is particularly evident in *Wenxin diaolong*. Since the "Great Commentary" represents not a single but an amalgam of different modes of cosmological thinking—Confucian, Daoist, yin-yang, and *wuxing*—Liu's concept of literature accordingly contains diverse elements associated with all these modes.

Following Liu Xie, most later critics adopt the *wen*-Dao model for their reconceptualizations of literature. However, not all of them are quite as eclectic as Liu Xie in their interpretation of the Dao. Some critics like Zhong Hong, Xiao Tong, Ye Xie, and Zhang Xuecheng show a singular interest in the impact of the ultimate cosmological process on literature. When the term Dao is explicitly employed in their writings, it carries few moralist implications of the Confucian Dao. Instead it seems to hark back to the early Daoist notion of the amoral cosmological Dao. Other critics, especially the *guan Dao* and the *zai Dao* advocates in Tang and Song times, embrace the neo-Confucian notion of the Dao. Unlike the Dao in *Analects,* the neo-Confucian Dao entails a very conspicuous metaphysical dimension reminiscent of cosmological discussions in the "Great Commentary." Influenced by this neo-Confucian notion of the Dao, these critics display an eclectic tendency similar to Liu Xie's as they discuss literature in relation to the cosmological as well as the moralist Confucian Dao. Unlike Liu Xie, however, they usually foreground the transmission of the moralist Confucian Dao and discuss the cosmological Dao merely for the purpose of demonstrating the sacred origin of the Confucian Dao.

In this chapter I have chosen not to discuss Buddhist worldviews introduced from India during the Han. This choice is largely the result of my reflection on the long-standing debates on the influence of Buddhist cosmological thinking or the lack thereof in *Wenxin diaolong*. The critics who emphasize such an influence usually cite Liu's life experiences as a tonsured Buddhist monk and identify various Buddhist terms and concepts used in his discussion of certain critical issues. Some of them go so far as to argue that Liu Xie's Dao is exclusively the Buddhist Dao. Rejecting such an argument, many critics point to the notable absence of an unambiguous Buddhist definition or description of the Dao. In contrast to this absence, they underscore the elaborate description of the Confucian Dao that spans the first three chapters.

In my opinion, these two opposing views are illuminating in their own ways because they help us to see two important characteristics concerning the Buddhist influence on *Wenxin diaolong* and on Chinese literary thought at large. The first characteristic is that the influence of Buddhist worldviews is quite conspicuous in the discussion of particular critical issues. In *Wenxin diaolong* and many later texts, a great many Buddhist ideas, terms, and images are used as metaphors or analogues for understanding the creative and receptive processes and for establishing ranks of literary excellence. The second characteristic is that the influence of Buddhist worldviews has not penetrated to the level of theoretical conceptualization of literature. They have not inspired any influential statements and tenets like *"Shi yan zhi," "Wen yi guan Dao,"* and *"Wen yi zai Dao."* Indeed, the origins, nature, and functions of literature are seldom discussed in Buddhist terms. This shows that Buddhist worldviews have not influenced the development of Chinese literary criticism so profoundly as indigenous Chinese worldviews. Considering these two characteristics, it seems appropriate not to foreground Buddhist worldviews when discussing the overall orientation of Chinese poetics. For this reason, I have decided to postpone my discussion of Buddhist worldviews until I explore the issue of deconstruction in chapter 8.

Having said so much about the affinities between cosmological thinking and literary thought, I must stress that I do not mean to suggest a simplistic causal relationship between them. Besides the worldviews examined above, there are other factors that influence the way critics formulate their concepts of literature. Some factors, such as the changing roles of speech and writing, are intrinsic to literary development itself. Others have more to do with different social and political worlds in which critics lived. With these qualifications, I should reiterate that it is hard to overestimate the influence of Chinese worldviews on Chinese literary thought. Given the weight of evidence shown above, we have reason to argue at least that Chinese worldviews have effectively opened up the "epistemes" for different ways of thinking about literature.

CHAPTER 4

The Systematics of
Western and Chinese Poetics
Common Denominators, Differentiae,
and Cosmological Paradigms

O N THE BASIS OF MY FINDINGS IN THE FIRST THREE CHAP-
ters, I will now reflect on the systematics of Western and Chinese
poetics. The systematics of a critical tradition may be construed as a
broad set of inherent relationships among the major literary concepts
and theories developed in that tradition. It is constituted by one or
more common denominators that unify diverse literary concepts and
theories into a meaningful whole and differentiae that set particular
concepts and theories apart from one other. Both common denomi-
nators and differentiae are grounded in cosmological paradigms
specific to a given cultural tradition. By comparing these common de-
nominators, differentiae, and underlying cosmological paradigms, we
shall be able to mutually illuminate the systematics of Western and
Chinese poetics.

COMMON DENOMINATORS

The conception of literature in relation to truth constitutes a common
denominator of Western poetics. This core belief may be seen to un-
derlie and unify Western critical theory from Plato to our time. West-
ern critics tend to see literature, a specific form of reality, in relation
to a presumed ultimate reality—be it the Platonic Idea, the Aristote-
lian Form, the Judeo-Christian God, the creative Mind, the Cogito,
the *langue* as the semiotic essence, or *différance*. As they evaluate the
nature of literature in terms of its truthfulness or untruthfulness to,
or its negation of, that reality, they make different kinds of untruth-

claims, truth-claims, or antitruth-claims about literature. These claims form the very foundation of the major critical schools examined in chapter 1. It is true that not all major Western critical schools are known for making such broad, lofty untruth-claims, truth-claims, or antitruth-claims for literature. For instance, the medieval criticism and the eighteenth-century neoclassical criticism are concerned not so much with abstract questions about literature and truth as with practical issues such as *allegoresis* and artistic decorum. Nonetheless, the major conceptual models used by medieval and neoclassical critics are grounded in the existing paradigms of truth. The famous medieval fourfold model of scriptural interpretation is apparently derived from a dualistic, hierarchical paradigm of truth. The progression from the literal, through the moral and the allegorical, and finally up to the anagogic sense—signifies something similar to the climb up the ascending levels of truth depicted in Plato's *Republic*. In neoclassical criticism, the model of artistic decorum and perfection is also grounded on a dualistic, though less metaphysical, paradigm of truth. The rules and ideals of literature are formulated in terms of the best possible representation of the truth of human or physical nature perfectly embodied in the finest classical works. In the critical writings of Boileau, Dryden, Samuel Johnson, Pope, and other neoclassical critics, we can clearly see the extent to which their debates on poetic rules and dramatic "unities" are framed by their concern with the representation of truth. In a way, these examples of practical criticism speak even more eloquently than loud untruth-claims, truth-claims, or antitruth-claims to the centrality of truth in Western poetics.

By contrast, the conception of literature as a harmonizing process is a common denominator of traditional Chinese poetics since the earliest times. Traditional Chinese critics do not conceive of literature as a form of knowledge that enables, obstructs, or renders impossible the cognizance of the ultimate truth. Instead, they regard literature as a cyclical, harmonizing process. This process has its ultimate origin in the external world, works its way through the internal world, and produces a counterimpact on the external world. As it completes this cycle, it brings into harmony all phenomena and experiences involved— the natural and the human, the external and the internal, the public and the private, the sensory and the suprasensory, and so on. This core belief unifies the major Chinese concepts of literature discussed in chapter 2. It is articulated first by various *"Shi yan zhi"* statements and later by various tenets about *wen* and the Dao. During Tang and Song times, these *wen*-Dao tenets emerge as dominant, pervasive models for thinking about literature. Later, in Ming and Qing times, many critics shy away from talking about *wen* and the Dao and focus their attention on practical issues, such as the periodization of the literary past, the imitation and canonization of particular literary periods, the founding of poetry and prose schools modeled on particular ancient masters, and the formulation of rules for poetry and prose. Nonetheless, they cannot escape from the influence of the *wen*-Dao tenets developed by their Tang and Song predecessors. Seen in a broad historical perspective, all the practical issues mentioned above are an outgrowth of the investigation of *wentong* 文統 (the transmission of literature) begun in the Southern Song. This investigation is in turn a critical endeavor inspired by the study of *daotong* 道統 (the transmission of the Confucian Dao) in the neo-Confucian sociopolitical discourse. So in the final analysis, the practical issues addressed by Ming and Qing critics are framed by the neo-Confucian paradigms of *wen* and the Dao. This aptly attests to the pervasive presence of the *wen*-Dao model, one that crystallizes the core belief about literature in Chinese poetics.

DIFFERENTIAE

In Western poetics, the change of critical locus means a shift of attention from one to another among the four critical coordinates: the universe, the artist, the work, and the reader. In chapter 1, we have observed a continual shift in the central criterion for literary judgment, from the universe in classical and neoclassical criticism, to the artist or author in Romantic criticism, to textual meanings in practical criticism and New Criticism, to the reading process in phenomenological criticism, and to the mode of linguistic signification in structuralism and deconstruction. While this pattern of changing loci holds true for Western poetics as a whole, there are three important differences between pre-twentieth-century and twentieth-century ways of conceptualizing the four coordinates.

The first difference concerns the critical perspective from which the four coordinates are examined. Most pre-twentieth-century critics examine the four coordinates from the point of traditional philosophy or theology. For instance, Plato and Aristotle conceptualize the universe in terms of their own speculative philosophies. Wordsworth examines and theorizes about the poet and poetic imagination through the overlapping prisms of German metaphysics, British associationist philosophy, and his own creative experiences. Coleridge investigates and defines the nature of the poetic text in light of the then prevalent philosophical and theological views of symbol and allegory. By contrast, twentieth-century critics often seek to view the four coordinates from the multiple perspectives provided by new modern disciplines. Those disciplines are highly specialized, often rigorously empirical, and traditionally unrelated to literary studies. For example, consider the reconceptualization of subjective consciousness by psychoanalytic critics and the reconceptualization of the text by structuralists and deconstructionists on the basis of Saussurian linguistics.

The second difference involves the interaction among the four coordinates. Pre-twentieth-century critics usually treat the four coordinates as static constants and focus on one of them as a center of reference point. In contrast, many twentieth-century critics go beyond this convention and regard the dynamic interaction between two or more coordinates as the locus of their investigation. The phenomenological critics, for instance, direct their attention to the interplay of text, authorial consciousness, and readerly consciousness in the process of reading. For their part deconstructionists seek to "de-reify" the four coordinates by playing them against one another. In their exercise of textual deconstruction, they have practically transformed the four coordinates from static, self-contained entities into mutually implicating signs.

The third difference concerns the switch of the conceptual models used for examining the four coordinates. Pre-twentieth-century critics usually investigate a particular coordinate by using conceptual models closely associated with it. In examining the creative process, for instance, Romantic critics almost invariably adapt conceptual models from established studies of the mind. Seldom, if ever, do pre-twentieth-century critics take the liberty of switching conceptual models around (applying a linguistic model, say, to the study of the "universe"). By contrast, many twentieth-century critics examine a coordinate within conceptual models traditionally unrelated to it and originally used for the investigation of a different coordinate. Consider, for instance, Lacan's application of Freud to the analysis of language. Another notable example is the application of the Derridean textual model by Marxist, feminist, and other poststructuralist critics to study social, ethnic, racial, gender, and class issues—issues traditionally subsumed under the coordinate "universe."

In Chinese poetics, the change of critical locus does not occur along the same axis as in Western poetics. What marks one critical concept or theory from others is not its emphasis on any of these four coordinates, but its unique understanding of the interaction between literature and specific ongoing processes in the realms of heaven, earth, and man. In other words, the change of critical locus in Chinese poetics means a shift of attention to the interaction of different internal and external processes. In each of the four early concepts of literature, for instance, we can observe a distinctive pattern of interacting processes set in motion by the act of public, performative / verbal communication or private belletristic creation.

The change of critical locus in early Chinese poetics is not marked by the kind of radically antithetical tendencies seen in Western poetics. For instance, the relationships among the four early concepts of literature examined in chapter 2 are mutually complementary rather than antithetical. While a critic emphasizes literature's interaction with specific ongoing processes, he often touches upon its interaction with other processes as well. Even if he ignores certain ongoing processes, he does not consider them at odds with those processes he emphasizes. For example, the Confucian-minded author of the "Great Preface" focuses on literature's interaction with various sociopolitical processes, and meanwhile acknowledges literature's indirect effects on "ghosts and spirits." He ignores but does not dispute literature's interaction with natural processes. The fact that Liu Xie can smoothly codify earlier concepts of literature into a comprehensive critical system attests to their mutual complementality.

Among the concepts of literature developed after Liu Xie, however, we take note of some degree of antithetical tension. Although the *guan Dao* and *zai Dao* advocates conceptualize *wen* in relation to the neo-Confucian Dao, they disagree with one another about the value of *wen*. In Ming and Qing times, there emerge critical schools that compete with one another ever more self-consciously. But in their relentless mutual attacks, these schools do not focus on challenging one another's understanding about the nature of literature. They have not shown any strong interest in launching abstract theoretical debates on the *guan Dao* and *zai Dao* tenets. Instead they tend to argue about how to rank past literary periods and individual writers, how to distinguish and evaluate particular genres, and how to define themselves against the literary traditions. So their disagreements about the *wen-Dao* relationship do not evolve into something like the continuous, intense quarrel about the nature of literature seen in Western poetics.[1]

COSMOLOGICAL PARADIGMS

The common denominators and differentiae of Western and Chinese poetics are respectively grounded in dualistic and nondualistic cosmological paradigms.

Western critics entertain a core belief in literature as untruth, truth, or antitruth largely because they examine the nature of literature through the dualistic cosmological paradigms developed in Western metaphysics. As shown in chapter 1, Plato sets up a hierarchical opposition between the ultimate existence (Being) and relative existences (beings). When examining literature within this cosmological paradigm, he naturally regards it, an imitation of beings, as untruthful copy or simply untruth thrice removed from Being. Like Plato, many Western philosophers such as Aristotle, Kant, Hegel, and others are themselves literary theoreticians of the highest order. So it is little wonder that they often take the lead in reconceptualizing literature within variant dualistic cosmological paradigms developed by themselves. In so doing, they introduce new concepts of literature as untruth, truth, or antitruth, and thereby charter a new course for the development of Western poetics.

The close affinity between Western philosophy and poetics is reflected also in corresponding shifts of orientation in those two realms of thought. While Western philosophers redirect their search for the ultimate truth or antitruth from the universe, to the individual mind, to the rhetorical structures of language, to the subject-object perceptual interaction, to the semiotic system, and to the play of *différance*, Western critics correspondingly change their critical locus from the universe, to the artist, to the work, to the reading process, and to the mode of linguistic signification. Moreover, they correspondingly reconceptualize literature in terms of its artistic imitation, its spiritual revelation, its autotelic embodiment, its phenomenological manifestation, or its ceaseless deconstruction of the ultimate truth envisioned by their philosophical counterparts.

The dominance of dualistic cosmological paradigms provides an underlying unity for Western theory. The continuous mutual displacement of the four critical coordinates results in abrupt shifts of critical orientation in the development of Western poetics. However, these shifts of critical orientation, if seen in a broader philosophical perspective, merely mean the reordering of the hierarchy of the terms within the dualistic paradigms in question. For instance, the Romantic rebellion against the classical and neoclassical traditions amounts to little more than a reversal of these two terms—the universe and the individual mind. Whereas classical and neoclassical critics identify the former as the locus of ultimate truth and the latter as an instrument of imitating that truth, Romantic critics tend to reverse the relationship of the two terms. Paradoxically, this reversal does not destroy but actually ensures the continued dominance of the dualistic paradigms on which the mimetic tradition is founded. Any re-ordering of the four coordinates presupposes an acceptance of the dualistic paradigms that undergird them. This holds true even for the self-consciously anti-dualistic deconstruction. Insofar as its very existence depends on the prior existence of dualistic paradigms as the objects of its continual deconstruction, deconstruction is no less inscribed than other critical schools by dualistic paradigms. The case of deconstruction aptly demonstrates the extent to which dualistic paradigms determine the overall paramater for the development of Western poetics.

Traditional Chinese critics embrace a common belief in literature as a harmonizing process largely because they think about literature through nondualistic cosmological paradigms. As shown in chapter 3, traditional Chinese thinkers conceive of the ultimate reality, not as a transcendental entity diametrically opposed to the phenomenal world, but as an Ultimate Process that generates, sustains, controls, and unifies ongoing processes in all realms. The early Chinese worldviews discussed in chapter 3 furnish testimony to this nondualistic way of thinking. Those worldviews entail either a "naturalization" of conscious beings in the numinous realm (ancestral spirits, the high god, Heaven, etc.), or a "supernatualization" of actual processes in the worlds of nature and man (the cosmological *li,* Confucius' Dao of human history, the all-inclusive Dao of the *Changes*). These conceptions of the ultimate reality give rise to various nondualistic cosmological paradigms marked by an inseparable entwining of the "metaphysical" (*xingshang* 形上) and the "physical" (*xingxia* 形下).[2] Thinking through these nondualistic paradigms, Chinese critics naturally conceptualize literature within a resonantial network of internal and external processes and assess its value in terms of how effectively it harmonizes those processes and makes manifest the Ultimate Process itself.

We can also observe corresponding shifts of locus in the development of Chinese cosmology and poetics.[3] Broadly speaking, the development of Chinese cosmological thinking may be understood in terms of a continual rethinking of three fundamental questions. First, what form does the Ultimate Process assume? Ghosts and spirits, the high god, the cosmological *li,* the Confucian Dao, the Daoist Dao, the Dao of the *Changes,* the Dao of the neo-Confucians, or something else? Second, where does the Ultimate Process manifest itself most eminently? In the numinous realm, the world of nature, the human society, the mysterious symbols of the *Changes,* simultaneously in more than one of these realms, or somewhere else? Third, how best to integrate human life with the Ultimate Process? Through rituals and ceremonies, the rectification of human relationships, the contemplation of the Dao of the *Changes,* the neo-Confucian learning of the Dao, or other means? As shown in chapter 3, the rethinking of these three questions significantly influences the development of the major Chinese concepts of literature. As the privileged locale of the ultimate reality changes to a new realm, critical attention is redirected to the human interaction with the ongoing processes in that realm. Moreover, as the ultimate reality changes from the numinous spirits, to the early Confucian Dao, to the all-embracing Dao of the *Changes,* and to the neo-Confucian Dao, literature is reconceptualized as a process instrumental to integrating human life with the ultimate reality in its newly perceived form. This reconceptualization of literature leads to new ideas about its origin and function and about the dynamics of literary creation.

CULTURAL SPECIFICITY AND COMMONALITY

Our comparisons of the common denominators, differentiae, and cosmological paradigms in Western and Chinese poetics should help us to dispel some entrenched misconceptions with regard to the systematics or the alleged lack thereof in these two critical traditions. As shown above, Western poetics is anything but universalistic. Its entire system is permeated by beliefs, concerns, questions, and attitudes bounded by Western cultural and intellectual traditions. When contrasted with their Chinese counterparts, these beliefs, concerns, questions, and attitudes aptly accentuate the cultural specificity of Western poetics. Although few would openly declare that Western poetics is universalistic, it has long been so treated not only in Western but also in non-Western countries. While some scholars in the West indiscriminately apply Western critical theory to literary and cultural studies involving non-Western traditions, scholars of non-Western countries often attempt to re-present their own native critical traditions within the framework of Western poetics. Both practices apparently operate under the same assumption that Western poetics is universalistic. So long as we perceive the cultural specificity of Western poetics, we will see the need to reject this universalistic assumption and question all practices based on it.

Freed from the shackles of this universalistic assumption, we can reexamine Chinese poetics on its own terms and redefine its cultural specificity. In investigating the macrocosmic structures of Chinese poetics, we have discovered that Chinese is not "systemless" as has been long misconstrued. The interrelatedness of major Chinese concepts of literature reveals a critical system grounded in "process-based," non-dualistic cosmological paradigms. In light of this "process-based" systematics, we can perceive inner coherence on all levels of critical discourse. For instance, even Chinese critical terms, long considered elusive and logically unconnected, appear to manifest a coherent nomenclature. The *qi* 氣-related terms are an excellent case in point. The great majority of these terms describe human interaction with external processes on five different levels.[4] For instance, we have "*xueqi*" 血氣, "*qili*" 氣力, "*guqi*" 骨氣, and "*qizhi*" 氣質 on the physiological level; "*xiqi*" 喜氣, "*shuangqi*" 爽氣, and "*nuqi*" 怒氣 on the psychological level; "*zhiqi*" 志氣, "*haoqi*" 浩氣, "*zhengqi*" 正氣, and "*gangqi*" 剛氣 on the moral level; "*shenqi*" 神氣, "*lingqi*" 靈氣, "*qiqi*" 奇氣, and "*zhenqi*" 真氣 on the intuitive level; and "*caiqi*" 才氣, "*wenqi*" 文氣, and "*ciqi*" 辭氣 on the intellectual level.[5]

This nomenclature of *qi*-related terms strikes us as a microcosmic reflection of the "process-based" critical system described. The word "*qi*," a process that is more concrete than but sometimes used interchangeably with the Dao, aptly bears upon the core idea of "process" in traditional Chinese concepts of literature. Meanwhile, its multifarious, often protean, compounds attest to the dynamic interplay between external and internal processes on the five levels. Furthermore, the fact that many *qi*-related terms are used to describe at once the writer's creative process, the reader's aesthetic experience, the qualities of a work, and a work's impact on the external world shows that traditional Chinese critics conceptualize the major aspects of literary experience in terms of the interaction and harmonization of internal and external processes.[6]

Once we perceive a "process-based" critical system in Chinese poetics, we will feel obliged to debunk the widely accepted cliché that the "systemlessness" is a culture-specific feature of Chinese poetics. Traditional Chinese poetics strikes us as impressionistic, haphazard, and orderless only because we seek to understand it within an analytical framework grounded in the dualistic paradigms of Western critical thinking. But when we reexamine it within an interpretive framework grounded in nondualistic Chinese cosmological paradigms, we can find overwhelming evidence of its systematic coherence.

In stressing the cultural specificity of Western and Chinese poetics, I do not intend to denigrate one tradition for the purpose of aggrandizing the other, nor to emphasize the differences between the two to the neglect of their commonality. Quite the contrary, by dismissing the two major misconceptions about Western and Chinese poetics, I hope to redress the imbalance of received opinions of the two traditions and initiate a constructive dialogue between them on an equal basis. Such a dialogue should tell us much about their commonality as well. In the second part of this book, we shall see show how Western and Chinese critics share a common interest in a broad array of critical subjects and issues. We shall also note that they often develop similar strategies, methods, and procedures for exploring those subjects and issues. The similarities discussed in chapters 5 to 8 will bear witness to the common critical interest and wisdom of Western and Chinese critics. It is this deep commonality that makes it possible for Western and Chinese critics alike to appropriate ideas, terms, and strategies from each other and thereby invigorate their own critical traditions. Chapters 7 and 8 provide two equally illuminating examples of such a meaningful, productive encounter between the two traditions. In chapter 7, we will see how Fenollosa and Pound, looking to the East, discover a Chinese nonmimetic notion of written language and ingeniously appropriate it within the Western dualistic paradigm of metaphor. In chapter 8, we will see how Seng Zhao and his followers, looking to the west (India in this case), import the Mādhyamika Buddhism, a deconstructive philosophy developed within a broader dualistic philosophical tradition. Although Fenollosa and Pound hardly produce any significant impact on the basic dualistic paradigms of Western critical thinking, they admirably use their (mis)conception of the Chinese written character as a catalyst for the modernist reinvention of Western poetry. Similarly, even though the Mādhyamika and other Buddhist doctrines produce no full-fledged Buddhist concepts of literature and therefore pose no serious challenge to the basic "process-based" paradigms of Chinese critical thinking, they do provide Chinese critics with alternate terms, concepts, and models for examining issues such as literary creation and reception. From these two examples we can see that, while stressing the cultural specificity of Western and Chinese poetics, we should not lose sight of their deep commonality and explore the infinite potential for meaningful, fruitful dialogues between them. With this balanced awareness of cultural specificity and commonality, let us proceed to pursue four specific dialogues between Western and Chinese poetics.

PART II

Microcosmic Textures
of Western and Chinese Poetics

CHAPTER 5

Poetics of Harmony

Plato and Confucius on Poetry

PLATO (CA. 427–CA. 347 B.C.) AND CONFUCIUS (CA. 551–479 B.C.) lived only about half a century apart, but in two culturally unrelated worlds. The influence of these two thinkers on mankind can be measured only on the grandest scale of time and space. For about two and a half millennia, Plato's and Confucius' thoughts have shaped all the major aspects of life in the West and East Asia, respectively. To compare Platonic and Confucian thought is an expedition back to the fountainheads of Western and East Asian cultures. By comparing Plato's and Confucius' thoughts, we can observe similarities and differences between Western and East Asian cultures in their infancy and better understand why the two great traditions would develop as they have. For this reason, Plato-Confucius comparisons abound in the works of comparative philosophy.[1] While these comparisons cover a broad spectrum of intellectual interest, they seldom deal with the topic of poetry and aesthetics. To bring due attention to this topic, I shall consider the two thinkers' theories of poetry in relation to their broader educational, ethical, and philosophical concerns.

Plato's and Confucius' theories of poetry as we understand them today are the products of centuries of critical interpretation. Neither Plato nor Confucius consciously set out to formulate a theory of poetry. They both came to discuss poetry during dialogues with their friends or pupils. Plato's notion of poetry is not exactly the same as Confucius', with regard to both its ontological implications and its referential scope.[2] For Plato, poetry is a very broad category for works, composed by human beings or attributed to divine muses, which are usually rhymed, set to music, and cast in the form of an epic or a tragedy. Confucius did not entertain such a generalized notion of poetry, nor did he discuss so extensive a range of works in *Analects* (*Lunyu* 論語) as Plato did in his dialogues.[3] Confucius' attention is fixed not on poetry in general, but on *The Book of Poetry* (hereafter the *Poetry*) (*Shi jing* 詩經), the earliest Chinese anthology of ancient poems and songs. Ever since the Han, however, Confucius' remarks on the *Poetry* have customarily been considered to be comments on poetry in general as much as on a single anthology. Thanks to this ingenious identification of the *Poetry* with poetry,[4] Confucius' remarks have become an invaluable source of ideas about poetry and have taken on phenomenal significance as a coherent theory of poetry. In the Western critical tradition, Plato's conversational remarks on poetry have undergone a similar process of transformation into a coherent theory of poetry. In the discussion below, we will see that Plato's and Confucius' theories of poetry bear close similarities to each other, not only in terms of ideas expressed, but also in terms of their lasting influence on the Western and Chinese critical traditions as a whole.

PLATO'S AND CONFUCIUS' EDUCATIONAL SYSTEMS:
CULTIVATION OF INTELLECTUAL AND MORAL HARMONY

For both Plato and Confucius, poetry is not a pure belletristic pursuit separate from intellectual, moral, and utilitarian concerns. Rather, it is an integral part of a broad system of education they each seek to institute in the hope of producing an elite educated class to run an ideal government of the best, the wisest, and the most virtuous.[5] The model members of this elite class are for Plato philosophers or would-be philosophers and for Confucius *junzi* 君子 or gentlemen. Since Plato's and Confucius' theories of poetry are formulated in the broader contexts of their discussion of education, a brief comparison of their educational systems is necessary.

The core of Plato's educational system is a rigorous, highly programmatic cultivation of intellectual harmony through music and physical training (gymnastics), intellectual studies (mathematics, geometry, astronomy), and pure reasoning (dialectic)—a lifelong enterprise to be completed step by step by the young guardians of his ideal Republic.

The education of young guardians must begin with music, which Plato expressly claims includes literature. This is because young guardians are too weak bodily to develop rhythm and harmony through physical training. Gymnastics follows music. Of the numerous possible ways of training the body, Plato recommends a military gymnastics, characterized by the endurance of coarse food and physical hardship. For him, this simple gymnastic is the parent of health in the body as simple music is that of temperance in the soul.[6] A man who has been through such a gymnastic comes to possess not only an excellent physique but also the wisdom of not wishing to lengthen his own life beyond the point of its usefulness to the public.[7] Emphasizing a proper balance between gymnastic and music education, Plato notes that "the mere athlete becomes too much of a savage, and that the mere musician is melted and softened beyond what is good for him."[8] Having acquired hardiness through gymnastics and gentleness through music, a youth's soul will become so well-proportioned and harmonious that it "will move spontaneously towards the true being of everything."[9]

At this stage, however, young guardians are still too delicate mentally to deal with abstract reasoning. Before embarking on the contemplation of true being, they must also go through a rigorous training in arithmetic, geometry, and, to a lesser extent, astronomy. These three sciences serve in their own ways to prepare a youth for the dialectic, or pure reasoning. Arithmetic compels "the soul to reason about abstract number, and rebel against the introduction of visible or tangible objects into the argument."[10] As far as its finer abstract part is concerned, geometry leads the soul to turn its gaze toward "where is full of perfection of being."[11] According to Plato, astronomy, or the motion of solids, is the sister science of Pythagorean harmonics. It is to the eye as the latter is to the ear—both being wrongly concerned with the material and sensible rather than the eternal and immutable in heaven. Only if it is, as Benjamin Jowett observes, "studied with a view to the good and not after the fashion of the empirics" does it become a worthy subject of study for a youth.[12]

Young guardians are to have completed their training in these sciences as well as in music and gymnastics by the age of twenty. The best from the class of twenty-year-olds are promoted to the higher honor of being taught what Plato calls the "inter-communion and connection" of the sciences.[13] This select class is to have mastered the knowledge of "natural relationship of them [the sciences] to one another and to true being," and consequently have a comprehensive mind or dialectical talent by the age of thirty.[14] Then the most promising of this select class will be promoted to the still higher honor of being taught how to "give up the use of sight and the other senses and [be] in company with truth to attain absolute being."[15] After five years of such philosophical study, they will be sent back to the world and will hold military or other offices to be proved firm against temptations and adversities. Finally, when they reach fifty years of age, those who have distinguished themselves in political service and in the mastery of knowledge are ready at last to approach the absolute good through dialectic, the only science that does away with hypotheses and goes directly to the first principle. By means of dialectic or pure reasoning, they "raise the eye of the soul to the universal light which lightens all things, and behold the absolute good."[16] Notably, in the process they will not only bring about a transcendental transformation of the soul, but also find in the absolute good the "pattern according to which they are to order the State and the lives of individuals, and the remainder of their own lives also."[17] After they have performed their own duties and brought their like to be the rulers of the State, they will "depart to the Islands of the Blest and dwell there" and will be honored as demigods in public memorials and sacrifices.[18]

Like Plato, Confucius places the cultivation of harmony at the center of his educational system. What he wants his pupils to cultivate, however, is primarily moral harmony rather than intellectual harmony. Whereas the Platonic intellectual harmony culminates in the cognition of the absolute truth, Confucian moral harmony leads one toward the achievement of the supreme moral virtue of *ren* 仁, which is inclusive of but not limited to the meanings of goodness, humanity, benevolence, and many other virtues.[19] What unifies these concrete virtues is the ideal of perfect inward and outward harmony that can be achieved by man. Although Confucius seldom speaks of the manifestation of *ren* in individual persons, he regards the attainment of *ren* as the ultimate goal of his broad educational program.

Like Plato, Confucius believes that education should begin with the study of poetry due to its beneficial effects on the young mind. As to what comes after the study of poetry, however, Confucius holds a view quite different from Plato's. Whereas Plato next introduces physical education and abstract sciences, Confucius proceeds to his central task of moral education. For Confucius, moral education is not a matter of imposing on his disciples an elaborate set of ritualistic rules governing their inner and outer lives. Rather, it is a matter of helping them to cultivate a harmonious character and to establish a harmonious relationship with people of different social strata.

For Confucius, a gentleman is one who has successfully cultivated both inner and outer harmony. A gentleman displays the spirit of temperance under all circumstances. Temperance, a minor virtue to some, is of cardinal importance to Confucius, because it is the key to developing one's harmonious character. It means the avoidance of extremes in one's speech, action, and thought:

> There are three things that a gentleman, in following the Way, places above the rest: from every attitude, every gesture that he employs he must remove all trace of violence or arrogance; every look that he composes in his face must betoken good faith; from every word that he utters, from every intonation, he must remove all trace of coarseness or impropriety.[20]

君子所貴乎道者三。動容貌。斯遠暴慢矣。正顏色。斯近信矣。出辭氣。斯遠鄙倍矣。

As shown here, Confucius always has the golden mean or the Middle Course (*zhongdao* 中道) in the foremost of his mind when he depicts a gentleman. Even when praising a gentleman's moral character, Confucius stresses that his virtues are never developed to a fault. A gentleman is, like the Master himself, "affable yet firm, commanding but not harsh, polite but easy."[21] He is "proud but not quarrelsome" on some occasions, and "conciliatory but not accommodating" on others.[22]

After a gentleman has achieved harmony in temperament, learning, and conduct, Confucius believes, he should be entrusted with the responsibilities of the state. By conducting his private and public life in the spirit of propriety and temperance, he helps bring the entire society into harmony. In serving his parents, a gentleman wears an air of reverence and exerts his utmost; in serving his superiors, he is punctilious and ready to lay down his own life; in dealing with friends, he is always true to his words; in treating his inferiors, he always generously provides for their needs and exacts their service in a fair manner,[23] and when facing Heaven, great men, and divine sages, he always stands in awe.[24] Thanks to his adoption of these proper attitudes, he comes to enjoy a harmonious relationship with all people. His filial piety wins the affection of his parents and enhances the familial harmony. His loyalty earns him trust from his superiors and contributes to the harmony between superiors and inferiors. His trustworthiness wins him friends and brothers from the "Four Seas" and hence strengthens his bond with his equals.[25] His generosity and compassion gain the respect and support of the multitude and help promote peace and harmony in the society at large. In short, his inward harmony will radiate far and wide, reaching from his individual self to the family to the state and to the entire world.

Unlike Plato, Confucius does not prescribe a definite timetable for his program of moral education. There are no indications that he expects his disciples to attain a certain kind of moral harmony by a given time. However, Confucius does cherish in his mind a broad pattern of spiritual progress, which is akin to Plato's in some ways. He hints at that pattern when he talks about his own spiritual progress:

> The Master said, At fifteen I set my heart upon learning. At thirty, I had planted my feet firm upon the ground. At forty, I no longer suffered from perplexities. At fifty, I knew what were the biddings of Heaven. At sixty, I heard them with docile ear. At seventy, I could follow the dictates of my own heart; for what I desired no longer overstepped the boundaries of right.[26]

> 子曰。吾十有五而志於學，三十而立。四十而不惑。五十而知天命。六十而耳順。七十而從心所欲。不踰矩。

If we place this and other passages cited above alongside what we have read in the *Republic,* we can see that Plato and Confucius design their schemes of education with the comparable objectives of achieving inner and outer harmony. While Plato emphasizes the achievement of the harmony of the mind in ever higher realms of human thought, Confucius stresses the expansion of inner moral harmony to ever broader realms of human existence. Furthermore, we can see that both thinkers ascribe to comparable broad time frames for one's spiritual progress. They both believe that one's spiritual life begins with education in poetry and arts, progresses through the development of inward and outward harmony in the course of middle age, and culminates in the attainment of absolute knowledge or spontaneous awareness of the heavenly will.

THE USE OF POETRY:
BENEFICIAL VS. HARMFUL EFFECTS

Both Plato and Confucius have mixed views about the use of poetry in their educational systems. On the one hand, they endorse the use of poetry as a good tool for cultivating intellectual or moral harmony. They hold that poetic harmony produces a more subtle and efficacious impression on one's consciousness than other types of harmony. On the other hand, they regard poetry as one of the least important subjects of study and give it no more than an auxiliary role in their respective educational systems. Moreover, they fear the harmful effects of poetry stemming from its appeal to emotion and sensual pleasures. To prevent such harmful effects, they seek to ban the use of poetry from later stages of education or to weed out the influence of bad poetry.

In the third book of the *Republic,* Plato gives a detailed explanation of the usefulness of poetry and music:

> Hence, Glaucon, I continued, the decisive importance of education in poetry and music: rhythm and harmony sink deep into the recesses of the soul and take the strongest hold there, bringing that grace of body and mind which is only to be found in one who is brought up in the right way. Moreover, a proper training in this kind makes a man quick to perceive any defect or ugliness in art or in nature. Such deformity will rightly disgust him. Approving all that is lovely, he will welcome it home with joy into his soul, and nourished thereby, grow into a man of noble spirit. All that is ugly and disgraceful he will rightly condemn and abhor while he is still too young to understand the reason; and when reason comes, he will greet her as a friend with whom his education has made him long familiar.
>
> I agree, he said; that is the purpose of education in literature and music.[27]

Here Plato endorses the use of poetry and music for two reasons. First, they can arouse in the young a healthy aversion to the inharmonious and the ugly. Second, they can bring about the grace of body and mind. Through poetry and music, Plato maintains, the grace of harmony and rhythm "shall flow into the eye and the ear, like a health-giving breeze from a purer region, and insensibly draw the soul from the earliest years into likeness and sympathy with the beauty of reason."[28] Among poems and music suitable for the young, he particularly extols two simple kinds: those about a brave man who "meets the blows of fortune with a firm step and a determination to endure," and those about a prudent man who acts moderately and wisely in the time of triumph.[29]

Plato rejects the use of poetry for later stages of education as vehemently as he endorses it for the initial stage of education. In book 10 of the *Republic,* Plato delivers his well-known condemnation of poetry:

> I think, he said, that we may fairly designate him as the imitator of that which the others make.
>
> Good, I said; then you call him who is third in the descent from nature an imitator?

Certainly, he said.

And the tragic poet is an imitator, and therefore, like all other imitators, he is thrice removed from the king and from the truth?

That appears to be so.[30]

While in early works he censures some particular poems merely for their imitations of evil, Plato here condemns poetry wholesale for its act of imitation, notwithstanding its possible imitation of good morals. He criticizes poetry not for ethical reasons, but on philosophical grounds. Poetry is not to be admitted into his ideal republic because of two related epistemological reasons. First, poetic imitation does not lead the soul beyond particular objects of sense to an apprehension of universals or ideas of which the absolute truth is constitutive. As Richard Kannicht points out, for Plato "the absolute primacy of truth attained philosophically (i.e. dialectically *via* recourse to the Ideas) entails the rejection of mimetic poetry, since by representing the given world it merely repeats it and to that extent remains in doubtful distance from the truth of Ideas."[31] Second, poetic imitation excites passions in the base part of the soul, while keeping in check the reason of the better part of the soul. In this regard, Plato writes that the imitative poet "awakens and nourishes and strengthens the feelings and impairs the reason . . . [and] implants an evil constitution, for he indulges the irrational nature."[32]

Probably because this broad attack on poetry occurs in the last book of the *Republic,* it is often misconstrued to represent Plato's final view of poetry. In any case, it is treated as such in many widely used critical anthologies, where the above passage is presented in isolation from Plato's more positive comments on poetry.[33] This inevitably gives rise to the common misconception of Plato as an avowed enemy of poetry among students of Western poetics.

Plato's negative view advanced in book 10 of the *Republic* should not be seen as superseding his fairly positive view of poetry in his early dialogues and in the early books of the *Republic.* Instead, his two conflicting views should be placed alongside each other as two different competing sides of his theory of poetry, each of which was to exert tremendous influence on Western criticism at different historical periods. Plato's shift to the negative view indicates not a final conclusion, but another new perspective on poetry developed after he became a disciple of Socrates.[34] Apart from the influence of Socrates, his adoption of this new perspective also has something to do with the changing contexts of his discussions. In discussing the education for young guardians in the early books of the *Republic,* it is natural that Plato distinguishes good and bad poetry and lays down the principle for the proper use of poetry. When the context of his dialogue changes to his theory of ideas in book 10, it is quite sensible for him to denounce poetry's bondage to the world of senses.

In light of Plato's idea of philosophical mission as a double journey—first the ascent to the world of ideas and then the descent back to the world of senses[35]—we can better understand his two conflicting views of poetry. He takes a positive view of poetry when he sees it from the perspective of the ascent and recognizes its usefulness as a stepping-stone to higher strata of spiritual harmony. However, when seeing poetry from the perspective of the descent and confronting its degenerate nature as an imitation, he cannot but embrace a negative view and propose to banish it from his ideal republic. But in so doing, he means only to expose the inferiority of poetry to transcendental ideas, not to ban the use of it in the sensible world altogether. In fact, according to Plato, when philosopher-kings descend back to the sensible world, they should seek to reorder that world after the pattern found in the absolute good. Poetry, among other things of sense, is to be re-created with a view to illustrating the existence of universals beyond the sensible world.

Such a revisionist view of poetry is evident in Plato's *Timaeus, Laws,* and other dialogues written after the *Republic.* The following passage from *Timaeus* is representative of Plato's revisionist view of poetry in his later dialogues:

> Moreover, so much of music as is adapted to the sound of the voice and to the sense of hearing is granted to us for the sake of harmony; and harmony, which has motions akin to the revolutions of our souls, is not regarded by the intelligent votary of the Muses as given by them with a view to irrational pleasure, which is deemed to be the purpose of it in our day, but as meant to correct any discord which may have arisen in the course of the soul, and to be our ally in bringing her into harmony and agreement with herself; and rhythm too was given by them for the same reason, on account of the irregular and graceless ways which prevail among mankind generally, and to help us against them.[36]

This passage amounts to something of a reversal of the view of poetry put forward in book 10 of the *Republic.* In book 10, poetry is condemned for its dealing with appearances of sense instead of the suprasensible truth. But here, the sound of the voice and the sense of hearing bring no disgrace to poetry. On the contrary, they are described as constitutive of poetic harmony akin to "revolutions of the soul." Poetry is censured in book 10 for its arousal of passions or the "irrational principle." Here its harmony and rhythm are endorsed as a welcome ally in correcting any discord in the soul and "bringing her into harmony with herself." As William C. Greene points out, Plato comes to befriend himself to poetry again in his later dialogues because he himself appears there as "a poet who has achieved a greater degree of truth and hence a greater seriousness of purpose" of poetry.[37] In light of this reaffirmation of poetry's usefulness for training the philosophical mind, Plato in the *Laws* begins all over again to discuss the educational use of poetry just as in the early books of the *Republic*. Once more, he sees fit to acknowledge education as being "first given through Apollo and the Muses,"[38] to distinguish good and bad kinds of poetry and music, to urge the poet to portray the character of good men,[39] and to advocate a rigorous exercise of censorship to guard against the abusive use of poetry.[40]

Like Plato, Confucius considers poetry to be a useful tool for helping the young to cultivate inward and outward harmony. Whereas Plato believes that good poetry imparts the grace of harmony and rhythm into the soul of the young, Confucius holds that good poetry can teach the young how to regulate their inward feelings and bring themselves in harmony with other people. This view of poetry is expressed clearly in his best known remark on the *Poetry:*

> How come you, little ones, do not study the *Poetry?* The *Poetry* may help to inspire, to observe, to keep company, and to express grievances. It may be used in the service of one's father at home and in the service of one's lord abroad. Furthermore, it may broaden our knowledge of the names of birds, beasts, plants, and trees.[41]

子曰。小子何莫學詩。詩。可以興。可以觀。可以群。可
以怨。邇之事父。遠之事君。多識於鳥獸草木之名。

Except for the least important use of the *Poetry* as a literacy primer, all the functions of the *Poetry* discussed here are geared toward enhancing inward and outward harmony. Confucius not only explicitly mentions the use of the *Poetry* for regulating father-son and lord-subject relationships, but also sets forth the four important ways in which the *Poetry* can function to enhance broader human relationships: *xing* 興 (to inspire), *guan* 觀 (to observe), *qun* 群 (to keep company), and *yuan* 怨 (to air grievances). Although no one can claim to know the exact meanings of these four terms, exegetes and critics have offered countless glosses and commentaries over the past two millennia. As we examine the best known of those glosses and commentaries, we will find that each of these four terms pertains to the achievement of inward and outward harmony.

Xing, here rendered "to inspire," has been glossed as "to introduce comparisons and brings categories together" by Kong Anguo 孔安國 (Han Dynasty) and "to evoke the heart's intent" by Zhu Xi 朱熹 (1130–1200).[42] These two glosses speak to the two different beneficial effects the *Poetry* produces on the reader: to evoke his moral consciousness and to help him express himself properly with poetic metaphors. It is important to note that, according to Confucius, the *Poetry* evokes moral ideas rather than crude emotions.[43] Apparently, Confucius stresses the evocation of moral consciousness because he believes that in the process one can channel one's emotions into moral sentiments and achieve an inward harmony of feelings and thoughts.[44]

Guan is glossed as "to observe the rise and decline of moral customs" by Zheng Xuan 鄭玄 (127–200)[45] and "to observe the success and failures [of government]" by Zhu Xi.[46] Huang Kan 皇侃 (488–545) explains Zheng Xuan's gloss of *guan* in the context of the *Poetry:* "The *Poetry* contains the songs of different states and therein the rise and fall of social customs may be observed and understood."[47] In light of the glosses by Zheng Xuan and Zhu Xi, it is generally assumed that Confucius takes the *Poetry* to be a mirror in which the reader can see reflections of both the social harmony of a well-governed state and the chaos of an ill-governed state. By observing the depictions of good and bad governments in the *Poetry,* he believes that one can learn, as Wang Fuzhi 王夫之 (1619–1692) says, "to make use of praise and satire to establish a code of rightness."[48]

Qun is glossed as "to keep company and try to improve one another" by Kong Anguo[49] and "to be accommodating but not to follow the tide of bad customs" by Zhu Xi.[50] In glossing this term, the exegetes undoubtedly bear in mind this remark by Confucius: "Men who keep company all day long but never mention rightness and who are given to petty acts of cleverness, are indeed difficult."[51] The exegetes assume that by the term *qun* Confucius means not only a rejection of bad human company, but also an establishment of good human company governed by moral rightness as exemplified in the *Poetry*.

Yuan is glossed as "to remonstrate with the lord by means of grievances" by Kong Anguo and as "to air grievances without being angry" by Zhu Xi. If taken literally, this term would mean simply "to air grievances" and would give the wrong suggestion that Confucius encourages people to vent their grievances by means of poetry. This is, of course, in contradiction to Confucius' advocacy of propriety and emotional restraint.[52] In order to prevent such a misunderstanding, some exegetes stress the subtle manner in which people express grievances toward their rulers in the *Poetry*. For instance, Zhang Juzheng 張居正 writes that the *Poetry* "brings forth sorrows and grievances from beneath earnest admonitions, yet keeps the sentiment of loyalty. Having learnt this, one will know how to handle grievances."[53]

Based on the glosses of the four terms,[54] we can see that Confucius encourages the study of the *Poetry* largely as an aid to one's cultivation of moral harmony. Like Plato, Confucius regards the study of the *Poetry* as the initial stage in cultivating one's moral harmony. Confucius says, "Let a man be inspired by the *Poetry*, set straight by the rituals, and perfected by music."[55] According to the interpretation of Bao Xian 包咸 (6 B.C.– A.D. 65), to be "inspired by the *Poetry*" is to have one's moral cultivation initiated by reading the *Poetry*, and to be "set straight by rituals" is to have oneself established on firm moral ground. To be "perfected by music," Liu Baonan 劉寶楠 (1791–1855) explains, is to have one's moral qualities refined and brought to completion by music.[56] All in all, Confucius stresses the importance of moral education with the help of rituals, and regards the *Poetry* merely as a means of fostering proper sentiments conducive to moral cultivation.

Judging by his arrangements of the subjects of education, Confucius undoubtedly assigns an auxiliary role to the study of the *Poetry*. When mentioning the subjects in the order of learning, he places the *Poetry* and arts before other subjects: "The Master took four subjects for his teaching: culture, conduct of affairs, loyalty to superiors, and the keeping of promise."[57] Of these four subjects, the first encompasses literature and the arts in the broadest sense, and the next three cover the major aspects of moral education. This sequence from literature to moral education is also reflected in another passage. "A gentleman," he says, "who is widely versed in letters and at the same time knows how to submit his learning to the restraints of ritual is not likely, I think, to go far wrong."[58] However, when talking about those subjects in order of their importance, he places literature and arts last. For instance, he says to his disciples, "Set your mind on the Way, base yourself upon morality, place your dependence on the Good, and dabble in polite arts."[59] Although Confucius himself does not explain the reason for placing poetry and polite arts at the bottom of his educational program,[60] it is nonetheless not difficult to see why he chooses to do so. In denouncing licentious content and florid rhetoric in some works of the *Poetry*, he betrays a deep fear of the harmful effects produced by an uncontrolled use of poetry and arts. Although he does not translate this fear into a sweeping injunction against poetry as Plato does in book 10 of the *Republic,* he feels impelled to lay down strict moral and aesthetic principles for poetry and arts in general. I shall discuss these moral and aesthetic principles later.

ADMIRATION FOR POETRY:
THE ULTIMATE GOOD IN THE BEAUTIFUL

Plato and Confucius admire poetry and arts as much as they fear them for their unparalleled power of transformation. Alongside the instances of one's mind being corrupted and led astray by poetry and arts, they both envision circumstances where one's mind is lifted to the realm of the ultimate good by poetry and arts. In observing such circumstances, they emphasize how poetry and arts enable one to suspend one's senses and achieve a direct communion with the ultimate reality in the course of artistic intuition. In praising this transforming power, they reverse their customary views of poetry and arts and consider them instrumental to achieving the highest form of intellectual or moral harmony.[61]

Contrary to the common conception of Plato as the enemy of poetry, we can find in his early dialogues an impassioned glorification of poetry that has been largely neglected by literary critics. In the following passages from *Phaedrus* and *Symposium,* for instance, he praises ideal poetry with the same fervor as the high Romantics will do more than two millennia later. Not only is poetry not called an imitation thrice removed from the truth, it is lauded as an embodiment of the truth. Likewise, not only is the ideal poet not denigrated as the artificer of falsehood, he is acclaimed as the maker or creator worthy of the title of philosopher.

> SOCRATES: Go and tell Lysias that to the fountain and school of the Nymphs we went down, and were bidden by them to him and to other composers of speeches—to Homer and other writers of poems, whether set to music or not; . . . to all of them we are to say that if their compositions are based on the knowledge of the truth, and they can defend or prove them . . . then they are to be called, not only poets, orators, legislators, but worthy of a higher name, befitting the serious pursuit of their life.
>
> PHAEDRUS: What name would you assign to them?
>
> SOCRATES: Wise, I may not call them; for that is a great name which

> belongs to God alone,—lovers of wisdom or philosophers
> is their modest and befitting title. (*Phaedrus*, 278)[62]

> She answers me as follows: 'There is poetry, which, as you know, is
> complex and manifold. All creation or passage of non-being into being
> is poetry or making, and the processes of all art are creative; and the
> masters of arts are all poets or makers.'
> 'Very true.' (*Symposium*, 205)[63]

In these two passages Plato lavishes upon the ideal poet a whole array
of eulogistic terms. The praise of poets as "lovers of wisdom," "legis-
lators," "makers," "creators," and "philosophers" is what most people
expect to see in the writings of Romantics, not those of Plato. Given
the common misconception of Plato's views of poetry, one may be quite
surprised to find these adulatory terms in such abundance in his writ-
ings. To understand why Plato chooses to praise poetry in such un-
qualified terms, we must consider his views on particular beautiful
things, universal beautiful forms, the absolute beauty, and love. In his
early dialogues written before the development of his theory of ideas,
Plato conceives of the absolute truth as absolute beauty, which unifies
all beautiful forms lying behind the beautiful things. For him, love is
the divine outflow of the absolute beauty to beautiful forms and
through them to beautiful things. It is also the divine in the soul of
man that inspires him to search for absolute beauty through the steps
described as follows:

> He who from these ascending under the influence of true love, begins
> to perceive that beauty . . . to begin from the beauties of earth and
> mount upwards for the sake that other beauty, using these as steps only,
> and from one going on to two, and from two to all fair forms, and from
> fair forms to fair practices, and from fair practices to fair notions, un-
> til from fair notions he arrives at the notion of absolute beauty, and at
> last knows what the essence of beauty is. This, my dear Socrates, said
> the stranger of Manitineia, is that life above all others man should live,
> in the contemplation of beauty absolute.[64]

This process of searching for absolute beauty seems analogous to the
process of ascending toward the absolute truth set forth in the *Repub-
lic*. Both processes are characterized by the passage from the concrete
to the abstract, from the particular to the universal, and from the uni-
versal to the absolute. The major difference between these two processes
is that the former is a direct, unmediated leap from aesthetic experi-

ence to transcendental knowledge and the latter is a gradual ascent toward the same destination through the acquisition of the harmonies of the senses, the body, the intellect, and the soul. Considering the proximity of aesthetic experience to transcendental knowledge in the search for absolute beauty, it makes good sense for Plato to assign, among other honorable appellations, the name of philosopher to the poet. Inasmuch as the poet is inspired by the divine love of beauty and in turn inspires the same in others, Plato sees fit to declare in *Symposium,* "Love is a good poet and accomplished in all the fine arts."[65]

When Plato praises the ideal poet and poetry and talks about the direct leap to transcendental knowledge through aesthetic experience or the love of beauty, he is not thinking of any real poets nor any existent poetical works. To him, all poets of earlier times and his times, including Homer the greatest master, fall far short of the ideal of a true poet. None of their works measure up to the ideal of true poetry. Consequently, he chooses to identify the ideal poet with the creating deity in *Timaeus* and philosophers who are "'true' servants of Eros, beauty, and the Muse."[66] Meanwhile, he unhesitatingly shows his low regard for real mimetic poets by listing them as the sixth of nine orders of lives possible for fallen souls.[67] This ranking is far below the first order of philosophers, and the "only people more lowly than the poets are manual laborers, sophists, and tyrants, in that order."[68] Yet, in spite of his deliberate exclusion of real poets and poetry from his praises, what Plato has said about the ideal poet and poetry does become the source of the worship of real poets and poetry in the Renaissance and the Romantic era.[69]

It is true that in the later dialogues Plato, having developed his theory of ideas and expounded intellect and reason as a favored means of achieving transcendental knowledge, no longer speaks so admiringly of the poet and poetry as he did in the early dialogues. Nevertheless, insofar as he always sees the absolute truth, the absolute beauty, and the absolute good as being one and never jettisons his theory of beauty, Plato may be assumed to believe, in his later as well as early life, that the absolute "can be approached either by a hypothetical science of dialectic or by the direct intuition of the lover of beauty,"[70] even though the lover of beauty is, to him, more a philosopher than a real poet.

Like Plato, Confucius holds poetry and arts in the highest esteem when he comes to consider their aesthetic impact. In the three passages examined below, Confucius observes the transforming effects of poetry and music on his own moral consciousness and identifies such aesthetic experience with self-forgotten spontaneity, the highest form of moral harmony in his philosophical system. In so doing, he virtually moves poetry and arts from the peripheral to the central part of his teachings:

> When the Master heard the *Shao* in the state of Qi, he became oblivious of the taste of meat for three months. He said, "I never expected that music could be brought to perfection like this."[71]

子在齊聞韶。三月不知肉味。曰。不圖為樂之至於斯也。

Nowhere else in *Analects* is Confucius overwhelmed with joy or sadness, admiration or disgust to such a great extent. Confucius is known to be very fond of meat. When he admitted his pupils, the only thing he would accept from them is a bundle of meat—be it called gift or tuition. So in his case, the forgetting of the taste of meat for three months can be taken as a metaphorical statement about the transformation of his state of consciousness. For a modern critic influenced by Kantian aesthetics, this mental transformation of Confucius may seem to exemplify pure aesthetic experience, as it is marked by its purge of sensuous pleasure (the palate for meat) and by its enduring effect (three months). But he praises the *Shao* elsewhere as "being perfectly beautiful and perfectly good."[72] Apparently, he takes the *Shao* to be a supreme example of aesthetic and moral perfection, not aesthetic perfection alone. Like Plato, he holds that moral virtue and aesthetic beauty are not at odds, but bound up with each other. The perfectly good must be perfectly beautiful. Just as Plato speaks of his world of ideas as being absolutely good and absolutely beautiful, Confucius lauds his idealized Golden Age in both moral and aesthetic terms:

> The Master said, "Great was Yao as a lord. Greatness is only for heaven, yet Yao matched it. How sublime! People could not find a name for it. Noble and grand are his accomplishments! Luminous are his cultural embellishments!"[73]

子曰。大哉堯之為君也。巍巍乎唯天為大。唯堯則之。蕩蕩乎民無能名焉。巍巍乎其有成功也。煥乎其有文章。

The case of Confucius' being transported by the *Shao* is not the only instance of an intense state of moral consciousness interfused with aesthetic experience. If we recall Confucius' description of his own spiritual progress, we see that the self-forgotten spontaneity, the highest form of moral consciousness he achieves at the age of seventy, is akin, if not entirely identical, to a heightened state of aesthetic experience untainted by specific utilitarian ends or purposiveness.

This merging of the highest moral consciousness with aesthetic experience becomes even more evident in the passage cited below.[74] The passage is part of a conversation Confucius has with four of his disciples: Zilu 子路, Ran You 冉有, Gongxi Hua 公西華, and Zeng Xi 曾皙. Confucius asks these four pupils to tell him what employment they would seek if their merits were recognized by someone. The first replies that he would ask to lead a country of a thousand warriors threatened by powerful enemies and hit by natural calamities, promising to endow the people with courage and to teach them the way of right conduct in three years. The second pupil replies that he would ask to govern a region of roughly sixty to seventy leagues and promise to have the people well provided for in the space of three years. The third replies that he would like to assume the duty of a junior assistant in performing various courtly ceremonies. Then, the fourth is called upon to give his reply:

Zeng Xi, what about you?

The notes of the zithern he was softly fingering died away; he put it down, rose and replied saying, I fear my words will not be so well chosen as those of the other three. The Master said, What harm is there in that? All that matters is that each should name his desire.

Zeng Xi said, At the end of spring, when the making of the Spring Clothes has been completed, to go with five times six newly-capped youths and six times seven uncapped boys, perform the lustration in the river I, take the air at the Rain Dance altars, and then go home singing. The Master heaved a deep sigh and said, I am with Dian.[75]

點。爾何如。鼓瑟希。鏗爾。舍瑟而作。對曰。異乎三子者之撰。子曰。何傷乎。亦各言其志也。曰。莫春者。春服既成。冠者五六人。童子六七人。浴乎沂。風乎舞雩。詠而歸。夫子喟然歎曰。吾與點也。

This is perhaps one of the most heatedly debated passages in *Analects*. Why does Confucius express a subtle disapproval of the first three pupils' choices, which all seem to be in line with his customary emphasis on active participation in politics and on the observance of rituals? Why does he give an explicit endorsement of Zeng Xi's choice, which seems all too similar to the course of nonaction advocated by Daoists? His disagreement with the first three is not too difficult to understand, as he himself explains shortly to Zeng Xi that he disagrees with them because they were asking for a kingdom or an official post and lacked the virtue of yielding (*rang* 讓). In other words, Confucius disapproves of their choices of purposive action because they are not untainted by personal ambitions. As to his agreement with Zeng Xi, Confucius gives no explanation and leaves posterity speculating about it ever since. Of the countless interpretations given by later Confucians, the most noteworthy are, as Wing-tsit Chan says, "that Zeng Xi was enjoying the harmony of the universe (Wang Chong), that he was wisely refraining from officialdom at the time of chaos (Huang Kan), that he was thinking of the 'kingly way' whereas other pupils were thinking of the government of feudal states (Han Yu), that he was in the midst of the universal operation of the Principle of Nature (Zhu Xi), and that he was expressing freedom of the spirit (Wang Yangming)."[76] All these interpretations are perceptive in their own ways and, together, they constitute a threefold explanation of Confucius' agreement with Zeng Xi. First, Zeng Xi's choice represents a course of nonpurposive life that leaves no room for egotistic desires and pursuits. Second, such a nonpurposive life exemplifies the way of sage-kings, who do not rule by purposive actions but reign through the moral influence emanating from their own unself-conscious life. Third, such a nonpurposive life leads to the state of self-forgotten spontaneity, in which one enjoys ultimate harmony with all things, whether that harmony is called "harmony of the universe," "Principle of Nature," or "freedom of spirit."

Interestingly, when Plato discusses the ultimate transformation of the soul, he comes to embrace three similar ideals: noncontentiousness, philosopher-kings, and the ultimate harmony. He maintains that after one has achieved harmony with all the universals or ideas, one becomes a philosopher-king who is willing but not eager to rule. Just as Confucius praises the nonpurposive life of Zeng Xi who stands above political ambition, Plato glorifies the contemplative, noncontentious life of a philosopher-king who "looks down upon the life of political ambition"[77] and who, like Confucius' sage-kings, "are most reluctant to govern."[78]

Having grasped the philosophical significance of Zeng Xi's ideal nonpurposive life, we can now consider the relationship of such a life with aesthetic activities. Just as Xu Fuguan points out, what Zeng Xi proposes to do is, essentially, aesthetic activity.[79] As Zeng Xi depicts the lustration in the river and the altar visit in the spirit of a springtime excursion, we have good reason to assume that he engages himself in these activities for aesthetic pleasure rather than a ceremonial purpose. His depiction of the humming and singing of poetry only serves to confirm the aesthetic orientation of his proposed life. Inasmuch as Confucius endorses such an aesthetically oriented life as an ideal way to the attainment of self-forgotten spontaneity, he seems to be doing what Plato does in *Phaedrus* and *Symposium*—celebrating artistic intuition as the means of achieving the blessed form of consciousness and moving poetry and arts to the center of his teachings.

MORAL AND AESTHETIC PRINCIPLES: SIMPLICITY IN CONTENT AND FORM

Both Plato and Confucius judge poetical and musical works in light of their positive and negative effects on the maintenance of harmony at various levels. On the one hand, they find in some works examples of harmonious relationship in the realms of gods or men, and encourage the young to study those works. On the other hand, they both see in other poems many undesirable elements that confuse one's perception of the Ideas (divine harmony), or upset one's mental equilibrium and incline one to inappropriate actions. On the grounds of these negative effects, Plato proposes to censor various kinds of poetry and banish the poet from his ideal Republic. Confucius was widely believed by premodern scholars to have edited out thousands of poems on moral grounds and thus reduced the extant corpus of the *Poetry* to merely 305 pieces. Though discredited as a mere myth by most modern scholars, this belief should not be dismissed offhandedly. Considering Confucius' harsh verdicts on licentious works, it is at least a plausible conjecture of what Confucius would like to do with the undesirable poems in the *Poetry.* In judging the content and form of poetry and music, Plato and Confucius both adhere to the same golden principle of simplicity. For them, simplicity leads to the good and the beautiful, as multiplicity leads to the bad and the ugly. There are plenty of examples that tell us how these two ancient thinkers apply their similar moral-aesthetic standards to the evaluation of particular works.

In the first two books of the *Republic,* Plato identifies the lives of gods and good men as good content of poetry and music. For Plato, simplicity in content means that gods must be singularly good—devoid of any traces of evil in deeds or words—and remain so under all circumstances. Any contrary depiction of their lives is condemned by him as the usurpation of simplicity by multiplicity or duplicity. Among numerous examples of such tampering with godly simplicity, he cites the battle of gods, the metamorphosis of gods by magic or illusions, the terrifying words and scenes about Hades, and the unseemly lamentations and laughter, drunkenness, softness, and indolence in the works of Homer, Aeschylus, and others. For Plato, these blatant adulterations of the singular goodness in poetry are no small matter, as they are bound to corrupt the souls of the young, the hope of his ideal Republic. He is particularly fearful that these untruths would cause the young to form an erroneous notion of the gods and admire patricides, fratricides, and other violent acts willfully attributed to those gods; and that the young would ape the unbecoming languages and deeds falsely represented in poetical works, and act in ways that not only upset the harmony of their own souls but threaten the harmony of the State at large. In view of this grave danger, Plato makes the censorship of poetry his first order of business in the building of his Republic:

> Then the first thing will be to establish a censorship of the writers of fiction, and let the censors receive any tale of fiction which is good, and reject the bad; and will desire mothers and nurses to tell their children the authorized ones only. Let them fashion the mind with such tales, even more fondly than they mould the body with their hands; but most of those which are now in use must be discarded.[80]

The scope of Plato's proposed censorship encompasses form as well as content of poetry. As Mihail I. Spariosu points out, Plato believes that poetry can "affect the soul of the future guardians not only through its content or tales (*logoi, mythoi*), but also through its diction (*lexis*) or its manner of presentation."[81] In other words, the form of poetry is, to Plato, inseparably bound up with its content. "Beauty of style and harmony and grace and good rhythm depend on simplicity," he announces, "—I mean the true simplicity of a rightly and nobly ordered mind and character."[82] Conversely, he argues that "ugliness and discord and inharmonious motion are nearly allied to ill words and ill nature."[83] Given this straightforward identification of form with content, it is all but certain that Plato would establish simplicity as the criterion of good form and denounce elaborate multiplicity as the trademark of bad form.

This is exactly what Plato does when he discusses the style of dramatic imitation. According to him, no one should allow himself to play more than one character type in a narrative or dramatic representation because "the same person will hardly be able to play a serious part in life, and at the same time to be an imitator and imitate many other parts as well."[84] So for those who wish to imitate all, he gives this practical advice: "They should imitate from youth upward only those characters which are suitable to their profession—the courageous, temperate, holy, free, and the like."[85] Although he admits that a pantomimic performer may have the miraculous power of imitating anything and holding spellbound children and their attendants alike, Plato contends that "we must inform him that in our State those such as he are not permitted to exist; the law will not allow them."[86] Analogous to his criticism of the mixed style of imitation is his opposition to the mixed style of harmony and meter. He censures the "multiplicity of notes or panharmonic scale" and agrees to banish "the artificers of lyres with three corners and complex scales, or the makers of any other many-stringed curiously harmonized instruments."[87] The only instruments to remain in his State are the simple "lyre and harp for use in the city" and a pipe for the use by shepherds in the country.[88] He subjects the use of meter to the same rules, as he warns people "not to seek out complex systems of meter, or meters of every kind, but rather to discover what rhythms are the expressions of a courageous and harmonious life."[89]

In discussing the works of the *Poetry,* Confucius judges them by a moral-aesthetic standard of simplicity comparable to that of Plato in many ways. Like Plato, he regards singular moral goodness as the hallmark of good poetry. Just as Plato commends the proper portrayals of gods in some of Homer's works, Confucius praises the wholesome contents of the *Poetry* as a whole: "The Master said, *Three Hundred Poems*[90] may be summed up in this phrase: 'no departing from the right'."[91] When he discusses "The Osprey," the first and most famous poem in this poetical collection, he speaks admiringly of its fine moral-aesthetic qualities:

> The Master said, The Ospreys! Pleasure not carried to the point of debauch; grief not carried to the point of self-injury.[92]

子曰。關雎。樂而不淫。哀而不傷。

This judgment of the poem is a moral as well as aesthetic one. Confucius praises its observance of the principle of the Middle Course in the avoidance of emotional extremes. In the meantime he tacitly refers to the absence of excesses in form and style. The word *yin* 淫, rendered here as "debauch," originally meant "excessive" in the time of Confucius, and only later takes on the meaning of "debauched." In explaining this passage, traditional Chinese commentators tend to interpret this word in these two senses alternately. Taking the word *yin* in its original sense, we can assume that Confucius is commenting on the absence of excesses in the poem's form and style as well as its contents.[93] This being the case, we should consider this passage to be a moral-aesthetic rather than a pure moral judgment. This is the appropriate way to interpret the passage as it is in keeping with the typical fusion of morality and aesthetics in *Analects*. For Confucius as for Plato, moral and aesthetic qualities are one and the same. Although Confucius does not discuss the affinity between the good and the beautiful on an abstract conceptual level as does Plato, he does applaud the fusion of the two in the best artistic works:

> The Master spoke of the *Shao* as being perfectly beautiful and perfectly good.[94]

子謂韶盡美矣。又盡善也。

In *Analects* Confucius consistently associates simplicity with the morally good and aesthetically desirable, and multiplicity with the morally bad and aesthetically undesirable. Whereas he takes the first piece of the *Poetry* as exemplary of simplicity, he regards the songs of Zheng as typical of "excessiveness":

> Do away with the tunes of Zheng and keep the flatterers at bay. The Tunes of Zheng are excessive and the flatterers are dangerous.[95]

放鄭聲。遠佞人。鄭聲淫。佞人殆。

In another passage, Confucius delivers an even more forthright denunciation of multiplicity: "I hate purple that usurps red."[96] Here he denounces purple because it is a mixed color that results from the adulteration of the pure color of red. Apparently he uses red as a metaphor for the virtue of simplicity, and purple as a metaphor for the vice of multiplicity or duplicity in moral as well as aesthetic matters. This seems truly analogous to Plato's view on simplicity and multiplicity in poetic imitation, melodies, and meters.

Whether or not Confucius edited the *Poetry* and expunged thousands of poems as is alleged, he would certainly be sympathetic to the idea of censoring works that fail to meet his moral-aesthetic standards. His desire to do away with the songs of Zheng is a clear indication of how he would censor poetry if he were in an official position to do so. In a way, Confucius may be seen to practice a measure of censorship in the name of "rectification." In addition to his attempt to eradicate the songs of Zheng, he seeks to rectify the music, songs, and hymns in his home state, Lu. "The Master said, 'After I returned from Wei to Lu, music was rectified, odes and hymns put to their proper use.'"97 Moreover, he sets himself to rectify language itself, the very raw material for poetry and other literary arts:

> If language is incorrect, then what is said does not concord with what was meant; and if what is said does not concord with what was meant, what is to be done cannot be effected. If what is to be done cannot be effected, then rites and music will not flourish. If rites and music do not flourish, then mutilations and lesser punishments will go astray. And if mutilations and lesser punishments go astray, then the people have nowhere to put hand or foot.98

> 名不正。則言不順。言不順。則事不成。事不成。則禮
> 樂不興。禮樂不興。則刑罰不中。刑罰不中。則民無所
> 錯足也。

Like Plato's censorship of poetry, Confucius' rectification of language is motivated by the concern over the dire consequences of misrepresentation of reality. Just as Plato dreads that poetic misrepresentation of gods will lead to imitation of evil conduct by his ingenuous guardians, Confucius fears that linguistic misrepresentation of sociopolitical reality will lead to a willful destruction of the hierarchical sociopolitical structure. Unless language is rectified and made to represent reality truthfully, Confucius believes, there cannot be order and harmony in human relationships, let alone stable social and political institutions.99

In rectifying the use of language, Confucius adopts the same moral-aesthetic standard of simplicity as he does in judging poetry, music, and arts. According to him, simple language is the language for a gentleman:

> The Master said, A gentleman is ashamed to let his words outrun his deeds.100

> 子曰。君子恥其言而過其行。

> The Master said, In official speeches all that matters is to get one's meaning through.101

> 子曰。辭達而已矣。

Here Confucius shows that a gentleman uses language carefully and sparingly in official businesses, and never lets himself use more words than necessary to describe his thoughts and deeds. Conversely, he maintains that clever, contrived language is the language of a base man scheming for his own gains:

> The Master said, Artful words and an ingratiating countenance, they scarcely have anything to do with the Humane.[102]

子曰。巧言令色。鮮矣仁。

> The master said, What need he to be a good talker? Those who down others with claptrap are seldom popular.[103]

子曰。焉用佞。御人以口給。屢自憎於人。

Like Plato, Confucius is particularly mindful that his censure of multiplicity should not be mistaken for a denial of beauty. Whereas Plato cautions that simplicity is not naive, Confucius warns his pupils against equating his denunciation of purple with an indiscriminate rejection of beautiful patterns. To correct such a misunderstanding of his idea by Ji Zicheng 棘子成, he says, "Culture is like substance; substance is like culture. If shorn of hairs, the skin of a tiger or leopard resembles that of a dog or sheep."[104] In addition, he makes clear that his denunciation of artful language does not mean an exclusion of refined language. To the extent that refined language helps to convey meanings forcefully, he endorses the use of it even in official writings. In preparing a government ordinance, he says, it is best to have it revised, embellished, and given elegant finishing touches by persons like his disciples Ziyou 子由 and Zichan 子產 who have a special talent for language.[105]

PATTERNS OF HARMONY: VERTICAL
ELEVATION VS. HORIZONTAL EXPANSION

In sum, it seems appropriate first to consider why there are so many similarities between Plato's and Confucius' theories of poetry, and then to set forth the underlying difference between the two theories.

As shown above, Plato and Confucius hold similar views on poetry with regard to its educational value, its social functions, its aesthetic power, and the moral-aesthetic standards for evaluating it. All these similarities stem from a common overriding concern with harmony.

Both Plato and Confucius have harmony in the forefront of their minds when they formulate their views of poetry. They both acknowledge the educational value of poetry because they consider it conducive to the development of inward harmony in the young. They both assign to poetry a status considerably lower than other subjects of education because they find poetic harmony to be of a less significant kind than the intellectual or moral harmony. However, when they take note of the transforming aesthetic experience afforded by poetry in certain circumstances, they both identify such aesthetic experience with the attainment of blessed harmony with the ultimate reality—the truth and the will of Heaven. In judging both content and forms of particular poetical works, they both adopt the stringent moral-aesthetic standards of simplicity, as they believe that simplicity leads to harmony and order not only in the mind of an individual, but also in the affairs of human society at large. Moreover, to ensure that poetry will contribute to the enhancement of inward and outward harmony, they both seek to exercise a rigorous censorship and expunge whatever is not singly good in content and what is excessive or overly elaborate in form.

While Plato's and Confucius' common concern with harmony gives rise to those similar views, their different views of the ultimate reality lead them to pursue harmony and develop their theories of poetry along different axes. Benjamin Schwartz gives an excellent analysis of the fundamental difference between Plato's and Confucius' views of the ultimate reality:

> In Plato we find a yawning abyss between a truth arrived at through the apodictic necessity of the dialectic and of mathematical reasoning and a world of "opinion" derived haphazardly from an observation of the chaos of ordinary human experience. Confucius does not rise from the chaos of the world of particulars to a realm of eternal forms since, in his view, the *tao* remains indissolubly linked to the empirical world.[106]

For Plato, the transcendental truth is to be arrived at by pursuing harmony along a vertical axis.[107] In discussing Plato's system of education, we have already caught a glimpse of his ascending scale of harmonies— from that of poetry at the bottom, through those of gymnastic, mathematics, geometry, astronomy, and dialectic, to that of divine sphere at the apex. In *Timaeus,* Plato depicts this scale of harmonies from the opposite direction, as he traces the originative harmony in God, through its manifestation in celestial movements, to the sublunary harmonies of human thought, sensations, and physical bodies.

By contrast, Confucius believes that the Dao is to be realized by extending harmony along a horizontal axis.[108] Unlike Plato, he does not conceive the Dao to be a transcendental entity which, like Plato's God, is to be transmitted through a vertical chain of beings by the pure thinking of a philosopher-king. Instead, he regards the Dao as an "immanent" principle of ideal human order to be realized in the midst of one's private and social life. For him, the realization of the Dao means first to achieve perfect inward harmony of self and then to establish perfect harmony with all other people at home and abroad in a manner appropriate to one's status in a hierarchical society. If one achieves such perfect inward and outward harmony, Confucius believes, one will attain to the ideal of *ren* and become one with the Dao at work in all human relationships. When such a person becomes a ruler, he must of necessity bring about the realization of the Dao in all levels of human existence and hence achieve a long-lasting peace and prosperity in his state. Although Confucius himself does not expound his concept of harmony in these terms, he is believed by Zhu Xi to have set forth a process of extending the concentric circles of harmony from within one's heart to the entire world:

> Things being investigated, knowledge became complete. Their knowledge being complete, their thoughts were sincere. Their thoughts being sincere, their hearts were then rectified. Their hearts being rectified, their persons were cultivated. Their persons being cultivated, their families were regulated. Their families being regulated, their States were rightly governed. Their States being rightly governed, the whole kingdom was made tranquil and happy.[109]

物格而後知至。知至而後意誠。意誠而後心正。心正而後身脩。身脩而後家齊。家齊而後國治。國治而後天下平。

This passage comes from the *Great Learning* (*Daxue* 大學), originally a chapter from the *Book of Rites* (*Liji* 禮記) and later made one of the four Confucian canonical books by Zhu Xi. Although this passage is not likely to have come from the mouth of Confucius as Zhu Xi argues,[110] it does present concisely Confucius' horizontal pattern of harmony, upon which his educational and sociopolitical programs as well as his theory of poetry are founded.

Plato's vertical and Confucius' horizontal patterns of harmony reveal two different paths leading to the attainment of the ultimate harmony. Plato's vertical pattern betokens an epistemological process. For him, to climb up the scale of harmonies means to gain ever more abstract and rarefied forms of knowledge until one enters the threshold of pure thinking and the reality of Being. Within this vertical pattern of harmony—or to be exact, "logo-rational harmony," as Spariosu calls it[111]—action is of secondary importance. As David L. Hall and Roger T. Ames point out, Plato and his idealist followers interpret "praxis as activity in accordance with the normative principles of knowledge."[112] For Plato, active sociopolitical life mainly serves these two purposes: to test the effects of such epistemological pursuits on the character of younger learners, and to reorganize human society on the model of the absolute knowledge.[113]

In contrast, Confucius' horizontal pattern traces a primarily existential process.[114] For Confucius, to expand the concentric circles of harmony means to live a moral private life, to practice filial piety and other virtues in one's family, to conduct social and political affairs properly, and thereby to bring order to the state and peace to the world.[115] Within this horizontal pattern of harmony, epistemological pursuit is of secondary importance.[116] It is true that Zhu Xi, in editing and elucidating the *Great Learning*, attaches more importance to the acquisition of knowledge than most Confucian thinkers, including Confucius himself. He chooses to gloss *gewu* 格物 as "to investigate things" and *zhizhi* 致知 as "to extend one's knowledge" and to take these two initial steps as the core of the horizontal pattern of harmony set forth in the *Great Learning*. Still, Zhu's idea of investigating things and extending knowledge is anything but identical to Plato's idea of pure epistemological pursuit.[117] While Plato believes that the attainment of absolute knowledge is in and of itself the end and reward of epistemological pursuit, Zhu Xi holds that the extension of knowledge to the utmost—namely the grasp of the *li* 理, the absolute principle of all things,—marks only the beginning of an ideal ethical way of living that promises to bring about perfect harmony in ever broadening realms of human life. The fact that Zhu Xi, arguably the greatest Confucian advocate of knowledge, still holds epistemology in subordination to the ethical ideal of living is a testimony to the secondary importance of pure epistemological pursuit in Confucius' horizontal pattern of harmony.[118]

Plato's and Confucius' theories of poetry, built on their vertical and horizontal patterns of harmony, inevitably exhibit a fundamental difference between an epistemological and an existential understanding of poetry. All of Plato's views on poetry are, in essence, comments on the validity, effectiveness, and usefulness of poetry as a means of knowing the absolute truth. His denunciation of poetry in book 10 of the *Republic* is an indictment of its false, invalid presentation of the truth. His conditional acceptance of poetry in books 2 and 3 of the *Republic* and in *Timaeus* and the *Laws* is a tacit admission of its usefulness in preparing the young for the acquisition of higher forms of knowledge. His praise of poetry in *Phaedrus* and the *Symposium* is an acknowledgement of its direct contact with absolute beauty and truth. His moral-aesthetic standards of simplicity are an indication of his concern over erroneous perceptions of truth, absolute or otherwise, caused by the multiplicity in poetic content and style. His censorship of poetry is an expression of his fear of the ruination of the young's epistemological capability by its untruthful presentation of reality.

Conversely, all Confucius' views of poetry are assessments of the applicability of the *Poetry* to real life as a model for ethical living. Just as Plato always asks himself the question of whether and how poetry can be useful in the cognition of the truth, Confucius always concerns himself with the question of how the *Poetry* can be used to guide various aspects of one's inner and outer life. In defining the functions of the *Poetry*, he focuses exclusively on the positive effects it can produce on an individual's emotional and ethical life (the evocation of moral sentiments), on his sociopolitical life (the distinction of good and bad customs), on his relationship with friends and equals (the keeping of good company), on his family life (the proper service to parents), on his communicative skills (the mastery of diplomatic protocol), and on his interaction with the rulers (the proper expression of grievances). He takes the attainment of the state of nonpurposive yet moral existence, not the direct intuition of the truth, to be the greatest possible effect poetry can produce on one's life. He introduces the moral-aesthetic standards of simplicity, not for an epistemological reason as does Plato, but out of concern for the orderliness of life in a hierarchical feudal society. Whereas Plato imposes the moral-aesthetic standards of simplicity as an antidote to distortions of truth stemming from unethical, multiple modes of presentation in poetry and the arts, Confucius enacts the same as a safeguard against the usurpation of the order of sociopolitical life resulting from the artful use of language.

This discussion can be considered a study of "similarities in dissimilarity." All of the similarities examined arise from Plato's and Confucius' common overriding concern with harmony. The fundamental dissimilarity against which these similarities should be seen is this sharp contrast: Plato's vertical pattern of abstract intellectual harmony versus Confucius' horizontal pattern of moral harmony. To be more specific, we may say that their theories of poetry are similar in many areas of particular concerns but fundamentally different in the basic account of the nature of poetry. Poetry is presumed to be an epistemological process in Plato's theory and largely an existential process in Confucius'. These two different presumptions constitute the grounds not only for the two thinkers' various claims about poetry, but also the subsequent development of mimetic theories of literature in the West and of nonmimetic theories of literature in China.

CHAPTER 6

Poetics of Imagination
Wordsworth and Liu Xie on Literary Creation

W ORDSWORTH IS PROBABLY THE FIRST WESTERN CRITIC
who consciously aims to relocate the locus of criticism to the au-
thor. He seeks to place the artist at the center of criticism mainly be-
cause he accords paramount importance to the creative process, an is-
sue largely ignored in classical and neoclassical criticism. In his critical
writings and poems, he assiduously expounds the significance of the
creative process in various terms—psychological, aesthetic, epistemo-
logical, philosophical, and theological—within the all-embracing no-
tion of imagination.[1] His pioneering view of the creative process helps
earn him a preeminent place in Western criticism.

In establishing the artist's inner life as the locus of criticism, Words-
worth brings himself closer to the Chinese critical tradition than any
earlier Western critic. His theory of literary creation bears striking sim-
ilarities to Liu Xie's.[2] In examining the creative process, they focus on
the same array of issues: stages of literary creation, the interchange
of powerful emotions and tranquil moods, the alternation between
unconscious responses and conscious endeavors, the fusion of feelings
and images, the sensory engagement with *natura naturata* (external na-
ture), the suprasensory communion with *natura naturans* (the essence
of nature), and the interplay of sensory and suprasensory experiences
throughout the creative process.

In this chapter I will compare Wordsworth and Liu Xie on these is-
sues, showing how they treat each of them in a similar fashion. I also
will attempt to distinguish the broad conceptual frameworks within
which they work, and to trace their different conceptual frameworks

to different cosmological paradigms established by Western and Chinese thinkers. With due attention to differences as well as similarities, I hope to demonstrate both the cross-cultural relevance and the cultural specificity of their theories of literary creation.

WORDSWORTH AND LIU XIE
ON THE FOUR STAGES OF LITERARY CREATION

Wordsworth and Liu Xie both conceive of literary creation as a sustained process that transforms inner emotions into an artistic work of language. In this creative process, they both perceive four distinct stages: initial emotional response, restoration of tranquility, contemplation of perceptive and emotive experiences, and compositional execution.

In his "Preface to *Lyrical Ballads* (1800)," Wordsworth revolts against the neoclassical mimetic tradition and redefines poetry as "the spontaneous overflow of powerful feelings."[3] To justify his revolutionary expressive concept of poetry, he reconceptualizes literary creation as a four-stage process that engenders and transforms inward feelings into written words. He calls the first stage "the spontaneous overflow of powerful feelings." According to him, these powerful feelings are unmediated responses to "incidents and situations from common life."[4] In the conditions of low and rustic life, he argues, one can find the finest of spontaneous feelings "because the essential passions of the heart find a better soil in which they can attain their maturity"[5] and because these passions "exist in a state of greater simplicity, and consequently may be more accurately contemplated, and more forcibly communicated."[6]

The second stage is the restoration of mental equilibrium or what he calls "tranquility," which follows the initial emotional response. He does not elaborate on this mental state and merely mentions it as the necessary condition in which perceptive and emotive experiences are to be recollected and contemplated. He writes, "I have said that Poetry is the spontaneous overflow of powerful feelings: it takes its origin from emotion recollected in tranquility."[7] Only when emotional responses are "recollected in tranquility," Wordsworth believes, can they be purged of crude elements and become the staple of fine poetry.

The third stage constitutes something of a reversal of the second: a change from tranquility to the emergence of a new emotion. For Wordsworth, this new emotion arises from a modification of the initial emotions by "our thoughts, which are indeed the representatives of our past feelings" in the course of contemplation:

> The emotion is contemplated till by a species of reaction the tranquil-
> ity gradually disappears, and an emotion, similar to that which was be-
> fore the subject of contemplation, is gradually produced, and does it-
> self actually exist in the mind.[8]

Here Wordsworth is not interested in drawing a clear-cut distinction between the new emotion and the old one. He states only that the new emotion is "kindred to that which was before the subject of contem-plation."[9] Nonetheless, this statement tells us that, to Wordsworth, contemplation is the key factor separating the two: One exists before contemplation, and the other after it. Thus, by examining what Words-worth has said about the transforming effect of contemplation, we can get an idea of what he thinks distinguishes the new emotion from the old one. "By the repetition and continuance of this act [of contem-plation]," he tells us, "our feelings will be connected with important subjects"[10] and "the passions of men are incorporated with the beau-tiful and permanent forms of nature."[11] Judging by these remarks, Wordsworth may be assumed to believe that the new emotion exists in a form that embodies a fusion of subject and object, feelings and "permanent forms of nature." In fact, his remark that this new emo-tion "does itself actually exist in the mind" strongly suggests a mental vision or envisagement rather than a formless sensation.

The fourth stage is the voluntary description of this new emotion or envisagement in harmonious metrical language:

> In this mood successful composition generally begins, and in a mood
> similar to this it is carried on; but the emotion, of whatever kind and
> in whatever degree, from various causes is qualified by various pleas-
> ures, so that in describing any passions whatsoever, which are volun-
> tarily described, the mind will upon the whole be in a state of enjoy-
> ment. . . . Now the music of harmonious metrical language, the sense
> of difficulty overcome, and the blind association of pleasure which has
> been previously received from works of rhyme or meter of the same or
> similar construction, all these imperceptibly make up a complex feel-
> ing of delight, which is of the most important use in tempering the
> painful feeling which will always be found intermingled with powerful
> descriptions of the deeper passions.[12]

Interestingly, this lengthy passage tells us very little about the essential task of the fourth stage: the translation of a mental envisagement into a work of language. Wordsworth does not discuss any of the issues cru-cial to successful compositional execution—say, the development of proper mental habits, the cultivation of linguistic talent, or training in the art of composition. Instead, he is content merely to describe the "state of enjoyment" during the final stage of composition. His only reference to poetic language concerns the use of rhyme and meter. When he talks about rhyme and meter, he is concerned solely with their contribution to that "state of enjoyment." For him, rhyme and meter merely serve to remove unpleasant painful feelings and enhance aesthetic pleasure in the course of composition.

In conceptualizing this four-stage process of literary creation, Wordsworth draws extensively from "eighteenth century speculations on the emotional origin of language, prevalent ideas about the nature and value of primitive poetry, together with the results of a century of developments in Longinian doctrines."[13] He appropriates the positive views of primitivism by Herder, maybe Rousseau, and others to justify his emphasis on emotion and his adaptation of rustic speech as the poetic language par excellence. He adopts the associationist ideas of Locke, Hartley, and others to explain the complex processes of recollection and reflection. Moreover, he avails himself of Longinian doctrines to illuminate the aesthetic pleasure of composition.

Of all these ideas, primitive theories of poetry are considered by many to have exerted the greatest influence on Wordsworth. It is true that he frequently makes use of primitive poetry to illustrate an ideal process of literary creation. However, like his claim for the rustic qualities of *Lyrical Ballads,* Wordsworth's praise of primitive poetry in the Preface should be taken with a grain of salt. He uses primitive theories of poetry mainly as a convenient weapon against the predominant neoclassical tradition, and actually aims to develop a new theory of literature for the literati. As we shall see in the next section, his conception of the four-stage process is grounded on his own creative experience as much as anything else. Without his personal experience as a poet, he probably could not have so keenly observed the four stages and so deftly integrated disparate eighteenth-century ideas into a comprehensive theory of literary invention, a theory that would replace mimesis as the frame of critical reference for himself as well as other Romantics.[14]

Liu Xie makes a comparable effort to develop a comprehensive theory of literary invention in the *Literary Mind and the Carving of Dragons.* Like Wordsworth, he considers literary invention to be a complex, sustained process of transforming internal feelings and thoughts into external patterns of language. "When the affections (*qing*) are aroused," he writes, "language gives them [external] form. When the inherent principle (*li*) comes forth, pattern (*wen*) is manifest. We follow a course from what is latent and arrive at the manifest. According to what lies within, there is a correlation to what lies without" 夫情動而言形，理發而文見；蓋沿隱以至顯。因內而符外者也 (*WXDL* 27 / 1–4).[15] Moreover, he too perceives four similar stages of literary invention: initial emotional response, the state of mental tranquility, inward contemplation leading to the fusion of feelings and images, and the final compositional execution.

Much as Wordsworth does in the 1800 Preface, Liu Xie traces the origin of literary invention to a spontaneous emotional response to the outside world. Like Wordsworth, he emphasizes the involuntary nature of such a response. "When spring appears with the incoming year," he writes, "feelings of delight and ease infuse us; in the billowing luxuriance of early summer, the mind, too, becomes burdened" 是以獻歲發春，悅豫之情暢；滔滔孟夏，鬱陶之心凝 (*WXDL* 46 / 13–16).[16] After describing universal emotional reactions to the four seasonal processes, he seeks to distinguish what a poet feels from the emotions of ordinary people. According to him, what marks a poet's emotional response is his susceptibility to endless categorical associations (*lianlei* 聯類).

Like Wordsworth, Liu believes that the second stage is a state of tranquility and mental concentration following the initial emotional response. Liu tells us more about this second stage than Wordsworth, characterizing it as a stage when a writer's inner spirit transcends the normal restrictions of time and space and roams in the wonderland of images:

> The ancients observed "The physical body is by the rivers and lakes, but the mind remains below the gatetowers of Wei." This is what is called spirit and thought (*shensi*). In the thought process of writing, the spirit goes afar. In the state of silence and mental concentration, thought reaches to a thousand years ago. With a slight change of one's facial expression, one's vision may have already crossed ten thousand leagues. (*WXDL* 26 / 1–10)

> 古人云：形在江海之上，心存魏闕之下。神思之謂也。文之思也，其神遠矣！故寂然凝慮。思接千載；悄焉動容，視通萬里。

For Liu as for Wordsworth, the third stage is the rise of a new emotion. Liu obviously has this new emotion in mind when he remarks, "If one thinks of climbing a mountain, one fills the mountain with one's feelings" 登山則情滿於山 (*WXDL* 26 / 44). This new emotion is not identical with the initial emotion because it is "the experience of the mind, not an empirical experience."[17] Liu offers a detailed description of the interaction between the inward spirit and external things:

> When the workings of thought are at their most miraculous, the spirit wanders along with things. The spirit dwells in the breast; the intent and bodily gusto (*qi*) control the bolt of its outlet. Things come in through the ear and eye; the ordering of words governs the pivot and trigger of their influx. When the pivot and trigger allow passage, things have no hidden appearance. When the bolt of the outlet is closed, the spirit is hidden. (*WXDL* 26 / 15–24)

> 故思理為妙，神與物游。神居胸臆，而志氣統其關鍵；物沿耳目，而辭令管其樞機。樞機方通，則物無隱貌；關鍵將塞，則神有遯心。

For Liu, this interaction between the spirit and things is made possible by a simultaneous, well-coordinated activation of several processes— the physiological-moral process that controls and guides the outward thrust of the spirit, the perceptual-psychological process that commands the influx of sensory impressions, and the intellectual-linguistic process that mediates both the outbound spirit and the inbound images.

For Liu as for Wordsworth, the third stage culminates in a fusion of spirit and things, feelings and images into a nebulous poetic vision. Liu denotes this poetic vision with the vaguely defined term *yixiang* and gives a vivid description of it:

> In the midst of chanting and singing, one has already conjured up the sounds of pearl and jade. Right before one's eyelashes the shades of wind-blown clouds have unfurled. This is the result of the workings of thought. (*WXDL* 26 / 11–14)

> 吟詠之間，吐納珠玉之聲；眉睫之前，卷舒風雲之色：其思理之致乎！

Like Wordsworth, Liu believes that the fourth stage is voluntary compositional execution, through which the author seeks to capture his poetic vision in the medium of language. However, Wordsworth and Liu Xie seem to hold different opinions about the difficulty of this fourth and final stage. Influenced by primitive theories of poetry,

Wordsworth believes that genuine, "accurately contemplated" passions would always come accompanied by the natural, perfect language for their expression. For him, the writer's voluntary effort is limited primarily to adding the superimposed charm of metrics to that spontaneous poetic speech. By contrast, Liu stresses the immense difficulty of this final stage. "When one holds up the writing brush," he writes, "one's vital force is twice stronger than the words that come. When a piece is complete, one expresses only half of what was originally in the mind. Why? Ideas roam in the realm of emptiness and thus can easily appear extraordinary. Language is substantial and thus hard to be used deftly" 方其搦翰，氣倍辭前，暨乎篇成，半折心始，何則？意翻空而易奇，言徵實而難巧也 (*WXDL* 26 / 48–54).

WORDSWORTH ON THE MUTUAL INGRAINING OF SENSORY AND SUPRASENSORY EXPERIENCES

For Wordsworth and Liu Xie alike, literary creation involves two fundamental types of experiences: the sensory engagement with *natura naturata* and the suprasensory union with *natura naturans*. The former experience denotes mental activities that arise from man's contact with the outer nature through the five senses. It includes not only all forms of sensory impressions but also feelings and thoughts derived from those impressions. The latter experience refers to mental activities that transcend the boundaries of time and space and reach the innermost nature. In examining the creative process, both Wordsworth and Liu Xie pay close attention to the interaction of these two experiences. Here let us first consider how Wordsworth observes the interplay of the two experiences at four different stages of literary creation.

In the 1800 and 1850 Prefaces, Wordsworth preoccupies himself with sensory experiences and almost completely ignores suprasensory experiences. His references to the latter are limited to remarks about "a certain colouring of imagination"[18] thrown over a composition and about a poet's propensity to "contemplate similar volitions and passions as manifested in the goings-on of the Universe, and habitually impelled to create them where he does not find them."[19] As M. H. Abrams rightly points out, "Only in his poetry, not in his criticism, does Wordsworth make the transition from the eighteenth-century view of man and nature to the concept that the mind is creative in perception, and an integral part of an organically inner-related universe."[20] Indeed, it is only in poems like "Tintern Abbey" and the *Prelude* that he redresses his neglect of suprasensory experience and gives a more balanced discussion of creative experiences than in the 1800 Preface.

In the opening passage of book 12 of the *Prelude,* he sketches a broader conceptual scheme than what he uses to distinguish the four stages of literary creation in the prefaces:

> From nature doth emotion come, and moods
> Of calmness equally are nature's gift,
> This is her glory; these two attributes
> Are sister horns that constitute her strength;
> This twofold influence is the sun and shower
> Of all her bounties, both in origin
> And end alike benignant. Hence it is,
> That Genius which exists by interchange
> Of peace and excitation, finds in her
> His best and purest Friend, from her receives
> That energy by which he seeks the truth,
> Is rouz'd, aspires, grasps, struggles, wishes, craves,
> From her that happy stillness of the mind
> Which fits him to receive it, when unsought.[21]

This conceptual scheme is constituted by three interlocking sets of dynamic relationships: the succession of involuntary acts ("receive it, when unsought") and conscious endeavors ("aspires, grasps, struggles, wishes, craves"), emotion and "moods of calmness," and the intertwining of these two affective conditions with suprasensory experiences ("seeks the truth").[22] If in the 1800 and 1850 Prefaces Wordsworth distinguishes the development of the four stages in terms of merely a continuous interchange of involuntary responses and voluntary endeavors, emotion and "moods of calmness," here in his poems he consistently seeks to show the presence of the suprasensory within those seemingly pure sensory experiences.

For Wordsworth, sensory and suprasensory experiences are mutually ingrained throughout the creative process. Even at the first stage when one engages the outer nature directly through one's senses, one cannot but come under the sway of a transcendental power. In "Expostulation and Reply," he describes his own engagement with external nature as an experience filled with suprasensory significance:

> One morning thus, by Estwaite lake,
> When life was sweet, I knew not why,
> To me my good friend Matthew spake,

And thus I made reply:
"The eye—it cannot choose but see;
We cannot bid the ear be still;
Our bodies feel, where'er they be,
Against or with our will.
"Nor less I deem that there are Powers
Which of themselves our minds impress;
That we can feed this mind of ours
In a wise passiveness . . ."23

In describing this direct contact with external nature, Wordsworth emphasizes its natural, involuntary characteristics. His biological and psychological makeup is such that he cannot bid his eyes not to see, his ears not to hear, and his body not to feel when confronting images of nature. In examining poems like this one, Lilian Furst says, "The essential point to grasp is that expression of feeling was never an end in itself to Wordsworth, but rather a means subordinate to a higher purpose."24 Here, the higher purpose to which Wordsworth subordinates his involuntary emotions is the awakening of his innate divine power, which "as an agent of the one great Mind, / Creates, creator and receiver both, / Working but in alliance with the works / Which it beholds."25 However, amidst the excitation of emotions, Wordsworth maintains that this divine power gave him only joys of sensations and a sense of intimacy with external nature:

. . . The sounding cataract
Haunted me like a passion: the tall rock,
The mountain, and the deep and gloomy wood,
Their colours and their forms, were then to me
An appetite; a feeling and a love,
That had no need of a remoter charm,
By thought supplied, nor any interest
Unborrowed from the eye.26

While such sweet sensations "had no need of a remoter charm" or "any interest / Unborrowed from the eye" during his early childhood, Wordsworth contends that they contain the very seed of the "remoter charm" or the suprasensory experience to be sought in later life:

Thus, often in those fits of vulgar joy
Which, through all seasons, on a child's pursuits
Are prompt attendants, 'mid that giddy bliss
Which, like a tempest, works along the blood

And is forgotten; . . .
Until maturer seasons call'd them forth
To impregnate and to elevate the mind.[27]

By "maturer seasons," Wordsworth apparently refers to the advent of his conscious, contemplative life marked by a habitual recollection of the sweet sensations of yore in "moods of calmness." Through the recollection of these sensations, Wordsworth contends, we awaken the innate divine power that can "feed this mind of ours" and enable us to penetrate the spirit of all things. This change from spontaneous emotion to "moods of calmness" corresponds to the progression from the first to the second stage of literary invention.

As a poet recollects his own affective engagement with external nature at this second stage, Wordsworth believes, he can achieve a suprasensory union with the innermost nature. While in the 1800 and 1850 Prefaces Wordsworth makes no mention of suprasensory dimensions of recollection, he makes them the focus of his attention in "Tintern Abbey":

These beauteous forms,
Through a long absence, have not been to me
As is a landscape to a blind man's eye:
But oft, in lonely rooms, and 'mid the din
Of towns and cities, I have owed to them
In hours of weariness, sensations sweet,
Felt in the blood, and felt along the heart;
And passing even into my purer mind,
With tranquil restoration:—feelings too
Of unremembered pleasure; such, perhaps,
As have no slight or trivial influence
On that best portion of a good man's life,
His little, nameless, unremembered acts
Of kindness and of love. Nor less, I trust,
To them I may have owed another gift,
Of aspect more sublime; that blessed mood
In which the burthen of the mystery,
In which the heavy and the weary weight
Of all this unintelligible world,
Is lightened:—that serene and blessed mood,
In which the affections gently lead us on—
Until, the breath of this corporeal frame
And even the motion of our human blood
Almost suspended, we are laid asleep

In body, and become a living soul:
While with an eye made quiet by the power
Of harmony, and the deep power of joy,
We see into the life of things.[28]

In this state of "wise passiveness," the divine power begins to pro-
duce its magic effect, transforming what Locke, Hobbes, and other
British empiricists would call mechanical memory into a suprasen-
sory experience of the Absolute Being. Under the impact of this di-
vine power, Wordsworth tells us, his recollection of the "beauteous
forms" of nature—along with joyful intimacy accompanying the erst-
while perception of them—metamorphoses into "sensations sweet, /
Felt in the blood, and felt along the heart." As these sweet sensations
purify our mind, Wordsworth continues, they will gently lead us on
until we reach a "blessed mood" in which we will find ourselves "laid
asleep / In body" and become "a living soul." For Wordsworth, the cul-
mination of this suprasensory experience is the act of seeing and hence
knowing the Truth—"the life of things."

To Wordsworth, the divine power responsible for this miraculous
transmutation of recollection into a suprasensory experience is incip-
ient in the human mind as well as nature, and is brought into activity
by man's sensory perception of and emotional interaction with nature.
In his famous "infant babe" passage of the *Prelude,* he calls this divine
power the "first poetic spirit of our human life" which effects the "filial
bond / Of nature that connects him [infant babe] with the world."[29]
According to him, this divine power "[i]s most abated or suppressed"
in their conscious lives, but in some (poets like himself) is retained and
enhanced through tranquil recollection. He traces the origin of this di-
vine power to the Absolute Being and praises Him for infusing it into
the innermost essence of both man and nature:

Wisdom and Spirit of the universe!
Thou soul that art the Eternity of Thought!
That giv'st to forms and images a breath
And everlasting motion! not in vain
By day or star-light thus from my first dawn
Of Childhood didst Thou intertwine for me
The passions that build up our human Soul;
Not with the mean and vulgar works of Man,
But with high objects, with enduring things,
With life and nature, purifying thus
The elements of feeling and of thought,

And sanctifying, by such discipline,
Both pain and fear, until we recognize
A grandeur in the beatings of the heart.[30]

This idea of the divine power is essentially identical to Coleridge's idea of primary imagination. "The primary IMAGINATION," Coleridge writes, "I hold to be the living power and prime Agent of all human Perception, and as a repetition in the finite mind of the eternal act of creation in the infinite I AM."[31] This passage seems a fitting description of the modus operandi and origin of the Wordsworthian divine power. Like the Coleridgean primary imagination, the Wordsworthian divine power is "the living and prime Agent of all human Perception" because its connects us "with high objects, with enduring things, / With life and nature." It, too, is "a repetition in the finite mind of the eternal act of creation in the infinite I AM," as it makes humans capable of bringing all things into a living whole in their finite minds. Indeed, it has its origin in the "Wisdom and Spirit of the universe," as does the Coleridgean primary imagination in the "infinite I AM."[32]

Of course, there remain important differences between Coleridge's and Wordsworth's ideas. Coleridge's idea is primarily an epistemological one, formulated under the strong influence of German metaphysics. Wordsworth's is more existential as it is developed largely in the context of his personal quest for spiritual union between man and nature. Coleridge's prominent concerns are the mind and understanding rather than the heart and sensibility; Wordsworth's are the opposite. Another important difference is that Coleridge sees the primary imagination as an unconscious act of perception, whereas Wordsworth believes that the divine power is at work not only in spontaneous sensory engagements with nature, but also in self-conscious recollection of these engagements.[33]

According to Wordsworth, the rise of a new emotion at the third stage of literary invention is the result of the alternation, modification, and transformation of one's perceptive and emotive experiences by a willful "modifying and endowing" power. In the following passage, he describes how this power enabled him to change the look of external nature:

A plastic power
Abode with me, a forming hand
. . . but for the most
Subservient strictly to the external things

> With which it commun'd. An auxiliar light
> Came from my mind which on the setting sun
> Bestow'd new splendor, the melodious birds,
> The gentle breezes, fountains that ran on,
> Murmuring so sweetly in themselves, obey'd
> A like dominion; and the midnight storm
> Grew darker in the presence of my eye.[34]

This "plastic power" is none other than the divine power at work in the first two stages, but in a new, dynamic mode of operation. If tranquil recollection lays Wordsworth "asleep / In body" and lets him receive the spirit of nature in his "wise passiveness," this plastic power prompts him to bestow his own spirituality upon nature, thus lifting him into the role of a creator. Using his own poetical lines "O Cuckoo! shall I call thee Bird / Or but a wandering Voice?" as an example, Wordsworth shows how he was enabled by this plastic power to transform what is actual into a new ideal existence.[35] The process responsible for transforming a real bird into an intangible voice, he explains, is "carried on either by conferring additional properties upon an object, or abstracting from it some of those which it actually possesses, and thus enabling it to react upon the mind which hath performed the process, like a new existence."[36] This passage recalls Coleridge's description of secondary imagination:

> The secondary I consider as an echo of the former, coexisting with the conscious will, yet still as identical with the primary in the *kind* of its agency, and differing only in *degree,* and in the *mode* of its operation. It dissolves, diffuses, dissipates, in order to recreate; or where this process is rendered impossible, yet still, at all events it struggles to idealize and to unify. It is essentially *vital,* even as all objects (as objects) are essentially fixed and dead.[37]

The Wordsworthian "plastic power" is quite close to the Coleridgean secondary imagination. Like the latter, it is also distinguished by its vital, idealizing thrust and by its modification, transformation, and recreation of real existence. If we decide to apply the term "imagination" to this Wordsworthian plastic power, we may characterize it as a dynamic "creative imagination"—as opposed to the "perceptive imagination" at work during his tranquil recollection.

In his poetry Wordsworth pays more attention to perceptive imagination than creative imagination. This reflects an important difference between Wordsworth's and Coleridge's views on the relationship of these two types of imagination. For Coleridge, secondary imagination is superior to primary imagination because of the dynamic exercise of conscious will. Although he concedes that primary imagination entails a higher degree of divinity than secondary imagination and calls the latter "an echo of the former," he argues that the coexisting conscious will in secondary imagination more than compensates for its loss in degree of divinity. Coleridge regards the rise of conscious will as a "fortunate fall" in the Schillerian vein: It affords the poet the freedom and "the means of transforming finitude and embodying unconscious *poesie* within the conscious forms of art."[38] For Coleridge, this "willful" recreation represents a higher and loftier mode of imagination's operation than unconscious perception. If the latter brings together external things largely unmodified, the former melts and dissipates all "dead and fixed" forms, reveals the inner spirit of nature, and interfuses it with that of the human mind.

By contrast, Wordsworth perceives little qualitative difference between perceptive and creative imagination. Wordsworth's deemphasis of the difference between the two is consistent with his stance on the distinction between fancy and imagination. Disputing Coleridge's absolute differentiation of fancy and imagination, he writes, "Yet it is not the less true that Fancy, as she is an active, is also, under her own laws and in her own spirit, a creative faculty. In what manner Fancy ambitiously aims at a rivalship with Imagination, and Imagination stoops to work with the materials of Fancy, might be illustrated from the compositions of all eloquent writers, whether in prose or verse."[39] Wordsworth's reluctance to draw clear-cut distinctions between perceptive and creative imagination has much to do with his view on the mutual spirituality between man and nature:

How exquisitely the individual Mind,
And the progressive powers perhaps no less
Of the whole species to the external world
Is fitted, and how exquisitely too,
Theme this but little heard of among men,
The external world is fitted to the mind
And the creation (by no lower name
Can it be called) which they with blended might
Accomplish: this is my great argument.[40]

For Wordsworth, the spirit of nature flows into the human soul as much as the spirit of man infuses nature's innermost essence. He speaks of nature as both "creator and receiver," and man as half-creating and half-perceiving the mighty world. Commenting on this scheme of mutual spirituality in Wordsworth, E. D. Hirsch writes, "The reciprocity of subject and object is a true one, for both sides actively participate. Each side gives and receives, so that the process itself is simultaneously one of activity and passivity."[41] So, within this scheme, the difference of perceptive and creative imagination only attests to varying perspectives on the mutual spiritual flow. If the spirit of nature is seen on the active, creating side, then perceptive imagination is at work in the state of "wise passiveness."

> . . . I would walk alone,
> In storm and tempest, or in starlight nights
> Beneath the quiet Heavens; and, at that time,
> Have felt whate'er there is of power in sound
> To breathe an elevated mood, by form
> Or image unprofaned; and I would stand,
> Beneath some rock, listening to sounds that are
> The ghostly language of the ancient earth,
> Or make their dim abode in distant winds.
> Thence did I drink the visionary power.[42]

Conversely, if it is seen on the passive, receptive side, creative imagination is in full swing, exerting its plastic or, in Coleridge's word, "esemplastic" power:

> The Power, which these
> Acknowledge when thus moved, which Nature thus
> Thrust forth upon the senses, is the express
> Resemblance, in the fullness of its strength
> Made visible, a genuine Counterpart
> And Brother of the glorious faculty
> Which higher minds bear with them as their own.
> This is the very spirit in which they deal
> With all the objects of the universe:
> They from their native selves can send abroad
> Like transformation; for themselves create
> A like existence. . . . [43]

Probably because Wordsworth sees perceptive imagination as essentially identical with the creative one, he deems it fit to focus on perceptive imagination. Thus, we can locate only a limited number of poetical passages about a poet's dynamic re-creation of the world at the third stage.

Wordsworth largely neglects the fourth stage in his poems, just as he did in the 1800 Preface. This neglect reflects not only his reaction against the neoclassical preoccupation with methods, rules, and decorum of composition, but also his inheritance of the popular renaissance notion of the poet as Maker who "maketh his worke by the patterne which he had erst conceyved in his mynde, which patterne is his inward word."[44] Explaining this renaissance notion, Heninger writes, "This concept of God as maker working from preconceived forms was transferred undiminished and applied to the poet. Sidney, for example, goes on in his *Defense of Poesie* to state flatly: 'The skill of ech [poetic] Artificer standeth in that *Idea,* or force conceit of the worke, and not in the worke it self."[45] Like Sidney, Wordsworth believes that the essence of poetry lies in what is conceived in the poet's mind—be it called "inward word," "Idea," "conceit," or envisagement—not in language. Just as W. J. B. Owen observes, for Wordsworth "once the appropriate state of mind is achieved, then if nothing extraneous intervenes, authentic utterance is assured."[46] Because he considers language to be an inherent, unmediated manifestation of the mind, he naturally concentrates on the achievement of the ideal envisagement and largely sets aside the issue of compositional execution.[47]

LIU XIE ON THE MUTUAL GENERATION OF SENSORY AND SUPRASENSORY EXPERIENCES

Like Wordsworth, Liu Xie does not examine the creative process merely in terms of the interchange of emotion and the "moods of calmness," unconscious responses and conscious endeavors. He also explores the creative process in light of the interplay of sensory and suprasensory experiences through its four stages.[48]

In discussing the first stage, Liu focuses on sensory experiences of man's direct emotional engagement with external nature as does Wordsworth. However, while Wordsworth sees in this emotional engagement the "seed" of suprasensory experience to be brought to fruition by tranquil recollection, Liu considers this emotional engagement is in and of itself a pure sensory experience. In chapter 46 ("Wuse" 物色 [Sensuous Colors]), he pursues a step-by-step, comprehensive examination of man's direct emotional engagement with external nature and the analogical poetic mode born of this engagement. He begins by describing this engagement and characterizing it as a natural and involuntary phenomenon, similar to any living thing's response to the cycle of seasonal changes. Next, he seeks evidence of such an engagement in the *Shijing*. For him, it is most faithfully preserved in the construction of a typical line in the *Shijing* ballads: a juxtaposition of nature's images and man's emotive utterances—highly expressive *lianmianzi* 連綿字 or reduplicatives—made in response to those objects. Citing the juxtaposition of willow and poplar with *yiyi* 依依, the rain and snow with *biaobiao* 瀌瀌, he shows us how vividly and faithfully *Shijing* poets captured their emotional engagements with external nature in these lines. Then, he goes on to consider how a correlative or analogical mode of thinking was born out of these engagements and how it was adopted and developed by literati poets like Qu Yuan as their mode of presentation. "By the time *Lisao* appeared to take the place of [the *Shijing*]," Liu observes, "the poets probed analogical categories and thereby extended the range [of their emotional expression]" 及離騷代興，觸類而長 (*WXDL* 46 / 51–52). Turning to his own time, he notes the ascendancy of a new descriptive mode grounded in the new aesthetic ideal of "descriptive verisimilitude," but stresses that the analogical mode of the *Shijing* and *Chuci* remains an indispensable model for the integration of nature's images and man's emotions. Since he does not even mention the *shen* or the inner spirit throughout his discussion, it is quite fitting for him to talk about the interaction between man and nature solely on the sensory level in the concluding verse of chapter 46:

The mountains in folds with rivers winding,	山沓水匝，
Mixed trees where the clouds merge:	樹雜雲合。
When the eyes have roamed over them,	目既往還，
The mind expresses them.	心亦吐納。
The days of spring pass slowly,	春日遲遲，
The winds of autumn howl.	秋風颯颯。
Our emotions go out as a gift,	情往似贈，
And poetic inspiration comes back like an answer.	興來如答。
(*WXDL* 46 / 115–23)[49]	

While he confines his discussion to the realm of sensory experience in chapter 46, Liu hints that an emotional engagement with the external world may lead to a suprasensory experience should "a poet, in responding to external objects, make categorical associations without an end" 詩人感物，聯類不窮 (*WXDL* 46 / 29–30). At the beginning of chapter 26 ("Shensi" 神思 ["Spirit and Thought"]), Liu Xie describes how such a suprasensory experience ushers in the second stage of literary creation:

In the thought process of writing, the spirit goes afar. In the state of silence and mental concentration, thought reaches to a thousand years ago. With a slight change of one's facial expression, one's vision may have already crossed ten thousand leagues. (*WXDL* 26 / 6–9)

文之思也，其神遠矣！故寂然凝慮，思接千載；悄然動容，視通萬理。

Reading this passage, we cannot but think of a similar description of an imaginative flight of mind by Shakespeare: "The poet's eye, in a fine frenzy rolling, Doth glance from heaven to earth, from earth to heaven / And as imagination bodies forth / The forms of things unknown, the poet's pen turns them to shapes, and gives to airy nothing / A local habitation and a name."[50] Comparing these two descriptions, we note a common recognition of the poet's transcendence of the confines of time or space in his moments of mental concentration. We see also a difference with respect to the relationship of the eye to this suprasensory experience. Shakespeare considers the open eye to be the window through which "imagination bodies forth / The forms of things unknown." In other words, the eye is instrumental to the flight of the suprasensory imagination. Liu does not entertain this idea of achieving suprasensory experience through the help of the eye. His phrase "one's vision" is a reference to an intuitive flight of the mind, unmediated by the eye.

This exclusion of sensory experience distinguishes Liu's observation of the "emptiness and stillness" from Wordsworth's description of tranquil recollection. For Wordsworth, sensory and suprasensory experiences are closely intertwined. It is through a recollection of his sensory experiences that he laid himself "asleep / In body" and obtained the transcendental vision of "the life of all things." By contrast, Liu believes that a suprasensory union with all things cannot be achieved until after sensory experiences have been suspended. If Liu only implies this suspension of sense experiences by the phrase "silence and mental concentration," Lu Ji explicitly describes how the poet would cut off his sensory experiences in the hope of achieving a suprasensory communion with all things:

> This is how it begins: perception is 其始也，皆收視反聽，
> held back and listening is reverted.
> Engrossed in thought, one searches 耽思傍訊，
> all sides.

His essence galloping to the world's 精騖八極，
eight boundaries,
His mind soaring across ten 心游萬仞。
thousand yards.[51]

The contrast between the line "perception is held back and listening is reverted" and Wordsworth's statement "with an eye . . . / We see into the life of things" is truly remarkable. It brings into sharp relief the fundamental difference between Liu Xie's and Lu Ji's views of "emptiness and stillness" and Wordsworth's understanding of the significance of tranquil recollection.

If the second stage represents a sublimation of man's emotional engagement with concrete natural phenomena into a suprasensory communion with the subtlest of all things, the third stage constitutes the reverse course of transforming the nebulous undifferentiated state of this suprasensory communion into a concrete mental picture of images and feelings. Lu Ji depicts this process of transformation in a broad outline: "Emotions that are fuzzy become clear; things become luminous and appear one after another" 情曈曨而彌鮮，物昭晰而互進.[52] For his part, Liu Xie offers a detailed discussion of the interplay of the physiological, psychological, and linguistic processes at work in the course of this transformation. According to him, these processes belong to sensory experiences because they entail the exertion of vital bodily force (*qi* 氣) and the linguistic capability to recall, select, and reorganize the data of sensory experiences "coming along through the ear and the eye" as well as feelings and thoughts derived from those experiences. However, unlike the sensory experiences at the first stage, these processes are not born of involuntary emotional responses to the real world. Rather, they arise from conscious mental efforts to draw images and feelings from the treasure houses of memory and knowledge and to blend them in ways that best embody the mysterious suprasensory communion in "emptiness and stillness."

In saying "the spirit dwells in the breast," Liu obviously means to stress the impact of a suprasensory communion on these processes. To indicate their end product as an embodiment of the suprasensory communion, he calls it "idea-image" (*yixiang* 意象). Judging by his subsequent citation of Daoist views on the idea-language relationship, we can tell that he employs the word "idea" (*yi*) not so much in its ordinary sense of "meaning" or "intent" as in its philosophical sense of the ultimate ontological reality as used by Wang Bi 王弼 (226–249). Liu's invention of the compound "idea-image" is obviously inspired by Wang

Bi's explanation of the category of *xiang* 象 in his commentaries on the *Book of Changes* as the intermediary between the old dichotomy of *yi* 意 and *yan* 言 set up earlier by Zhuang Zi. By inventing this compound, he probably intends to steer us toward a recognition of *yi,* the ontological reality, embodied in the artistic envisagement that emerges at the third stage. As has just been shown, he contends that the embodiment of *yi* consists in a perfect fusion of images and feelings.[53] In his concluding verse to the chapter, he reiterates the importance of a fusion of images and feelings: "When the spirit comes into play, images commune with one another; and feelings bring about a transformation of their contents" 神用象通，情變所孕 (*WXDL* 26 / 127–28 / 339). Comparing these lines with the concluding verse to chapter 46 ("Sensuous Color"), we can see a great difference between a categorical interaction between man and nature at the first stage and the fusion of the innermost essences of both at the third stage.

Whereas Wordsworth leaves the fourth stage largely undiscussed, Liu pays as much attention to it as to the third stage. For him, to capture the *yijing* or artistic vision in language is no less difficult than to form it in the mind. A successful compositional execution depends not only on a mastery of compositional art but also on the aid of mysterious inspiration from the suprasensory realm. Liu holds a balanced view of these two opposite yet complementary dimensions of compositional execution. On the one hand, he recommends systematic training and practice in all aspects of composition: the integration of content and form (chapter 32), the choice of genres and structures on the ground of their inherent dynamics (chapter 30), the exploitation of musical elements (chapter 33), the construction of parallelisms (chapter 36), the incorporation of allusions (chapter 38), and so on.[54] That he devotes an entire chapter to each of these aspects underscores the degree of importance he attaches to them. On the other hand, he maintains that such training and practice, though indispensable to everyone, cannot alone produce great works of literature. Only if guided by an inspiration arising from a suprasensory communion with the object(s) of art, he argues, can a well-trained author produce a literary work completely identical to the artistic vision in the mind. He shows the impact of this inspiration through his allusions to Zhuang Zi's fables of the butcher and the wheelwright, which are discussed in the next section.

In formulating his views on the roles of conscious learning and practice and unconscious inspiration at the fourth stage, Liu is greatly influenced by Lu Ji. In *Wen fu* 文賦 (A Rhapsody on Literature), after discussing the importance of mastering a host of compositional and rhetorical principles, Lu Ji turns his attention to the play of inspiration:

> At the conjunction of stirring and response, 若夫應感之會。
> At the demarcation between blockage 通塞之紀。
> and passage,
> What comes cannot be halted, 來不可遏。
> What goes off cannot be stopped. 去不可止。
> When it hides, it is like a shadow 藏若景滅。
> disappearing,
> When it moves, it is like an echo rising. 行猶響起。
> When Heaven's motive impulses move swiftly 方天機之駿利。
> on the best course,
> What confusion is there that cannot be put 夫何紛而不理。
> in order?

This passage has exerted a great influence not only on Liu Xie but on virtually all Chinese critics who seek to understand the nature of this suprasensory experience. In traditional Chinese literary criticism, we can find as many descriptions and comments about it as we can about the other type of suprasensory experience at the second stage. In depicting the latter, critics tend to focus on the initial state of "emptiness and stillness" and subsequent roaming of the mind. In depicting the former, they usually stress the suddenness of its visitation, its complete possession of the author, and its powerful and irresistible guidance through the compositional process. Nowadays, their remarks on these two types of suprasensory experience are appropriately distinguished as the "theory of emptiness and stillness" (*xujing shuo* 虛靜說) and the "theory of inspiration" (*ganxing shuo* 感與說).[55] The "theory of inspiration" is often erroneously identified with Plato's theory of divine inspiration in the *Ion*. Unlike Plato's theory, it is not meant to indicate the origin of literature in a divine muse, but to show the decisive role of suprasensory experience in the perfect consummation of a long, sustained creative process.

WORDSWORTH'S PATTERN OF MUTUAL INGRAINING AND PLATO'S ALLEGORY OF THE CAVE

In comparing Wordsworth's and Liu Xie's observations on sensory and suprasensory experiences through the four stages, we can see that they conceive of the interaction between the two experiences in two different ways—that of mutual ingraining and that of mutual generation.

These two patterns are grounded in two different sets of philosophical assumptions made by early Western and Chinese thinkers about the relationship between inner self and its relationship to perceptual process and the ultimate reality.

The Wordsworthian creative process is remarkably analogous to the process of Wordsworth's own spiritual growth. As shown above, his poems, especially the *Prelude,* reveal three phases of his spiritual growth—a sensitive though unself-conscious child, a reflective youth, and a mature, philosophical poet. Interestingly, this spiritual growth may be seen as the creative process writ large. The addition of the subtitle *"or growth of a poet's mind"* to his spiritual autobiography the *Prelude* aptly speaks to this close analogue between the teleology of his spiritual life and the etiology of literary creation envisioned by himself.

Considering this close analogue, we may very well apply Hirsch's comments on the progressive interplay of emotion and imagination in Wordsworth's own spiritual life to characterize Wordsworth's conception of literary creation:

> There is always an element of emotion in Imagination, but emotion, as such, is only the first stage of Imagination. . . . The teleology of the cosmos is expressed in the teleology of the individual mind. For Wordsworth this development begins with the "unconscious" feelings of childhood and culminates in the poetic or philosophical mind. Yet, the final stage is not cut off from the emotions which started the development on its true path. The final stage is "feeling intellect." There is emotion both in the present, higher experience of nature and also in the remembrance of past emotion. But the emotion is different in the final stage; it is mediated by consciousness and knowledge. It is less direct and intense but more constant. It is emotion along with awareness of emotion. This stage comprehends both the "thing Contemplated" and "the Mind and Man Contemplating." As in all organic development, Imagination advances and yet remains the same.[56]

Parallel to this teleology of his spiritual life, Wordsworth conceptualizes the literary process in terms of a progressive interplay between sensory and suprasensory experiences. He believes that sensory (perceptive and emotive) and suprasensory (imaginative or visionary) experiences are mutually ingrained throughout the creative process. One experience necessarily involves and activates the other. Utterly sensory as it may appear to most others, a direct, spontaneous emotive encounter with external nature is seen by Wordsworth as the very seed

of suprasensory experience, to be brought to fruition by tranquil rec-
ollection. Whereas many of his contemporaries associated such "moods
of calmness" with the exercise of mechanical memory, he calls it the
"blessed mood," or "that happy stillness of the mind, / Which fits him
to receive it [the truth], when unsought." Next, the "moods of calm-
ness" lead to the rise of a new emotion, imparting creative energy to a
poet who then "aspires, grasps, struggles, wishes, craves." By asserting
his conscious will to reorder the sensory data of images, feelings, and
thoughts, he brings into active play the divine power of his own mind
and forms the universe anew like a divine creator. For Wordsworth,
this continual mutual ingraining of sensory and suprasensory experi-
ences betokens not a static, nonprogressive reciprocity but a steady in-
tensification of a poet's awareness of the suprasensory elements in his
own perceptive and emotive experiences.

This pattern of mutual ingraining is rooted in Western philosoph-
ical assumptions about the interplay of sensory and suprasensory ele-
ments in human perception. These assumptions may be traced to Plato's
remarks on the eye as the means of communion between the soul and
the external world. In his famous Parable of the Cave in book 7 of the
Republic, Plato gives a somewhat metaphorical description of eyesight
as a means of attaining suprasensory truth:

> And now look again, and see what will naturally follow if the prisoners
> are released and disabused of their error. At first, when any of them is
> liberated and compelled suddenly to stand up and turn his neck round
> and walk and look towards the light, he will be unable to see the reali-
> ties of which in his former state he had seen the shadows; and then con-
> ceive some one saying to him, that what he saw before was an illusion,
> but that now, when he is approaching nearer to being and his eye is
> turned towards more real existence, he has a clearer vision,—what will
> be his reply?[57]

Commenting on this passage, Gerald F. Else says, "The development
of the freed prisoner's power of sight, culminating in his ability to look
directly at the sun, is explicitly identified with the soul's progress in di-
alectic, ending in its vision."[58] In *Timaeus,* Plato gives a more theo-
retical analysis of human perception. He identifies it as "pure fire" from
the soul, or the visual current which "issues forth, like to like, and co-
alesces with it [external object] and is formed into a single homoge-
neous body in a direct line with the eyes, in whatever quarter the stream
issuing from within strikes upon any object it encounters outside."[59]

With these and other similar passages, Plato sets up a broad cos-mological-epistemological paradigm through which most Western critics subsequently examine the interplay of the sensory and the suprasensory in creative imagination.[60] Employing this paradigm, they tend to focus on and argue with one another over the relationship of the eye to suprasensory experience. Ralph Waldo Emerson's exaltation and William Blake's condemnation of the eye represent polar oppo-sites. For Emerson, the eye is the embodiment of the transcendental experience. Hence he celebrates the dissolution of his whole being into a "transparent eye-ball":

> Standing on the bare ground,—my head bathed by the blithe air, and uplifted into infinite space,—all mean egotism vanishes, I become a transparent eye-ball. I am nothing. I see all. The currents of the Uni-versal Being circulate through me; I am part or particle of God.[61]

By contrast, Blake condemns the eye as an impediment to transcen-dental experience:

> I assert for Myself that I do not behold the Outward Creation and that to me it is a hindrance and not Action it is as the Dirt upon my feet. No part of Me. 'What' it will be Question'd, 'When the Sun rises, do you not see a round disc of fire somewhat like a Guinea?' O no, no. I see an Innumerable company of the Heavenly host crying, 'Holy, Holy, Holy is the Lord God Almighty.' I question not my Corporeal or Vege-tative Eye any more than I would Question a Window concerning a Sight. I look through it and not with it.[62]

Paradoxically, in saying that the eye is that *through* which he looks to God, Blake actually affirms the indispensability of the eye as a gateway to suprasensory experience. This paradoxical denial of the eye only serves to underscore the extent to which Plato has influenced the ways later thinkers view the relationship of the eye, or broadly speaking, sen-sory experience as a whole, to suprasensory experience.

In adopting Plato's onto-epistemological paradigm, Wordsworth takes a more balanced view of the eye. For him, it is not a "transpar-ent eye-ball"—a total embodiment of the transcendental essence. Nor is it a "Vegetable Eye"—an impediment to the transcendental experi-ence. Rather, he sees the eye as something that cannot be identified ex-clusively with either the suprasensory or the sensory:

There is creation in the eye,
Nor less in all the other senses; powers
They are that colour, model, and combine
The things perceived with such an absolute
Essential energy that we may say
That those most godlike faculties of ours
At one and the same moment are the mind
and the mind's minister. In many a walk
At evening or by moonlight, or reclined
At midday upon beds of forest moss,
Have we to Nature and her impulses
Of our whole being made free gift, and when
Our trance had left us, oft have we, by aid
Of the impressions which it left behind,
Looked inward on ourselves, and learned, perhaps,
Something of what we are . . .[63]

Here, by observing its sensory perception and its latent transcendental powers, Wordsworth conceives the eye to be an essential epistemological medium for the knowledge of the absolute Being as suggested by Plato in the allegory of the cave. Through this medium, Wordsworth tells us that a poet or *vates* like himself can experience both the sensory and the suprasensory, awaken to the mutual ingraining of the two in the cosmos as well as in his own mind, and achieve a union with Nature and God in that blessed moment of awakening.[64]

LIU XIE'S PATTERN OF MUTUAL GENERATION
AND ZHUANG ZI'S PARABLE OF BUTCHER DING

As shown above, Liu discerns a pattern of mutual generation between sensory and suprasensory experiences. For him, literary creation is none other than a continuous process of mutual generation of sensory and suprasensory experiences. Emotional response to external nature leads to a state of "emptiness and stillness," in which the mind embarks on a suprasensory roaming. After this suprasensory process has reached its culmination, what follows is an essentially sensory process of recalling, mediating, and selecting images. When this process of inward perception and contemplation ends with the formation of a unified envisagement, there comes another spell of suprasensory enthrallment in which the writer will spontaneously execute a faultless, seamless translation of his envisagement into language. Like the state of "emptiness and stillness," this second type of suprasensory experience does not come to everyone. It comes only to those who are capable of mental quiescence and intuitive awareness and have mastered all the important skills of composition through persistent, painstaking efforts.

This pattern of mutual generation is grounded in Chinese philosophical assumptions about the relationship between visual perception and intuitive awareness. Just as we have traced Wordsworth's pattern of mutual ingraining to Plato's allegory of the cave, we can find the origin of Liu's pattern of mutual generation in Zhuang Zi's Parable of Butcher Ding, to which Liu makes an explicit reference in the "Spirit and Thought" passage cited earlier. Now, let us take a look at Zhuang Zi's parable and assess its influence on Liu:

> Cook Ding was cutting up an ox for Lord Wenhui. At every touch of his hand, every heave of his shoulder, every move of his feet, every thrust of his knee—zip! zoop! He slithered the knife along with a zing, and all was in perfect rhythm, as though he were performing the dance of the Mulberry Grove or keeping time to the Jingshou music.
> "Ah, this is marvelous!" said Lord Wenhui. "Imagine skill reaching such heights!"
> Cook Ding laid down his knife and replied, "What I care about is the Way, which goes beyond skill. When I first began cutting up oxen, all I could see was the ox itself. After three years I no longer saw the whole ox—now I go at it by spirit and don't look with my eyes. Perception and understanding have come to a stop and spirit moves where it wants. I go along with the natural makeup, strike in the big hollows, guide the knife through the big openings, and follow things as they are. So I never touch the smallest ligament or tendon, much less a main joint."[65]

To this passage we can trace the two types of suprasensory experience described by Liu. What Liu has said about the state of "emptiness and stillness" is obviously modeled on Zhuang Zi's account of the butcher's mental preparation: the closing of his eyes, his suspension of understanding, his suprasensory or intuitive union with the ox, and the free roaming of his mind. By the same token, what Liu has told us about suprasensory enthrallment at the final stage is undoubtedly inspired by Zhuang Zi's description of the butcher's spontaneous, absolutely faultless execution of his job beyond any explanation in terms of skills. Moreover, Liu's view of the interdependence between sensory and suprasensory experiences, between spontaneity and conscious endeavor, and between natural talent and learning, may also be traced to this passage. While Zhuang Zi indicated that the butcher could "go at it [an ox] by spirit" only after years of visual contact with oxen, Liu holds that the writer could not enter into a communion with all things without any prior emotional engagement with external nature. In the last paragraph, Zhuang Zi shows that the inspired moment of spontaneous execution did not preclude the use of senses by the butcher. Similarly, Liu contends that the final stage of compositional execution involves an active interplay of spontaneous inspiration and conscious intellectual-linguistic endeavors by the writer.

Apart from the Parable of Butcher Ding, Liu makes subtle references to many other philosophical texts in his "Spirit and Thought" passage. For instance, his description of "emptiness and stillness" (*xujing* 虛靜) echoes Lao Zi's and Xun Zi's discussions of that thoughtless state as the precondition for one's union with the Dao, the ultimate reality.[66] His phrase "shaping and turning [as on a potter's wheel] literary thought" (*taojun wensi* 陶鈞文思) brings to mind the story in *Zhuang Zi* of Wheelwright Bian, who described how he reached a divinelike skill in his trade through decades of conscious endeavor.[67] In like manner, his phrase "wielding the ax" (*yunjin* 運斤) alludes not only to the Parable of Butcher Ding but also to a similar story meant to illustrate the same kind of miracle that arises from one's suprasensory union with the spirit of all things. The story is that of Carpenter Shi who had such an intuitive skill that he could wield his ax effortlessly to remove a speck of plaster from his friend's nose.[68] All these references and allusions leave no doubt about the origin of Liu's pattern of mutual generation in Chinese philosophical discourses on human perception and understanding.

In closing this chapter, it seems appropriate to make some general remarks about the cross-cultural relevance and cultural specificity of Wordsworth's and Liu Xie's theories of literary creation. In the course of my discussion, I have shown numerous parallels between the two theories. Wordsworth and Liu Xie conceive of four similar stages of literary creation, marked by a gradual transformation of emotion into a work of language. They both explore this creative process in terms of a progressive interplay between three sets of opposite yet complementary mental conditions: emotion and the "moods of calmness," unconscious response and conscious endeavor, and sensory and suprasensory experiences. It is truly significant that these two critics, living nearly one and a half millennia apart and working in unrelated cultural traditions, would come to focus on these same sets of mental conditions and stress their interrelatedness in their theories of literary creation.

This shows that these mental conditions pertain to common aspects of literary creation as a basic human experience and that what the two critics have said about them has a relevance beyond the boundaries of Western and Chinese criticism. Thus, by comparing their views, I believe we can work toward a better understanding of literary creation in a cross-cultural perspective.

I also have addressed differences between the two theories, especially those pertaining to the broad conceptual patterns used by Wordsworth and Liu Xie to examine the interplay of sensory and suprasensory experiences. Since their conceptual models are respectively rooted in Plato's and Zhuang Zi's cosmological paradigms, it is best to account for their conceptual differences in light of these two paradigms. In my opinion, the fundamental differences between the two paradigms concern the ultimate ground for the union of man and nature and the roles of human perception and consciousness in achieving that union.

For Plato, God is the ultimate ground for the union of man and nature. On the one hand, God's divinity flows through the human eye into nature, giving it an inner spiritual essence akin to what He imparts to the human soul. On the other hand, this spiritualized inner nature acts upon the human soul, helping it to know the spirituality of its own as well as that of the spiritual nature. Both being emanations of God, nature and the human soul are akin to each other and can be brought into a living unity with each other and with God. This is to be achieved by man's exercising his divine gift of perceiving, knowing, and thereby repeating "in the finite mind the eternal act of creation in the infinite I AM."

For Zhuang Zi, the ultimate ground for the union of man and nature is the Dao, an everlasting natural process of change that generates and sustains all things. As the Dao is anything but an absolute transcendental subject like God, it is out of the question for him to conceive of the union of man and nature on the ground of common emanations from a supreme subject. Neither nature's nor man's innermost essence is a form of subjective spirituality but rather the impersonal, amoral, and completely natural process of the Dao. Hence, the union of man and nature is not to be achieved through an exertion of one's consciousness to see, know, and create. On the contrary, it is to be achieved by suspending one's perception and thought and letting the Dao work its way through nature and man unhindered.[69] For him, human perception, thought, and language are often a hindrance to the suprasensory union of man and nature. They are useful only to the extent that they help induce intuitive awareness, a state beyond thought and language, in which man becomes one with the Dao operating in all things under heaven and through which he is enabled to render his envisagement into a work of art.

These differences between the two cosmological paradigms are reflected in the differences between Wordsworth's and Liu Xie's conceptual models. Wordsworth's is distinguished by his emphasis on the spiritual flow between nature and man, on the revelation of a transcendental God through this mutual spirituality,[70] on the pivotal roles of human perception and emotion in achieving a suprasensory union between man and nature, and on a poet's need to reflect on this mutual ingraining of sensory and suprasensory experiences in the course of literary creation. By contrast, Liu Xie's is characterized by his emphasis on the mutual resonance between nature's changing phenomena and man's perceptual and emotive experiences, on the crucial role of intuitive awareness in achieving the union of nature and man, on the revelation of the Dao through such a union, on the rhythmic mutual generation of sensory and suprasensory experiences, and on a poet's total immersion in these experiences without contemplating and philosophizing about them. These different emphases speak eloquently to the cultural specificity of the two theories.

CHAPTER 7

Poetics of Dynamic Force
*Fenollosa, Pound, and Chinese
Critics on the Chinese Written Character*

IN COMPARATIVE STUDIES OF WESTERN AND CHINESE POET-
ics, perhaps no work has attracted more enthusiastic acclaim and
more unsympathetic criticism than the essay "The Chinese Written
Character as a Medium for Poetry," written by Ernest Fenollosa and
edited for publication by Ezra Pound.[1] Andrew Welsh calls the essay
"one of the high points of modern poetics" and devotes a long chap-
ter to Fenollosa and Pound's theory of the ideogram in his book, *Roots
of the Lyric.*[2] Welsh's remark seems to sum up all the laudatory com-
ments on the essay in Western literary circles. On the contrary, James
J. Y. Liu argues that the essay perpetuates the fallacy outside Sinological
circles, namely that "Chinese characters are pictograms or ideograms,"
and begins his book *The Art of Chinese Poetry* with a critique of Fenol-
losa and Pound's misrepresentation of Chinese characters.[3] Such an un-
complimentary view of the essay is widely held in Sinological circles.[4]
In reading the essay, we tend to follow one side or the other of these
polarized views—often depending on our disciplinary allegiance—and
pay almost exclusive attention to the pictorial aspect of Chinese char-
acters. Consequently, we lose sight of what informs Fenollosa and
Pound's discussion of Chinese characters: an aesthetic ideal centering
on the concept of dynamic force. The neglect of this aesthetics of
dynamic force prevents us from seeing Fenollosa and Pound's insight
into the etymological, aesthetic, and calligraphic aspects of Chinese
characters, and thus we let pass an excellent opportunity to explore the
full significance of their views in a cross-cultural, cross-disciplinary
context.

THE DYNAMIC FORCE OF NATURE
IN THE MORPHOLOGICAL, SYNTACTICAL,
AND ETYMOLOGICAL ASPECTS OF THE
CHINESE WRITTEN CHARACTER

To correct Fenollosa and Pound's overstatements about the pictorial quality of the Chinese language is a justifiable and indeed necessary task in the teaching of Chinese.[5] However, it would be a deplorable mistake to dismiss Fenollosa's essay merely because it perpetuates the pictorial myth about Chinese characters. This is especially true if we approach the essay from a literary point of view.

To grasp the literary values of this essay, we must dismiss the overly harsh charge against Fenollosa for his perpetuation of the pictorial myth. Throughout the essay, Fenollosa cites Chinese characters and comments on "their semi-pictorial effects" only a few times. Even when doing so, he stresses that Chinese characters are "based upon a vivid shorthand picture of the operations of nature"[6] and that "their ideographic roots carry in them a verbal idea of action."[7] Placing this essay under close scrutiny, we find that it is not concerned, as it seems in the eyes of many critics, with the pictorial quality of Chinese characters for its own sake. Rather, it is a comprehensive inquiry into the dynamic force of nature revealed pictorially or otherwise in the Chinese language. In fact, as early as 1916, Pound called attention to this central concern of the essay when he asked a friend to "see Fenollosa's big essay on verbs, mostly on verbs."[8]

In analyzing the syntactic organization of Chinese characters, Fenollosa seeks to show how effectively a Chinese sentence conjures up "transferences of force from agent to object."[9] He holds that a Chinese sentence does not involve what they called "weakness of formalism" (articles, inflections, conjugation, and intransitiveness, etc.). As a result, he sees "literally the parts of speech growing up, budding forth one from another,"[10] a process that closely replicates the transferences of force in nature. The bulk of Fenollosa's essay is devoted to an analysis of how the Chinese character evokes the dynamic force of nature as a result of its ideogrammic, morphological, and syntactical organization.

In considering Chinese parts of speech, Fenollosa again focuses on the evocation of dynamic force in nature. According to him, Chinese nouns are superior to their counterparts in Western languages because their ideogrammic forms are virtually "meeting points, of actions, cross-sections cut through actions, snapshots."[11] He regards Chinese verbs as an ideal embodiment of natural force because they contain no passive voice or copula which subtracts the directness and intensity of natural force. Chinese adjectives are laudable because they are derived from and, in many cases, interchangeable with verbs. As Chinese adjectives always retain "a substratum of verbal meaning," they are anything but "bloodless adjectival abstraction."[12] By the same token, Chinese prepositions and conjunctions are worthy of praise because "they usually serve to mediate actions between verbs, and therefore they are necessarily themselves actions."[13] In the opinion of Fenollosa, even Chinese pronouns are pregnant with verbal qualities as shown in the ideogrammic combination of two forms of "I" in Chinese (*wo* 我 and *wu* 吾).[14]

Fenollosa sees the evidence of verbal power first in the etymologies of Chinese characters. When he examines "primitive Chinese characters" (simple pictograms or ideograms), he seeks to represent them as "shorthand pictures of actions and processes."[15] When he discusses complex Chinese characters (composite ideograms), he argues that two or more ideograms "added together do not produce a third thing but suggest some fundamental relation between them."[16]

In focusing his attention on its dynamic force, Fenollosa captures, consciously or not, the quintessential quality of the Chinese written character in terms of both its etymological evolution and the aesthetic use of it in calligraphy as well as literature. The evocation of dynamic force is what distinguishes the evolution of Chinese characters from those of other ancient pictorial languages like the Egyptian hieroglyphic.[17] Many early Chinese characters, in the Oracle Bone Script or the Bronze Script, often assumed a pictorial form reminiscent of Egyptian hieroglyphic (see figure 2). Over time they gradually evolved into an abstract shorthand of the dynamic force of things. This symbolic feature became truly prominent in the Small Seal Script introduced in the Qin (see figure 4).[18] To illustrate this evolution from pictorial representation to symbolic evocation of dynamic force of things, let us observe four different scripts for the following characters cited in Fenollosa's essay.

While both the Oracle Bone Script and Bronze Script pictorially represent an erect man, the act of seeing, and a horse, the Small Seal Script symbolically sketches, as Fenollosa argues, abstract rhythms of movements.[19] What we observe in the latter are not concrete physical things but a shorthand of dynamic postures and movements: a man standing, a man squatting and looking around, and a horse galloping with fluttering mane. Besides this well-known example, Fenollosa's descriptions of the dynamic force in the three characters in figure 3 are also clearly borne out by their Small Seal Script form.

	MAN	SEE	HORSE
Oracle Bone Script	🄴	𗀤	𩡋
Bronze Script	🄵	𗀥	𩡌
Small Seal Script	🄶	𗀦	𩡍
Modern Script	人	見	馬

Figure 2.

Note: These three characters in four Chinese scripts are reproduced respectively from (1) Xu Zhongshu 徐中舒, ed., *Jiaguwen zidian* 甲骨文字典 (A Dictionary of Oracle Bone Inscriptions) (Chengdu: Sichuan cishu chubanshe, 1988); (2) Rong Geng 容庚, ed., *Jinwen bian jinwen xubian* 金文編金文續編 (A Collection of Bronze Inscriptions and an Addendum) (Rpt. Taipei: Hongshi chubanshe, 1974); (3) Xu Shen 許慎 (30-124), *Shuo wen jiezi zhu* 説文解字注 (Explanations of Simple and Compound Characters, with Annotations), annot. Duan Yucai 段玉裁 (1735-1815) (Rpt. Yangzhou: Jiangsu Guangling guji keyinshe, 1997); and (4) Fenollosa and Pound, *Chinese Written Character*, p. 8.

As we examine closely these characters, we can see in them a visible presence of the natural force described by Fenollosa. Fenollosa's etymological interpretation of Chinese characters is not always accurate, but it normally cuts to the heart of the matter—the inner dynamics of Chinese etymology. Fenollosa's categorization of this inner dynamics as "things in motion, motion in things" is quite insightful. While the character 馬 (horse) typifies "things in motion"[20] or a display of force in full swing, the three characters in figure 3 exemplify the "motion in things" or an equilibrium of dynamic force in stationary things. All in all, Fenollosa's analysis of Chinese characters threw light on "the deliberate neglect of realistic representation"[21] and the revelation of natural force in the graphic formation of the Chinese written character (see figure 4).[22]

FENOLLOSA AND TRADITIONAL CHINESE SCHOLARSHIP ON THE WRITTEN CHARACTER

There seems to be an unannounced but readily discernible reason for some Sinologists to cast scorn on Fenollosa's essay: It is a blatant trans-

SMALL SEAL SCRIPT	FENOLLOSA'S DESCRIPTIONS
 𤯚	The sun underlying the bursting forth of plants = spring
 𤲬	"Rice field" plus "struggle" = male
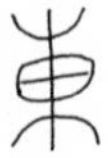 東 ᵃ	The sun sign tangled in the branches of the tree sign = east[b]

Figure 3.

[a] These three characters are reproduced from Xu, *Shuowen jiezi zhu*, p. 47, 271, and 698.
[b] Fenollosa, *Chinese Written Character*, p. 10.

gression of the professional knowledge of Sinologists by an amateur who hardly knows Chinese. Although they may seem ridiculously naïve to some Sinologists, Fenollosa's explanations of Chinese written characters are in fact firmly grounded in traditional Chinese studies of characters, or *wenzixue* 文字學. Fenollosa's indebtedness to traditional Chinese *wenzixue,* for both his errors and insights, has been largely neglected by scholars and demands our attention here.

Fenollosa himself declares that his essay "represents for the first time a Japanese school of study in Chinese culture" and that he studied "for many years as a private student under Professor Kainan Mori, . . . probably the greatest living authority on Chinese poetry."[23] If we examine Fenollosa's essay in relation to traditional Chinese *wenzixue,* we shall discover that the two fallacies of which Fenollosa has been accused— pictorial myth and indiscreet ideogrammic explanations—are actually not of Fenollosa's own making, but of Xu Shen's 許慎 (30–124), the very founder of traditional Chinese *wenzixue.*

Xu Shen is the compiler of the first comprehensive Chinese dictionary, *Explanations of Simple and Compound Characters* (*Shuowen jie zi* 説文解字 hereafter *Simple and Compound Characters*). In this

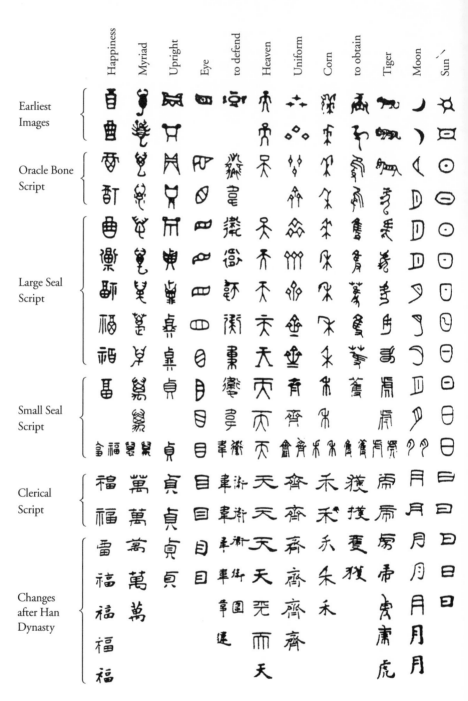

Figure 4. Table of Chinese Characters. Adapted from Chiang Yee, *Chinese Calligraphy: an Introduction to Its Aesthetic and Technique* (Cambridge: Harvard Univ. Press, 1966), p. 34.

dictionary Xu has collected as many as 9,353 characters in the Small Seal Script. Under these main entries, he has also included 1,163 variant characters in older Large Seal Script, also known as *Guzhou* 古 籀 Script. In explaining a character, Xu typically defines its meaning and then analyzes its ideogrammic structure. Often he also gives a homonym to indicate the pronunciation and cites a few words from a classic to support his explanations. In the preface to the dictionary, he presents a comprehensive explanation on the origins and evolution of written characters and expounds the *liushu* 六 書, or the Six Methods of Character Formation.[24] In compiling *Simple and Compound Characters,* Xu single-handedly establishes, defines, and delimits the field of *wenzixue,* or the study of written characters. Most if not all subsequent studies of characters continue the three tasks begun by Xu: to explain individual characters, to discuss the origins of characters, and to distinguish the relationship of the Six Methods.[25] In pursuing these three tasks, the compilers of these studies often take Xu's dictionary as their points of departure and raise questions about his errors and inaccuracies.

A complaint frequently made against Xu is that he persistently overemphasizes visual elements at the expense of phonetic ones in his analysis of characters. Although he acknowledges the presence of phonetic elements in three of the Six Methods, he considers the roles of phonetic elements supplementary to those played by visual elements. His overriding emphasis on pictograms and ideograms is aptly reflected in the ways he categorizes characters. In *Simple and Compound Characters,* he categorizes the mass of 9,353 characters under 540 radicals. All but a handful of those radicals are pictographs or ideograms. Even in that handful of phonetic radicals, he seeks to identify pictogrammic and ideogrammic elements therein so that he can group them with other pictogram-radicals or ideogram-radicals. Thanks to this maneuver, he manages to arrange all the radicals in a sequence based almost solely on the consideration of their graphic configurations. Apparently, Xu should be held responsible in some ways for the so-called "pictorial myth" of which Fenollosa is accused.

Standing at the end of a long line of Xu's loyal followers is Fenollosa. Like Xu, Fenollosa devotes himself to unlocking the pictogrammic and ideogrammic clues in characters, albeit for the different purpose of reinventing Western poetry. Again, like Xu, he downplays the importance of phonetic values. "It is true that the pictorial clue of many Chinese ideographs can not now be traced," he argues, "and even Chinese lexicographers admit that combinations frequently contribute only a phonetic value. But I find it incredible that any such minute subdivision of the idea could have ever existed alone as abstract sound without the concrete character. It contradicts the law of evolution. Complex ideas arise only gradually, as the power of holding them arises. The paucity of Chinese sound could not so hold them."[26]

Another frequently registered complaint against Xu is that he tends to allow himself too much liberty in explaining the structure of a character. He is found to have committed anachronistic errors of various kinds. As he grounds his explanations on the relatively late Small Seal Script rather than the oldest available scripts, he is particularly prone to misinterpret the pictogrammic and ideogrammic clues of a character. Indeed, by checking his explanations against the older bronze and oracle inscriptions, Qing and twentieth-century scholars have found numerous errors and inaccuracies. Xu commits the worst kind of anachronistic error when he seeks to explain a character in light of the sociopolitical and cosmological concerns of his own time. The most notorious example of such an error is none other than his explanation of "*yi*" (one), the very first character of the dictionary. Although this single horizontal stroke is self-evidently an ideogram indicating the simple idea of "one," he goes to great lengths to explain it in terms of the cosmological principle of Oneness.[27] Another example is his explanation of the character *wang* 王 (king, kingship), an exalted term in the Han Confucian cosmology espoused by Dong Zhongshu 董仲舒. Adopting Dong's gloss, Xu writes, "Dong Zhongshu says, 'The ancient inventors of characters wrote three [horizontal] strokes and linked them in the middle by a [vertical] stroke, and they called this character "*wang*." The three strokes are heaven, earth, man. That which participates in and reaches through the three is *wang* (king)'" 董仲舒曰。古之造文者。三畫而連其中謂之王.[28] These errors of Xu make us think of the error made by Fenollosa when glossing "*xin*" 信. To explain the combination of 亻 and 言 in this character, Fenollosa finds it handy to use the English idiom "to stand by": "Man and word, man standing by his word, man of his word, truth, sincere, unwavering."[29] Cavalier as it may seem to the Chinese, this gloss is not substantially worse a transgression than Xu's gloss of "*yi*." This being the case, we should perhaps forgive Fenollosa's transgressions as leniently as we would Xu's. After all, Fenollosa is concerned with, as he himself declares, "not linguistics, but poetics."

All in all, Fenollosa has displayed a greater willingness than Xu, his ultimate master, in ignoring phonetic elements and indulging in fanciful ideogrammic explanations. However, this may very well be the result of the influence of Xu's radical successors on Fenollosa through his Japanese teacher. In his essay, Fenollosa himself intimates a close connection between China's Song Dynasty with the Japanese school of Chinese studies headed by his teacher Kainan Mori. This has led to the speculation that this Japanese school is "developed from China in the Song Dynasty when Wang Anshi's *Zishuo* dominated."[30] *Zishuo* 字 說 (Discourse on Characters), an influential, now lost work on characters by the prominent Song politician and poet Wang Anshi 王安石 (1021–1086), is best known and often ridiculed for its unabashed disregard of phonetic values and for its far-fetched ideographic explanations. Leaving to literary historians the questions of whether and how Wang's ideas might have influenced Kainan Mori and, indirectly, Fenollosa, we can say that Fenollosa's ideogrammic analysis does display a buoyant, imaginary quality characteristic of Wang's approach, even though Fenollosa's errors often seem less glaring than Wang's.

A recognition of Wang's possible influence may also help us identify the sources of Fenollosa's notion of the "verbal ideal of action" in characters. Although characters had long been seen by calligraphers as an embodiment of nature's dynamic force, Wang Anshi was probably the first lexicographer to explicitly trace the structural principles of characters to dynamic configurations of nature.[31] In his "Memorial on the Submission of *Discourse on Characters*" ("Jin *Zishuo* biao" 進字說表, Wang writes, "While characters were made by man, in their origin they came from nature. Phoenixes and birds have patterns, and the Chart from the River have diagrams. These were not created by man; man merely imitated them. Thus, such positions as above and below, within and without, beginning and end, front and back, center and side, left and right, are all the positionings of nature" 字雖人之所制，本實出 於自然。鳳鳥有文，河圖有書，非人為也，人則效此。故上下內 外，初終前後，中偏左右，自然之位也.[32] Echoes of these remarks can be clearly heard in Fenollosa's essay. Indeed, Fenollosa's remarks about the dynamics of Chinese characters—"the meeting points, of actions, cross-actions cut through actions, snapshots"[33]—seem to be an elucidation of Wang's remarks on the dynamic spatial figuring of characters.

Having examined Fenollosa's indebtedness to traditional Chinese *wenzixue,* we may argue that his essay constitutes a unique offshoot of traditional Chinese scholarship on the written character, marked by its doubly cross-cultural character—a creative English representation of traditional Chinese scholarship transmitted and interpreted by Japanese scholars.

THE EVOCATION OF DYNAMIC FORCE
IN THE POETIC USE OF CHINESE WRITTEN CHARACTERS

Since Fenollosa makes it clear that he is interested in "not linguistics, but poetics," it is incumbent upon us to go beyond the criticism of his linguistic fallacies and assess the value of his essay in terms of its critical perceptiveness. Fenollosa's anatomy of Chinese characters is intended mainly to demonstrate a feature unseen in any other living written languages—their ability to preserve and augment the dynamic force latent in their etymological roots. In winding up his ideogrammic analysis of Chinese characters, Fenollosa writes,

> In this Chinese shows its advantage. Its etymology is constantly visible. It retains the creative impulse and process, visible and at work.[34]

If understood with reference to the ordinary process of writing or reading Chinese, these remarks would prove to be erroneous. The Chinese respond to their modern printed characters as abstract linguistic signs in basically the same way as Westerners do their noncharacter equivalents in any Western language. Seldom do the Chinese pause to think about etymological components of a character, and still less do they contemplate the "creative impulses and process" embedded in the structure of a character in the normal course of writing or reading.

However, if we revisit traditional Chinese critics' remarks on both the poetic and calligraphic use of characters, we will find that Fenollosa's remarks are not at all off the mark. On the contrary, in stressing ideogrammic configurations as a source of visual appeal, dynamic force, and poetic inspiration, Fenollosa has come amazingly close to traditional Chinese critics.

First, let us examine what Liu Xie has said about the noncalligraphic use of characters in belletristic writing. Although the standardization of Chinese characters in Qin and Han times led to a substantial loss of their pictorial appeal, Chinese scholars continued for a long time to see an aesthetic value in the structure of characters for belletristic writing. In "The Choice of Written Characters" ("Lianzi" 煉字), a largely neglected chapter of *Literary Mind*, Liu Xie gives an eloquent expression to this view of characters. He begins by sketching the entire history of characters since its invention by Cang Jie 倉頡. Judging by the myths, legends, anecdotes, and historical events chosen for this historical sketch, Liu obviously aims to emphasize two points. The first is that written characters have been used with great reverence throughout Chinese history. The second is that written characters have been valued for different reasons over time—primarily for their magico-religious power in remote antiquity, for their ritualistic usefulness in Zhou times, for their functions to regulate sociopolitical realities in Qin and Han times, and for their aesthetic effects in his own time (*WXDL* 39 / 1–85). In view of this luminous history of characters, Liu goes on to stress their importance to belletristic writing:

> The mind sends off its sound in speech; speech assumes its form in written characters. In chanting, our accomplishment lies in [the use of] *gong* and *shang* (tones). In writing, we attribute what we have accomplished to the shapes of characters. (*WXDL* 39 / 89–93)

心既託聲於言，言亦寄形於字，諷誦則績在宮商，臨文則能歸字形矣。

In tracing from the heart's intent to speech and to written characters, Liu does not perceive, as Plato would, a process of degeneration or adulteration from an original entity. Instead he discerns a process of an incipient condition reaching ever fuller actualization. What lies in the heart registers a measure of actualization when it is sent off in words, and reaches fuller actualization when verbalization in turn "assumes its form to written characters."[35] Given this primary importance of characters, Liu finds it necessary to lay down four strict rules to prevent their misuse:

> The first is to avoid odd and strange characters. The second is to use sparingly characters with the same radicals. The third is to weigh carefully the repeated use of the same character. The fourth is to balance the use of simple and complex characters. (*WXDL* 39 / 96–99)

一避詭異，二省聯邊，三權重出，四調單複。

As we go through Liu's ensuing explanation of these four rules (*WXDL* 39 / 100– 136), it is not difficult to see that he is concerned with mainly graphic configurations of characters, not their semantic meanings as misconstrued by some critics. Like Fenollosa, he is interested in maximizing the visual appeal of characters. Moreover, like Fenollosa, he emphasizes visual appeal not for its own sake, but for the purpose of evoking dynamic force in a literary work. "If both sounds and the patterning of characters are luminous and spirited, / The patterns of ink will dance with great vigor" 聲書昭精，墨采騰奮 (*WXDL* 39 / 175–176), writes Liu in the concluding verse for the chapter.[36]

Unlike Fenollosa, Liu does not regard the structure of characters as a meaningful source of poetic inspiration. However, he does acknowledge that some cultured men of his time composed riddles (*miyu* 謎語) by "observing and analyzing the structure of characters" 體目文字 (*WXDL* 15 / 102). Tracing the origins of such riddles, Liu notes that, "after the time of Wei-Jin, people disliked jokers and jesters. Cultured men transformed the 'enigmas' into riddles" 自魏晉以來，頗非俳優，而君子嘲謔，化為謎語 (*WXDL* 15 / 95–98). Liu seems to have a mixed opinion about riddles. While he speaks favorably of those who used riddles effectively in sociopolitical satire (*WXDL* 15 / 106–110), he ridicules those who employed them merely to "show refinement and cleverness in the manipulation of thoughts" 巧以弄思 (*WXDL* 15 / 104).[37] "While cunning and clever," Liu continues, "they miss the important point. When we reexamine the enigmas of the ancients, we find that they are perfectly logical and concerned with what is important. When did the ancients indulge in the childish burlesques, aiming at thigh-slapping merriment?" 雖有小巧，用乖遠大。觀夫古之為隱，理周要務，豈為童稚之戲謔，搏髀而笑哉! (*WXDL* 15 / 114–120).[38] Although it is praised for its satirical function by critics like Liu Xie, the genre of ideogram-based riddles cannot outgrow its tarnished reputation as a shallow form of entertainment employed by jesters.[39] Influenced by this uncomplimentary view of the genre, traditional Chinese poets certainly would not think of ideogrammic structures as a medium of serious poetic expression. Interestingly, it was not until Fenollosa and Pound's ideas were recycled back into China that Chinese poets began to seriously look into ideogrammic structures as a credible source of poetic inspiration.[40]

THE EVOCATION OF DYNAMIC FORCE IN THE CALLIGRAPHIC WRITING OF CHINESE WRITTEN CHARACTERS

If interpreted in the context of the historical development of Chinese calligraphy, Fenollosa's remarks on the dynamic force of characters would strike us as even more perceptive. In many ways, Liu Xie's discussion of characters is an isolated phenomenon in Chinese poetics. After him, few literary critics would consider the exploitation of ideogrammic structures to be important or even relevant to the writing of a poetic or prose composition. The subject of written characters simply disappears in the major critical writings after Liu Xie. How shall we explain the disappearance of this subject from literary criticism? It may be easily construed to have resulted from a degeneration of characters from "shorthand pictures of actions and processes"[41] into abstract, lifeless signs. Those familiar with Chinese artistic traditions, however, would rather consider it the result of an elevation of characters through the rise of calligraphy. In developing calligraphy as a dignified form of art that rivals poetry, Chinese calligraphers and calligraphy critics have in effect taken over from their literary counterparts the business of preserving, codifying, and augmenting the dynamic force of written characters. This business would remain largely the monopoly of calligraphers and calligraphy critics until the movement to integrate poetry, painting, and calligraphy in Yuan times.[42]

To Chinese calligraphers, the evocation of dynamic force is an aesthetic ideal that can be traced in the ancient seal scripts. From early times to the present day, ancient seal script has never ceased to be admired, practiced, and perfected by Chinese calligraphers and art connoisseurs. "A Song for the Stone Drum" ("Shi gu ge" 石鼓歌), a poem written by Han Yu 韓愈 (768–824) to praise the inscriptions on a Zhou stone drum (see figure 5), is testimony to how Chinese calligraphers looked on the ancient seal script as the perfect model for evoking the dynamic force of nature:

How can time not leave these characters with missing strokes?	年深豈免有缺畫，
But they still look like sharp daggers that pierce live crocodiles,	快劍斬斷生蛟鼉。
Like phoenix mates dancing, like angels hovering down,	鸞翔鳳翥眾仙下，
Like trees of jade and coral with interlocking branches,	珊瑚碧樹交枝柯。
Like golden cord and iron chain tied together tight,	金繩鐵索鎖鈕壯，
Like incense-tripods flung in the sea, like dragons mounting heaven.[43]	古鼎躍水龍騰梭。

Here, Han Yu praises the ancient seal script for the same reason Fenollosa does the Chinese character in general—its powerful evocation of natural force. Like Fenollosa, Han Yu discusses the inner dynamics of characters in terms of both the release and equilibrium of natural force.

Figure 5. Part of the Stone Drum Inscription, based on a rubbing from the Ming Dynasty. Reproduced from Gao Ming 高明. *Zhong-guo gu wenzixue tonglun* 中國古文字學通論 (A Comprehensive Survey of the Studies on Chinese Ancient Characters)(Beijing: Beijing Univ. Press, 1996), p. 20.

He envisions some character strokes as "things in motion" and praises them with phrases such as "like sharp daggers that pierce live crocodiles," "like phoenix mates dancing," "like angels hovering down," and "like dragons mounting heaven." He conceives other strokes as "motions in things" and likens them to "trees of jade and coral with interlocking branches" and "golden cord and iron chain tied together tight." If in ancient seal script we see the preservation of dynamic force praised by Fenollosa, we witness in later calligraphic styles an amelioration of dynamic force into dynamic beauty as suggested by the following remarks by Fenollosa:

> Thus a word, instead of growing gradually poorer and poorer as with us, becomes richer and still more rich from age to age, almost consciously luminous.[44]

As writing instruments and materials changed from cutters and hard objects to brushes and silk or paper, there emerged four new calligraphic styles in Han and Wei-Jin times (see figure 6): clerical style (*lishu* 隸 書), regular style (*kaishu* 楷書), running style (*xingshu* 行書), and cursive style (*caoshu* 草書).[45] These four calligraphic styles are capable of expressing an increasingly wider range of dynamic movements.[46]

Of these four styles, the first two are valued for their nuanced expressions of movement within the contour of a character, the other two are particularly favored by the literati for their unbridled tour de force from character to character and line to line.[47] Indeed, the running style and cursive style have opened up great possibilities for diversifying the breadth of strokes, altering the balance among different radicals within a character, adjusting space among different characters, varying the size of characters, controlling the force and speed of the brush, and changing the modes of direction for a column of characters or for an entire piece (see figures 7 and 8). In these two styles, the cursive in particular, the movement of the brush breaks through the confine of the outline of a single character, and therefore does not merely evoke the force released by or latent in a single object or a cluster of objects. As an abstract rhythm of art, it aims at revealing the Dao, the ultimate cosmic principle, which generates and sustains all forces in nature. This leap from a manifestation of local force to an evocation of the cosmic principle marks the process of Chinese characters becoming, in the words of Fenollosa, "richer and still more rich from age to age, almost consciously luminous" in the realm of calligraphy.[48]

	MAN	SEE	HORSE
Clerical Style	人	見	馬
Regular Style	人	見	馬
Running Style	人	見	馬
Cursive Style	人	見	馬

Figure 6.

Note: Examples of these four calligraphic styles are reproduced from *Lidai shufa zihui* 歷代書法字彙 (Dictionary of Chinese Calligraphic Styles in Successive Dynasties), ed. Datong shuju (Taipei: Datong shuju, 1981).

SHI (DYNAMIC FORCE) IN TRADITIONAL CHINESE CALLIGRAPHY CRITICISM

Shi 勢 (dynamic force) has been the center of reference in Chinese calligraphy criticism from its very beginning.[49] A description of the conscious evocation of dynamic force in calligraphy dates back to, at least, sometime around 200 B.C. Li Si is believed to be the first to set forth a method of dynamic brushwork and liken such brushwork to various displays of dynamic force in nature:

> The right method in the use of the brush is to give it a quick turn first and then bring it down swiftly like the flight of a hawk or a roc. Let it proceed naturally and do not work it over. The advance of the brush is as free as a swimming fish in water, and the swing of it, as rising clouds over a great mountain. Rolling and stretching, now light and now heavy. By deep contemplation on these essentials the truth of its own accord will be revealed.

> 夫用筆之法，先急回，後疾下，鷹望鵬逝，信之自然，不得重改；送腳如游魚得水，舞筆如景山與雲，或卷或舒，乍輕乍重。善深思之，此理可見矣。[50]

These remarks attributed to Li Si help set the direction for the development of Chinese calligraphy as an art of dynamic brushwork, and herald the rise of *shi* as an issue of overriding importance in calligraphy criticism. Cai Yong 蔡邕 (132–192) is said to have written, among other works on calligraphy, the "Nine Momentums" ("Jiushi"

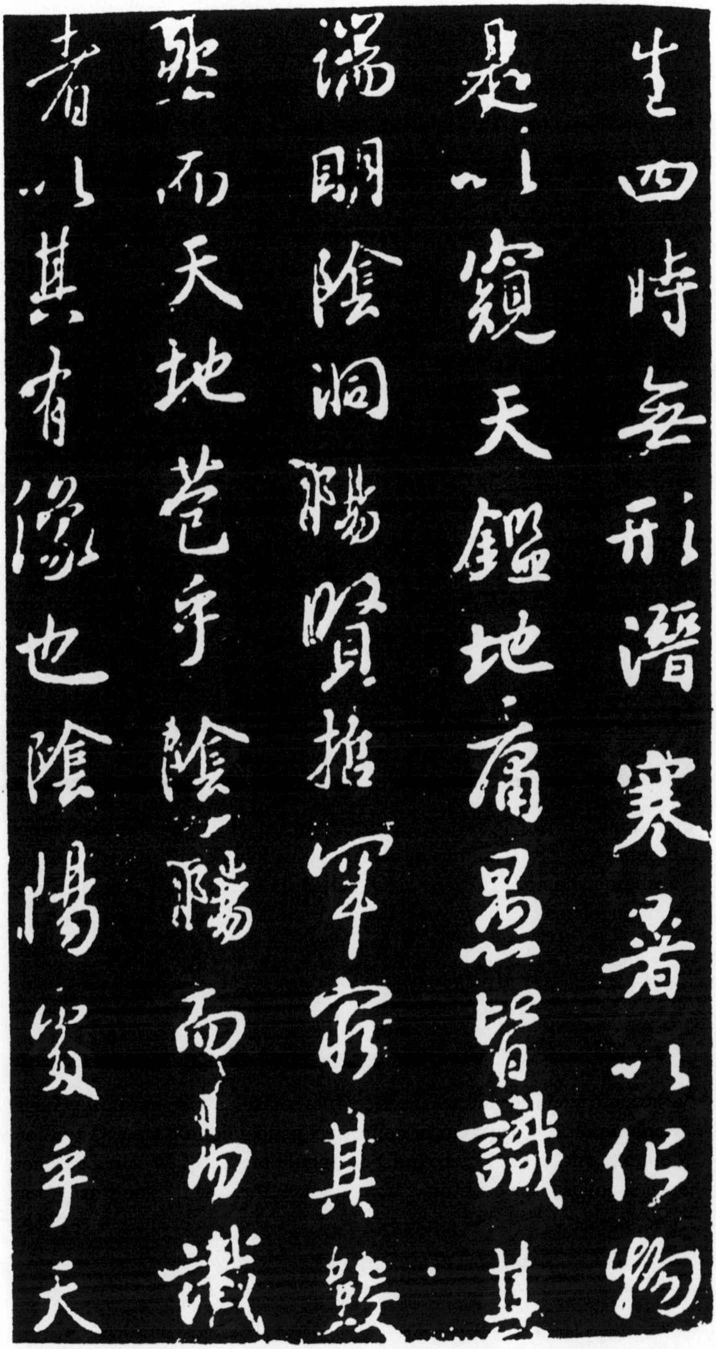

生四時無形潛寒暑以化物

是以窺天鑑地，庸愚皆識其

端；明陰洞陽，賢哲罕窮其數。

聚而天地苞乎陰陽而易識

者以其有像也。陰陽處乎天

Figure 7. Running Style. Preface to the *Sacred Teaching of Monk Sanzang of the Tang Dynasty*. Rubbing of an inscription in running style. Reproduced from Frederick W. Mote and Hung-lam Chu, eds., "Calligraphy and the East Asian Book," *The Gest Library Journal* 2, no. 2, special catalogue issue (1988): 33.

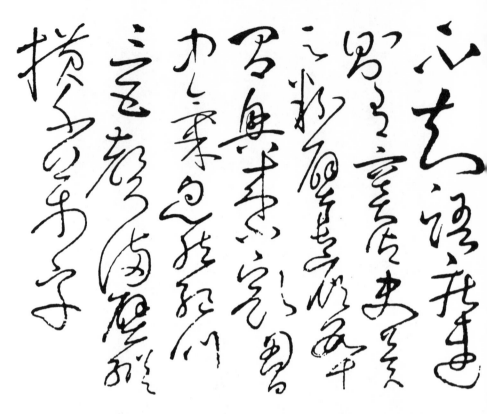

Figure 8. Cursive Style. Part of an autobiography by Huai Su 懷素, a Buddhist monk and a great Tang calligrapher known for his energized cursive style or "crazy cursive" *(kuangcao* 狂草*)*. Reproduced from Chiang Yee, *Chinese Calligraphy: An Introduction to Its Aesthetic and Technique* (Cambridge: Harvard Univ. Press, 1966), p. 34.

九勢), a treatise devoted to the discussion of *shi*. His daughter Cai Yan 蔡琰 (ca. 178–?) gives an account of his description of *shi* in the treatise:

As calligraphy arises naturally and establishes itself, yin and yang forces are generated. When yin and yang are generated, there emerge concrete forms with their latent force (*shi*). [When writing,] hide the beginning, protect the end, and concentrate your strength on the inside of characters. If you launch your brush with strength, you will bring forth the beauty of sinews and flesh. Therefore it is said: "when the momentum (*shi*) arrives, it cannot be stopped; when the momentum (*shi*) departs, it cannot be arrested. But if the brushwork is feeble, the strange and the abnormal will be produced.[51]

書肇於自然既立，陰陽生焉。陰陽既生，形勢出矣。藏頭
護尾，力在字中，下筆用力，肌膚之麗。故曰，勢來不可
止，勢去不可遏。惟筆軟則奇怪生焉。

Influenced by such early notions of *shi,* traditional Chinese calligraphy critics conceive of calligraphic writing as an act that evokes and trans-mits dynamic forces of nature. Whether they discuss the dynamics of individual strokes or the momentum of an entire piece, the movement of the brush or the process of the mind, they usually approach their subjects and make their critical comments from the perspective of the effectiveness of *shi.* In laying down rules and laws on any aspect of Chinese calligraphy, they set their eye on the attainment of *shi* and, wherever they can, correlate this calligraphic *shi* with concrete forces of nature.

Lady Wei Shuo 衛鑠 (272–349), third in descent from Cai Yong in the lineage of famous Chinese calligraphers, correlates individual strokes with concrete forces of nature:

[一], is like a line of clouds *stretching* a thousand miles, not distinct but having form;	一 如千里陣云， 隱隱然， 其實有形，
[、], like a rock *falling* from a high peak, *bounding* but about to crumble.	、 如高峰墜石， 磕磕然， 實如崩也；
[／], is *clean-cut* like [the horn of] a rhinoceros and [the tusk of] an elephant;	／ 陸斷犀象；
[＼] a *shot* from a *crossbow* one hundred *jun* in strength.	＼ 百鈞弩發；
[丨], an *old vine* ten thousand years of age.	丨 萬歲枯藤；
[～], *breaking waves* and rumbling thunder.	一 崩浪雷奔；
[乛], sinews and joints of a strong crossbow.[52]	乛 勁弩筋節

For his part, Chen Si 陳思 (Song Dynasty) codifies the inner dynamics of eight basic strokes contained in the character *yong* 永, and establishes his "Eight Laws of the Character *Yong*" (*Yong zi ba fa* 永字八法):

> The first stroke [`], a spot, is *ce* 側; the second [⌐], horizontal, is *le* 勒; the third [⺅], vertical, is *nu* 努, the fourth [⺅], up-stroke, is *ti* 趯; the fifth [⺅], left above, is *ce* 策; the sixth [⺅], left below, is *lue* 掠; the seventh [⺅], right above, is *zhuo* 啄; the eighth [永], right below, is *zhe* 磔.[53]

Turning to the issue of how to combine strokes into a character, Li Chun 李淳 (Ming Dynasty) establishes his "Eighty-four Laws" as he lists as many ways to achieve within a character an equilibrium of multifarious forces inherent in individual strokes. To impart a dynamic life to a character, Chinese calligraphers do not merely tap the "motion in things" codified in individual strokes. They also seek to model the overall shape of a character on the dynamic movement of a concrete thing. "When one wants to construct the shape of a character," writes Cai Yong, "one must model it on a concrete thing. It can be like the shape of a bird, or like a worm that is eating grains, or like mountains or trees" 凡欲結構字體，皆須象其一物，若鳥之形，若蟲食禾，若山若樹.[54] True to these remarks by Cai, the Yuan calligrapher Zhao Zi'ang 趙子昂 observed and sketched different figures of a mouse (𠄏 𠄏 𠄏 𠄏) so as to transform the character 為 into a living image of dynamic movement.[55]

Chinese calligraphy critics not only consistently correlate individual strokes and characters with powerful images of nature, but also conceptualize all other aspects of calligraphy in terms of *shi* or the play of dynamic force. To grasp this paramount importance of *shi,* let us examine Wang Xizhi's 王羲之 (ca. 321–ca. 379) comments on Lady Wei's "The Diagram of the Battle Array of the Brush":

> Paper is battle ground; brush is sword and shield; ink is armor; inkstone is a city wall and a moat; the heart's intent is the general; technical skills are lower-ranking generals; and structure is the strategy. Lifting the brush heralds life or death; moving the brush executes a military order; and whatever comes under the brush is killed![56]

> 夫紙者，陣也；筆者，刀稍也；墨者，鍪甲也；水硯者，城池也；心意者，將軍也；本領者，副將也；結構者，謀略也；颺筆者，吉凶也；出入者。號令也；屈折者，殺戮也。

This elaborate analogy of calligraphy with a military battle sets forth before our eyes the convergence of varied dynamic forces—the positioning of paper, the movement of brush, the flow of ink, the process of the mind, the structuring of characters and lines—in a spontaneous moment of executing a piece of calligraphy. This analogy drives home not only the paramount importance of *shi* in all aspects of Chinese calligraphy, but also the indivisibility of *shi* in terms of subject and object. The equilibrium of *shi* is found in paper and ink as much as in the meditative mind of the calligrapher. The release of *shi* propels the movement of the brush as much as the creative process of the calligrapher. This passage is a perfect example to show how Chinese calligraphy critics consider *shi* the cardinal principle governing all aspects of Chinese calligraphy.

THE FENOLLOSA ESSAY AND THE
POUNDIAN THEORY OF KINETIC IMAGE

The greatest importance of Fenollosa's essay lies in the role it has played in the reinvention of modern Western poetry, a role achieved through the editing and publication of the essay by Ezra Pound. The discovery of dynamic force in the Chinese character was truly a revelation to Pound, as it "seemed to confirm and to justify his theories of the poetic Image."[57] Prior to this discovery, Pound had already been searching for ways to reinvent modern poetry by energizing the phanopoetic tradition in Western poetry. The absence of dynamic force was what he saw as the essential deficiency of Western pictorialism from the Alexandrian figure-poems attributed to Simmias of Rhodes (ca. 300 B.C.), from George Herbert's wings to the mouse-tail in *Alice's Adventures in Wonderland*. It is his recognition of this deficiency that led him to depart from the early Three-Point Imagist Tenets and to develop a theory of kinetic Image in the light of Vorticist aesthetics.[58] "The image is not an idea," he declares. 'It is a radiant node or cluster; it is what I can, and must perforce, call a Vortex, from which and through which, and into which, ideas are constantly rushing."[59]

To reformulate the Imagist poetics, Pound not only draws from Vorticist aesthetics but also develops a "super-position" method modeled on Japanese haiku.[60] To understand how Japanese haiku helps him to create a kinetic Image that measures up to his aesthetic ideal, we need only read his account of the long compositional history of "In a Station of the Metro":

Three years ago in Paris I got out of a 'metro' train at La Concorde, and saw suddenly a beautiful face and another and another . . . and I tried all that day for words for what that had meant for me . . . And that evening . . . I found suddenly the expression . . . Not in speech but in sudden splotches of colour . . . but it was a word, the beginning for me of a new language in colour . . .

I wrote a thirty-line poem and destroyed it because it was what we call work of the second intensity. Six months later I made a poem half that length; a year later I made the following hokku-like sentence.

> The apparition of these faces in a crowd;
> Petals on a wet, black bough.

. . . In a poem of this sort, one is trying to record the precise instant when a thing outward and objective transforms itself, or darts into a thing inward and subjective.[61]

A less known source of inspiration for Pound's reinvention of Imagist poetics is Chinese art and poetry. In his recent study of Pound, Zhao-ming Qian ably documents how Pound came into contact with the Chinese traditions through his association with a number of prominent Orientalists.[62] By Qian's account, Pound was first introduced to Chinese art by Laurence Binyon (1869–1908), an English poet and the assistant keeper for the collection of Far Eastern paintings and prints at the British Museum. During his early London years, Pound and his bride-to-be, Dorothy Shakespear, frequently visited the British Museum, where she would draw pictures after Chinese models while he would view various artworks, probably including those in the 1910–1912 Exhibition of Chinese and Japanese Art organized by Binyon. In all likelihood Pound attended Binyon's lectures on "Oriental & European Art" in 1909 and read his *The Flight of the Dragon: An Essay on the Theory and Practice of Art in China and Japan Based on Original Sources*, published in 1911. At any rate, until 1914 Pound "regularly lunched in Binyon's group at the Vienna Café near the British Museum . . . [and] would have many chances to listen to the English champion of Oriental art dilate on his favorite subjects."[63]

If Binyon was Pound's primary teacher of Chinese art, then Allen Upward (1863–1926) was Pound's mentor on Chinese poetry. When Pound was introduced to Upward in London in 1911, Upward "had already made a name for himself as a poet and a writer of original thought."[64] Although Upward's admiration for Confucius may have inspired Pound's lifelong interest in Confucianism, his enduring influence on Pound was in the area of Chinese poetry. This influence may be attributed to two important events. The first was the publication of Upward's "Scented Leaves from a Chinese Jar," a sequence of poems based on Chinese works, in the journal *Poetry* in September 1913. In these poems, Pound found what had earlier fascinated him in Japanese haiku—sharp, contrasting colors and the evocative juxtaposition of emotions and images. On 17 September 1913, the day he received the *Poetry* and read Upward's poems, Pound wrote to Dorothy, "The chinese things in 'Poetry' are worth the price of admission."[65] In view of Pound's enthusiastic responses, one might agree with K. L. Goodwin that those poems of Upward are the "earliest poems claimed by Pound as 'imagistic'."[66] At any rate, Pound did set out to compose 'imagistic' poems in the Upwardian fashion—that is, to make them up "out of his head, using a certain amount of Chinese reminiscence" as told by Upward himself.[67] For instance, in "A Song of Degrees," published in the November issue of the *Poetry,* Pound seeks to evoke the power of Chinese colors: "Rest me with Chinese colours, / For I think the glass is evil."[68] The second event was Upward's initiation of Pound into the study of Herbert Allen Giles' *A History of Chinese Literature* (1901). This event took place when Pound went to visit Upward immediately after his first meeting with the widow of Fenollosa on 29 September 1913. The purpose of Pound's visit was, in part at least, to prepare for the discussion of Fenollosa's manuscripts on Chinese poetry at the next meeting with Mrs. Fenollosa. Indeed, Pound was to have read through many chapters of Giles' book by the time of the second meeting and be ready for an intelligent discussion of Fenollosa's work on Chinese poetry. The reading of Giles' *History* proved extremely beneficial to Pound. From the book he derived a general knowledge of Chinese literary history, which was indispensable to his efforts to convince Mrs. Fenollosa of his capability to edit her husband's works. More importantly, he found many elements crucial to his revitalization of Imagist poetry. In the poems of Qu Yuan 屈原 (ca. 340 B.C.–ca. 278 B.C.), the first great Chinese literatus-poet, he saw what he would like the Imagist poetry to achieve: a free adaptation of meter to sense, a blending of the real and mythical, and a perfect balance between nature images and emotions. In the poems of Liu Che 劉徹 (r. 106 B.C.–86 B.C.), Emperor Wu of the Former Han Dynasty, Pound noticed the picturesque or painterly use of verbs to suggest emotions. "In the Chinese models provided by Giles (notably Qu Yuan and Liu Che)," Zhao Ming Qian observes, "Pound found an art more objective than the Greek, more suggestive than the Provençal, more precise than the modern French, and more brilliant and resourceful than the medieval Japanese. To illustrate his Imagist theories now, he would have to include, among other things, the Chinese voice."[69]

This Chinese voice Pound does include and, in fact, accentuate in *Des Imagistes,* the first anthology of Imagist poetry he compiled in October 1913. In addition to Upward's "Scented Leaves from a Chinese Jar," Pound includes four poems composed by himself on Chinese models—"After Ch'u Yuan (Qu Yuan)," "Liu Ch'e" (Liu Che), "The Fan-Piece, for her Imperial Lord," and "Ts'ai Ch'ih." Pound's newfound enthusiasm for Chinese poetry seems to have even superseded his longstanding fondness of Greek poetry, as he wrote only two poems on Greek models for the anthology. In any case, by foregrounding Chinese models in the first Imagist anthology, as Qian remarks, "Pound had actually pointed out to the Imagist movement a new direction and a new possibility—the possibility of drawing on the robust Imagistic traditions of the Chinese."[70]

The "robust" or kinetic Image of Chinese poetry plays a key role in Pound's transition from old Imagist to new Vorticist notion of Image. If Pound had long ago noted the dynamic linear rhythms in Chinese paintings during his visits to the British museum, and if he had subsequently observed the dynamic interplay of images and emotions in the Chinese poems discussed in Giles' book, he was to find even more compelling evidence of kinetic Image in Fenollosa's notebooks on Chinese poetry. In late 1919 Mrs. Fenollosa transferred to Pound the bulk of her late husband's records and manuscripts: "eight notebooks in all [on Chinese poetry], plus the volumes of notes on *Noh* drama, plus the books in which he was drafting his lectures on Chinese poetics, plus a sheaf of loose sheets."[71] As far as Chinese materials are concerned, they come in two large parts: those on poetry and those on poetics. Each of these two parts was an important source of inspiration for Pound's endeavor to make Imagist poetry more intense and dynamic. Working through Fenollosa's notebooks on poetry, Pound selected and translated many poems out of a corpus of 150 or so. His *ver-libre* translations of these poems were put together as an anthology entitled *Cathay.* In rendering these poems, Pound displays a remarkable, uncanny capability to grasp the spirit of the original and successfully reveal the "dynamic force of the universe"[72] embodied therein. For instance, when he translated the poems by Li Bo 李白 (701–762) or "Rihaku" (Japanese transliteration of his name used in Fenollosa's notebook), regarded by some as the greatest Chinese poet, Pound "was able to go beneath Fenollosa's fragmented gloss to 'a radiant node or cluster' in the original poetry," and indeed his rendition usually "captures for us both Li Bo's visual imagination and his poetic energy."[73] By tapping the kinetic Image in Chinese poetry, Pound succeeds in translating into reality his Vorticist notion of "a radiant node or cluster." Apparently, his Vorticist ideas guide him to discover and appreciate kinetic Images in Chinese poems. Conversely, his reevocation of kinetic Chinese Images in his translation enables him to demonstrate the power and effects of his Vorticist poetics. Pound himself seemed keenly aware of the compatible and mutually enhancing influences exerted on him by Chinese kinetic Images and Vorticism. "Pound himself saw the compatibility of the two influences," Dasenbrock notes, "and in the period of Vorticism he constantly drew parallels between his two sources of inspiration."[74]

Of Fenollosa's writings on Chinese poetics, the essay "The Chinese Written Character as a Medium for Poetry" most attracts Pound's attention. Pound was undoubtedly captivated by numerous parallels between Fenollosa's views of the Chinese written character and his maturing Imagist-Vorticist ideals. Fenollosa's depiction of pictorial "operations of nature" in simple ideogram must have reminded him of the dynamic painterly qualities of Chinese poems, especially the use of "picturesque," animating verbs seen in Liu Che's and Li Bo's poems. Fenollosa's analysis of the "compounding process" in the making of compound ideograms must have struck him as identical to the powerful juxtaposition of images and emotions in Qu Yuan. Moreover, Fenollosa's remark that ideograms call forth real things as "the meeting points, of actions, cross-actions cut through actions, snapshots" must have made him think of his own definition of a Vorticist Image: "It is a radiant node or cluster; . . . from which and through which, and into which, ideas are constantly rushing." Since what Fenollosa had said about the written character so neatly corresponds with what he discovered in the Chinese poems and wished to re-create in his own works, it is only too natural that he would assiduously edit Fenollosa's essay and publish it as a kind of manifesto for the Imagist-Vorticist movement.

To Pound, the essay most eloquently articulated the revolutionary principles of modernist poetry he himself wished to establish. Although Pound had already formed his Imagist-Vorticist ideals before he read Fenollosa's essay, he sincerely and enthusiastically praised the essay as "a study of the fundamentals of all aesthetics" and credited Fenollosa with ushering in "many modes of thought since fruitful in 'new' Western painting and poetry."[75] Yielding the honor of a movement founder to Fenollosa, Pound writes, "He [Fenollosa] was a forerunner without knowing it and without being known as such. . . . The vitality of his outlook can be judged from the fact although this essay was written some time before his death in 1908 I have not had to change the allusions to Western conditions. The later movements in art have corroborated his theories."[76] For Pound, the visual manifestation of dynamic force in the Chinese character is undreamt-of evidence attesting to not only the historical precedence but also to the universal relevance of his own theory. By editing and publishing Fenollosa's essay, Pound seeks to show that the kinetic Image is not just what he thinks poetry should be, but actually what poetry originally was many millennia before. As Fenollosa's essay is written largely from the point of view of reception, it would be an ideal complement to his earlier discussions of dynamic force from the angle of poetic creation. So, his publication of Fenollosa's essay may be seen as a self-conscious effort to round out his own aesthetics of dynamic force.

WRITTEN LANGUAGE, COSMOLOGY, AND AESTHETIC IDEALS

The conception of written language, a locus where Fenollosan-Poundian and Chinese aesthetics of dynamic force cross paths, is also a place where we can trace the fundamental difference between them. To distinguish the cultural specificity of these two aesthetic theories, we will do well to consider how they each arise from a distinctive concept of written language and follow a course of development largely predetermined by that concept.

It is important to note at the outset that Fenollosa and Pound themselves are aware of the fundamental difference between the dynamic force they see in Chinese characters and the dynamic force they seek to evoke in their own poetry. In observing the dynamic force in Chinese characters, they stress that it was *natural* rather than *subjective* force. "In reading Chinese, we do not seem to be juggling with mental counters, but to be watching *things* work out their own fate."[77] Moreover, they note that Chinese characters reveal not only the dynamic force of individual phenomena but, more importantly, "the whole harmonious framework of nature."[78] However, once they begin to relate those discoveries to their own tradition, they immediately introduce the concept of metaphor and reinterpret their discoveries within the dualistic paradigm of the seen and unseen, signifier and signified, and object and subject:

Yet the Chinese language with its peculiar materials has passed over from the seen to the unseen by exactly the same process which all ancient races employed. This process is metaphor, the use of material images to suggest immaterial relations.[79]

Here Fenollosa and Pound seem to reinvent the Chinese written language in a way reminiscent of "the Renaissance emblematists' understanding of Egyptian hieroglyphs as images used by Egyptian priests to foreshadow divine ideas."[80] For them, the "immaterial relations" are neither monistic God nor the Dao, the ultimate cosmic process operating through the Chinese artists as well as their works. Rather, the "immaterial relations" are "our forgotten mental processes."[81] By "our forgotten mental processes," Fenollosa and Pound refer to the ways prehistoric people unconsciously communed with the divine forces inhabiting natural images. If more than a century earlier Schiller lamented man's irrevocable loss of his original contact with the divine, Pound still strives to reintuit polytheistic gods abiding within or behind the dynamic force of poetic Image. Thanks to this "metaphorization" of the dynamic force in Chinese characters, Pound can not only bring Fenollosa's essay in line with the theories of primitive languages developed since the eighteenth century but also sanction the new path of his own visionary quest.

The Fenollosan-Poundian aesthetics of dynamic force is deeply rooted in the mimetic concept of written language, even though it represents a radical attempt to break away from it. In the West, written language is generally considered to be only a *representation* of speech, which is in turn a *representation* of the Logos or the absolute subject. This "twofold" mimetic view of written language not only dominates avowedly mimetic theories from Plato and Aristotle to the neoclassicists, but also inscribes all Romantic and post-Romantic attempts to demolish it. To counter neoclassical diction, Wordsworth advocates the use of low and rustic speech because he believes "such a language, arising out of repeated experience and regular feelings, is a more permanent, and a far more philosophical language."[82] For Coleridge, it is not oral speech of the uneducated but written symbols by a poetic genius that can make the absolute subject present in language itself:

> . . . a Symbol is characterized by a translucence of the Special in the Individual or of the General in the Especial or of the Universal in the General. Above all by the translucence of the Eternal through and in the Temporal. It always partakes of the Reality which it renders intel-

ligible; and while it enunciates the whole, abides itself as a living part in that Unity, of which it is the representative.[83]

Wordsworth's and Coleridge's attempts to reinvent mimetic poetry are inscribed by the very mimetic concept they rebelled against because they still operated within the value system of signifier and signified. Their poetic innovations consist chiefly in reversing the orders of speech and writing, signifier and signifier, and in arguing for the presence of the absolute subject in language itself. Although Pound renounces the Coleridgean faith in the translucence of the monistic Eternal in poetic language, he nonetheless regards poetic Image as "Vortex, from which and through which, and into which, *ideas* are constantly rushing."[84] In asserting that poetry is "an emotional and intellectual complex in an instant of time"[85] and that "a thing outward and objective transforms itself, or darts into a thing inward and subjective" during that precise instant, Pound reaffirms the primacy of the subject and interprets the dynamic force in poetry as the élan vital toward the subjective. Indeed, while the Romantics search for the monolithic reification of the absolute subject in a landscape, Pound strives to envision "a cosmic pattern of ceaseless transformations between seemingly discrete entities; and the visionary experience of gods inhabiting the landscape."[86] Considering this epistemological orientation, the Fenollosan-Poundian aesthetics is, in the final analysis, an aesthetics of subjective force.

The Chinese aesthetics of dynamic force is predicated on an essentially nonmimetic concept of the written language.[87] In the Chinese tradition, characters have been regarded from the very earliest as an embodiment of the forces of nature. This "essentialist" concept of the written language is crystallized in various myths about the origins of characters.[88] Among these myths, two are most prominent. The first is about the creation of the protocharacters—trigrams and hexagrams—as told in the "Great Commentary" to the *Book of Changes*. As demonstrated in chapters 2 and 3, this myth is intended primarily to show that those protocharacters were born of, and thus coeval with, the divine forces of nature. The second myth is about the invention of full-fledged characters by Cang Jie, the scribe of the Yellow Emperor (Huang Di 黃帝). In the postface to his dictionary, Xu Shen gives a detailed account of both myths:

> In the days of antiquity when Bao Xi [Fu Xi] ruled as king over the subcelestial realm, gazing up he observed the phenomena of the heavens, looking down he observed the patterns on earth. He noticed how the

markings of birds and beasts were appropriate to the earth [around them]. Close at hand he took them [his impressions] from his own person. Further removed he took them from other creatures. Thereupon he undertook to create the Eight Trigrams of the *I*, as a means to transmit these patterns and phenomena.

Later Shen Nong knotted cords to bring about order, thus giving regularity to affairs. When the various occupations multiplied and proliferated, ornament and artifice arose and thrived. Huang Di's scribe Cang Jie saw the traces of the footprints of birds and beasts. He recognized that these partiform structures could be distinguished and differentiated one from another. Thus he first created writing. The hundred craftsmen were thereby regulated, and the myriad groups were thereby scrutinized. In all likelihood, he took it [this idea] from the *Guai* trigram.

古者庖犧氏之王天下也。仰則觀象於天。俯則觀法於地。
視為烏獸之文。與地之宜。近取諸身。遠取諸物。於是始
作易八卦。以垂憲象。及神農氏結繩為治。而統其事。庶
業其繁。飾偽萌生。黃帝之史倉頡見烏獸蹏迻之跡。知分
理之可相別異也。初造書契。百工以乂。萬品以察。蓋取
諸夬。89

Xu begins by repeating almost verbatim the description of Fu Xi in the "Great Commentary." Then, he proceeds to show how closely Cang Jie imitated the actions of Fu Xi—observing the "footprints of birds and beasts," distinguishing the patterns of nature revealed therein, and setting down those patterns in graphic symbols. By retelling the myth of Cang Jie in this fashion, Xu strives to establish that Cang Jie's characters are essentially identical to Fu Xi's trigrams. As if to make clear this point, he states explicitly that Cang Jie got his idea of the written character from the *Guai* 夬 trigram. We may recall that trigrams are depicted in the "Great Commentary" as "divine things" embodying the forces and processes of nature. In tracing Cang Jie's characters to the *Guai* trigram, Xu apparently aims to transfer to the former the claim of divine origin and efficacy originally made for the latter.90

By modeling his account of Cang Jie on the myth of Fu Xi, Xu Shen firmly establishes a reifying view that writing embodies at once patterns of concrete natural phenomena and the Dao, the ultimate principle governing all forces and processes of nature. This view of writing lays the ground for making similar reifying claims for literature, painting, calligraphy, and other forms of plastic arts. As shown in chapter 2, Liu Xie is the first one to establish a systematic view of literature (*wen*) as an embodiment of the Dao by appropriating the myths of Fu Xi and other creators of the trigrams and hexagrams. Here, let us see how Liu proceeds from his grand notion of *wen* to correlate the three major artistic patterns (*wen*) with the Five Agents, a set of cosmic co-ordinates codified under the Dao:

> Three main patterns are involved in the creation of literature: the color pattern, made up of the five colors; the sound pattern, made up of the five sounds; and the emotional pattern, made up of the five emotions. It is the mixing of the five basic colors which produces elegant embroidery; it is the harmonizing of the five basic sounds which creates ancient music such as the pieces "Shao" and "Xia" and it is the expression of the five emotions which gives us the essence of literature. All these processes are natural results of the operation of the spiritual principle. (*WXDL* 31 / 18–29)[91]

故立文之道，其理有三：一曰形文，五色是也；二曰
聲文，五音是也；三曰情文，五性是也。五色雜而成
黼黻，五音比而成韶夏，五情發而為辭章，神理之數也。

It seems that here the term *wen* also allows a narrower interpretation as a referent to literature itself. If so, Liu may be assumed to think of three major dimensions of literature as well: the musical, the visual, and the emotional. At any rate, his conception of the three patterns reminds us of three of Aristotle's six elements of tragedy (*melos, opsis,* and *lexis*) and Pound's adaptation of them to lyric (*melopoeia, phanopoeia,* and *logopoeia*).[92] However, whereas Aristotle and Pound use their categories mainly as three major aspects or modes of representation, Liu Xie considers his three patterns to have co-risen with the operations of nature itself. Cherishing this concept of writing, literature, and arts as dynamic patterns (*wen*) of nature, it is only natural that Liu Xie and other Chinese critics would regard the evocation of nature's force as their aesthetic ideal. Liu Xie's remarks on literature, along with those on Chinese calligraphy by Li Si, Lady Wei, and others, have shown how this aesthetic ideal of dynamic force—whether it is couched in terms of *shi* (momentum), *qi* (vital breath), or *shen* (spirit)—informs the discussion of numerous aspects of Chinese literature and arts, from the most general principles to the minutest rules. Given this, Chinese aesthetics should be distinguished as an aesthetics of natural force.

To sum up, this study has revealed many facets of the cross-cultural significance of the Fenollosan-Poundian theory of Chinese characters.

Looking at their theory from the Chinese side, we have found the entrenched accusation of "pictorial myth" to be unduly harsh because they are primarily concerned with the dynamic force, not pure pictorialism, of Chinese characters. The criticism of their ideogrammic explanations is also unnecessarily relentless and definitely unbalanced in that their transgressions have not been weighed against the same ones committed by their Chinese predecessors, especially Xu Shen, the founder of Chinese *wenzixue*. In going beyond those traditional criticisms, we have discovered in the Fenollosan-Poundian theory some real gems of critical insight. Probably without knowing it themselves, they have illuminated the history of both literary and calligraphic use of characters and, moreover, captured the quintessence of Chinese aesthetic ideal of dynamic force as expressed in literary and calligraphy criticism.

Looking at their theory from the Western side, we have demonstrated the special relationship of Fenollosa's essay to Pound's formulation and articulation of an Imagist-Vorticist aesthetic of dynamic force. Our investigation of this relationship serves not only to reaffirm the enthusiastic acclaim accorded Fenollosa's essay in Western criticism, but also to underscore the importance of the Chinese aesthetics of dynamic force as a catalyst for the modernist poetic revolution led by Pound.

This study is, of course, not all praise for Fenollosa and Pound's theory of the Chinese character. It has identified a hitherto unnoticed error—their "metaphorizing" appropriation of Chinese views of the dynamic force in characters. In investigating this error, we have come to a recognition of the fundamental difference between the Fenollosan-Poundian and Chinese aesthetics of dynamic force, a difference deeply grounded in Western mimetic and Chinese nonmimetic notions of written language. This recognition, in turn, makes us realize that such errors of distortion are practically bound to occur in the mutual borrowing of ideas across disparate cultural traditions. Moreover, it compels us to grapple with the broader theoretic problem about how to assess such errors of distortion.

To evaluate Fenollosa and Pound's "metaphorizing" can be a difficult task for a comparatist. If from the Chinese side one looks for an undistorted presentation of Chinese linguistic and aesthetic views, one may deplore it as an error that seems to undo their insightful appreciation of the dynamic force of Chinese characters latent in their ideogrammic roots. On the other hand, if one looks at the same matter from the Western side, one may hail it as a fortunate error. Thanks to this error,

Fenollosa and Pound do not just render the dynamic beauty of Chinese characters relevant to Western poetics, but actually make it a source of inspiration for a wide range of attempts at reinventing modern poetry, extending from Pound's own ideogrammic methods to e. e. cummings' typographical experiments and to more radical deconstructions of words by concrete poets.

CHAPTER 8

Poetics of Deconstruction
Derrida and Mādhyamika Buddhists
on Language and Ontotheologies

IN THE EYE OF JACQUES DERRIDA, FENOLLOSA AND POUND'S poetics of dynamic force represents the first major challenge to the entrenched tradition of Western poetics. "[Pound's] irreducibly graphic poetics," writes Derrida, "was with that of Mallarmé, the first break in the most entrenched Western tradition. The fascination that the Chinese ideogram exercised on Pound's writing may thus be given all its historical significance."[1] In foregrounding Pound's fascination with the Chinese written character, Derrida intends not merely to show the genesis of Pound's modernist poetics. He also attempts to reappropriate the Chinese written character as the other, against which he can pit Western phonocentrism and logocentrism. While Pound identifies the Chinese written character as an ancient antecedent of his Imagist-Vorticist poetics, Derrida sees it as convincing proof of the invalidity of all phonocentric claims upon which Western ontotheologies rest. He observes that "we have known for a long time that largely nonphonetic scripts like Chinese or Japanese . . . remained structurally dominated by the ideogram or algebra and we thus have the testimony of a powerful movement of civilization developing outside of all logocentrism."[2] In comparing the Chinese written character to algebra, Derrida reveals a profound ignorance of it. Of course, this ignorance is of little hindrance to his treating it as the imagined other. Fanciful though it is, his reappropriation of the Chinese written character reflects a broad trajectory from modernist to postmodernist challenges to the Western literary, intellectual, and cultural traditions.

It is quite extraordinary that the Chinese written character has played such an important role of the other in the development of both West-ern modernist and postmodernist movements. Derrida's view of the Chinese written character, like Fenollosa and Pound's, has been the sub-ject of intense debates. Responses to his views are predictably similar to the critiques of the Fenollosa-Pound essay. Some critics focus on crit-icizing Derrida's misconceptions of the Chinese language, especially his problematic assumption of its nonphonetic nature.[3] Others turn their attention to the parallels between Derrida's and Chinese Daoist thinkers' views on the nature of language and reality.[4] Among the studies of the latter category, Chinese texts chosen for comparison are almost exclu-sively the writings of Lao Zi and Zhuang Zi, the two founders of Chi-nese Daoism. As demonstrated below, these two Daoist masters' views bear far less resemblance to Derrida's than those of Chinese Mād-hyamika Buddhists. For this reason, I propose to undertake a com-parative study of Derrida and Chinese Mādhyamika Buddhism.

Mādhyamika Buddhism was founded by the Indian thinker Nā-gārjuna (fl. early second century A.D.) and established in China by Seng Zhao 僧肇 (374–414) and Ji Zang 吉藏 (549–623). It flourished in Ko-rea from the sixth to the fifteenth century and in Japan from the sev-enth to the twelfth century.[5] Derrida's deconstructive philosophy and Mādhyamika Buddhism are historically and geographically far apart from each other. However, many important parallels in method, strat-egy, and rationale exist between the two. Recently, a number of schol-ars have discovered significant parallels in the Derridean negation and the Mādhyamika *prasaṅga* (*reductio ad absurdum*), and have carefully compared the logic of negativity central to both traditions.[6] I shall fo-cus my attention on a number of noteworthy parallels in the Derridean and Mādhyamika linguistic and ontotheological deconstructions. Mād-hyamika texts chosen for comparison are mostly writings of Seng Zhao and Ji Zang.[7]

LEXICAL-SYNTACTICAL DECONSTRUCTION:
DERRIDA'S WORD-GAME AND SENG ZHAO'S WORD-MAZE

Both the Derridean and Mādhyamika theories are cast in terms of disagreements over language with idealists and materialists. Hence, language occupies a central position in their philosophical systems. To begin with, let me examine how Derrida and Seng Zhao perform lexical-syntactical deconstructions.

Derrida's handling of words has often been compared to a sleight of hand. In his writings, Derrida plays with words the way a magician plays with objects. He takes special delight in juggling opposite meanings within a word and creating a dizzying illusion of presence and absence, affirmation and denial. To figure out the secrets of his word-game, let us now look at the ways he plays meanings against one another at typographic, morphological, orthographic, semantic, etymological, and syntactic levels.

Derrida's typographic deconstruction is the most eye-catching or "eye-twitching" of all his word-games. By writing the words "writing," "encasing," and "screening" as "wriTing," "encAsing," and "screeNing,"[8] he puts their conceptual meanings *sous rature* (under erasure). With these deliberately misplaced capitalizations, Derrida not only delays our recognition of these words, but also injects doubt into our minds as to whether these words are meant to mean what they ordinarily mean. As we cannot figure out what "Ting," "Asing," and "Ning" stand for, we are left to assume that these embedded nonsensical signs function like overstrikes—"~~writing~~," "~~encasing~~" and "~~screening~~"—making those words signify simultaneously what they do and do not mean under normal circumstances.

Derrida's morphological deconstruction is less visually conspicuous but more thought-provoking. At the mention of morphological deconstruction, we immediately think of the very name by which Derrida prefers to let his philosophy be known. The word "deconstruct" results from a combination of two opposing morphemes: "de" (to undo, to destroy) and "construct" (to do, to build).[9] Violently yoked together, these two opposing morphemes come under a more dramatic kind of erasure than typographical deconstruction. Our response to this word, when first heard, is a dramatic sense of tension arising from a bizarre coexistence of destructive and constructive forces, a sense hitherto unconceptualized by any existent words. To bring our attention to the tension of opposite meanings latent in morphology, Derrida does not merely cast opposite morphemes into a new word like "deconstruct." More often, he hyphenates or brackets conflicting morphemes of an existing word, and thereby compels us to perceive the word not as a lifeless concept but as a vortex of conflicting meanings. For instance, in his *Dissemination,* he hyphenates the two morphemes of the word "preface," and discusses conflicts between "pre" and "face" in respect to temporal sequence. Then, he associates "pre-face" with its pseudo-synonym "pre-text" and conceives of a conflict between a substitution and an original implicated in the two morphemes of "pre-face."[10]

Derrida's orthographic deconstruction is, of course, best represented by his well-known coinage of "*différance.*" As we shall discuss the significance of *différance* in the next section, we can move on to consider Derrida's semantic deconstruction. To put words *sous rature*, Derrida exploits the semantic discrepancies as much as he manipulates morphological contrariety. If a word contains discrepant meanings within itself, he seeks to bring them into our consciousness. By so doing, he hopes to put us on guard against letting the word be overdetermined at the expense of its double entendre. His analysis of the opposite meanings of "to break" and "to join" in the French word *la brisure* is a typical example:

> you have, I suppose, dreamt of finding a single word for designating difference and articulation. I have perhaps located it by chance in *Robert*[*'s Dictionary*]. . . . This word is *brisure* [joint, break]"—broken, cracked part. Cf. breach, crack, fracture, fault, split, fragment, [*brèche, cassure, fracture, faille, fente, fragment.*]—Hinged articulation of two parts of wood- or metal-work. The hinge, the *brisure* [folding-joint] of a shutter. Cf. joint."[11]

To accentuate a word's semantic contrariness, Derrida often goes beyond its common usage and digs into its rich semantic sediments in writings of disparate types and different times. It is often a formidable task to track down such a semantic investigation because it threads through a great many texts without following a predetermined route. A case in point is his semantic investigation of the Greek word "*pharmakon*" in his lengthy essay "Plato's Pharmacy" in *Dissemination*. He starts with the undecidability of the word between "remedy" and "drug," "cure," and "poison." Then, by way of an anagrammatical twist, he goes into the mythical figure "Pharmaricia" and the word "*pharmakeos*" (sorcerer, magician). In the course of this semantic investigation, he pursues the manifold meanings of *pharmakon* through "such 'other' domains as medicine, painting, politics, farming, law, sexuality, festivity, and family relations."[12] The result is a startling revelation of *pharmakon*'s double entendre pertaining to a wide range of philosophical issues such as speech and writing, literal and figurative meanings, and paternity and language.

Such a rigorous semantic deconstruction seems to have already crossed the boundary of semantics into the field of etymology. To expose the "in-tension" of conflicting forces within a word, Derrida often avails himself of etymological deconstruction. He traces a word to its etymological roots of opposite import and thus invalidates the monolithic conceptualization of the word in question. For instance, he traces his neologism *archia* on the one hand to the Greek *arche,* meaning foundation, order, and principles (as reserved in words like *archi*tecture and hier*archy*), and on the other hand to the Greek *aporia,* meaning excess resistant to order or logic.[13] Notably, this etymological deconstruction attests to the co-arising of order and disorder, passion and logic. Like many other words of similar "in-tension," *archia* becomes a prized deconstructive term for Derrida.

Derrida's syntactical deconstructions are far less frequent and far less varied than his lexical deconstructions. They usually are intended to enhance the effects of lexical deconstructions. For instance, to drive home the significance of his orthographic deconstruction, Derrida deliberately deconstructs the syntax of his concluding statement in his seminal essay *"Différance":*

> Such is the question: the alliance of speech and Being in the unique word, in the finally proper name. And such is the question inscribed in the simulated affirmation of *différance.* It bears (on) each member of this sentence: "Being / speaks / always and everywhere / throughout / language."[14]

When he cuts his concluding statement into pieces, Derrida virtually destroys its syntax and what is inherent in it—a hierarchical order of subject-predicate-object. As a result, the lexical elements are freed from the binding syntax and become equal, free-floating components. These lexical elements may easily exchange positions and bring forth meanings contradictory to that of the original syntax:

> language / throughout / always and everywhere / speaks / Being /
> Being / speaks / language / always and everywhere / throughout /

Insofar as this mangled syntax results in such heterogeneous, opposite meanings, it may very well be assumed to reaffirm the significance of *différance:* an exposure of the pluralistic, contradictory import within any concept and a proof of the impossibility of self-presence within language. Indeed, this deconstructed sentence deals with none other than the issue of language and Being. Just as *différance* shows Being (signified) to be always deferred in time and differentiated in space by language (signifier), this deconstructed syntax enacts a play of signifier and signified caused by that ineluctable gap in space and time. Indeed, the syntactical interchangeability of "Being / speaks / language / . . ." and "language / speaks / Being . . ." aptly highlights Derrida's deconstructive conception of Being. When he casts Being into this deconstructed syntax, he intends to demonstrate that Being is not a self-present, transcendental signified lodged in the traditional copula-syntax (Being *is* . . .) of an ontotheological discourse. For Derrida, Being is nothing more than a signifier that "speaks / language"—speaking and respeaking, writing and rewriting itself perpetually and indeterminately like *différance.* Moreover, the syntactical interchangeability of "Being / speaks / language / . . ." and "language / speaks / Being . . ." emblemizes the infinite circularity in the movement of Being as a sign.

Now, let us examine how words and syntax are handled in the writings of Seng Zhao.[15] In the spirit of the Mādhyamika deconstruction, Seng Zhao seeks to "deconceptualize" and "deessentialize" some key Chinese ontological terms just as Derrida does many Western ones. Many Chinese characters (*zi* 字) can function independently as meaningful, self-contained words or combine with another character, often those of its opposite import, to form binomes (*shuangyin zi* 雙音字), rough equivalents of compound words in a Western language. For example, the characters *fang* and *yuan,* when alone, denote "square(ness)" and "circle(ness)"; but, when combined as a binome (*fangyuan* 方圓), mean literally "area" or "scope." To give another example, the characters *chang* and *duan* denote "length(y)iness" and "short(ness)" respectively; but together they form a binome (*changduan* 長短) indicating measurement of length. To a Derridean deconstructionist, these binomes pregnant with "in-tension" and contradictions entail a free play of conflicting signifiers and hence demonstrate the workings of *différance.* One can imagine that the Derridean deconstructionist would not hesitate to perform a sleight of hand between the ontotheological implications of "square(ness)" and "circle(ness)."[16] For Seng Zhao, however, there is a much simpler approach to destroying the conceptuality of an ontotheological term. Instead of reviving the dormant conflicts within an already conceptualized binome like *fangyuan,* he seeks to turn some ontotheological terms into *new* binomes which, like *différance,* are intended for no other purpose than to annul those terms. For instance, to demolish the ontotheological terms of "existence" (*you* 有) and "nonexistence" (*wu* 無), he renders them into binomes by combining them with the character *fei* 非 or *bu* 不, each of which can be taken as a prefix ("non") or a verb ("to be not") depending on the context and the way one interprets it. Whatever its grammatical function, the added character *fei* or *bu* causes the reified *you* and *wu* to become strongly negative binomes pointing to their opposites:

you 有 ("exist")—*fei wu* 非 無 or *bu wu* 不 無 ("not nonexist")

wu 無 ("nonexist")—*fei you* 非 有 or *bu you* 不 有 ("not exist")[17]

For Seng Zhao, these negative binomes provide a convenient way to point to the provisional states of "exist" and "nonexist" without affirming them as self-present entities. By referring to the phenomenal world negatively as "not nonexist" (*fei wu* 非 無 or *bu wu* 不 無), Seng Zhao believes, one can extricate oneself from the otherwise unavoidable reification of phenomena in the act of calling it "existence" (*you* 有). Conversely, by referring to the state of *wu* 無 negatively as "not exist" (*fei you* 非 有), one can forestall the essentialization of the name *wu* itself. Seng Zhao's use of these negative binomes reminds us of Derrida's yoking of opposite concepts: "good / evil, intelligible / sensible, high / low, life / death."[18] As compared with these yoked phrases, Seng Zhao's binomes seem to produce a greater deessentializing effect. They seem to more effectively inhibit one's capacity to conceptualize than do Derrida's lexical deconstructions. However, while Seng Zhao more successfully taxes our conceptualizing capability with his deconstructive binomes, he does not utilize as many means of lexical deconstruction as Derrida does.

To realize the extent to which Seng Zhao's lexical deconstruction plays havoc with our mind, we must show how Seng Zhao's binomes, already disorienting in and of themselves, become even more so when they crowd together in a sentence. The following sentence, Seng Zhao's rebuttal of the idea of "original nonexistence" (*benwu* 本 無) is a typical example:

[According to the School of Original Nonexistence], "not exist" means that "exist" is none other than "nonexist." "Not nonexist" means that "nonexist" is nothing but "nonexist" . . . [Seng Zhao argues] "Not exist" simply means no real (absolute) existence; and "not nonexist," no real (absolute) nonexistence.[19]

故	非	有	有	即	無	非	無	無	即	無	直
gu^1	fei^2	you^3	you^4	ji^5	wu^6	fei^7	wu^8	wu^9	ji^{10}	wu^{11}	zhi^{12}

以	非	有	非	真	有	非	無	非	真	無	耳[20]
yi^{13}	fei^{14}	you^{15}	fei^{16}	$zhen^{17}$	you^{18}	fei^{19}	wu^{20}	fei^{21}	$zhen^{22}$	wu^{23}	er^{24}

Going over these repetitions of *you* and *wu* in this paragraph, we cannot help thinking of how Zhuang Zi seeks to dehypostatize *you* 有 and *wu* 無 through a playful crowding of the two terms into a rather ambiguous sentence:

> There is a beginning. There is a not yet beginning to be a beginning. There is a not yet beginning to be a not yet beginning to be a beginning. There is being. There is nonbeing. There is a not yet beginning to nonbeing. There is a not yet beginning to be a not yet beginning to nonbeing. Suddenly there is nonbeing. But I don't know, when it comes to nonbeing, which is really being and which is nonbeing.[21]

有 始 也 者 ， 有 未 始 有 始 也 者 ， 有 未 始 有 夫 未 始 有 始 也 ， 有 有 也 者 ， 有 無 也 者 ， 有 未 始 有 無 也 者 ， 有 未 始 有 夫 未 始 有 無 也 者 。 俄 而 有 無 矣 ， 而 未 知 有 無 之 果 有 孰 無 孰 也 。

One can hardly miss the serious point Zhuang Zi wants to make through these playful remarks. The point is that *you* and *wu,* usually taken as opposite entities, are in fact indistinguishable and neither can be seen to precede or rule the other. This is because they are each part of the Dao, a constant, eternal process of change or transformation. According to Zhuang Zi, a wise man is one who can rise above the differentiation of things and leap to the undifferentiated totality of Dao. As compared with Zhuang Zi's remarks, Seng Zhao's passage is less playful but more negative. In my opinion, this has much to do with Seng Zhao's introduction through the word *fei* of a purely negative force not present in Zhuang Zi's remarks. By introducing this negative force, Seng Zhao wishes to avoid affirming, however implicitly, a higher totality like the Dao, in the course of demolishing both *you* and *wu* as ontotheological totalities. The very goal of his deconstruction is to demonstrate the impossibility of conceiving such a totality either in or through language. Given this, Seng Zhao's deconstruction of *you* and *wu* is unquestionably far closer than Zhuang Zi's to Derrida's deconstruction of ontotheological terms. Indeed, *fei you* 非 有 and *fei wu* 非 無 are de-essentializing binomes seldom seen in Daoist texts but used extensively in Buddhist texts. These binomes are called *zheyu* 遮 語 (words of negation) and a deconstructive presentation of the ultimate reality like Seng Zhao's is called *zhequan* 遮 詮 (presentation by means of negation) by the Chan Buddhists of later times.[22]

In Seng Zhao's passage, of the twenty-four characters numbered for convenient reference, there are only six particles, on which the classical Chinese language depends for the formation of a syntax. Among these six particles, there are five "adverbial" particles *(1, 5, 10, 12, 13),* roughly corresponding to the English "thus," "namely," "simply," and "with" and one exclamatory particle *(24).* Only the exclamatory particle *er* can be regarded as a final particle that functions to mark off a syntactic unit like a comma or period.[23] With the syntax-forming particles kept to a minimum, this passage seems to be an almost orderless recurrence of these three characters: *fei* ("non"), *you* ("exist"), and *wu* ("nonexist"). Compounding the difficulty of comprehension is the fact that *fei, you,* and *wu* can function either as nouns or verbs. Thus, when reading such a passage in the unpunctuated original, even an initiated reader may find his or her conceptual understanding held in check. One may easily get entangled in a maze of words—the semantic concatenation of which one must sort out and the syntactic functions of which one must decipher before one can get out. Seng Zhao's word-maze undoubtedly measures up to "a *grouped* textual field,"[24] the ideal of Derridean lexical-syntactical deconstruction. Like Derrida's word-game, it dislodges our habits of conceptual thinking, and this usually occurs when Seng Zhao sets himself to deconceptualize important ontotheological terms. What distinguishes Seng Zhao's word-maze from Derrida's word-game is his unwillingness to indulge in prolix, convoluted wordplay and establish such textual proliferation as an anti-ontotheological mode of discourse. For Seng Zhao, lexical-syntactic deconstructions are not of great significance in and of themselves. They are merely a means of breaking through conceptuality and attaining a transformed state of consciousness. This essential difference between Derrida's word-game and Seng Zhao's word-maze will become clearer as we proceed to examine the different philosophical agendas behind these two kinds of deconstructive textual practices.

FROM LINGUISTIC TO ONTOTHEOLOGICAL
DECONSTRUCTIONS: DERRIDA'S *DIFFÉRANCE*
AND THE MĀDHYAMIKA *DIFFERENTIAM*

Derrida's word-game and Seng Zhao's word-maze exploit the codependence of opposite elements at different levels of language. Through such lexical-theological deconstructions, Derrida and Seng Zhao aim to demonstrate that language is not a matter of signifiers "presencing" signifieds as self-identities, but a perpetual play of mutually dependent signifiers. For both Derrida and Seng Zhao, this codependence in linguistic signification precludes the possibility of any pure self-presence not only in language per se but in all language-thought constructs in the domain of philosophy and religion. They believe that all claims of ontotheological essence in and / or through language are necessarily invalid insofar as they go against the codependent rule of linguistic signification. By virtue of this reasoning, Derrida and Seng Zhao proceed from linguistic deconstruction to critiques of ontotheologies.

Derrida uses the play of a sign to disprove the self-present truth of Being valorized by all Western ontologists and theologians:

> One cannot get round that responses [what is Sign in the sense of Being], except by challenging the very form of the question and beginning to think that the sign is that ill-named thing, the only one, that escapes the instituting question of philosophy: "what is . . . ?"[25]

Here Derrida crosses out the name of Being twice (first calling it "ill-named thing," then overstriking it), and puts the copula *sous rature.* This is because the rule of a sign forbids our conception of Being as a self-present "thing" or our description of it with a copula. As a sign, "Being" must also signify "Nonbeing(s)." By the same token, the copula "is," once posited as a sign, must denote "is not" as well. Owing to this codependent rule, a sign, Derrida holds, escapes—and in fact displaces—the instituting question of "What is. . . . " For him, it is the question "What is Being?" that gives rise to all the wrongheaded pursuits of the phantom of a self-present truth in Western ontotheologies.

Derrida holds that Western idealists from Plato to Heidegger operate through a false conception of language. They all invoke the logos, a linguistic sign, as an intermediary between the transcendental and sensible, the divine and the human. Socrates in the *Phaedo,* Derrida observes, "tells of his fear of being blinded by looking at things directly. . . . And he tells how, instead of turning directly to things, he turned rather to *logoi* in order to examine there the truth of beings."[26] To vindicate the logos as an embodiment of "truth of beings," Plato and later idealists adopt a twofold strategy—to banish its corporeal *gram* and to reify its intangible *phonè.* Although the term "logos" contains the meaning of language as a whole, they do not employ it pertaining to the graphic form of language. This banishment of the *gram* from the logos stems from the fear that the visibly corporeal *gram* will contaminate the *phonè,* the transcendental signified. Plato unequivocally expresses such a fear when he denounces the birth of writing by the resourceful god Theuth:

> But when they came to letters, This, said Theuth, will make the Egyptians wiser and give them better memories; it is a specific both for the

memory and for the wit. Thamus replied: O most ingenious Theuth, the parent or inventor of an art is not always the best judge of the utility or inutility of his own inventions to the users of them. And in this instance, you who are the father of letters, from a paternal love of your own children have been led to attribute to them a quality which they cannot have; for this discovery of yours will create forgetfulness in the learners' souls, because they will not use their memories; they will trust to the external written characters and not remember of themselves. The specific which you have discovered is an aid not to the memory, but to reminiscence, and you give your disciples not truth, but only the semblance of truth; they will be hearers of many things and will have learned nothing; they will appear to be omniscient and will generally know nothing; they will be tiresome company, having the show of wisdom without reality.[27]

Or in the words of Derrida, Plato denounces the *gram* as "the intrusion of an artful technique, a forced entry of a totally original sort, an archetypal violence: eruption of the *outside* within the *inside*, breaching into the interiority of the soul, the living self-presence of the soul within the true logos, the help that speech lends to itself."[28] While Plato and later idealists banish the *gram* as "an orphan or a bastard," they reify the *phonè* as "the legitimate and high-born son of the 'father of logos'"[29]—on the ground of the "proximity of voice and being, of voice and the meaning of being, of voice and the ideality of meaning."[30] As a result of such a phonocentric reification, the logos has assumed the ontotheological significance of, as Gayatri Chakravorty notes, "the Word, the Divine Mind, the infinite understanding of God, and infinitely creative subjectivity, and closer to our time, the self-presence of full self-consciousness."[31]

In the opinion of Derrida, the phonocentric reification of the logos presents a paradox. While such a reification is intended to forestall "the eruption of the *outside* within the inside," it actually exposes the *outside* within the inside of all Western idealist metaphysics. For Derrida, the reason cannot be simpler. The privileged *phonè* is as much a linguistic sign as the denigrated *gram* and is subject to the same rules of linguistic signification governing the *gram*. So, the logos is by necessity a linguistic sign external to the transcendental absolute. As such, it inevitably inscribes all metaphysics within a space of externality and precludes the possibility of any intrinsic absolute presence.

To expose how Western metaphysics "finds inscribed, rather than inscribing itself, within a space [the externality of the logos] which it seeks but is unable to control,"[32] Derrida coins the word *"différance."*

This neologism constitutes on the one hand the nominal form for the French verb *différer,* which means both "to differ" and "to defer," and on the other a dissimulation of the French noun (*différence*). Simple and playful as it seems, this neologism spells out Derrida's deconstructive theory of linguistic signification. First, *différance* calls into question the privileging of the *phonè* by the idealists, because it is not the *phonè* but the *gram* of the word that makes its meaning understood. If heard but not read in French, *différance* is bound to be confused with the noun *différence.* Second, *différance* underscores the prerequisite for linguistic signification. A sign cannot exist unless it *differs* spatially and is *deferred* temporally from the signified. This ever receding gap between the signifier and the signified disproves the alleged fusion of the *phonè* and the ontotheological essence in the logos. Third, the Latin root of *différance* ("differre" in the sense of "to scatter, disperse") denotes the necessary play of opposing referents in linguistic signification. A name must contain its disputant meaning(s) in order to exist as a name (i.e., *A* cannot be called *A* unless *A* also signifies the existence of *non-A*). So a name signifies absence as well as presence. This being the case, what a name signifies cannot be the pure signified of presence, but another signifier which in turn signifies absence as well as presence.[33] This goes on and on to infinitude. It follows that the very possibility of the transcendental signified or the ontotheological presence is to be denied. Given this operation of *différance.* Derrida contends that logocentric concepts—"*eidos, arche, telos, energeia, ousia* [essence, existence, substance, subject], *aletheia, transcendentality, consciousness or conscience, God,* and so forth"[34]—are all caught in an infinite circularity of signifiers and will never be able to presence the transcendental absolute.

Like Derrida, Mādhyamika thinkers seek to demolish the ontotheological arguments by the Buddhist essentialists by exposing their false conception of language. Whereas Derrida invalidates the alleged self-nature of the logos by demonstrating the *phonè* as a conventional sign in *différance.* Mādhyamika thinkers nullify the "intrinsic identity" (*svalakṣana*) of the Name of Nonexistence by showing its conventionality.[35] Candrakīrti, a great Indian Mādhyamika thinker of the seventh century, repudiates the essentialist claim of the intrinsic nature of the Name of Nonexistence. In the opinion of a Buddhist essentialist, that the phrases "body of a statue" and "head of Rahū" exist—despite that neither an inanimate statue has a body nor does Rahū (a demon) have a head—attests to the nonrepresentational, intrinsic identity of language. In response to such an essentialist view, Candrakīrti writes:

When the words "body" and "head" normally occur in grammatical connection with companion entities like "hand" or "mind," the thought produced on the basis of the words "body" and "head" alone carries an expectation of the companion entities in the form, "Whose body?" and "Whose head?" . . . Furthermore, the terms "statue" and "Rahū," which are the qualifiers, actually exist as part of conventional usage, and are accepted without analysis, as in the conventional designation "person." Therefore your example is incorrect.[36]

Here, Candrakīrti considers the two phrases to be no more than ordinary words that can convey a meaning only through conventional association established by grammatical connections. He believes that "whatever meaning they [words] had was acquired by a process of mutual dependence (*parasparāpekṣā siddhi*), with one word depending for its meaning on the network of those that were used before it."[37] These remarks of Candrakīrti are reminiscent of Derrida's theory of *différance*. Like Derrida, he conceives of linguistic signification as an interplay of signifiers, and argues on that ground against the notion that a word has an intrinsic essence within itself.

It is important to note that Candrakīrti's analysis of linguistic signification is based on his commonsense observations whereas Derrida's is developed from modern theories of semiology. For a more systematically developed Buddhist theory of language, we must turn to the differentiation theory of meaning (*apoha*) developed by Dignāga (c. 480–540), a phenomenal Indian Buddhist logician, under the influence of the early Mādhyamika school.[38] Whereas Candrakīrti explores the mutual dependence of words within a grammatical construction, Dignāga looks into the mutual dependence of opposing elements within a single word and yields fresh insight into the nature of linguistic signification: "Indeed the name can express its own meaning only by repudiating the opposite meaning, as for instance the words 'to have an origin' designate their own meaning only through a contrast with things having no origin or eternal."[39] This statement seems at first sight to be an affirmation of the self-present meaning of a name. A closer examination of it reveals that Dignāga is actually arguing the opposite because he sees the very condition for any name to establish a meaning is the existence of a disputant meaning. This necessary dependence of a meaning upon its contrary is sufficient disproof of the alleged intrinsic meaning of a name. The deconstructive significance of this statement becomes much clearer in the following commentary by Jinendrabuddhi: "Indeed the aim of the text of Dignāga is that the word 'expresses *per differentiam*' its own meaning. . . . (The words express only negations, only differences!), because a pure affirmation without any (implied) negation is senseless."[40] This commentary helps convince us that Dignāga indeed conceives of linguistic signification as a process of negation and difference akin to that of *différance*.[41] Considering this, it seems no accident that Jinendrabuddhi uses *differentiam* to characterize Dignāga's differentiation theory of meaning, just as Derrida uses *différance* to typify his own. Moreover, like Derrida, Dignāga and other Buddhist logicians go from linguistic deconstruction to ontological negation (*arthātmaka-apoha*). While Derrida annuls "*eidos, arche, telos, energeia, ousia . . .*" through a demonstration of *différance* in those sacred names, they disprove the essence of language through a revelation of *differentiam* in ontotheological names.

Although Chinese Mādhyamika Buddhists do not develop such sophisticated theories like their Indian counterparts, they nevertheless go to great lengths to argue the impossibility of ontotheological presence in or through language. Seng Zhao repeatedly emphasizes this insufficiency of language in his writings, and is generally believed to have authored an essay called "Nirvāna Is Nameless" ("Niepan wuming lun" 涅盤無名論) on this subject.[42] In that essay he writes,

> Nirvāna, as the Dao, is silent, tranquil, insubstantial, and vast. It cannot be attained through a name. Subtle and without a phenomenal form, it cannot be known by the heart / mind.[43]

> 夫涅盤之為道也。寂寥虛曠。不可以名得。微妙無相。不可以有心知。

This passage reminds us of Lao Zi's well-known description of the Dao: "The way [Dao] that can be spoken of is not the constant way. The name which can be named is not the constant Name."[44] We also think of similar remarks by Zhuang Zi: "We can use words to talk about the coarseness of things and we can use our minds to visualize the fineness of things. But what words cannot describe and the mind cannot succeed in visualizing—this has nothing to do with coarseness or fineness."[45] These echoes of *Lao* [*Zi*] and *Zhuang* [*Zi*] testify to Seng Zhao's debt to the two Daoist masters.[46] In *Biographies of Eminent Buddhist Monks* (*Gao seng zhuan* 高僧傳), Hui Jiao 慧皎 (497–554) gives an account of Seng Zhao's fascination with *Lao Zi* and *Zhuang Zi*:

> [Seng Zhao] was fond of what is mysterious and subtle. He cherished *Zhuang* and *Lao* as the ultimate essence in the mind. Once he read the

chapters on *De* (virtue, power) in *Lao Zi* and sighed, "Beautiful as they are, they have not reached perfection in dealing with the mysterious spiritual realm." Later, when he saw the *Old* [*Translation of the*] *Virmalakīrti-nirdeśa sūtra,* he was elated and bowed to receive it. As he read through it with zest, he said that not until then did he know where to take refuge."[47]

[僧肇]愛好玄微，每以莊老為心要。嘗讀老子德章，乃嘆曰：美則美矣，然期神冥之方，猶未盡善也。"後見舊維摩經，歡喜頂受，披尋翫味，乃言始知所歸矣。

Based on Hui Jiao's account, Seng Zhao outgrew his interest in Daoism and eventually found his intellectual and spiritual moorings in *Virmalakīrti-nirdeśa sūtra* and Mādhyamika writings. As we can see in his own preface to his annotation of the *Virmalakīrti-nirdeśa sūtra,* it is largely the Buddhist view of language that attracted him away from Daoism.[48] Despite his numerous allusions to *Lao* and *Zhuang,* I would argue, Seng Zhao's view of language is essentially Buddhist and differs considerably from those of the two Daoist masters. This important difference, however, is very difficult to detect even for people living close to Seng Zhao's time. To counter the widespread misconception that Seng Zhao's views of language and thought are identical to Lao Zi's and Zhuang Zi's, Yuan Kang 元康 (Tang Dynasty), the major annotator of Seng Zhao's texts, finds it necessary to declare that "Master Zhao borrowed words from *Zhuang* and *Lao* in order to rectify the Dao. But how could this be taken to mean that he embraced *Zhuang* and *Lao* as the Dharma."[49] Explaining Seng Zhao's use of the phrase "divine Dao" (*shendao* 神道), Yuan Kang continues, "This shows Master Zhao's ultimate intention and makes it clear what is different from *Zhuang* and *Lao.* 'Divine Dao' means the miraculous Dao, namely, the Buddhist Dao . . . How could one assume that he does not have his own doctrinal principles (*li* 理) and uses those of *Zhuang* and *Lao* as Buddhist principles (*Foli* 佛理)?"[50] While we do come across such claims of difference in the commentaries on Seng Zhao's texts, we are hard put to find a clear exposition of the differences under discussion. Thus, here we have to find out on our own what essential difference lies between Seng Zhao's view of language and those of Zhuang Zi and Lao Zi.

In my opinion, an essential difference may be seen between Lao Zi's and Zhuang Zi's totalizing tendencies and Seng Zhao's antitotalizing tendency.[51] For Lao Zi and Zhuang Zi, language, though incapable of embodying the ontotheological reality *in* itself, can nevertheless be the springboard for a leap beyond language and conceptuality to that reality. In other words, they still affirm the possibility of approaching the ontotheological reality *through* language. In contrast to his famous words, "The way [Dao] that can be spoken of is not the real way," Lao Zi unambiguously *speaks of* the ultimate cosmological origin as the Dao:

There is a thing confusedly formed,	有物混成，
Born before heaven and earth.	先天地生。
Silent and void	寂漠！
It stands alone and does not change,	獨立不改，
Goes round and does not weary.	周行不殆，
It is capable of being the mother of the world.	可以為天下母。
I know not its name	吾不知其名，
So I style it "the way."[52]	字之曰道。

Likewise, despite all his dismissals of language, Zhuang Zi affirms its usefulness in pointing to the ultimate reality. In the passage cited earlier, he charts out a linear process of linguistic-mental process: a recognition of the "coarseness of things" (their appearances), a grasp of "fineness of things" (their intrinsic qualities), and an intuitive union with "what is beyond the coarseness and fineness"—the Dao, the ultimate reality. Zhuang Zi's famous comparison of language to a fish trap is an affirmation of language as an expedient of pointing to the totality of the Dao.[53]

By contrast, Seng Zhao's view of language is far more negative than Lao Zi's and Zhuang Zi's. If Lao Zi's and Zhuang Zi's criticisms of language are motivated by their desires to reach the totality of the Dao,[54] Seng Zhao's is intended not only to dispose of all attempts to find ontotheological presence in or through language, but to forestall the emergence of any new ontotheological totality from an incomplete deconstruction of language and thought like Lao Zi's and Zhuang Zi's. So, instead of comparing language to a useful fish trap for "catching" an ontotheological totality, he considers it an impediment to true enlightenment and emphasizes a total disposal of it:

The path of words and speech is cut off. The source of the mind's activities is eliminated.[55]

言語道斷。心行處滅。

It is significant that Seng Zhao subjects to deconstruction not only language but also the mind's activities (*xinxing* 心行), which is endorsed or even privileged by Zhuang Zi as the means of achieving an intuitive union with the totalistic Dao. Seng Zhao's antitotalizing tendency also is reflected in the way he uses language. If Lao Zi and Zhuang Zi employ the nebulous symbols (*xiang* 象), paradox, and relativistic rhetoric to suggest the totality of the Dao, Seng Zhao stays clear of such figurative forms and instead profusely uses statements of double negation, a discourse form based on the Mādhyamika deconstructive logic. This discourse form, hitherto scarcely used in the native Chinese traditions, consists in a simultaneous negation of two diametrically opposite ontotheological views without affirming a third one. Needless to say, this discourse form results in a far more thorough deconstruction of language and thought than do Lao Zi's and Zhuang Zi's relativistic rhetoric. Commenting on Seng Zhao's use of this discourse form, Yuan Kang says, "speech is by nature that which is used to eliminate words and nullify the mind's activities. As for words, they are by nature the means of eliminating words."[56] These remarks aptly point to a most radical deconstructive exercise not seen in *Lao Zi* and *Zhuang Zi* but prominent in Seng Zhao's writings. As we shall see next, this exercise serves him well in his efforts to eliminate all linguistic and mental constructs.

This brief comparison, I hope, will help us distinguish Seng Zhao's view of language from Lao Zi's and Zhuang Zi's and place it firmly in the antitotalizing tradition of Nāgārjuna and Candrakīrti. Like his Indian predecessors, Seng Zhao consistently exploits the codependent rule of linguistic signification to demolish all attempts to find ontotheological presence in or through language:

> Things do not become actualitized because they have acquired names. Names do not assume reality because they have been applied to things. Therefore, the absolute truth itself lies tranquil beyond any elucidation through names. How could one say that writings and words could express it?[57]

是以物不即名而就實。名不即物而履真。然則真諦獨靜於
名教之外。豈曰文言之能辯哉。

For Seng Zhao, "name" and "thing" are locked in a codependent relationship of the signifier and the signified, and allow no space for the existence of an absolute truth. When one perceives "thing" as a signified, its actuality cannot be presenced by its signifier, that is, a "name." If, on the contrary, one considers "name" as a signified, its so-called essence cannot be matched by its signifier "things." On the ground of this inevitable gap between "name" and "thing," Seng Zhao argues that all claims of "name" or "thing" as absolute truth are mere illusions and that it is utterly impossible to conceive of an absolute truth in and / or through language. Seng Zhao reaffirms this rationale of ontotheological deconstruction when he writes:

> If we look for a thing through a name, we shall find that there is no actuality in that thing which would correspond to the name. If we look for the name through a thing, we shall find that the name is not capable of helping us to discover a thing. A thing that has no actuality corresponding to a name is not a thing. A name that is not capable of discovering a thing is not a name. Consequently, a name does not correspond to an actuality and an actuality does not correspond to a name. As name and actuality do not correspond to each other, how can the myriad things exist?[58]

夫以名求物。物無當名之實。以物求名。名無得物之功。
物無當名之實。非物也。名無得物之功。非名也。是以名
不當實。實不當名。名實無當。萬物安在。

The way Seng Zhao plays the "name" and "thing" against each other recalls how Derrida exploits the gap between signifiers and signifieds with his play of *différance* for the same purpose of invalidating the reification of either. As we shall see later, Seng Zhao spares no efforts expounding the impossibility of finding ontotheological presence in or through language. In view of his exploitation of linguistic codependence, his relentless antitotalizing drive, and his deconstructive and self-deconstructive strategies to be examined below, I may confidently reiterate that Seng Zhao's philosophy is far closer to Derrida's than those of Lao Zi and Zhuang Zi.

DERRIDA'S DOUBLE SÉANCE
AND THE MĀDHYAMIKA DOUBLE NEGATION

Both the Derridean *différance* and the Mādhyamika *differentiam* illuminate the mutual dependence of signified and signifier, referent and nonreferent, presence and absence. On the ground of this mutual dependence, both Derrida and Mādhyamika thinkers believe that intrinsic identity cannot be claimed for either the signified / referent / presence side or the signifier / nonreferent / absence side. They hold that all ontotheologies are necessarily false insofar as they ascribe intrinsic identity to one or the other side of this paradigm. According to both Derrida and Seng Zhao, all ontotheologies err in reifying one side or another of their respective philosophical dualisms—the logos vs. Matter, Name vs. Thing, Being vs. beings, Nonexistence vs. Existence, etc.— as essence (a transcendental signified) and denigrating the other side as representation (a signifier). Hence, all Western and Buddhist ontotheologies fall into two opposing camps. Those who valorize "the logos" or "the Name of Nonexistence" are Western idealists and Buddhist Essentialists. Those who valorize "Matter" or "Thing" are Western materialists and Buddhist Realists.

For Derrida and Mādhyamika thinkers alike, the paradigm of mutual dependence of linguistic signification not only exposes the erroneousness of all ontotheologies but also provides a very convenient way to deconstruct them. All one has to do is to overturn the hierarchization of these two sides in a given philosophical system. Both Derrida and Seng Zhao readily apply the codependent paradigm to stage a two-pronged attack on these two opposing camps. They launch the first prong against the reification of the logos by Western idealists and of the Name of Nonexistence by Buddhist essentialists. They direct the second prong against the counterreification of Matter by Western materialists and of the Thing by Buddhist realists. We have already seen how Derrida and Mādhyamika thinkers launch such a deconstructive attack against Western idealisms and Buddhist essentialisms. Now, let us see how they return to deconstruct Western materialisms and Buddhist realisms.

While Derrida seeks to overturn the superiority of the *phonè* at the first phase of his deconstruction, he re-marks the *gram* at the second phase to prevent the reinstitution of logocentrism in the form of materialism. He writes, "Nothing would be more ridiculously mystifying than such an ethical or axiological reversal, returning a prerogative or some elder's right to writing."[59] He perceives the "counterprivileging" of the *gram*, the ostensibly corporeal signifier, as emblematic of a metaphysical reification in the form of materialism. Such a reification is not dissimilar to that of the *phonè* as the transcendental signified by idealists:

> . . . the concept of matter has been defined as absolute exterior or radical heterogeneity. I am not even sure that there can be a "concept" of an absolute exterior. If I have not very often used the word "matter," it is not, as you know, because of some idealist or spiritualist kind of reservation. It is that in the logic of the phase of overturning this concept has been too often reinvested with "logocentric" values, values associ-

ated with those of thing, reality, presence in general, sensible presence, for example, substantial plenitude, content, referent, etc. Realism or sensualism—"empiricism,"—are modifications of logocentrism. (I have often insisted on the fact that "writing" or the "text" are not reducible *either* to the sensible or visible presence of the graphic or the "literal.") In short, the signifier "matter" appears to me problematical only at the moment when its reinscription cannot avoid making of it a new fundamental principle which by means of theoretical regression, would be reinstituted into a "transcendental signified."[60]

In this passage, Derrida aims to show how easily the rehabilitation of a signifier may go overboard and result in the reinstitution of logocentric value such as "thing, reality, [or] presence in general." Derrida mentions the materialist texts of Marx and Lenin as a typical case.[61] There, the signifier of "matter" has become the absolute cosmological and sociohistorical principle. In other words, the signifier is reified and turned into a transcendental signified no less fictitious than the logos subscribed by most idealists from Plato to Heidegger. To prevent his own *grammatology* from being "reinvested with 'logocentric' values," Derrida advocates a simultaneous deconstruction of the *gram* and the *phonè* and calls such a practice "biface or biphase," "double séance," or "double register in grammatological practice"[62]

The Mādhyamika double negation bears close resemblance to the Derridean "double séance." At one phase, they seek to reduce ontotheological Names "to mere conventional negative signs of differentiation" and thereby deconstruct all Essentialist schools "whose valuation of Speech and of Names [Non-Being] had all the character of religious veneration—for whom the Word was an eternal positive Ens existing in an eternal union with the things denoted by it."[63] At the other phase, they seek to reduce the Physical Phenomenon to a mere language-thought construct and thereby destroy all realist schools which valorize Existence as the eternal Ens—what Derrida calls "thing, reality or presence in general."

Mādhyamika thinkers pursue double negation more evenhandedly than Derrida does. Derrida concentrates his attacks on idealisms and seldom takes on idealisms and materialism simultaneously as he claimed. By contrast, Mādhyamika thinkers almost invariably seek to negate essentialisms and realisms in the same breath. After all, it is in reaction against these two opposite positions that the Mādhyamika arose and developed as a deconstructive philosophy. This exercise of double negation is the very raison d'être of the existence of Mādhyamika Buddhism and thus abounds in various Mādhyamika texts. In "The

Emptiness of the Unreal" ("Bu zhen kong lun" 不真空論), for instance, Seng Zhao pursues a simultaneous two-pronged deconstruction of the two opposite camps of Chinese Buddhism in his time—Name-valorizing schools vs. Thing-valorizing ones.[64] First, he criticizes the School of Nonexistence of Mind (*Xinwu zong* 心無宗) led by Zhi Mindu 支愍度 (fl. 326) for its reification of the mind as "Nonexistence":

> The Nonexistence of the Mind [School] turns the mind into "nonexistence" in the face of the myriad phenomena, but the myriad phenomena are not necessarily "nonexistence." Thus, it succeeds in attaining divine quietude, but errs on not treating phenomena as insubstantial.[65]

> 心無者。無心於萬物。萬物未嘗無。此得在於神靜。失在於物虛。

In Seng Zhao's view, this school slips into an essentialization of the empty mind because it focuses its attention on the mind to the neglect of the phenomenal world. The failure to treat the mind and the phenomena as coequal and codependent inevitably leads to a privileging of one over the other. If this school valorizes the "nonexistence" of the mind over the "existence" of matter, Seng Zhao maintains, the School of Matter as It Is (*Jise zong* 即色宗) represented by Zhi Daolin 支道林 (314–366) does just the opposite:

> The Matter as It Is [School] understands that matter does not become what it is by itself. [Although] we know that matter which displays itself as such is not matter, those who talk about matter take matter to be as it is. But how can matter become what it is through itself? Those people merely say that matter does not become what it is by itself, but do not understand that matter is not matter at all.[66]

> 即色者。明色不自色。故雖色而非色也。夫言色者。但當色即色。豈待色色而後為色哉。此直語色不自色。未領色之非色也。

According to Seng Zhao, this school ends up with an ontotheological position privileging the "existence" of matter because it fails to grasp the insubstantial, illusory nature of matter. Insofar as matter depends on nonmatter for its very existence, it is as much nonmatter as it is matter. After his attack on the School of Matter as It Is, Seng Zhao returns to take on yet another Name-valorizing school—the School of

Original Nonexistence (*Benwu zong* 本無宗) founded by Zhu Fatai 竺法汰 (320–387) and Dao An 道安 (312–385).

> The Original Nonexistence [School] is more often than not disposed to revere "nonexistence." Whenever they speak, they honor "nonexistence." For them, "not exist" means that existence is nothing but nonexistence; and "not nonexist" means that nonexistence is too nothing but nonexistence. If we look for the original meanings of these terms, "not exist" should mean no real existence; and "not nonexist," no real nonexistence.[67]

> 本無者。情尚於無。多觸言以賓無。故非有。有即無。非無。無亦無。尋夫立文之本旨者。直以非有。非真有。非無。非真無耳。

Seng Zhao concludes that this school is "nothing but a talk partial to nonexistence," just like the School of Nonexistence of the Mind. Its reification of "nonexistence" as an ontotheological entity results from a failure to recognize "nonexistence" as unreal and pursue a simultaneous double negation of both "existence" and "nonexistence."

Although only three Buddhist schools are singled out for criticism, Seng Zhao might very well have had in mind all of the "Six Leagues and Seven Schools" (*liujia qizong* 六家七宗) that allegedly existed in his day.[68] Like the three schools criticized by Seng Zhao, the remaining four schools of Prajñā learning (*boruo xue* 般若學) alternatively valorize Nonexistence and Existence. Besides, Seng Zhao might also intend to direct his ontotheological deconstruction against Nonexistence-reifying neo-Daoism of Wang Bi 王弼 (266–249) and the Existence-reifying neo-Daoism of Guo Xiang 郭象 (d. 312). While Wang Bi hypostatizes the name of "Dao" of Lao Zi as Original Nonexistence (*benwu* 本無), Guo Xiang valorizes the "self-being-so" (*ziran* 自然) of Zhuang Zi as the ultimate Existence. The close correspondence between these two neo-Daoist schools with the two Buddhist camps has attracted the attention of many scholars. Some suggest that Wang Bi and Guo Xiang might have been inspired by Buddhist sources to conceptualize "nonexistence" (*wu*) and "existence" (*yu*) as ultimate ontotheological entities.[69] Others argue that Wang's and Guo's doctrines influenced considerably the debates on "nonexistence" and "existence" among the two Buddhist camps.[70] Apparently accepting this latter view, Walter Liebenthal contends that Seng Zhao's two-pronged attack on the three Buddhist schools "had no relation to Indian Buddhist controversies" but grew out of the neo-Daoists' debates on Existence (*you*) and Nonexistence (*wu*).[71] Neither of these two views is conclusive, but they each speak to the mutual interaction and mutual influence of the Buddhist and neo-Daoist schools in Wei-Jin times.[72] Considering this, it is appropriate to assume that Seng Zhao's double negation is, if not actually intended for, readily applicable to Wang's and Guo's neo-Daoist doctrines.

Derrida and the Mādhyamika thinkers not only double-negate Name-reifying and Matter-reifying ontotheologies in similar fashions, but also theorize about their double negation in similar terms of "neither / nor." In *Positions,* Derrida double-negates a host of conceptual opposites endowed with ontotheological significance, and then sums up the principle of his biphase deconstruction as a practice of "neither / nor":

> . . . the *pharmakon* is neither remedy nor poison, neither good nor evil, neither the inside nor the outside, neither speech nor writing; the *supplement* is neither a plus nor a minus, neither an outside nor the complement of an inside, neither accident nor essence, etc.; the *hymen* is neither confusion nor distinction, neither identity nor difference, neither consummation nor virginity, neither the veil nor unveiling, neither the inside nor the outside, etc; the gram is neither a signifier nor a signified, neither a sign nor a thing, neither a presence nor an absence, neither a position nor a negation, etc.; *spacing* is neither space nor time; the incision is neither the incised integrity of a beginning, or of a simple cutting into, nor simple secondarity. Neither / nor, that is simultaneously either *or*. . . .[73]

Likewise, Seng Zhao characterizes the Mādhyamika double negation of the Name and Thing as an exercise of "neither-this-nor-that" logic:

> The *Chung lun* [Treatise on the Middle Doctrine, *Mādhyamika śāstra* by Nāgārjuna] says, "Things are neither this or that." . . . Thus 'this' and 'that' do not definitely refer to a particular name, but deluded people would believe that they necessarily do. This being the case, [the distinction] between 'this' and 'that' is from the beginning nonexistent, but to the deluded it is from the beginning not nonexistent. If we realize that 'this' and 'that' do not exist, is there anything that can be regarded as existent? Thus we know that things are not real; they are from the beginning only temporary names."[74]

故中觀云。物無彼此……此彼莫定乎一名。而惑者懷必然之志。然則彼此初非有。惑者初非無。既悟彼此之非有。有何物而可有哉。故知萬物非真。假號久矣。

This passage is yet another innovative reappropriation of *Zhuang Zi* by Seng Zhao. In *Zhuang Zi,* "this" and "that" are played off by each other to lift us to the totality of Dao, which includes both "this" and "that" in a perpetual process of transformation.[75] But here, "this" and "that" do not merely refer to one-sided human judgments as in *Zhuang Zi.* More importantly, they represent the two opposite fundamental ontotheological positions under which various existing philosophical schools can be subsumed. By exercising his "neither / nor" logic to dispose of "this" and "that," Seng Zhao aims to accomplish what Derrida will try to do more than a millennium later—to deconstruct all existing ontotheological positions without creating one of his own.

DECONSTRUCTIVE FORMULA:
DERRIDA'S *TETRALPHARMAKON*
AND THE MĀDHYAMIKA TETRALEMMA

Not only do Derrida and Mādhyamika thinkers theorize about their deconstructive logic in the same terms of "neither / nor," they also seek to distinguish their deconstructive formulas from other modes of philosophical thinking by invoking the same symbolic number of four. In *Dissemination,* Derrida self-consciously defines his deconstructionism against other philosophical schools "through its insistence upon squares, crossroads, and other four-sided figures . . . [and its] violent but imperceptible displacement of the 'triangular'—Dialectical, Trinitarian, Oedipal—foundations of Western thought."[76] First, Derrida restates the different symbolic numbers adopted in ontotheological discourses. Numbers One and Two represent the classical opposition of Being and beings and its attendant duplicities ("remedy / poison, good / evil, intelligible / sensible, high / low, mind / matter, life / death, inside / outside, speech / writing, etc.").[77] Number Three emerges as a resolution of the duplicities—in religion as the Trinity (Hegel's word), in Kant as a lifeless "'triadic' form (Triplicität)" (Schelling's word), in Schelling as the quasi-dialectic triplicity, and in Hegel as the living triplicity.[78] Then, Derrida compares his deconstructive enterprise to "a pharmacy in which it is no longer possible to count by ones, by twos, or by threes."[79] There, all the twos "can be neither reduced to unity, nor derived from a primary simplicity, nor dialectically sublated or internalized into a third term."[80] Similarly, all the threes "no longer give us the ideality of the speculative opposition but rather the effect of a strategic re-mark."[81] While destroying the dualistic and trinitarian horizons, Derrida envisions his operation of *différance* or textual dissemination as "a fourth term" and "the supplementary four (neither a cross nor a closed square)."[82] Indeed, Derrida is so fascinated with the idea of a fourth term that he renames *pharmakon*—one of his archexamples of *différance*—as *tetralpharmakon.*[83] To elaborate on the significance of this fourth term, he cites the following passage from Philippe Sollers' *Nombres:* "Even though it is only a triangle open on its fourth side, the splayed square loosens up the obsidionality of the triangle and the circle which in their ternary rhythm (Oedipus, Trinity, Dialectics) have always governed metaphysics. It loosens them up; that is, it de-limits them, reinscribes them, re-cites them."[84]

That a fourth term marks off Mādhyamika Buddhism from other philosophical systems is self-evident in the very name for which the Mādhyamika deconstruction is best known—*catuṣkoṭi*, commonly rendered as tetralemma or the four-cornered method of argument. Like Derrida, Mādhyamika thinkers believe the number four represents a negation of the preceding three numbers representative of all ontotheological positions. To nullify the three existing kinds of ontotheological claims, Nāgārjuna introduces the "neither / nor" as a fourth term:

> The world is finite.
> The world is infinite.
> The world is both finite and infinite.
> The world is neither finite nor infinite.[85]

Like Derrida, Nāgārjuna and other Mādhyamika thinkers aim to destroy not only the fundamental opposition of Being and Nonbeing but all its attendant duplicities and triplicities. Indeed, just as Derrida rules against counting "by ones, by twos, or by threes" in his pursuit of *tetralpharmakon,* Nāgārjuna consistently disposes of the ontotheological ones, twos, and threes in his exercise of tetralemma. He casts out— among numerous other sets—the ones, twos, and threes regarding the extension of the world, the form of soul, the finality of death, and other important philosophical issues.[86]

SELF-DECONSTRUCTIVE COURSE:
DERRIDA'S "SUPERNUMERARY"
AND THE MĀDHYAMIKA OCTOLEMMA

When Derrida and the Mādhyamika thinkers reach the fourth term in their deconstructive process, they still face the danger of getting trapped in a new dualism between the three preceding terms and their own fourth terms. Unless this new dualism is disposed of, their deconstructive terms themselves are bound to become a fixed ontotheological thesis. To overcome such an ontotheological reinscription, both Derrida and Mādhyamika thinkers undertake self-deconstruction. Derrida sloughs conceptuality off his deconstructive terms and sees to it that they get "imprinted and fractured" by their own logic. He writes:

> The motif of *différance,* when marked by a silent *a,* in effect plays neither the role of a "concept," nor simply of a "word." This does not prevent it from producing conceptual effects and verbal or nominal concretions. Which, moreover—although this is not immediately noticeable—are simultaneously imprinted and fractured by the corner of this "letter," by the incessant work of its strange "logic."[87]

> [*Différance*] cannot be elevated into a master-word or a master-concept . . . it blocks every relationship to theology. . . .[88]

> In the final analysis *dissemination* means nothing, and cannot be reassembled into a definition. . . . If dissemination, seminal *différance* cannot be summarized into an exact conceptual tenor, it is because the force and form of its disruption *explode* the semantic horizon.[89]

Like Derrida, Mādhyamika thinkers stress the importance of abolishing their own arguments and positions. In grappling with the same problem of reinscription, they, too, attempt to turn their deconstructive terms against themselves. For instance, they use the term *śūnyata* to deconstruct itself and develop a self-deconstructive doctrine of *śūnyata-śūnyata* ("the emptiness of the emptiness"). From the writings of Nāgārjuna and Candrakīrti, we can find these comments on *śūnyata-śūnyata:*

> "Empty" [*śūnya*], "non-empty" [*aśūnya*], "both" [*śūnya* and *aśūnya*], "neither" [*śūnya* nor *aśūnya*]—these should not be declared. It is expressed only for the purpose of communication.[90]

> This statement (viz. that nothing has self-existence) is not self-existent. . . . Just as a magically formed phantom could deny a phantom. . . . Just so (is) this negation.[91]

> Emptiness is not a property, or universal mark, of entities, because then its substratum would be nonempty, and one would have a fixed conviction (*drsti*) about it. In fact, it is a mere medicine, a means of escape from all fixed conviction. . . . It is not a positive standpoint, but a mere turning away from all views and thought-constructions.[92]

In the writings of Chinese Mādhyamika thinkers, we can also find examples of self-deconstruction. Seng Zhao's deconceptualizing of his own deconstructive terms *fei you* ("not exist") and *fei wu* ("not nonexist") is an excellent case in point. In order to forestall the emergence of these two terms as new ontotheological theses, he seeks to cleanse them of their incipient conceptuality:

> To say "not exist" is to mean that there is no existence, not that there is a "nonexistence." To say "not nonexist" is to mean that there is no nonexistence, not that there is a "non-nonexistence." "Not exist" is not a nonexistence. "Not nonexist" is not a "non-nonexistence."[93]

> 言其非有者。言其非是有。非謂是非有。言其非無者。言
> 其非是無。非謂是非無。非有非非有。非無非非無。

Neither Derrida nor Mādhyamika thinkers believe that they can truly abolish their own arguments merely by disclaiming them. Therefore, they both launch into a sustained, rigorous process of self-deconstruction. For Derrida, a true abandonment of positions, whether his own or others', must be achieved through a kinesis of mutual negations. To distinguish this deconstructive kinesis from the teleological kinesis, particularly the Hegelian one, Derrida characterizes it as a process of infinite regress. He contends that *"différance . . .* is not a pure nominal entity, and unceasingly dislocates itself in a chain of differing and deferring substitutions."[94] For Derrida, the term "trace" best captures the infinitude and the drifting nature of his deconstructive kinesis. "The trace is in fact the absolute origin of sense in general. Which amounts to saying once again that there is no absolute origin of sense in general. The trace is the *différance.*"[95] Like the "trace" described here, the Derridean deconstructive kinesis reaches no destination—always drifting amidst the phantoms of "the absolute origin of sense." It does not at any stage bear fruits comparable to the syntheses born of the Hegelian kinesis. To emphasize the barren nature of his deconstructive kinesis, Derrida compares it to "a sowing that does not produce plants, but is simply infinitely repeated" and to "a semination that is not *in*semination but *dis*semination, seed spilled in vain, an emission that cannot return to its origin in the father."[96]

Mādhyamika thinkers, especially later Chinese masters, also seek to subject their own tetralemma to a deconstructive kinesis. They also believe that they must treat *catuṣkoṭi* as "mere medicine" and "magically formed phantom" rather than a positive entity. Although Seng Zhao does not explicitly mention the deconstruction of *catuṣkoṭi*, he nevertheless advances the idea of a deconstructive kinesis when he stresses that one "communes with the spirit in between existence and nonexistence" in such a way that "one never gets trapped by what is determinable."[97] By pursuing such a deconstructive kinesis, Mādhyamika thinkers seek to avoid any attachment to a fixed conviction while undoing all views and thought constructions.

In their pursuit of deconstructive kinesis, Mādhyamika thinkers follow a direction totally different from that of Derrida. Whereas Derrida views his as a random drift, they treat theirs as a decidedly directional operation leading to an ultimate stasis, beyond language and conceptuality. We can discern this distinguishing trait of Mādhyamika deconstructive kinesis in the doctrine of Three Levels of Two Truths (*sanchong erdi* 三重二諦), presumably developed by Fa Lang 法朗 (fl. 610), the teacher of Ji Zang. This doctrine divides all philosophical positions, including Mādhyamika tetralemma, into the mundane truths and absolute truths on three levels of spiritual progress:

THREE LEVELS OF TWO TRUTHS

Mundane	*Absolute*
1. Existence	2. Nonexistence
3. Both Existence and Nonexistence	4. Neither Existence nor Nonexistence
5. BOTH (Both Existence and Nonexistence) AND (Neither Existence nor Nonexistence)	6. NEITHER (Both Existence and Nonexistence) NOR (Neither Existence nor Nonexistence)[98]

The first lemma (existence) represents the mundane truth, and the second lemma (nonexistence) represents the absolute truth on the first and the lowest level. The third lemma (both existence and nonexistence) combines the first two lemmas and registers as the mundane truth on the second level. The fourth lemma (neither existence nor nonexistence) negates the third lemma and reaches the absolute truth on the second level. Then, just as the third lemma combines the first and second lemmas, the fifth lemma combines the third and fourth lemmas and becomes the mundane truth on the third level. Significantly, this fifth lemma represents the initial stage of Ji Zang's deconstruction of his own *catuṣkoṭi* (tetralemma). The sixth lemma completes this self-deconstruction through the negation of the fifth lemma and rises to the absolute truth on the third level.

For Ji Zang, this deconstructive kinesis is a means of mind-cleansing "not limited to three levels but to be employed progressively to infinite levels until one is free of conceptual attachment."[99] In his *Profound Treatise of Mahāyāna* (*Dacheng xuanlun* 大 乘 玄 論), he develops his teacher's scheme into an even grander scheme of Four Levels of Two Truths (*sichong erdi* 四 重 二 諦). Expounding this new scheme, Ji Zang writes,

> They [other schools] regard "existence" as the mundane truth and "emptiness" as the absolute truth. Now it is clear to us that "both existence and emptiness" is the mundane truth and that "neither emptiness nor existence" is the absolute truth. On the third level, [let us call] "both emptiness and existence" as the "Two" and "neither emptiness nor existence as the "Negative Two." They both [the "Two" and the "Negative Two"] are the mundane truth [the fifth lemma]. The "Neither 'Two' nor 'Negative Two'" is the absolute truth [the sixth lemma]. On the fourth level, these Three Levels of the Two Truths are all the categories of teaching. In speaking of these "Three Categories," the purpose is to inspire an awakening to the "Negative Three." Only if the state of no attachment and no gain is reached can we call it the principle [i.e., the eighth lemma as the absolute truth on the fourth level].[100]

他但以有為世諦。空為諦。今明。若有若空皆是世諦。非
空有非有始名真諦。三者空有為二。非空有為不二。二與
不二皆是世諦。非二非不二名為真諦。四者此三種二諦皆
是教門。説此三門為令悟不三。無所依得始名為理。

Here Ji Zang does not explicitly describe the seventh lemma *sanmeng* 三 門 (the "Three Categories") and the eighth lemma *busan* 不 三 (the "Negative Three") as he does the previous six lemmas. However, if we can see the fourth level as analogous to the third and the second, we may then figure out what the seventh and the eighth lemmas are constituted of.

> *Seventh lemma:*
> BOTH [Both (Both Existence and Emptiness) and (Neither Existence nor Emptiness)]
> AND [Neither (Both Existence and Emptiness) nor (Neither Existence nor nonexistence)]

Simply put, the seventh lemma represents a "both / and" affirmation of the fifth and sixth lemmas on the preceding level.

Eighth lemma:
NEITHER [Both (Both Existence and Emptiness) and (Neither Existence nor Emptiness)]
NOR [Neither (Both Existence and Emptiness) nor (Neither Existence nor Nonexistence)]

In other words, the eighth lemma constitutes a "neither / nor" negation of the fifth and the sixth lemmas.[101]

The seventh and eighth lemmas, like their counterparts at earlier levels, are taken as mundane and absolute truths at the fourth level. In order to explain the eighth lemma intelligibly, some scholars choose to describe it as a succession of negations instead of setting forth all its lemmas as I just did above. For instance, in the preface to his annotations to *Profound Meaning of the Three Treatises* (*San lun xuanyi* 三論 玄義), Han Tingjie 韓廷傑 gives this description of the eighth lemma:

> Not existence, not emptiness [fourth lemma], neither the Two nor the Negative Two [sixth lemma], not "neither the Two nor the Negative Two" [eighth lemma][102]

非有，非空，非二非不二，非非二非不二。

While Jing Zang conveniently uses his four numeric symbols ("Two," "Negative Two," "Three," "Negative Three") in setting forth his deconstructive kinesis beyond the tetralemma, he seldom employs them when deconstructing specific ontotheological concepts. For instance, when he deconstructs birth / extinction (*shengmie* 生滅), two of the eight primary binary ontotheological terms constantly negated by Mādhyamika thinkers, Ji Zang makes no use of the numeric symbols. This shows that he usually does not pursue his deconstructive kinesis any further than the fourth lemma. By the time he reaches the stage of *catuṣkoṭi*, his mind seems to have been rendered incapable of much further language-thought formulations.[103]

For Ji Zang, how far one should pursue the deconstructive kinesis depends on how effectively it renders one speechless and thoughtless. In his *Profound Meaning of Three Treatises,* he elucidates this view of a deconstructive kinesis: "*San Lun* [Three Treatises] doctrine teaches that each thesis that may be proposed concerning the nature of truth must be negated by its antithesis, the whole process advancing step by step until total negation has been achieved . . . until everything that may be predicated about truth has been negated."[104] "This forgetting of words and this elimination of thought," Ji Zang believes, "is the [ulti-mate] absolute truth."[105] When the deconstructive kinesis reaches this final stage, one attains the state of enlightenment.

Given this ultimate soteriological goal, the Mādhyamika thinkers would not set their deconstructive kinesis adrift among traces of traces, less would they delight in an infinite play of deconstructions, and still less would they compare their deconstructive enterprise to a fruitless dissemination. As Derrida and Ji Zang perceive their deconstructive kinesis in radically different lights, they naturally describe it with differ-ent numeric symbols. Derrida invokes Sollers' "supernumerary" in the last section of *Dissemination* and concludes the book with this math-ematical formula: "$(1 + 2 + 3 + 4)^2 \ldots$" Here, with a squaring for-mula, Derrida seems to indicate the nonlinear drift of his decon-structive kinesis. With "$\ldots$" after the squaring formula, he seems to symbolize the perpetual delays of an outcome and hence the fruitful-ness of his deconstructive kinesis. In contrast to Derrida's aimless, fruit-less "supernumerary," Ji Zang's "octolemma" can be conceived of as a linear progression: 1-2-3-4-5-6-7-8. This simple formula betokens the reverse of Derrida's formula. It stands for the directional character, the finite duration, the *fruitful* promise of the Mādhyamika deconstruc-tive kinesis.

THE "END" OF PHILOSOPHY: THE OUTCOME OF THE
DERRIDEAN AND THE MĀDHYAMIKA DECONSTRUCTIONS

Having examined the important parallels in the Derridean and Mād-hyamika deconstructive theories, we can now reflect on some funda-mental differences between these two deconstructive enterprises. The two deconstructive kineses reveal that the Derridean and Mādhyamika deconstructive programs differ from each other with respect to their directions and goals.

In their rigorous pursuits of deconstruction and self-deconstruction, the Derridean and Mādhyamika philosophies inevitably reach a point where philosophy ends and "nonphilosophy" begins. In the case of Der-rida, "nonphilosophy" takes the form of infinite textual proliferation beyond comprehension. This is the consequence Derrida knows he has to bear. "To risk meaning nothing is to start to play, and first to enter into the play of *différance*. . . ."[106] However, it would be wrong to think that Derrida delights in such a consequence of "non-sense," because he confesses that "'meaning-to-say-nothing' is not, you will agree, the most assured of exercises"[107] and he regrets that his deconstructive discourse has provoked "resistance or out-of-hand rejection even on the part of the best informed readers."[108] His is a dilemma between "true to his own word" and "meaning-to-say-nothing." If he practices what he preaches, he falls to "meaning-to-say-nothing." If he tries to avoid "meaning-to-say-nothing," he goes against his own word and becomes a half-hearted deconstructionist. While we can sense a frequent wavering between these two choices in Derrida's early writings, we feel that he seems more inclined to risk "meaning-to-say-nothing" in his later works. For instance, his *Glas* seems to exemplify a work "entangled in hundreds of pages of a writing simultaneously insistent and elliptical . . . carrying off each concept into an interminable chain of differences, surrounding or confusing itself with so many precautions, references, notes, citations, collages, supplements."[109] However, the "non-sense" that results from such verbiage takes on a philosophical meaning of its kind, even though it is intended to negate philosophical meanings and positions. As to how to interpret the meaning of the Derridean "non-sense," critics are quite divided. Many take the meaning to be that of antiphilosophy or even nihilism, and hold Derridean deconstructionism responsible for what they call the fads of denying humanistic values in present-day philosophical and literary studies. Some are more sympathetic to Derrida's deconstructive enterprise and seek to ascribe a positive philosophical purpose to the Derridean "non-sense." For instance, Coward holds that the Derridean "non-sense" is not an aimless linguistic play, but is "itself an ontological process."[110] While Derrida deconstructs "illusions of permanence, stasis, or presence" superimposed on language, Coward argues, he pursues the dynamic process of becoming of language as "the means for the realization of the whole ('the sign')."[111] When Derrida's faithful execution of his deconstructive theory results in nearly pure verbiage, one cannot resist doubting his claim that he does not "believe in what today is so easily called the death of philosophy."[112] One may even assume that he has jettisoned, along with ontotheologies, philosophy itself, and led himself into the prison-house of language, or even the abyss of nihilism.

Whether or not we interpret the Derridean "non-sense" in a negative or positive light, we would agree that it is fundamentally different from the kind of "non-sense" arising from Seng Zhao's lexical-syntactical deconstructions. Mādhyamika deconstructions and self-deconstructions follow a clearly directional path, defined by step-by-step negations of lemmas.[113] In the case of the Mādhyamika Buddhism, "nonphilosophy" is synonymous with religious enlightenment beyond language and conceptuality. For Mādhyamika thinkers, it is not a consequence to be dreaded but to be celebrated. The Mādhyamika deconstruction is geared to none other than this dawning of Nirvāṇa upon the death of language, conceptuality, and philosophy. In light of this, we can very well see the transformation of the Chinese Mādhyamika into the Ch'an (Zen) Buddhism—"a practical, anti-intellectual, irrational, unconventional and dramatic religious movement"[114]—as a doctrinal fulfillment of the soteriological promise of the Mādhyamika Buddhism.[115]

This positive, soteriological outcome of Mādhyamika deconstructions and self-deconstructions is not lost on Western thinkers seeking to cope with "the sense of loss of foundations in contemporary science and philosophy."[116] In their collaborative work, *The Embodied Mind,* three cognitive scientists, Francisco J. Varela, Evan Thompson, and Eleanor Rosch, employ the term "mindfulness / awareness" to describe the ultimate positive outcome of Mādhyamika thinking, and explore the possibility of attaining the same kind of transformative experience in Western postmodern conditions. They believe that their endeavor is not only possible but highly desirable because it will help to "develop direct and personal insight into the groundlessness of our own experience" and to transcend Western philosophy that "has been more concerned with the rational understanding of life and mind than with the relevance of a pragmatic method for transforming human experience."[117]

In the opinion of the three cognitive scientists, the Mādhyamika "mindfulness / awareness" approximates what the Italian philosopher Gianni Vattimo calls Nietzsche's "theory of a possibly active, or positive, nihilism"[118]—"that is, a kind of thought that would give up the modernist quest for foundations, yet without criticizing this quest in the name of another, truer foundation."[119] They believe that Nietzsche, Heidegger, and their postmodernist descendants like Derrida all failed to realize the positive potential of their deconstructivisms or nihilisms largely because "there is no methodological basis for a middle way between objectivism and subjectivism (both forms of absolutism)."[120] Specifically, they point out that this lack of middle ground, or "entre-deux" as they call it, prevents Western nihilism of all persuasions from following "through its own inner logic and motivation and so stop[ping] short of transforming its partial realization of groundlessness into the philosophical and experiential possibilities of *śūnyata.*"[121]

By adopting the Mādhyamika "mindfulness / awareness" to make up for the lack of the "entre-deux" in Western postmodernist thought, the three cognitive scientists seek to accomplish two ambitious goals. The first goal is to redirect all the intellectually oriented deconstructivisms to "transformative approaches to experience, especially those concerned not with escape from the world or the discovery of some hidden, true self but with releasing the everyday world from the clutches of the grasping mind and its desire for an absolute ground."[122] The second is to spell out the high ethical, if not outright soteriological, promise of Western postmodernist deconstructivisms, which they believe can be achieved through the "mindfulness / awareness" tradition:

> Let us restate why we think ethics in the mindfulness / awareness tradition, and indeed, the mindfulness / awareness tradition itself, are so important to the modern world. There is a profound discovery of groundlessness in our culture—in science, in the humanities, in society, and in the uncertainties of people's daily lives. This is generally seen as something negative—by everyone from the prophets of our time to ordinary people struggling to find meaning in their lives. Taking groundlessness as negative, as a loss, leads to a sense of alienation, despair, loss of heart, and nihilism. The cure that is generally espoused in our culture is to find a new grounding (or return to older grounds). The mindfulness / awareness tradition points the way to a radically different resolution. In Buddhism, we have a case study showing that when groundlessness is embraced and followed through to its ultimate conclusions, the outcome is an unconditional sense of intrinsic goodness that manifests itself in the world as spontaneous compassion. We feel, therefore, that the solution for the sense of nihilistic alienation in our culture is not to try to find a new ground; it is to find a disciplined and genuine means to pursue groundlessness, to go further into groundlessness. Because of the preeminent place science occupies in our culture, science must be involved in this pursuit.[123]

The two goals of the three cognitive scientists are truly as ambitious as any contemporary Western thinker dares to set himself to accomplish. They strive to bring about nothing less than a radical reorientation of the entire Western philosophical tradition and a formulation of a noble ethics for nihilism, the most dreaded abyss of Western thought. Needless to say, many trained in Western thought will question, doubt, challenge, or denounce their sweeping moral and (anti-)philosophical claims and their warm embrace of an alien mindfulness / awareness tradition.

This discussion has demonstrated four important parallels in the Derridean and Mādhyamika theories: (1) Both Derrida and Mādhyamika thinkers develop deconstructive theories of meaning based on the similar ideas of *différance* and *differentiam,* and seek to nullify the logos and the Name of Nonexistence reified by Western idealists and Buddhist essentialists; (2) they both apply the same theories of meaning to deconstruct the Matter and Existence reified by Western materialists and Buddhist realists; (3) they both conceive of their double negation as an exercise of "neither / nor" logic and set forth their deconstructive formulas in similar terms of *tetralpharmakon* and tetralemma or *catuṣkoṭi;* and (4) they both abolish their own *tetralpharmakon* and tetralemma and embark on their self-deconstructive course along an aimless "supernumerary" and along a linear "octolemma." While examining these four parallels, I have identified and explained fundamental differences between the Derridean and Mādhyamika, between the neo-Daoist and Mādhyamika philosophies, in light of their deconstructive goals. In presenting the response to Mādhyamika and Zen Buddhism by the three contemporary cognitive scientists, I intend not to defend or repudiate their positions, but to applaud their efforts to engage a genuine dialogue between Western and East Asian traditions. However controversial it may be, their project shows that an examination of important parallels in postmodernist and Mādhyamika theories can be not only a meaningful intellectual inquiry but also a broad cross-cultural dialogue fraught with social and moral implications for contemporary life.

This dialogue also has a close bearing on literary scholarship. As briefly discussed in chapter 1, Derridean thought undergirds all the variant modes of critical thinking in the postmodernist movement. Its impact on Western poetics has been examined thoroughly. Although the influence of Mādhyamika Buddhism on Chinese poetics is not nearly as extensive as that of Derridean thought on Western poetics, it is by no means insignificant and should not remain unrecognized and unexamined. In her study of Wang Wei, Pauline Yu rightly points out the important influence of Mādhyamika Buddhism on Chinese poetry.[124] Apart from her brief discussion, however, few efforts have been made to explore the Mādhyamika connection to Chinese poetics in the Western-language scholarship. Similarly, not until recently did scholars in China begin to trace the elements of Mādhyamika Buddhism in critical texts like Liu Xie's *Literary Mind.*[125] In a recent Chinese-language article, I myself attempt to analyze some conspicuously contradictory statements in the *Literary Mind* in terms of the Mādhyamika logic. Instead of being faults of argumentation as often assumed, I argue that these statements are clear evidence of Liu Xie's ingenious adaptation of the Mādhyamika middle way (*zhong-dao* 中道) to accommodate opposing critical views and trends.[126] Due to lack of space here, I shall wait for a future occasion to present my findings in English and further demonstrate the relevance of Derrida-Mādhyamika comparisons to our studies of Western and Chinese poetics.

Epilogue
Reflections: Intracultural, Cross-cultural,
and Transcultural Perspectives on Western
and Chinese Literary Criticism

I N THIS CLOSING CHAPTER, I SHALL ATTEMPT TO EXPLAIN
the intracultural, cross-cultural, and transcultural perspectives in-
troduced in this book. These three perspectives are intended to address
specific deficiencies in various comparative methods and to counter the
baneful influence of Orientalist and Occidentalist discourses.[1] Though
devised expressly for this project, they may have some theoretical rel-
evance and even practical applicability to similar projects in West-China
comparative studies. For this reason, I venture to share my reflections
on the raison d'être of the three perspectives and invite the reader to
assess his or her potential usefulness for battling various cultural and
racial biases that have long plagued West-China cultural comparisons
in general and West-China comparative literature in particular.[2]

INTRACULTURAL PERSPECTIVE:
ESTABLISHING RELIABLE GROUNDS
OF CROSS-CULTURAL COMPARISONS

Intracultural perspective is intended to help gain an understanding of
the root and historical development of one tradition without explicit
comparisons with another. All too often, Western and Chinese poet-
ics have been disengaged from their cultural contexts and hastily com-
pared as if they existed in a cultural vacuum. The results of such com-
parisons are often worse than dubious. As shown in the next section,
they tend to reinforce the polemics of similitude and the polemics of

difference lying at the core of Orientalist and Occidentalist discourses. To reverse this trend of superficial, misleading comparisons, we must first examine Western and Chinese critical traditions on their own terms and investigate the broader intellectual and cultural contexts in which they arose and developed. Only after such an intracultural inquiry should we begin to commit them to cross-cultural comparison.[3]

By coining the compound "intracultural," I wish to emphasize the dynamic interplay of "self-containedness" and "connectedness" to be achieved in my broad surveys of Western and Chinese critical traditions. The prefix "intra-" is essentially oxymoronic as it at once denotes self-containedness and connotes connectedness. For example, "intranet," a prominent neologism of our information age, denotes a self-contained system of electronic communication while it connotes the presence of, and hence a degree of connectedness with, other systems. If not for this implied presence of the other, the prefix "intra-" would be superfluous.

Similarly, my intracultural inquiry is, first and foremost, an endeavor to distinguish Western and Chinese poetics each as a largely self-contained system rooted in its own intellectual and cultural traditions. In examining the macrocosmic structures of the two critical systems, I have identified their distinctive sets of common denominators, *differentiae,* and cosmological paradigms. In discussing the microcosmic textures of the two systems, I have distinguished the conceptual models used in each system for exploring similar critical issues. I also have traced those models to their respective philosophical sources. In the meantime, I have sought to create a measure of connectedness through parallel arrangements of chapters and sections. I have paired off my investigations of the macrocosmic structures in chapters 1 and 2. When arranging individual sections in chapters 5 to 8, I have paired off my investigations of the microcosmic textures in a similar fashion. Examined in parallel, each tradition serves as a contrasting foil to accentuate the cultural specificity of the other. In this way, the two traditions become mutually connected and illuminated.

My findings in chapters 1–2 seem to attest to such effects of mutual illumination. If not for a keen awareness of their cross-cultural counterparts, I would not have come up with my own views of the overarching paradigms of Western and Chinese poetics. The discovery of the truth-centered paradigm in Western poetics enables me to modify M. H. Abrams' analytical scheme to better reflect the shifts of critical locus in Western poetics from Plato through the present day. Instead of taking the four coordinates (universe, artist, work, audience) as the constants of criticism in and of themselves, I have viewed their emergence and constant reconfigurations as engendered and propelled by the broader paradigmatic shifts of Western thinking about truth. By the same token, without my awareness of this truth-centered paradigm as its counterpart, I would not have discerned the process-centered paradigm of Chinese poetics. The recognition of this paradigm enables me to debunk the entrenched view that there is a deplorable lack of systematicity in Chinese poetics. When placed within a broad paradigm of interacting processes, a seemingly haphazard mass of critical statements emerges as a highly coherent systematic whole. As is the case with Western poetics, the shifts of critical locus in Chinese poetics often mirror the broader paradigmatic shifts of Chinese thinking about the dynamic relationship of external and internal processes. The findings of my intracultural inquiry may shed some light on the fundamental issues concerning the systematics, orientations, and philosophical foundations of Western and Chinese poetics. By addressing these fundamental issues, I hope to establish reliable grounds for my cross-cultural comparisons on a number of particular subjects.

CROSS-CULTURAL PERSPECTIVE: OVERCOMING THE POLEMICS OF SIMILITUDE AND POLEMICS OF DIFFERENCE

The cross-cultural perspective is intended to counter two broad types of polemics that have bedeviled much of West-China comparative studies. It is my belief that West-China comparative studies should not be merely an inquiry *across* geographical boundaries. More importantly, it should be an earnest endeavor to *cross* all the barriers of cultural biases. As we shall see below, to subject to comparison Western and Chinese cultures, on either macrocosmic or microcosmic scales, does not automatically help to bring down cultural barriers. On the contrary, if improperly conceived and conducted, such comparative studies may contribute to reinforcing racial stereotypes and cultural biases instead of demolishing them. In fact, intentionally or unintentionally, these studies often serve in their own ways the "purpose of conquering one cultural mode with another established mode."[4] Most of such prejudiced comparisons fall into two broad types: polemics of similitude and polemics of difference. It is to overcome these two polemics that I have sought to introduce the cross-cultural perspective.

The Two Polemics in
West-China Cultural Comparisons

First, let me consider the two polemics in broad West-China cultural comparisons. In my opinion, polemics of similitude, avidly pursued on both sides of the West-China cultural confrontation, arises from the deep anxiety for asserting or maintaining cultural superiority. In the West, there is a long tradition of polemic arguments on similarities of Chinese culture to Western culture, a tradition that traces back to the earliest substantial engagement with China by the Jesuits in the sixteenth century. The Jesuits' explanation of Confucian classics in Judeo-Christian terms constitutes a classic model of appropriating Chinese culture by Western thinkers for centuries to come.[5] Through such polemics of similitude, some missionaries aimed to show that Chinese culture is a primitive antecedent to Western culture and hence should be subordinated to the latter. Another important aim is to prove the universal validity of Western ideas, concepts, values, and norms by adducing their protean forms in the alien Chinese culture. If we survey the literary and intellectual discourses on China during the Renaissance, the Enlightenment, and the Romantic movement, we can find an overabundance of such efforts to harness, conquer, and subordinate the alien Chinese culture.[6] We may observe this deep anxiety for cultural dominance even among those who show a genuine interest in and considerable respect for Chinese culture.

On the side of China, we encounter a polemics of similitude of a different kind. If the Western polemics of similitude seeks to subordinate Chinese culture by treating it as its primitive antecedent, the Chinese polemics of similitude seeks to look at its antecedence to Western culture as proof of its cultural superiority. Whatever the West can boast of, the cliché goes, China has possessed not only in great abundance, but also for a longer time.[7] So long as the military might of the West could be kept at bay, this polemics of similitude worked rather conveniently to counter the Western threat to China's hitherto unchallenged cultural superiority. However, when the self-deceptive illusion of China's cultural superiority was gone with the smoke of the Opium War, a humble and self-redemptive polemics of similitude emerged to replace the older, arrogant kind. By dwelling upon the purported antecedence of Western ideas, values, and institutions in traditional China, the reform-minded Chinese thinkers in the late nineteenth and early twentieth centuries did not seek to reclaim China's superiority over the West. Rather, they aimed to salvage China's shattered self-esteem and convince the Chinese people that China could develop the finest things of the West because she had the seeds of them lying in the rich soils of her long history. In this regard, we immediately think of Liang Qichao's endeavors to locate the prototypes of the parliamentary institutions in ancient Chinese social structures, the notion of the rule of law in Guan Zi's writings, and the ideal of *minben zhuyi* 民本 主義 (the theory of the "people as the foundation [of Government]") in various pre-Qin texts.[8] Scholarly inaccurate and often downright erroneous, this polemics of similitude was intended at the time to help rally support for instituting literary, educational, and sociopolitical reforms.

Polemics of difference comes hand in hand with polemics of similitude and abounds on both sides of the West-China equation. It constitutes the alternate and often more pernicious means of asserting cultural superiority in both the West and China. What lies at the heart of polemics of difference is a condemnation of the absence in the other tradition of certain ideas, values, and institutions held sacred to one's own tradition. Polemics of difference, in its worst form, produces blatant racial stereotypes against other peoples.

In the West, polemics of difference came to dominate discourses on China in the second half of the nineteenth century, when the Western powers reached the height of their colonial conquests and finally brought China, the largest "pagan" country, to its knees. The main staple of this polemics is the so-called absence, or even deliberate disregard, of truth in China as well as other Asian countries:

> More uneradicable than the sins of the flesh is the falsity of the Chinese; . . . their disregard of truth has perhaps done more to lower their character than any other fault.[9]

> The ordinary speech of the Chinese is so full of insincerity . . . that it is very difficult to learn the truth in almost every case. In China it is literally true that a fact is the hardest thing in the world to get at.[10]

On the ground of what they saw as the absence or disregard of truth, they easily came to a wholesale denigration of the Chinese as a morally degenerate people completely different from Westerners. The Chinese, they concluded, are given to sins of the flesh, are full of falsity, and are completely devoid of any spirituality. Through deprecating the moral character of the Chinese, they sought to reaffirm their own moral and cultural superiority.

This polemics of difference has had a profound and lasting influence on the Western thinking about China ever since. Even though the most egregious of such racist remarks faded in subsequent Western ideological discourses on China, the basic assumptions of China's cultural and moral inferiority remained unchallenged and were often expressed in a subtle, disguised manner. Let us see, for example, the following two passages, one by Pearl S. Buck and one by William Haas:

> We are often puzzled by the lack of what we consider truth-telling on the part of Asians. It seems at times impossible to get facts from Asian persons. The difference here is that [we have come] to consider truth as factual . . . whereas for the Asian truth is contained in an ethic. When we inquire of an Asian as to what may have happened in a specific incident, we grow impatient because we cannot get from him a clear and simple statement of fact. But for him . . . human feelings and intentions are more important than mere material fact.[11]

> Facts are sacred to the Westerner; they are less so to the Oriental, who has always been more interested in the psychological and human aspects of phenomena. What to him is important, what, as a matter of fact, is real, is not the object in its supposed "objectivity," but its significance for man. So in dealing with the Oriental there arise continually situations for which the Westerner finds himself wholly unprepared and for which he may propose all-too-simple interpretations. . . . The readiness with which the Oriental gives erroneous information instead of confessing his ignorance is motivated by reluctance to disappoint; this motive often makes him give an answer which he considers agreeable to the questioner. In such cases and many others the desire to please and to feel obliging has a tendency to make one ignore plain facts.[12]

Though not as overtly accusatory as Sell Williams, Buck and Haas both advanced more or less the same racist arguments against the Asian peoples, deploring their disregard for truth and consequently their untrustworthiness and obsequiousness. In my opinion, their racist arguments are equally pernicious even though they are hidden behind a magnanimous explanation for the causes of these moral weaknesses. According to them, the causes are Asians' privileging of the feelings over objective truth, the sociopsychological over the scientific-intellectual. To anyone familiar with the Western value systems, this observation is anything but complimentary. In the West, feeling has long been considered an inferior part of the human soul to be controlled and ruled by reason or faith—the access to truth—in the mainstream Platonic and Judaic-

Christian traditions. Such is the most deeply entrenched view of feeling in the West despite the Romantics' attempt to elevate feeling by aligning it with divine imagination. Seen in this broad context of Western intellectual and ethical traditions, Buck's and Haas' remarks seem to be a thinly veiled condemnation of Asians' intellectual and moral inferiority due to their obsession with feeling at the expense of truth.

The Chinese side is not without the guilt of pursuing its own kind of polemics of difference. The worst forms of cultural bias and racial stereotypes against non-Han peoples are predicated on various polemics of difference. In both official and unofficial discourses in premodern China, non-Han peoples were often contemptuously referred to as "eastern barbarians" (*dongyi* 東夷), "southern barbarians" (*nanman* 南蠻), "western barbarians" (*xirong* 西戎), and "northern barbarians" (*beidi* 北狄). These peoples were regarded as barbarians or lesser human kinds for no other reason than that they lived on the fringes of the civilized Middle Kingdom and observed cultural customs radically different from those of the Han Chinese.[13] Later on, the generalized slur "barbarians" or *yi* 夷 was readily applied to Westerners on the same ground that their cultures were distant / different from and hence inferior to the Han Chinese culture. If the Western polemics of difference harps on the absence of regard for truth in the Chinese traditions, this Chinese polemics of difference feeds itself on the absence of moral censures against greed and voluptuousness. Like their Western counterparts, Chinese practitioners of polemics of difference sought to reaffirm their cultural and moral superiority through a sweeping denigration of the other side.

In the midst of this ugly exchange of polemics of difference, there occurred an anomaly in the first two decades of the twentieth century. At that time, the polemics of difference espoused by Western colonialists was embraced by Lu Xun 魯迅 (1881–1936) and many revolutionary-minded thinkers of the May Fourth Movement. They readily agreed that there was a deplorable absence of the ideas and values that had made the West strong and powerful—truth, science, and democracy, among others. While Liang Qichao and other earlier reformists pursued their polemics of similitude to expedite the integration of these ideas and values into the traditional Chinese culture, they sought to use their polemics of difference to demolish the traditional Chinese culture and make way for a wholesale import of Western ideas and values. Their hope was that China, through a total Westernization of her culture, could get back on her feet and become as strong and powerful as Western nations. It is truly an ironic twist of history that the Western colonialists' polemics of difference should become a sharp weapon in China's fight against Western colonization as well as her feudal past.

The Two Polemics in West-China Comparative Literature

In the field of West-China comparative literature, we can see many reflections of the polemics of similitude and the polemics of difference exposed and criticized above. Due to the limit of space, here I will discuss only the influence of these two polemics on the development of literary scholarship in China. Of the two kinds, the former wields a far more prevalent and consequential influence and hence deserves our special attention.

Seen in a broad outline, there have been two major phases in the continuing efforts to reexamine Chinese literature and criticism through comparisons with their Western counterparts. The first phase lasts from the late nineteenth century through the first half of the twentieth century. This phase is marked by the efforts to elucidate traditional Chinese critical concepts, redefine traditional literary genres, and rewrite Chinese literary history within the broad Western conceptual frameworks. As a notable early example of such efforts, we may mention Wang Guowei's reconceptualization of the notion of *yijing* 意境 (ideascape) with the Western subject-object dichotomy and his reclassification of Chinese dramatic works into the Western categories of tragedies and comedies.[14] For an equally well-known example from a later time, we may think of Zhu Guangqian's (1897–1986) 朱光潛 discussion of traditional Chinese aesthetics in terms of Croce's theory of intuition.[15] Of course, among the broad-based efforts to find structural similarities to the Western critical system, we can still hear the stressed voices of Chinese critics decrying the absence of certain all-important genres or concepts in the Chinese traditions. In this regard, we cannot but recall how Liang Qichao laments the absence of political novels and how Lu Xun condemns the suppression of the "demonic" Romantic ideal in traditional Chinese poetics.[16]

The second phase spans about two decades from the introduction of comparative literature as a discipline in the 1960s outside mainland China and in the late 1970s in mainland China. This phase is characterized by attempts to make text-to-text and author-to-author comparisons after the model of parallel study, one of the two prominent approaches used by Western, especially American, comparatists. If one looks through the journals or yearbooks of comparative literature published in mainland China, Taiwan, or Hong Kong from the 1960s through the late 1980s, one will find an overabundance of such comparative studies. Yet, in spite of the daunting number of publications, the results of the second phase are often far more problematic and far less inspiring than those of the first phase. This is due in part to the inappropriate application of the model of parallel study, a model that was originally developed for comparing works produced within the same cultural system and does not entail the consideration of the fundamental differences rooted in different cultural systems. The problem of methodology is compounded by the insufficient training of the comparatists in both Western and Chinese traditions. If the first phase represents concerted endeavors pursued by the finest Chinese scholars, firmly in command of traditional scholarship and truly conversant with Western literary theories, the second phase may be regarded as a popular movement by the educated multitude, many of whom originally work only in the field of Western or Chinese literature and hastily embark on the adventures of comparative studies. So it is not surprising that many comparative projects aim merely to find in Chinese texts surface resemblances to certain Western literary themes, motifs, or styles. More often than not, they choose to ignore the underlying differences grounded in different Western and Chinese conceptual models and cosmological paradigms. Consequently, they usually fail to reveal the raison d'être of resemblances and differences or to yield true theoretical insight into the issues under investigation.

In criticizing the overeagerness to fit broad Chinese literary concerns into Western theoretical categories or to locate specific text-to-text, author-to-author similarities, I do not mean to detract the achievements of early comparatists. Quite the contrary, we owe a great debt to them for, to say nothing else, our very ability to perceive the imperfections in their works and set higher goals for our own comparative work. If not for their pioneering efforts, Western and Chinese literary criticisms would not have been brought into the same purview of intellectual inquiry. Much less would we have reached a sophisticated stage of development when we can aim to go beyond polemics of similitude and polemics of difference and strive to be truly "cross-cultural" in the sense of crossing deeply entrenched cultural biases separating the West and China.

In chapters 4–8, I sought to establish this cross-cultural perspective by taking two steps to avoid the pitfalls of the two polemics noted above. The first is to anchor my comparisons on non-culture-specific issues.

Of the primary issues addressed—the formation of a critical system in chapter 4, the nature and use of poetic harmony in chapter 5, the creative process in chapter 6, the power of written language in chapter 7, and deconstructive logic and strategies in chapter 8—none are exclusively specific to either Western or Chinese tradition. Although these issues should not be essentialized as "human universals," they do point to the basic aspects of literary and intellectual experience that transcend both cultural and temporal boundaries. By centering my comparisons on these issues, I could be less susceptible to the two polemics than I would if I anchored my comparisons on issues that are essential to the Western tradition but irrelevant or negligible to the Chinese tradition—say, "representation" in chapter 5, "primary and secondary imagination" in chapter 6, "Imagism" in chapter 7, and "logocentrism and phonocentrism" in chapter 8. If so anchored, my comparisons are bound to be lopsided and would most likely degenerate into polemics of similitude or difference.

The second step is to assess the findings of my comparisons within the broad Western and Chinese intellectual horizons set forth in chapters 1–3 and in the ending sections of chapters 5–8. Thanks to these horizons established through the use of intracultural perspective, I can assess my findings of similarities and differences in a true cross-cultural fashion. First of all, I can appreciate the similarities, not as a confirmation of certain preexisting universals or the superiority of one particular tradition, but as a convergence of views and concerns that attests to the commonality of literary experience. By the same token, I can contemplate the differences, not as the ground for privileging one tradition over another, but as a testimony to divergent priorities in each tradition. Wai-lam Yip seems to have this kind of cross-cultural perspective in mind when he presents a diagram called "Cultural convergences and divergences"[17] (see figure 9).

In explaining this diagram, Yip maintains that "we must not apply all the structuring characteristics of circle *A* onto circle *B* or vice versa."[18] In other words, we must guard against the polemics of similitude that aims to force a cultural tradition into the mode of another. Meanwhile, Yip stresses the importance of examining and understanding each tradition on its own terms. "Quite often," he writes, "the parts (i.e, the divergences) can bring us closer than the resemblances to the root understanding of the two models."[19] It is noteworthy that the two circles are symmetrical in their sizes and in their participation in the shaded areas of resemblances. With this conspicuous symmetry, Yip obviously wants to emphasize the basis of equality for any truly "cross-cultural"

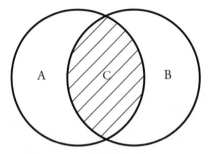

Figure 9.

dialogue. If not conceived and conducted on an equal basis, a comparison or contrast between two indigenous traditions is likely to degenerate into polemics of difference, one that aggrandizes one tradition at the expense of the other on the ground of its monopoly of certain ideas and values. While I have reservations about Yip's interpretation of the shaded areas of C as "the basis for establishing a fundamental model" or for "setting up any fundamental universals,"[20] I warmly applaud his diagram as a vivid presentation of a truly "cross-cultural" perspective to be used in West-China comparative poetics.

TRANSCULTURAL PERSPECTIVE:
THE EVALUATION OF SIMILARITIES AND DIFFERENCES

The establishment of a "cross-cultural" perspective makes possible, but by no means guarantees, the overcoming of the polemics of similitude or difference. In placing Western and Chinese traditions on equal footing, this perspective will certainly help prevent us from exaggerating either similarities and differences in favor of one particular tradition. It does not, however, provide a broader framework for assessing similarities and differences in ways that will forestall the two kinds of polemics. Let us return, for a moment, to Yip's diagram. In it, we can find no clues as to from which point of view we should look at the similarities and differences shown. We are left to conceive of three possible points of view: from A, B, or C. If we look at the similarities and differences solely from either A or B, we will be seeing two cultural traditions through the vistas of one, and hence become susceptible to the two polemics. On the other hand, if we focus our attention solely on C, we will be tempted to overemphasize the similarities to the point of

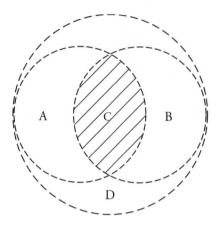

Figure 10.

essentializing them as "universals," and consequently neglect the examination of differences.

Since each of these three points of view are partial and limited, we need to establish a broader, transcultural perspective for assessing similarities and differences revealed by "cross-cultural" comparative studies. For this end, I propose to present a new diagram based on Yip's (see figure 10).

The new circle D encompasses both the intracultural (A and B) and "cross-cultural" (A, B, and C combined) perspectives discussed above. As suggested by its inclusiveness, this perspective is born of an effort to rise above the limitations and prejudices of any single tradition to a transcultural vantage point, from which we can assess similarities and differences without privileging, overtly or covertly, one tradition over another. Here, a brief statement on the philosophical ground for this transcultural perspective is necessary, even though such an explanation will inevitably bring up a theoretical issue too complex to address in this book—the current debate on multiculturalism and multiethnicism. The transcultural perspective as envisioned in this book is predicated on a positive interpretation of the historicity of cultures. Historicity of cultures means, first of all, that all cultures are products of human development under given historical circumstances. One culture may possess a set of ideas, values, and practices earnestly emulated by other cultures at a later historical time. But such a lead in the timeline of development is always temporary when viewed through the long vista of human history. No matter how far a culture is seen ahead of others, it is bound to be overtaken by those behind once it becomes self-complacent and does not regenerate itself by absorbing useful elements from other cultures. Similarly, no matter how much a culture is perceived to lag behind others, it can offer a great deal that enables us to have a better knowledge of our past and present and to chart a better course of future. Each culture always has the potential of regenerating itself and reaching or surpassing the level of development attained by other cultures. This historicity of cultures should preclude any culture and race from claiming superiority and exercising hegemony over other cultures and races. Thus, all cultural and racial biases based on a false claim of superiority should be thoroughly repudiated. Furthermore, as we learn to respect, appreciate, and learn from each and every culture, we can even go beyond this relativistic historical thinking to embrace a strongly positive transcultural vision—seeing all cultures and peoples as equal participants in the one and same course of human betterment. Idealistic as it is, this all-inclusive, transcultural vision can serve as a practical safeguard against the two polemics in our comparative studies.

In my opinion, West-China comparatists should not only develop this transcultural perspective in their works but also explain it carefully to the reader so that their discussions of similarities and differences will be interpreted within the intended transcultural framework. The failure to do so has resulted in countless cases of unfortunate misunderstandings, charges, and countercharges of cultural insensitivity and racist biases. One of the most celebrated of these cases is Chad Hansen's discussion of the absence of the concept of "truth" in Chinese philosophy. In his controversial article, "Chinese Language, Chinese Philosophy, and Truth," Hansen sets out to demonstrate through a semantic and syntactic analysis that "Chinese philosophy has no concept of truth."[21] While Donald Munro and A. C. Graham earlier discussed the absence in specific Chinese philosophical texts of a character identifiable with the Western word "truth," Hansen asserts that their views "can be freed from the single character limitation and generalized to all pre-Buddhist Chinese philosophy."[22] In making this sweeping assertion, he aims to reach even broader conclusions about the so-called different nature of Chinese intellectual activity, Chinese moral system, and Chinese norms of conduct. "'Chinese philosophy has no concept of truth,'" he declares, "is not a simple claim about the existence of some character; it is a claim about the fundamentally contrasting nature of Chinese intellectual activity."[23] Because "Chinese philosophy seldom employs semantic concepts such as truth, as distinct from pragmatic concepts," he suggests that "we may begin to wonder about the system of morality."[24] According to him, the Chinese moral system represents a form of utilitarianism that "conflicts with our 'intuitions'about these paradigm requirements of morality [truth-telling and promise-keeping]."[25] In consequence of this, he contends that the Chinese people observe different norms of speech and behavior. "Chinese treat utterances as actions with behavioral consequences," he writes, "not as conveying information for use in a rational decision process."[26] By contrast, "once we [Westerners] have the concept of a human as an independent, rational, purposive truth seeker, we then have reasons to treat humans with special respect."[27]

If we recall our earlier discussion of the polemics of difference by Williams, Haas, Buck, and others, we will understand why Hansen's thesis that "Chinese philosophy has no concept of truth" would stir up a long-lasting controversy that remains unabated to this day.[28] His observations run a gamut of perilous parallels to those Orientalists' value judgments on the Chinese culture and people: the lack of spirituality, disregard for truth, the emphasis on emotions, the deficiency in rational thinking, and the untrustworthy character. So it is not surprising that many scholars would read his article within the interpretive horizons of those Orientalists' value judgments and consider it an intellectual rationalization of the polemics of difference pursued by those people. No matter how wronged Hansen may feel by his critics, he bears the blame in considerable measure for this reading or what he would call misreading of his views. In my opinion, this interpretation (or misinterpretation) arises to a great extent from his failure to introduce a transcultural perspective for his discussion of the differences between Western and Chinese traditions. It is not that there are no important differences between them, nor that we should avoid any discussion of such differences for fear of evoking the ghosts of cultural imperialism and racial stereotypes. The issue is that we should try to view differences as indicative of equally valid alternatives within a broader framework of transcultural or universal human concerns and aspirations.

The peril of not having a transcultural perspective is also amply illustrated in a more recent case of charges and countercharges between the scholars of Chinese philosophy. In reviewing Randall Peerenboom's *Law and Morality in Ancient China: The Silk Manuscripts of Huang-Lao*, Carine Defoort takes issue with the author's tendency to overlook the obscurities and ambiguities in the original texts and ascribe "'transcendent'principles to Chinese philosophy" in the interest of meeting a "Cartesian demand for perfect clarity and strictly demarcated definitive criteria."[29] The thrust of her critique suggests that she identifies the author's arguments with what I have called the polemics of similitude, which appropriates Chinese indigenous ideas and values by forcing them into Western conceptual categories. This is certainly the way Peerenboom reads the review. For him, the review goes beyond normal academic discussion and launches a politically charged criticism "by raising the specter of cultural imperialism."[30] Apparently incensed, Peerenboom responds with an even more vociferous countercharge. The intensity of his response is aptly indicated by its title: "The Rational American and the Inscrutable Oriental as Seen from the Perspective of a Puzzled European: A Review (and Response) in Three Stereotypes—A Reply to Carine Defoort." From an opposite perspective, he argues that Defoort's review represents "a kind of reverse cultural imperialism" identical with what I have called the polemics of difference—one that relies "on the assumption that Chinese could never be so clever as to come up with similar solutions to similar problems as their Western counterparts."[31] In Defoort's review, he hears equally disturbing echoes of imperialistic rhetoric: "The poor Chinese are trapped in their own world views; unable to change, they are doomed to an endless round of totalitarian governments and despotic rulers who prefer rule of man to rule of law."[32]

In reviewing these two cases of controversy, I wish to show how easily we may find ourselves in a minefield of politically charged accusations and counteraccusations if we do not exert our utmost to steer away from the polemics of similitude or difference. These two polemics have dominated the field of East-West comparisons for so long that they inevitably cloud the interpretive horizons into which our discussions of similarities and differences are examined. Thus, in order to avoid the misinterpretation of our comparative studies, we must work hard to clear up the interpretive horizons and establish a broad transcultural perspective in which similarities and differences can be discussed without privileging, overtly or covertly, one tradition over another.

The establishment of this transcultural perspective is of crucial importance for this book because it deals with many of the touchiest issues in East-West comparisons, such as truth vs. process, transcendence vs. immanence, and intellect vs. feeling. As these issues have been at the core of the two polemics over the centuries, my discussion of them is hence very susceptible to being miscomprehended and associated with the two polemics. Consider, for instance, the comparisons I have made between the Western truth-centered and the Chinese process-centered concepts of literature in chapters 1–3, between Plato's vertical axis of intellectual harmony and Confucius' horizontal axis of moral harmony in chapter 4, between Wordsworth's and Liu Xie's schemes of sensory and suprasensory experiences in chapter 5, between Western and Chinese concepts of language and reality in chapter 6, and so forth. If placed within the Western value system—built upon the dichotomous hierarchization of "transcendental truth" over physical reality, intellect over feeling, and speech over writing—these comparisons will be perilously conducive to value judgments against the Chinese tradition. For example, my distinction of the Western truth-centered and the Chinese process-centered concepts of literature may seem to some an invitation to infer the superiority of the Western tradition and the inferiority of the Chinese tradition.

To prevent such an unfortunate association of this project with the two polemics it aims to battle, I have sought to assess the findings of my comparisons within a broad transcultural perspective as indicated by circle D. This transcultural perspective has enabled me to discuss similarities as meaningful convergences between two equal traditions, rather than in terms of the conformity of a "lesser" tradition to a "superior" one. Similarly, it has helped me to assess the various fundamental differences outside the Western value system, seeing them as indicative of equal, mutually illuminating alternatives. For example, it has guided me to see that a pursuit of truth and an integration with the Dao represent two equal alternatives to the same loftiest human goal of total union with the ultimate reality. Neither one should be regarded as superior to the other. By the same token, these two different ways of conceptualizing literature, centered upon truth and the Dao respectively, constitute two alternate and equal ways of understanding literature. Each sheds important light on the origins, formation, and functions of literature in its own way as does the other. Indeed, this transcultural perspective is particularly helpful for bringing recognition to the long neglect of the rich heritage of Chinese critical tradition. Once Western critics recognize this tradition as an equal counterpart to Western literary criticism, they will find a new, invaluable source of inspiration for the development and enrichment of their own tradition.

A final note about the new diagram and, in fact, about the entire book. I have drawn circles D as well as A and B in dotted rather than solid lines. With this change, I wish to underscore the dynamic openness of each circle for change and development. Circles A and B betoken not only cultural *fait accompli* of times past but also changing cultural practices of today and tomorrow. Part C, too, is set to change and develop. Along with the ever increasing contact, interaction, and mutual influence across cultures, this area of resemblances will certainly expand substantially. In my belief, this expansion will not lead to the rise of "universals" at the cost of the waning or death of different cultural traditions. Quite the contrary, it will serve only to stimulate further development and enrichment of each indigenous tradition involved. This dialectic interplay of mutual assimilation and mutual differentiation comes to the fore when we view circles A and B through all-inclusive circle D. In drawing circle D in dotted lines, I intend to emphasize that it is not a fixed domain of pragmatic objectives that can be fully realized. Rather, it is an open field of an idealistic vision that inspires, sustains, and guides our efforts to overcome all cultural bias and stereotypes and better understand our common humanity. While I have no illusion that our comparative studies can be absolutely free of prejudices and misunderstandings, I believe that, by setting our sight on the transcultural ideal, we will be able to get much closer to that ideal than we otherwise would. It is in the spirit of this transcultural ideal that this book has been conceived and written. I hope that it will be read in the same spirit and will be taken as an invitation to search for better ways to compare Western and Chinese poetics and the two cultural traditions at large.

Abbreviations

SBBY   *Sibu beiyao* 西部備要

SBCK   *Sibu congkan* 西部叢刊

SSJZ   Ruan Yuan 阮元 (1764–1849), comp. *Shisanjing zhushu* 十三經注疏 (Commentary and Subcommentary on the Thirteen Classics). 2 vols. Beijing: 1977.

WXDL   Zhu Yingping 朱迎平, ed. *Wenxin diaolong suoyin* 文心雕龍索引 (Indexes to *Wenxin diaolong*). Shanghai: Shanghai guji chubanshe, 1987.

XCZ   "Xici zhuan" 繫辭傳 (Commentary on the Appended Phrases). In *SSJZ*.

ZGLD   Guo Shaoyu 郭紹虞 and Wang Wensheng 王文生, eds. *Zhongguo lidai wenlun xuan* 中國歷代文論選 (An Anthology of Writings on Literature through the Ages). 4 vols. Shanghai: Shanghai guji chubanshe, 1979.

Notes

PROLOGUE

1. Traditional Chinese poetics is the focus of study in this book. There are only a few brief comments on twentieth-century Chinese literary criticism in the epilogue.
2. The compound "West-China" is used in this book as a convenient designator of the scope of inquiry. Although this compound has been widely used for the same purpose in works by other scholars, I wish to stress that there is no intention on my part to make China equivalent to the "East" in the compound "East-West." Like India, Japan, Korea, or any other Asian country, China is only part of the broadly and rather loosely defined sphere of the East.

CHAPTER 1: THE ORIENTATION OF WESTERN POETICS

1. M. H. Abrams, *The Mirror and the Lamp: Romantic Theory and the Critical Tradition* (London: Oxford, 1953), p. 6.
2. Pragmatic theories focus on the practical effects of literature on the audience. Unlike the other three theories, they are not grounded in a given set of broad truth-claims about literature. Theoretically, they can be seen as an offshoot of the mimetic theory with a special emphasis on the effects of imitation on the audience. Abrams demonstrates considerable foresight in including the audience in his diagram. The subsequent rise of the reader-response theories lends strong support to his identification of the audience as a primary coordinate of Western poetics, even though these theories are concerned with reading rather than the reader or audience per se.
3. David P. Richter, *The Critical Tradition: Classical Texts and Contemporary Trends* (New York: St. Martin, 1989), pp. 6–14, takes issue with some theoretical implications of Abrams' diagram and reviews the highlights of three other diagrams developed subsequently to compete with Abrams'. The first is R. S. Crane's concentric diagram that groups critical theories in terms of their interpretative approaches. See "Questions and Answers in Teaching of Literary Texts," in his *The Idea of the Humanities,* 2 vols. (Chicago: Univ. of Chicago Press, 1966). The second is Paul Hernadi's modification and expansion of Abrams' diagram by subsuming under the

four coordinates various contemporary as well as traditional disciplines related to literary studies. See his "Literary Theory: A Compass for Critics," *Critical Inquiry* (1976): 382. The third is Richard McKeon's arrangement of critical theories in terms of the modes of thought used by the critics. See "Imitation and Poetry," in his *Thought, Action and Passion* (Chicago: Univ. of Chicago Press, 1954). Walter A. Davis provides an exposition of McKeon's ideas in *The Act of Interpretation: A Critique of Literary Reason* (Chicago: Univ. of Chicago Press, 1978), pp. 88–119.

4. Abrams, *The Mirror and the Lamp*, p. 7.

5. Eliot Deutsch, *On Truth: An Ontological Theory* (Honolulu: Univ. of Hawai'i Press, 1979), p. 1. See also the concise bibliography of major studies on "truth" on pp. 123–124.

6. William C. Greene, "The Greek Criticism of Poetry: A Reconsideration," *Harvard Studies in Comparative Literature* 20 (1950): 21, 20. For an account of early Greek views of literature, see E. E. Sikes, *The Greek View of Poetry* (New York: Barnes & Noble, 1931), pp. 1–62; Rosemary Harriot, *Poetry and Criticism before Plato* (London: Methuen, 1969).

7. For contemporary studies of this ancient quarrel, see Thomas Gould, *The Ancient Quarrel between Poetry and Philosophy* (Princeton: Princeton Univ. Press, 1991); Richard Kannicht, *The Ancient Quarrel between Philosophy and Poetry* (Christchurch, New Zealand: Univ. of Canterbury, 1988); and Stanley Rosen, *The Quarrel Between Philosophy and Poetry: Studies in Ancient Thought* (New York: Routledge, 1988).

8. William C. Greene, "The Greek Criticism of Poetry," p. 24.

9. For Plato's construction of this cosmological scheme, see Plato, *Plato's Timaeus*, trans. Francis M. Cornford (Indianapolis, Ind.: Bobbs-Merrill, 1959).

10. Plato, *Republic*, bk. 10, 605, trans. and ed. Benjamin Jowett, *The Dialogues of Plato*, 2 vols. (New York: Random House, 1937), vol. 1, p. 863.

11. Plato, *Republic*, bk. 10, 599; Plato, *Dialogues*, vol. 1, p. 856.

12. Bertrand Russell, *A History of Western Philosophy: And Its Connection with Political and Social Circumstances from the Earliest Times to the Present Day* (New York: Simon & Schuster, 1945), p. 166. Immediately after these remarks, Russell offers a further elaboration on the lack of essential difference between Aristotle's forms and Plato's universals:

> The change that Aristotle makes in Plato's metaphysic is, it would seem, less than he represents it as being. This view is taken by Zeller, who, on the question of matter and form, says:
>
>> The final explanation of Aristotle's want of clearness on this subject is, however, to be found in the fact that he *had* only half emancipated himself, as we shall see, from Plato's tendency to hypostatise ideas. The 'Forms' had for him, as the 'Ideas' had Plato, a metaphysical existence of their own, as conditioning all individual things.

> And keenly as he followed the growth of ideas out of experience, it is none the less true that these ideas, especially at the point where they are farthest removed from experience and immediate perception, are metamorphosed in the end from a logical product of human thought into an immediate presentment of a supersensible world, and the object, in that sense, of an intellectual intuition.
>
> I do not see how Aristotle could have found a reply to this criticism (p. 166).

13. Aristotle, *The Poetics,* 1451 a-b; Stephen Halliwell, trans., *Aristotle: Poetics* (Cambridge, Mass.: Harvard Univ. Press, 1995), pp. 59–61.
14. William Wordsworth, "Preface to *Lyrical Ballads* (1850)," *The Prose Works of William Wordsworth,* eds. W. J. B. Owen and Jane Worthington Smyser, 3 vols. (Oxford: Clarendon, 1974), vol. 1, pp. 139, 141.
15. Similar claims for poetry as the locus of the truth were made contemporaneously by German romantics like Friedrich Schlegel and Friedrich W. J. Schelling. For a study of these claims, see Philippe Lacoue-Labarthe and Jean-Luc Nancy, *The Literary Absolute: The Theory of Literature in German Romanticism,* trans. Philip Barnard and Cheryl Lester (Albany State Univ. of New York Press, 1978).
16. On this Romantic notion of imagination and truth, W. P. Albrecht, *Hazlitt and the Creative Imagination* (Lawrence, Kansas: Univ. of Kansas Press, 1965), pp. 63–64: "By Hazlitt's time, the word *imagination* frequently meant a faculty which not only achieves a moral identification with others but perceives truth and reality: a creative faculty which, enabled by intense feeling to see otherwise unrevealed similitudes, selects, molds, and unifies concrete particulars to represent essential truth and provide aesthetic pleasure." See also David Bromwich, *Hazlitt, the Mind of a Critic* (Oxford: Oxford Univ. Press, 1985).
17. Percy Bysshe Shelley, "A Defence of Poetry," in *Shelley's Poetry and Prose: Authoritative Texts and Criticism,* eds. Donald H. Reiman and Sharon B. Powers (New York: Norton, 1977), p. 482.
18. Mathew Arnold, "The Study of Poetry," *The Complete Prose Works of Matthew Arnold,* ed. R. H. Super, 11 vols. (Ann Arbor: Univ. of Michigan Press, 1962), vol. 3, p. 171.
19. A notable exception is Coleridge who goes beyond the poet-worship to examine the intrinsic values of poetry. His writings on poetic language and symbol are widely viewed to have presaged the rise of text-oriented theories, including Anglo-Saxon practical criticism, New Criticism, and structuralism. See Emerson R. Marks, *Coleridge on the Language of Verse* (Princeton: Princeton Univ. Press, 1981), pp. 5–27.
20. Arnold, "The Study of Poetry," *Complete Prose Works,* vol. 3, pp. 161–62.
21. Arnold, "Wordsworth," *Complete Prose Works,* vol. 9, pp. 48–49.
22. Ibid., p. 54.

23. Among numerous essays that glorify Shakespeare as the world soul, see Johann Gottfried Herder, "Shakespeare," trans. Joyce P. Crick, modifications by H. B. Nisbet, and collected in H. B. Nisbet, *German Aesthetic and Literary Criticism: Winckelmann, Lessing, Hamann, Herder, Schiller, Goethe* (Cambridge: Cambridge Univ. Press, 1985), pp. 161–176; German text in Johann Gottfried Herder, *Sämmtliche Werke,* ed. Bernhard Suphan, 33 vols. (rpt. New York: Olms-Weidmann, 1994), vol. 5, pp. 208–231. See also Thomas Carlyle, "The Hero as Poet: Dante, Shakespeare," *On Heroes, Hero-Worship, & the Heroic in History,* notes and introduction by Michael K. Goldberg (Berkeley: Univ. of California Press, 1993), pp. 67–97.

24. As a philosophical term, *ontic* means "possessing or pertaining to real existence." This meaning seems to sum up what the following formalist critics want to say about literature.

25. T. S. Eliot, *Selected Essays* (New York: Harcourt and Brace, 1932), pp. 10–11.

26. Ibid., pp. 6, 8.

27. John Crowe Ransom, "Criticism Inc," *The World's Body* (New York: Scribner, 1938), p. 348.

28. Ibid., p. 347.

29. Cleanth Brooks, John Thibaut Purser, and Robert Penn Warren, "General Introduction," *An Approach to Literature: A Collection of Prose and Verse with Analyses and Discussions* (Baton Rouge: Louisiana State Univ. Press, 1936), p. 8.

30. Cleanth Brooks, "The Language of Paradox," *The Well-Wrought Urn: Studies in the Structure of Poetry* (New York: Renal, 1947), pp. 3–21.

31. Brooks, Purser, and Warren, "General Introduction," p. 8.

32. William K. Wimsatt, "The Concrete Universal," *The Verbal Icon: Studies in the Meaning of Poetry* (Lexington: Univ. of Kentucky Press, 1954), pp. 69–83.

33. René Wellek and Austin Warren, *Theory of Literature,* third edition (New York: Harcourt Brace Jovanovich, 1975), p. 156.

34. Wellek and Warren comment on these truths in *Theory of Literature,* pp. 92–93, 109.

35. M. Merleau-Ponty, *Phenomenology of Perception,* trans. Colin Smith (London: Routledge and Kegan Paul, 1962), pp. 219–221.

36. Georges Poulet, "Phenomenology of Reading," *New Literary History* 1 (1969): 59.

37. Eugene H. Falk, *The Poetics of Roman Ingarden* (Chapel Hill: Univ. of North Carolina Press, 1981), p. 35. Roman Ingarden, *The Cognition of the Literary Work of Art,* trans. Ruth Ann Crowley and Kenneth R. Olson (Evanston, Ill.: Northwestern Univ. Press, 1973), p. 14, gives a more theoretical exposition of this phenomenological concept of literature: "The literary work as such is a purely intentional formation which has the source of its being in the creative acts of consciousness of its author and its phys-

ical foundation in the text set down in writing or through other physical means of possible reproduction (for instance, the tape recorder). By virtue of the dual stratum of its language, the work is both intersubjectively accessible and reproducible, so that it becomes an intersubjective intentional subject, related to a community of readers. As such it is not a psychological phenomenon and is transcendent to all experiences of consciousness, those of the author as well as those of the reader."

38. Falk, *Poetics of Roman Ingarden*, p. 115. Cf. Roman Ingarden, *The Literary Work of Art: An Investigation on the Borderlines of Ontology, Logic, and Theory of Literature*, trans. George G. Grabowicz (Evanston, Ill.: Northwestern Univ. Press, 1973), p. 59: "In the first instance, the phonetic stratum, and in particular the manifold of word sounds, forms the external, fixed shell of the literary work, in which all the remaining strata find their external point of support or—if one will—their external expression."

39. Ingarden, *The Literary Work of Art*, pp. 291, 297–298. For a discussion of Ingarden's phenomenological notion of literary truth, see Peter J. McCormick, "Literary Truths," *Fictions, Philosophies, and the Problems of Poetics* (Ithaca, N.Y.: Cornell Univ. Press, 1988), pp. 78–106.

40. Ingarden, *The Literary Work of Art*, p. lxxix.

41. Falk, *Poetics of Roman Ingarden*, p. 115.

42. Ibid., p. 204.

43. For a list of these cognitive acts, see Falk, *Poetics of Roman Ingarden*, p. 132.

44. Georges Poulet, "Criticism and the Experience of Interiority," in *The Structuralist Controversy*, ed. Richard Macksey and Eugenio Donato (Baltimore: Johns Hopkins Univ. Press, 1970), p. 58.

45. Wolfgang Iser, *The Implied Reader: Patterns of Communication in Prose Fiction from Bunyan to Beckett* (Baltimore: Johns Hopkins Univ. Press, 1974), p. 294.

46. Iser, *Implied Reader*, p. 288.

47. Jonathan Culler, *Structuralist Poetics: Structuralism, Linguistics, and the Study of Literature* (Ithaca, N.Y.: Cornell Univ. Press, 1975), p. viii.

48. Roland Barthes, "The Structuralist Activity," in *Critical Essays*, trans. Richard Howard (Evanston, Ill.: Northwestern Univ. Press, 1972), pp. 214–215.

49. Ibid., p. 215.

50. As I shall closely examine Derrida's writings in chapter 8, here I will not cite and discuss specific passages and will give only a brief summary of his deconstructive thought.

51. This inevitable inscription of Western dualistic metaphysics on those who deconstruct it has been noted by many scholars. For instance, commenting on Nietzsche's deconstruction of Western metaphysics, Philippe Lacoue-Labarthe writes, "Nietzsche calls fiction the lie that is truth and calls into question the essentially Platonic, metaphysic break between appearance and reality as well as the whole system of oppositions it engen-

ders and by which it is accompanied: opinion / science, becoming / eternity, etc. The theme is well known: Nietzsche is the reversal of Platonism and hence still a Platonism—and ultimately the accomplishment of metaphysics itself." (*The Subject of Philosophy,* trans. Thomas Treizise et al [Minneapolis: Univ. of Minnesota Press, 1993], p. 5).

52. Paul de Man, *Allegories of Reading: Figural Language in Rousseau, Nietzsche, Rilke, and Proust* (New Haven: Yale Univ. Press, 1979), p. 115.

CHAPTER 2: THE ORIENTATION OF CHINESE POETICS

1. See James J. Y. Liu, *Chinese Theories of Literature* (Chicago: Univ. of Chicago Press, 1975), pp. 2–116.

2. M. H. Abrams, *The Mirror and the Lamp,* p. 6.

3. Ibid., p. 7.

4. Aware that Abrams' diagram cannot accommodate this cyclical process, Liu rearranges the four coordinates into a cyclical diagram, arguing that the four coordinates are "the four phases that constitute the whole artistic process" (*Chinese Theories of Literature,* p. 10).

5. The "Canon of Yao" is divided into two chapters (the "Canon of Yao" and the "Canon of Shun" ["Shun dian 舜典"]) in *Shang shu zhengyi* 尚書正義 (Correct Meanings of *Shang shu*), commentary by Kong Yingda 孔穎達 (574–648), collected in *Shisanjing zhushu* 十三經注疏 (Commentary and Subcommentary on the Thirteen Classics), comp. Ruan Yuan 阮元 (1764–1849), 2 vols. (Beijing: 1977, hereafter *SSJZ*). The *"Shi yan zhi"* statement appears in the latter chapter in this edition of the *Book of Documents.*

The dating of this chapter, along with some others, is a matter of long-standing debate among scholars. Gu Jiegang 顧頡剛 dates it as early as to the transitional period between the Western Zhou and the Eastern Zhou in his "Lun *jinwen Shangshu* zhuzuo shidai shu" 論今文尚書著作時代書 (A Letter on the Date of the Composition of *Shang shu*), collected in *Gushi bian* 古史辨 (Analysis of Ancient History), 7 vols. (rpt. Hong Kong: Taiping shuju, 1962), vol. 1, p. 200–206. Gu's dating is accepted by Zhu Ziqing 朱自清, *Shi yan zhi bian* 詩言志辨 (Analysis of "Poetry Expresses the Heart's Intent")(Beijing: Guji chubanshe, 1956), p. 9, and by Luo Genze 羅根澤, *Zhongguo wenxue piping shi* 中國文學批評史 (A History of Chinese Literary Criticism), 3 vols. (Shanghai: Gudian wenxue chubanshe, 1957–1961), vol. 1, p. 36. However, Qu Wanli 屈萬里, "*Shang shu* bu ke jin xin di cailiao" 尚書不可盡信的材料 (Material in *Shang shu* that is not fully trustworthy), *Xin shidai* 新時代 (New Era) 1.3 (1964), pp. 23–25, chooses to date this chapter to the end of the Warring States.

6. The word *zhi* has been translated as "earnest thought" in James Legge, *The Shoo King or the Book of Historical Documents, The Chinese Classics,*

vol. 3. (rpt. Taipei: Wenxin, 1971), p. 48, and as "the heart's intent" in Liu, *Chinese Theories of Literature*, p. 75. Liu's translation seems to be more appropriate because it avoids the rationalistic connotations of "earnest thought" and yet subtly implies moral inclination. However, the word *zhi* can take on a wide range of different meanings depending on the historical periods and particular contexts in which it is used. For this reason, Liu finds it necessary to render it as "emotional purport," "moral purpose," or "heart's wish" in other contexts (p. 184). Liu's translation has been adopted with slight modification ("heart / mind") in Pauline Yu, *The Readings of Imagery in the Chinese Tradition* (Princeton: Princeton Univ. Press, 1987), p. 31. For a discussion on the translation of *zhi*, see Stephen Owen, *Readings in Chinese Literary Thought* (Cambridge, Mass.: Harvard Univ. Press, 1992), pp. 26–29.

7. *Shang shu zhengyi, SSJZ*, vol. 1, p. 13.

8. This sequence of activities seems to correspond with what Mihail I. Spariosu calls the "archaic mythopoeic unity of poetry reciting, music making, and dancing, as well as ritualistic and dramatic performance" in ancient Greece. See his *The God of Many Names: Play, Poetry, and Power in Hellenic Thought from Homer to Aristotle* (Durham, N. C.: Duke Univ. Press, 1991), p. 141.

9. See Guo Shaoyu 郭紹虞 and Wang Wensheng 王文生 eds., *Zhonguo lidai wenlun xuan* 中國歷代文論選 (An Anthology of Writings on Literature through the Ages), 4 vols. (Shanghai: Shanghai guji chubanshe, 1979, hereafter *ZGLD*), vol. 1, p. 2.

10. These remarks of Kong Yingda appear in *Shang shu zhengyi*, in *SSJZ*, vol. 1, p. 132.

11. On the religious functions of the earliest Chinese dances, see Ye Shuxian 葉舒憲, *Shi jing di wenhua chanshi: Zhongguo shige di fasheng yanjiu* 詩經的文化闡釋——中國詩歌的發生研究 (A Cultural Exegesis of *Shi jing*: Studies on the Genesis of Chinese Poetry) (Wuhan: Hubei renmin chubanshe, 1994), pp. 9–17, 273–287.

12. Lü Buwei 呂不韋 (?–235 B.C.), *Lü shi chunqiu* (Spring and Autumn Annals of Mister Lü), annot. Chen Qiyou 陳奇猷 (Shanghai: Xuelin chubanshe, 1984), vol. 1, p. 284.

13. See Zheng Xuan 鄭玄 (127–200), annot., *Zhou li zhushu* 周禮注疏 (Commentary and Subcommentary on the *Rituals of Zhou*), juan 22, in *SSJZ*, vol. 1, pp. 788–789.

14. Zheng Xuan, annot., *Zhou li zhushu, juan* 23, in *SSJZ*, vol. 1, p. 793.

15. See Xu Zhongshu 徐中舒, ed. *Jiaguwen zidian* 甲骨文字典 (A Dictionary of Oracle Bone Graphs) (Chengdu: Sichuan cishu chubanshe, 1990), p. 678.

16. Chow Tse-tsung, "Early History of the Chinese World *Shih* (Poetry)," in *Wenlin: Studies in the Chinese Humanities*, ed. Chow Tse-tsung (Madi-

son: Univ. of Wisconsin Press, 1968), p. 195. Chow's argument seems to have been inspired by Yang Shuda's 楊樹達 (1884–1956) gloss of the word *shi* (poetry). See Yang Shuda, "Shi 'shi'" 釋詩" (Explaining the Word "Poetry"), in his *Jiweiju xiaoxue jinshi luncong* 積微居小學金石論叢 (Discussion on Philology and Bronze and Stone Drum Graphs from the Jiweiju Studio) (Beijing: Kexue chubanshe, 1995), pp. 25–26.

17. See Xu Zhongshu, *Jiaguwen zidian*, p. 125.

18. Wen Yiduo, *Wen Yiduo quanji* 聞一多全集 (Complete Works of Wen Yiduo) (Shanghai: Kaiming shudian, 1948), vol. 1, p. 185.

19. See Ch'en Shih-hsiang, "In Search of the Beginning of Chinese Literary Criticism," in *Semitic and Oriental Studies* (Berkeley: Univ. of California Publications in Semitic Philology, 1951), vol. 11, pp. 50–52. See also his discussion of the vestiges of religious dance in *xing* 興, a key Chinese critical term, in his article "The *Shih Ching:* Its Generic Significance in Chinese Literary Theory and Poetics," *Bulletin of the Institute of History and Philology* (*Academia Sinica*) 39, no. 1 (1968): 371–413 and reprinted in *Studies in Chinese Literary Genres,* ed. Cyril Birch (Berkeley: Univ. of California Press, 1974), pp. 8–41.

20. Chow Tse-tsung, "Early History of the Chinese Word *shih* (Poetry)," p. 207.

21. Zhu, *Shi yan zhi bian*, p. 4.

22. This belief of literature as a process in Chinese poetics has been noted by many scholars. For instance, Stephen Owen, *Traditional Chinese Poetry and Poetics: Omen of the World* (Madison: Univ. of Wisconsin Press, 1985), p. 59, observes that in traditional Chinese poetics, "The movement from the condition of the world or of the age, through the poet, into the poem, and finally to the reader was conceived not as a series of causes and effects but as an organic process of manifestation."

23. Kong Yingda, annot., *Chunqiu Zuo zhuan zhengyi* 春秋左傳正義 (Correct Meanings of the Zuo Commentary to Spring and Autumn Annals), in *SSJZ*, vol. 2, pp. 2107–2108.

24. Kong Yingda, annot., *Chunqiu Zuo zhuan zhengyi*, in *SSJZ*, vol. 2, p. 2109.

25. Zhu Ziqing, *Shi yan zhi bian*, p. 9. See also Min Ze 敏澤, "Woguo gu wenlun zhong de qinggan lun" 我國古文論中的情感論 (Theories of Emotion in Our Country's Ancient Writings on Literature), *Gudai wenxue lilun yanjiu* 古代文學理論研究 (Studies on Classical [Chinese] Literary Theory) 4 (1981), pp. 284–308.

26. Zhu Ziqing, *Shi yan zhi bian*, pp. 3–4.

27. The neglect of dance is particularly conspicuous in the passages from *Zuo Commentary* and *Speeches of the States* to be cited and discussed below. In these passages, music is seen to occupy the center of courtly ceremonies in lieu of dance.

28. Zhu Ziqing, *Shi yan zhi bian*, p. 8.

29. See Zheng Xuan, annot., *Zhou li zhushu, juan* 22, in *SSJZ*, vol. 1, p. 787.
30. *Shi yan zhi bian*, p. 6.
31. For a study of these two types of poetry, see Xia Chengtao 夏承濤, "'Caishi' yu 'fushi'" 采詩與賦詩 (On Collected Poetry and Presented Poetry), *Zhonghua wenshi luncong* 中華文史論叢 (Forum on Chinese Literature and History), 1 (1962), pp. 171–182. Dong Zhi'an 董治安, *Xian Qin wenxuan yu xian Qin wenxue* 先秦文獻與先秦文學 (Pre-Qin Texts and Pre-Qin Literature) (Jinan: Qi Lu shushe, 1994), provides four useful comparative charts on *yinshi* 引詩, *fushi* 賦詩, and *geshi* 歌詩 in the *Zuo Commentary* and *Speeches of the States*. The last two charts (pp. 35–45) identify the time, the speaker, and the title of the cited work for every single occurrence of *yinshi, fushi,* and *geshi* in the *Zuo Commentary* and in *Speeches of the States*, respectively.
32. For examples of the expression of these two types of moral-political *zhi* (intent), see Kong Yingda, annot., *Chunqiu Zuo zhuan zhengyi*, Wengong 13, in *SSJZ*, vol. 2, p. 1853, and Xianggong 27, in *SSJZ*, vol. 2, p. 1997, respectively.
33. In "Speeches of the Zhou" ("Zhou yu" 周語) in *Speeches of the States*, Duke Shao 邵公 urges King Li 厲王 (r. 878–842 B.C.) to examine the admonitions and remonstrations submitted by his subjects in the forms of poetry, music, and pithy sayings (*Guo yu*, annot. Wei Zhao 韋昭 [204–273], 2 vols. [Shanghai: Shanghai guji chubanshe, 1978], *juan* 1, vol. 1, pp. 9–10). This seems to be the first known explicit mention of music and poetry as means of observing popular sentiment and the state of governance, even though the practice of collecting admonitions and remonstrations from the populace can be traced to earlier times. The *Book of Documents*, for instance, notes, "Every year in the first month of spring, the herald with his wooden-tongued bell goes along the roads, proclaiming, 'Ye officers able to direct, be prepared with your admonitions'" (*Shangshu zhengyi, juan* 7, in *SSJZ*, vol. 1, p. 157; trans. James Legge, *The Shoo King*, in *Chinese Classics*, vol. 3, p. 164).
34. Kong Yingda, annot., *Chunqiu Zuo zhuan zhengyi*, Xianggong 29, in *SSJZ*, vol. 2, pp. 2006–2007. For previous translations, see James Legge, trans., *Ch'un Ts'ew with the Tso Chuen*, in *The Chinese Classics*, vol. 5, pp. 549–550; and Kenneth J. DeWoskin, *A Song for One or Two: Music and the Concepts of Art in Early China* (Ann Arbor: Center for Chinese Studies, Univ. of Michigan, 1982), pp. 22–24.
35. DeWoskin, *A Song for One or Two*, p. 23, n. 7, rightly points out that "the 'eight winds' may be either a reference to the eight 'timbres,' or instrumental voices . . . or a reference to the influence of the 'airs' of surrounding areas." I am inclined to accept the latter interpretation because it fits well with the context and conveys the idea of the spheres under particular ethico-sociopolitical influence. The phrase "eight winds" has no fixed ref-

erent and its meaning must be contextualized. In the passage from *Speeches of the States* to be cited below, "eight winds" occurs in a different context and takes on the meaning of a generalized reference to natural processes and forces.

36. Yan Zi is Grand Minister of the Qi state, to whom *Spring and Autumn Annals of Master Yan* (*Yan Zi Chunqiu* 晏子春秋) is attributed.

37. Kong Yingda, annot., *Chunqiu Zuo zhuan zhengyi*, Zhaogong 22, in *SSJZ*, vol. 2, pp. 2093–2094. For a previous translation, see Legge, trans., *Ch'un Ts'ew with the Tso Chuen*, in *The Chinese Classics*, vol. 5, p. 684.

38. For a previous translation, see ibid. For similar discussions of this function of music and poetry, see *Chunqiu Zuo zhuan zhengyi*, Zhaogong 1, in *SSJZ*, vol. 2, pp. 2024–2025; and "Chu yu 楚語," A, in *Guo yu, juan* 17, vol. 2, p. 528.

39. *Guo yu, juan* 4, vol. 1, pp. 128–130.

40. In this context, the term "eight winds" is a generalized reference to natural processes and forces. For a similar account of music's impact on the "winds" or natural processes and forces, see the remarks by Shi kuang 師曠 the great music master in "Jin yu" 晉語, 4, in *Guo yu, juan* 14, vol. 2, pp. 460–461.

41. *Guo yu, juan* 4, vol. 1, pp. 128–130.

42. Ibid. In addition to this passage, we can find in "Speeches of Zhou" another excellent example of the overriding concern with natural processes and forces during the Spring and Autumn period: the long speech made by Prince Jin 晉公子 to his father King Ling 靈王 in 549 B.C., about twenty-seven years earlier. In that speech, Prince Jin explains the systematic correlation of human society and natural processes and forces, and urges his father not to disrupt the order of nature (*Guo yu, juan* 3, vol. 1, pp. 101–112). For a discussion of the cosmological significance of this passage, see James A. Hart, "The Speech of Prince Chin: A Study of Early Chinese Cosmology," in *Explorations in Early Chinese Cosmology*, ed. Henry Rosemont (Chico, Cal.: Scholar Press, 1984), pp. 35–65. This book is published as volume L, No. 2, of *Journal of the American Academy of Religion Studies*.

43. This preface to the entire corpus of 305 poems is often called the "Great Preface" ("Da xu" 大序) as opposed to the "Lesser Prefaces" ("Xiao xu" 小序) that introduce individual poems in the corpus. The authorship of the "Great Preface" is a matter of speculation among traditional Chinese scholars. Some scholars consider it the work of Confucius' disciple Zi Xia 子夏 while others attribute it to Wei Hung 衛宏, a scholar living in the first century A.D. See Yong Rong 永瑢 (Qing Dynasty), et al., ed. *Siku quanshu zongmu* 四庫全書總目 (General Catalogue of the Imperial Library), 2 vols. (rpt. Beijing: Zhonghua shuju, 1965), *juan* 15, vol. 1, p. 119.

44. Owen, *Readings*, p. 37. For studies of this preface, see Steven Van Zoeren, *Poetry and Personality: Reading, Exegesis, and Hermeneutics in Traditional China* (Stanford: Stanford Univ. Press, 1991), pp. 80–115; Owen, *Read-

ings, pp. 37–49; and Haun Saussy, *The Problem of a Chinese Aesthetic* (Stanford: Stanford Univ. Press, 1993), pp. 74–105.

45. Kong Yingda, annot., *Mao shi zhengyi* 毛詩正義 (Correct Meanings of the Mao Text of the *Book of Poetry*), *juan* 1, in *SSJZ,* vol. 1, pp. 269–270.

46. See Kong Yingda, annot. *Liji zhengyi* 禮記正義 (Correct Meanings of the *Book of Rites*), *juan* 39, in *SSJZ,* vol. 2, p. 1545.

47. The key to understanding this order of decreasing importance is the phrase "*buzu* 不足" (not adequate), used here to introduce various lesser activities as supplements to the core activity of poetic verbalization. Interestingly, this *buzu* has the same function of indicating a graduated order as its antonym *zu* 足 (adequate) does in Confucius' remarks on *yan* (speech) and *wen* (embellishment) quoted in the *Zuo Commentary*—"Confucius said, 'The record contains this: words (*yan*) are to make one's intent (*zhi*) adequate (*zu*), and embellishment (*wen*) is to make one's words adequate (*zu*).' If one does not employ words, who can know his intent? If one employs words without embellishment, he will not go far." (Kong Yingda, annot., *Chunqiu Zuo zhuan zhengyi,* Xianggong 25, in *SSJZ,* vol. 2, p. 1985). Apparently, what embellishment is to words is analagous to what dance, songs, or chanting is to poetic verbalization in the "Great Preface."

48. Kong Yingda, annot., *Mao shi zhengyi, juan* 1, in *SSJZ,* vol. 1, p. 270.

49. It is ironic that his elevation of poetry over music is modeled on the argument for the elevation of music in the "Records of Music." There, the author seeks to align music with ethico-sociopolitical processes rather than natural processes. He demonstrates the paramount importance of music by elucidating its harmonizing effects on individuals, families, clans, and states. The author of the "Great Preface" makes a corresponding shift of emphasis to ethico-sociopolitical processes and justifies his elevation of poetry on the ground of its unparalleled efficacy in harmonizing these processes.

50. See Xiao Huarong 蕭華榮, "*Chunqiu* cheng shi yu Kongzi lun shi" 春秋稱詩與孔子論詩 (The Recitation of the *Poetry* in *Spring and Autumn Annals* and Confucius' Discussion of the *Poetry*), *Gudai wenxue lilun yanjiu* 古代文學理論研究 (Studies on Classical [Chinese] Literary Theory) 5 (1981), pp. 192–209.

51. See a chart of these references in Dong, *Xian Qin wenxuan yu xian Qin wenxue,* pp. 64–65.

52. *Lunyu yinde* 論語引得 (Concordance to the *Analects*), Harvard-Yenching Institute Sinological Index Series, supp. 16, (Beijing: Harvard-Yenching Institute, 1940), 8 / 8. For a different translation, see Confucius, *Analects,* trans. Arthur Waley (New York: Random House, 1938), VIII, 8, p. 134.

53. *Lunyu yinde,* 17/8. Cf. Confucius, *Analects,* XVII, 9, p. 212.

54. See the charts on the citation of the *Poetry* in *Mencius* and *Strategies of the States* in Dong, *Xian Qin wenxuan yu xian Qin wenxue,* pp. 65–66 and 88.

55. Kong Yingda, annot., *Mao shi zhengyi, juan* 1, in *SSJZ*, vol. 1, p. 272.
56. Ibid., p. 271.
57. Ibid.
58. Ibid., p. 270.
59. Ibid., p. 272.
60. Ibid.
61. Ibid.
62. For instance, Zhu Ziqing leaves out any discussion of *Wenxin diaolong* in his *Shi yan zhi bian*.
63. Zhu Yingping 朱迎平, ed., *Wenxin diaolong suoyin* 文心雕龍索引 (Indexes to *Wenxin diaolong*) (Shanghai: Shanghai guji chubanshe, 1987) 7/99–101, 107–108 (i.e. chapter 7/sentences 99–101; 107–108). Hereafter, where appropriate, *Wenxin diaolong* is referred to as *WXDL*, and its translation *Literary Mind and the Carving of Dragons* as the *Literary Mind*. The text of *WXDL* in this book is taken from Fan Wenlan 范文瀾, ed. *Wenxin diaolong zhu* 文心雕龍注 (Commentaries on *Wenxin diaolong*) (Beijing: Renmin wenxue chubanshe, 1958).

   Basing my translation on Fan's edition, I have also drawn from the glosses, annotations, commentaries, and translations given in other editions, including Huang Kan 黃侃 (1886–1935), *Wenxin diaolong zhaji* 文心雕龍札記 (Notes on *Wenxin diaolong*) (Shanghai, 1962; reprint, Taipei: Wenshizhe chubanshe, 1973); Lu Kanru 陸侃如 and Feng Yuanjun 馮沅君, eds., *Wenxin diaolong yizhu* 文心雕龍譯注 (Translation and Commentaries on *Wenxin diaolong*) 2 vols. (Jinan: Qi Lu shushe, 1981); Zhou Zhenfu 周振甫, *Wenxin diaolong zhushi* 文心雕龍注釋 (Commentaries and Explanations of *Wenxin diaolong*) (Beijing: Renmin wenxue chupanshe, 1981); Yang Mingzhao 楊明照, *Wenxin diaolong jiaozhu shiyi* 文心雕龍校注拾遺 (Supplements to the Collations and Commentaries on *Wenxin diaolong*) (Shanghai: Shanghai guji chubanshe, 1982); and Zhan Ying 詹鍈, ed., *Wenxin diaolong yizheng* 文心雕龍義證 (Investigation of the Meanings of *Wenxin diaolong*) 3 vols. (Shanghai: Shanghai guji chubanshe, 1989).

   For English translations of the *Literary Mind,* see Vincent Yu-chung Shih, trans., *The Literary Mind and the Carving of Dragons* (Hong Kong: Chinese Univ. Press, 1983), p. 43, and Owen, *Readings in Chinese Literary Thought,* pp. 183–298. In the course of translating this and other passages from the *Literary Mind,* I consulted Shih's and Owen's translations and benefited from their insights into the original work as well as their choices of words and expressions.

64. Compare this passage with the opposite view held by Plato: "I cannot help feeling, Phaedrus, that writing is unfortunately like painting; for the creations of the painter have the attitude of life, and yet if you ask them a question they preserve a solemn silence. And the same may be said of

speeches. You would imagine that they had intelligence, but if you want to know anything and put a question to one of them, the speaker always gives one unvarying answer. And when they have been once written down they are tumbled about anywhere among those who may or may not understand them, and know not to whom they should reply, to whom not; and, if, they are maltreated or abused, they have no parent to protect them; and they cannot protect or defend themselves." (*Phaedrus*, 275; Plato, *The Dialogues of Plato*, trans. and ed. Benjamin Jowett, 2 vols. [New York: Random House, 1937], vol. 1, pp. 278–279.)

65. Liu Xie's view on the creative process is a subject that has attracted much critical attention in the studies of *Wenxin diaolong*. For a summary of research in this area, see Xiong Lihui 熊黎輝, "Chuangzuo lun 創作論" (Theory of Literary Creation), in *Wenxin diaolong xue zonglan* 文心雕龍學綜覽 (A Comprehensive Survey of Studies on *Wenxin diaolong*), eds. *Wenxin diaolong xue zonglan* bianweihui (Shanghai: Shanghai shudian chubanshe, 1995), pp. 98–105. *Wenxin diaolong xue zonglan* is the fruit of many years of collaboration among scholars from all over the world and is an indispensable tool for research on the *Literary Mind.*

66. See, for instance, *WXDL* 5/58, 64; 6/48–49; 8/133–134; 15/40–41, 93–94; and 16/38–41.

67. I discussed in greater detail Liu's critical system in my article "*Wen* and and Construction of a Critical System in *Wenxin diaolong*," *Chinese Literature: Essays, Articles and Reviews* 22 (2000): 1–29.

68. It is important to stress that my following stratum-by-stratum analysis is meant only to distinguish Liu Xie's treatment of various external and internal processes, not to suggest that those processes are clear-cut, unrelated entities. On the contrary, they are interactive and interdependent within an intricate scheme.

69. To see this transformation clearly, one may compare Liu's account of the religious invocation to *shen*, the numinous spirits, by the earliest people in Chapter 10 ("Zhu Meng" 祝盟 [Sacrificial Prayers and Oaths of Agreement]) and his own description of the *shen*, the subtlest of the mind's operations, in chapter 26 ("Shensi").

70. To grasp this difference, one may compare Liu's account of the comments on music's effects on the "Seven Beginnings" (*qishi* 七始, namely, heaven, earth, man, and the four seasons) and the "Eight Winds" by Ji Zha and Shi Kuang 師曠 in chapter 7 ("Yuefu" 樂府 [*Yuefu* Poetry]), and his own discussion of the relevance of those natural processes to artistic creation in Chapter 46 ("Wuse").

71. See chapter 42 "Yangqi" 養氣 (The Nourishing of Vital Breath).

72. For a summary of the ongoing debates among Asian scholars on the Dao in *Wenxin diaolong*, see He Yi 何懿, "Yuan Dao" 原道, in *Wenxin diaolong xue zonglan*, pp. 137–147. For an interpretation of the Dao in *Wenxin*

diaolong as the Buddhist Dao, see Victor H. Mair, "Buddhism in *The Literary Mind and Ornate Rhetoric*," in *A Chinese Literary Mind: Culture, Creativity, and Rhetoric in Wenxin diaolong*, ed. Zong-qi Cai (Stanford: Stanford Univ. Press, 2000), pp. 63–81.

73. See Zhong Hong, "*Shipin* xu" 詩品序 (Preface to the *Grading of Poets*), *ZGLD*, vol. 1, p. 309.

74. Ibid.

75. Ibid.

76. Ibid., p. 308.

77. See Xiao Tong, "*Wenxuan* xu" 文選序 (Preface to the *Anthology of Refined Literature*), *ZGLD*, vol. 1, p. 329.

78. Ibid.

79. Ibid.

80. Ibid.

81. See Wang Tong, "Tiandi pian" 天地篇 (Chapter on Heaven and Earth), *Zhong shuo* 中説 (Sayings of [Wen] Zhong [Zi]), *ZGLD*, vol. 2, pp. 1–2.

82. For these critics' remarks on the *wen*-Dao relationship, see Liu Zongyuan, "Da Wei Zhongli lun shidao shu" 答韋中立論師道書 (A Letter on the Way of a Teacher in Reply to Wei Zhongli), *ZGLD*, vol. 2, pp. 144–148; Han Yu, "Da Liu Zhengfu shu" 答劉正夫書 (A Letter in Reply to Liu Zhengfu), *ZGLD*, vol. 2, pp. 115–119; and Li Han, "Changli xiansheng ji xu" 昌黎先生集序 (Preface to the *Collected Works of Mister Changli [Han Yu]*), *ZGLD*, vol. 2, pp. 121–122.

83. These critics' remarks on *wen* and the Dao will be discussed below.

84. *Hanyu da zidian* 漢語大詞典 (A Comprehensive Dictionary of Chinese), 12 vols. (Shanghai: Hanyu dazidian chupanshe, 1994), vol. 10, p. 132.

85. Han Yu, "Song Meng Dongye xu" 送孟東野序 (Words Given to Meng Dongye at Parting), *ZGLD*, vol. 2, pp. 125–126; Bai Jiuyi, "Yu Yuan Jiu shu" 與元九書 (A Letter to Yuan Jiu), *ZGLD*, vol. 2, pp. 96–102; Su Xun, "Zhongxiong zi Wenpu shuo" 仲兄字文甫説 (Remarks on Changing the *Zi* of My Second Elder Brother), *ZGLD*, vol. 2, pp. 268–269.

86. See Liu Zongyuan, "Da Wei Zhongli lun shidao shu," *ZGLD*, vol. 2, p. 144.

87. Shi Jie, "Shangcai fu shumi shu" 上蔡副樞密書 (A Letter to the Auxiliary Academician in the Bureau of Military Affairs of Shangcai), *ZGLD*, vol. 2, p. 252.

88. Zhou Dunyi, "Wenci" 文辭 (Literary Expressions), *Tongshu* 通書 (*Comprehensive Book*), *ZGLD*, vol. 2, p. 283.

89. See Pei Du 裴度, "Ji Li Ao shu" 寄李翱書 (A Letter to Li Ao), *ZGLD*, vol. 2, p. 158–162; Wang Yucheng 王禹偁, "Da Zhang Fu shu" 答張扶書 (A Letter in Reply to Zhang Fu), *ZGLD*, vol. 2, pp. 231–233; Zhi Yuan 智圓, "Song Shu Ji xu" 送庶幾序 (Words Given to Shu Ji at Parting), *ZGLD*, vol. 2, pp. 234–236; and Ouyang Xiu 歐陽修, "Da Wu Chong xiucai shu" 答吳充秀才書 (A Letter in Reply to Wu Chong the Recommended Candidate for Officialdom), *ZGLD*, vol. 2, pp. 255–258.

90. See Cheng Yi, *Yulu* 語錄 (Collected Sayings), *ZGLD*, vol. 2, p. 284.

91. For Li Zhi's views discussed in this paragraph, see Li Zhi 李贄, "Tongxin shuo" 童心說 (Theory of the Childlike Heart), *ZGLD*, vol. 3, p. 117–118.

92. For Jiao Hong's views discussed in this paragraph, see Jiao Hong, "Yu youren lun wen" 與友人論文 (Discussing *Wen* with Friends), *ZGLD*, vol. 3, p. 131.

93. For Yuan Mei's defense of parallel prose, see Yuan Mei, "Hu Zhiwei piantiwen xu" 胡稚威駢體文序 (Preface to the *Parallel Prose of Hu Zhiwei*), *ZGLD*, vol. 3, p. 460. See also Ruan Yuan's enthusiastic praise of parallel prose in his "Wenyan shuo" 文言說 (On Refined Expressions), *ZGLD*, vol. 3, p. 586.

94. See Duan Yucai, "Dai Dongyuan ji xu" 戴東原集序 (Preface to the *Collected Works of Dai Dongyuan*), *ZGLD*, vol. 3, p. 504.

95. See Zhang Xuecheng, "Yu Zhu Shaobai lunwen" 與朱少白論文 (Discussing *Wen* with Zhu Shaobai), *ZGLD*, vol. 3, p. 509.

96. See Ye Xie, "Neipian shang" 內篇上 (Inner Chapter, Part I), *Yuan shi* 原詩 (Origins of Poetry), *ZGLD*, vol. 3, p. 344.

97. See Ye, "Neipian xia" 內篇下 (Inner Chapter, Part II), *Yuan shi, ZGLD*, vol. 3, p. 346.

98. See Ibid., p. 353–354.

99. See Yao Nai, "*Shu An wenchao* xu" 述庵文鈔序 (Preface to *Writings of Shu An*), *ZGLD*, vol. 3, p. 499.

100. Yao, "Fu Lu Jiefei shu" 復魯絜非書 (A Letter in Reply to Lu Jiefei), *ZGLD*, vol. 3, p. 510.

101. Ibid.

102. See Yao, "Fu Lu Jiefei shu," *ZGLD*, vol. 3, p. 510–511.

103. See Ibid., p. 511.

104. Elliot Deutsch, *On Truth: An Ontological Theory On Truth*, p. 37.

105. In this body of writings on vernacular literature, there are few particularly noteworthy statements on *wen* and the Dao. For this reason, I have decided not to included them in this survey.

CHAPTER 3: EARLY CHINESE WORLDVIEWS
AND CONCEPTS OF LITERATURE

1. Of early Chinese worldviews, I shall focus on the ghosts- and spirits-centered worldviews of high antiquity, the *li*-centered worldview of the Western Zhou and the early Spring and Autumn period, Confucius' worldview, and the "organismic" worldview developed in the *Commentaries to the Book of Changes*. In selecting these worldviews for discussion in this chapter, I only intend to identify the most important sources of influence on the four concepts of literature discussed in the previous chapter. At the very outset I must emphasize that the development of these early Chinese worldviews should not be seen as a teleological process of ever newer and more advanced worldviews emerging to replace earlier

and lesser ones. In fact, there are times when some key elements of the dominant worldview of a bygone age reemerge at the core of a new worldview. For instance, the ancient notion of conscious supernatural beings, after being ignored or relegated to secondary importance for a long time by the *li*-centered, classical Confucian and Daoist worldviews, is restored to preeminence in the Dong Zhongshu's 董仲舒 cosmological scheme and in the so-called *chenwei* 讖緯 (prophetic pronouncements and the apocrypha of Confucian classics) prevalent in the early Eastern Han. Such examples show us that the development of early worldviews is far more complex than a unilinear progression.

2. Zheng Xuan, annot., *Zhou li zhushu, juan* 22, in *SSJZ*, vol. 1, p. 788.

3. See Sima Qian, comp., *Shi ji* 史記 (Records of the Historian) (Beijing: Zhonghua shuju, 1982), 1/1/12.

4. See Sima Qian, comp., *Shi ji*, 1/1/14.

5. This ancient religious worldview is to evolve into what Tu Wei-ming calls the "paradigmatic expression of this idea of man as the co-creator of heaven and earth" in the *Zhong yong* 中庸 (The Doctrine of the Mean): "Only those who are absolutely sincere can fully develop their nature. If they can fully develop their nature, they can then fully develop the nature of others. If they can fully develop the nature of others, they can then develop the nature of things. If they can develop the nature of things, they can assist in the transforming and nourishing process of Heaven and earth. If they can assist in the transforming and nourishing process of Heaven and earth, they can thus form a trinity with Heaven and earth" (Wingtsit Chan, trans. and comp., *A Source Book in Chinese Philosophy* [Princeton: Princeton Univ. Press, 1969], pp. 107–108). Tu Wei-ming's remark appears in his *Way, Learning, and Politics: Essays on the Confucian Intellectual* (Albany: State Univ. of New York Press, 1993), p. 2.

6. This intensely religious life is also reflected in the ubiquitous use of divination in the earliest times. Kong Yingda, annot., *Liji zhengyi, juan* 55, in *SSJZ*, vol. 2, p. 1644, provides an account of how the people of remote antiquity consulted the oracle with the help of yarrow stalks and tortoise shells for all their human activities, big or small.

7. See Sima Qian, comp., *Shi ji*, 1/1/12.

8. In the *Literary Mind*, Liu Xie devotes the first half of chapter 10, "Zhu meng" 祝盟 (Sacrificial Prayers and Oaths of Agreement), to examining the development of sacrificial prayers into a literary genre (*WXDL* 10/1–108). The examples he gives of earliest sacrificial prayers are brief words of prayer for a good harvest delivered by Shun and other legendary rulers. According to Liu, it was not until the Zhou times when words of praise were added to sacrificial prayers. Indeed, we can find an overabundance of words of praise in the Zhou hymns (*Zhou song* 周頌) of the *Book of Poetry*.

9. Eliot Deutsch, *On Truth: An Ontological Theory*, p. 14.

10. "Xici zhuan," A12, in Richard John Lynn, trans., *The Classic of Changes: A New Translation of the I Ching as Interpreted by Wang Bi* (New York: Columbia Univ. Press, 1994), p. 67. The Chinese text of "Xici zhuan" is taken from *Zhou yi yinde* 周易引得 (A Concordance to Yi Ching [Yi jing]), Harvard-Yenching Institute Sinological Index Series, Supplement no. 10 (rpt. Taipei: Chinese Materials and Research Aids Service Center, 1966). For an earlier translation of the complete *Book of Changes,* see Richard Wilhelm, trans., *The I Ching or Book of Changes,* translated from German into English by Cary F. Baynes (Princeton: Princeton Univ. Press, 1950).

11. Willard J. Peterson, "Making Connections: 'Commentary on the Attached Verbalizations' of the *Book of Changes,*" *Harvard Journal of Asiatic Studies* 42.1 (1982): 104.

12. Xu Shen 許慎 (30–124), *Shuowen jiezi zhu* 說文解字注 (Explanations of Simple and Compound Characters, with Annotations), annot. Duan Yucai 段玉裁 (1735–1815) (rpt. Yangzhou: Jiangsu Guangling guji keyinshe, 1997, 5A26, p. 201.

13. Xu Zhongshu 徐中舒, *Jiaguwen zidian* 甲骨文字典 (Dictionary of Oracle Bone Graphs) (Chengdu: Sichuan cishu chubanshe, 1990), pp. 630–631.

14. For a criticism of these explanations, see Victor H. Mair, "Old Sinitic *Mʸag, Old Persian Maguš, and English 'Magician,'" *Early China* 15 (1990): pp. 27–47, especially n. 31 on pp. 39–40.

15. Wang Yi, ed., *Chuci buzhu* 楚辭補注 (The Songs of the Chu, with Supplements and Annotations) (*SBBY* edn.), 2.1b–2a.

16. "Shi song" 釋頌 (An Explanation of *Song*), *Yanjingshi yiji* 罨經室一集 (A Collection from the Yanjing Studio) (*SBCK* edn.), 1.13.

17. Liang Qichao, "Shi sishi mingyi 釋四詩名義" (An Explanation of the Meanings of the Four Poetic Genres) in his *Yinbingshi heji: Zhuanji* 飲冰室合集，專集 (Combined Collections of Writings from the Yinbing Studio: Specialized Essays) (Shanghai: Zhonghua shuju, 1936), vol. 10, 74.92–97.

18. *Gu wuyi yu liushi kao* 古巫醫與六詩攷 (Study of Ancient Shaman-Doctors and the Six Poetic Genres and Modes) (Taipei: Jinglian chubanshe, 1986), pp. 265–268. *Weng* 甕 is an ancient container used for measurement.

19. See Zhang Binglin, *Wenshi* 文始 (Genesis of *Wen*) (Taipei: Taiwan Zhonghua shuju, 1970), 5.19a, p. 104; Chen Mengjia, "Shandai shenhua yu wushu 商代神話與巫術" (Myths and Shamanistic Arts in the Shang Dynasty), *Yanjing xuebao* 燕京學報, 20 (1936), pp. 572–574; Wang Guowei, *Song Yuan xiju kao* 宋元戲劇攷 (Study of Song and Yuan Drama) (Taipei: Yiwen yinshuguan, 1964), pp. 3–6; and Liu Shipei, "Wenxue chuyu wuzhu zhi guan shuo" 文學出於巫祝之官說 (An Explanation: Literature Came from the Officials in Charge of Shamanistic Incantations), *Zuo An waiji* 左盦外集 (Supplementary Collection of Zuo

An) *juan* 8, collected in *Liu Shenshu yishu* 劉申叔遺書 (Posthumous Publications of Liu Shenshu), 4 vols. (Taipei: Huashi, 1975), vol. 3, p. 1519.

20. See Ye Shuxian, *Shijing di wenhua chanshi,* pp. 439–530.

21. Kong Yinda, annot., *Liji zhengyi, juan* 54, in *SSJZ,* vol. 2, p. 1642.

22. Benjamin I. Schwartz, *The World of Thought in Ancient China* (Cambridge, Mass.: Harvard Belnap Press, 1985), p. 37.

23. Kwang-chih Chang, *Early Chinese Civilization: Anthropological Perspectives* (Cambridge, Mass.: Harvard Univ. Press, 1976), p. 190.

24. Schwartz, *World of Thought,* p. 32.

25. Ibid. p. 38. The brackets are mine.

26. By the estimate of Xu Fuguan 徐復觀, the word *tian* appears 148 times. More than 80 times it is used in reference to the high god as the highest moral authority. See Xu Fuguan, *Zhongguo renxinglun shi* 中國人性論史。先秦篇 (A History of Chinese Theories of Human Nature: the Pre-Qin Volume) (Taichung: Sili donghai daxue, 1963), pp. 36–40.

27. Schwartz, *World of Thought,* p. 48.

28. See, for instance, *Mao Shi yinde* 毛詩引得 (A Concordance to the Mao Text of the *Book of Poetry*), Harvard-Yenching Institute Sinological Index Series, Supplement no. 9 (rpt. Tokyo: Japanese Council for East Asian Studies, 1962), Poem 245, p. 62.

29. See *Mao Shi yinde,* Poems 54 and 255, p. 66–67.

30. See ibid., Poems 191–194, pp. 43–45.

31. In tracing this transformation of *li* in his *Zhongguo zhexueshi dagang* 中國哲學史大綱 (A General Outline of the History of Chinese Philosophy) (rpt. Beijing: Dongfang chubanshe, 1996), pp. 118–126, Hu Shi 胡適 (1891–1945) mentions the "Three Rites" as a typical example of purely religious rites of remote antiquity, and the "Five Rites" (*wuli* 五禮), the "Six Rites" (*liuli* 六禮), and the "Nine Rites" (九禮) as examples of the man-centered rites and ceremonies developed in the Zhou. He holds that most of the complex systems of rites depicted in the *Rituals of Zhou* and the *Book of Etiquette and Ceremonial* (*Yi li* 儀禮) have very limited religious significance and mainly serve to enhance the ethico-sociopolitical order (p. 119).

32. Kong Yinda, annot., *Chunqiu Zuo zhuan zhengyi,* Huangong 6, in *SSJZ,* vol. 2, p. 1750. Translation taken with modifications from James Legge, trans., *The Ch'un Ts'ew with the Tso Chuen,* in *Chinese Classics,* vol. 5, p. 48.

33. Kong Yinda, annot., *Chunqiu Zuo zhuan zhengyi,* Xigong 19, in *SSJZ,* vol. 2, p. 1810. Translation taken with modifications form Legge, *The Ch'un Ts'ew with the Tso Chuen,* vol. 5, p. 177.

34. Kong Yinda, annot., *Liji zhengyi, juan* 47, in *SSJZ,* vol. 2, p. 1595.

35. Ibid.

36. Kong Yinda, annot., *Chunqiu Zuo zhuan zhengyi,* Zhaogong 26, in *SSJZ,* vol. 2, p. 2115. Translation taken with modifications from Legge, *The Ch'un Ts'ew with the Tso Chuen,* vol. 5, p. 718.

37. Kong Yingda, annot., *Chunqiu Zuo zhuan zhengyi*, Yingong 11, in *SSJZ*, vol. 2, p. 1736. For a previous translation, see Legge, *The Ch'un Ts'ew with the Tso Chuen*, vol. 5, p. 33.

38. Kong Yingda, annot., *Chunqiu Zuo zhuan zhengyi*, Zhaogong 25, in *SSJZ*, vol. 2, p. 2107. For a previous translation, see Legge, *The Ch'un Ts'ew with the Tso Chuen*, vol. 5, p. 708.

39. This valorization of *li* as the ultimate cosmological principle is an example of the tendency commonly seen in the *Zuo Commentary* to extend the knowledge of human affairs to understand the ways of Heaven. Commenting on this tendency, Sima Qian writes, "*Spring and Autumn Annals* extends from what is seen to what is hidden, while the *Changes* concerns itself with what is hidden to make it manifest" 春秋推見至隱，易本隱之以顯. In explaining this remark, Yü Xi 虞喜 (Eastern Jin Dynasty) writes "*Spring and Autumn Annals* reaches the Dao of Heaven through human events and therefore [it is said] it extends from what is seen to what is hidden. The *Changes* proceeds from the Dao of Heaven to human events and therefore [it is said] it concerns itself with what is hidden to make it manifest" 春秋以人事通天道，是推見以至隱也，易以天道接人事，是本隱以之明顯也. See Sima Qian, comp., *Shi ji*, 9/117/3073. For a discussion on the valorization of *li* during the Spring and Autumn period, see Xu Fuguan, *Zhongguo renxinglun shi*, chapter 3, pp. 36–62.

40. Kong Yingda, annot., *Liji zhengyi, juan* 38, in *SSJZ*, vol. 2, p. 1537. *Juan* 38 is part of "Yue ji" 樂記 (Records of Music).

41. "Yue ji" 樂記 (Records of Music) provides an extensive discussion of the mutually complementary roles of *li* and *yue* in establishing the cosmological and ethico-sociopolitical orders. See Kong Yingda, annot., *Liji zhengyi, juan* 37–39, in *SSJZ*, vol. 2, pp. 1527–1548. For studies on the "Records of Music," see Yu Yuan 郁沅, "Lun 'Yueji' meixue sixiang di liang pai" 論樂記美學思想的兩派 (On the Two Schools of Aesthetics in the "Records of Music"), *Zhongguo wenyi sixiangshi luncong* 中國文藝思想史論叢 (Discussions on the History of Chinese Ideas of Art) 1 (1984), pp. 44–78; and Owen, *Readings*, pp. 50–56.

42. See *Lunyu yinde* 論語引得 (A Concordance to *Analects*), Harvard-Yenching Sinological Index, Supplement No. 16 (rpt. Shanghai: Shanghai guji chubanshe, 1986), p. 150.

43. Schwartz, *World of Thought*, p. 67.

44. *Lunyu yinde*, 3/19; trans. Waley, *Analects*, pp. 98–99.

45. Ibid., 12/5; trans. Waley, *Analects*, pp. 163–164.

46. Ibid., 13/4; trans. Waley, *Analects*, p. 172.

47. Ibid., 4/13; trans. Waley, *Analects*, p. 104. Waley also provides a paraphrase of this statement: "If I and my followers are right in saying that countries can be governed solely by correct carrying out of ritual and its basic principle of 'giving way to others,' there is obviously no case to be made out

for any other form of government. If on the other hand we are wrong, then ritual is useless. To say, as people often do, that ritual is all very well so long as it is not used as an instrument of government, is wholly to misunderstand the purpose of ritual" (p. 104).

48. *Lunyu yinde,* 3/26; trans. Waley, *Analects,* p. 101.
49. Ibid., 17/9; trans. Waley, *Analects,* p. 212
50. Ibid., 8/2; trans. Waley, *Analects,* p. 132.
51. Ibid., 12/1; trans. Waley, *Analects,* p. 162. The brackets are mine. On the spirituality of *li* in *Analects,* see Herbert Fingarette's thought-provoking, controversial book *Confucius: The Secular as Sacred* (New York: Harper Torchbooks, 1972).
52. Schwartz, *World of Thought,* p. 62.
53. *Lunyu yinde,* 5/13; trans. Waley, *Analects,* p. 110.
54. Ibid., 7/21; trans. Waley, *Analects,* p. 127.
55. Schwartz, *World of Thought,* p. 62.
56. The term "organismic" is used and popularized by Joseph Needham for reference to the all-embracing systems of correspondence and resonance among natural and human phenomena and processes developed during the Warring States period and the Han. While this term aptly conveys the idea of intricate, interactive relationships among all ongoing processes, it carries the alien association of Western biological science. For this reason, I have put the term in quotation marks.
57. For a study of these competing efforts to construct an all-embracing cosmological scheme, see John B. Henderson, *The Development and Decline of Chinese Cosmology* (New York: Columbia Univ. Press, 1984), pp. 1–58.
58. For a discussion of these *wuxing*-based cosmological schemes, see Xu Fuguan, *Zhongguo sixiangshi lunji xupian* 中國思想史論集續篇 (Collected Works on Chinese Intellectual History: A Sequel) (Taipei: Shibo wenhua chuban shiye youxian gongsi, 1982), chapters 4–11, pp. 50–111; and Schwartz, *World of Thought.* chapter 9, pp. 350–382. For a study of these correlative cosmologies in a West-China comparative perspective, see David L. Hall and Roger T. Ames, *Anticipating China: Thinking through the Narratives of Chinese and Western Culture* (Albany: State Univ. of New York Press, 1995), pp. 237–281.
59. Hellmut Wilhelm, *Change: Eight Lectures on the I Ching,* translated from German by Cary F. Baynes, collected in Hellmut Wilhelm and Richard Wilhelm, *Understanding the I Ching: The Wilhelm Lectures on the Book of Changes* (Princeton: Princeton Univ. Press, 1995), p. 17. The first chapter of this book, "Origins," provides a succinct account of the origins of the different strata of the *Changes.*
60. "Xici zhuan," A1, in Kong Yingda, annot., *Zhou yi zhengyi* 周易正義 (Correct Meanings of the *Book of Changes*), collected in *SSJZ,* vol. 1, pp. 75–76; trans. Lynn, *The Classic of Changes,* pp. 47–48.
61. Zhang Dainian 張岱年, *Zhongguo zhexue dagang* 中國哲學大綱 (A

General Outline of Chinese Philosophy) (Beijing: Zhongguo shehui kexue chubanshe, 1982), pp. 109–126, lists five distinguishing features of the bipolar cosmological principle as depicted by different Chinese thinkers. The first is the inevitability of the bipolar opposition of things. Nothing exists alone; all things are paired off as they alternately gravitate toward two poles (yin and yang). The second is the union of bipolar opposites as one. This union is understood in terms of the mutual dependence, mutual penetration, mutual transformation, mutual equality, and mutual identity of all bipolar opposites. The third is the mutual complementality of bipolar opposites. Neither yin nor yang can be complete without the other. The fourth is the interactive relationship between bipolar opposites and changes. All changes are seen to result from the interaction of bipolar opposites. The fifth concerns the relationship between the One and the Two (bipolar opposites). After listing these five features, Zhang discusses a chronologically arranged selection of passages that demonstrate those features of the bipolar principle. Zhang's list captures the major characteristics of the Chinese bipolar cosmological principle as a whole, even though there are some overlaps in his categories and subcategories. It is important to note that Chinese thinkers, in presenting their own versions of the bipolar principle, do not necessarily address all of the features listed above. In fact, they tend to emphasize some features over others.

62. "Xici zhuan," B6, *Zhou yi zhengyi*, in *SSJZ*, vol. 1, p. 89; trans. Lynn, *The Classic of Changes*, p. 86.

63. "Xici zhuan," A5, *Zhou yi zhengyi*, in *SSJZ*, vol. 1, p. 78; trans. Lynn, *The Classic of Changes*, p. 53.

64. "Xici zhuan," B10, *Zhou yi zhengyi*, in *SSJZ*, vol. 1, p. 90; trans. Lynn, *The Classic of Changes*, p. 92.

65. *Lao zi jiaoshi* 老子校釋 (Collations and Explanations of *Lao Zi*), annot. Zhu Qianzhi 朱謙之 (Beijing: Zhonghua shuju, 1984), chapter 42, p. 174; trans. D. C. Lau, *Lao Tzu: Tao Te Ching* (London: Penguin, 1963), p. 103.

66. Richard Wilhelm, *Lectures on the I Ching: Constancy and Change*, trans. from German by Irene Eber (Princeton: Princeton Univ. Press, 1979), pp. 6–7.

67. For a summary of the debate on the character of the "Great Commentary" from the Song to the late 1950s, see Peterson, "Making Connections," pp. 77–79. For an account of the most recent works on the "Great Commentary," see Chen Guying 陳鼓應 *Yi zhuan yu Daojia sixiang* 易傳與道家思想 (*Commentaries to the Book of Changes* and Daoist Thought) (Beijing: Sanlian shudian, 1996), pp. 232–276. Chen's book is the latest major work to emerge from the ongoing debate on the character of the "Great Commentary." Chen seeks to establish the Daoist character of the "Great Commentary" through textual collations. Comparing the standard text with the oldest extant silk text of the "Great Commentary" unearthed in the Mawangdui Tomb in the 1970s, Chen notes the absence in the

latter of several passages expounding Confucian ideas and regards those passages as latter-day interpolations into a text of Daoist origins. To demonstrate the Daoist origins of the "Great Commentary," Chen also traces the key philosophical concepts of the "Great Commentary" to a broad array of Daoist texts and presents the results of his textual collations in a convenient chart (pp. 225–231).

68. "Xici zhuan," B10, *Zhou yi zhengyi,* in *SSJZ,* vol. 1, p. 90; trans. Lynn, *The Classic of Changes,* pp. 92–93.

69. "Xici zhuan," B3, *Zhou yi zhengyi,* in *SSJZ,* vol. 1, p. 87; trans. Lynn, *The Classic of Changes,* p. 80.

70. "Xici zhuan," A2, *Zhou yi zhengyi,* in *SSJZ,* vol. 1, p. 77; trans. Lynn, *The Classic of Changes,* p. 50.

71. "Xici zhuan," A11, *Zhou yi zhengyi,* in *SSJZ,* vol. 1, p. 82; trans. Lynn, *The Classic of Changes,* pp. 65–66.

72. "Xici zhuan," B1, *Zhou yi zhengyi,* in *SSJZ,* vol. 1, p. 85; trans. Lynn, *The Classic of Changes,* p. 75.

73. Peterson, "Making Connections," p. 80. In order to emphasize the particular meanings of *xiang* used in the "Great Commentary," I have capitalized the word "Image."

74. Ibid.

75. "Xici zhuan," B3, *Zhou yi zhengyi,* in *SSJZ,* vol. 1, p. 86; trans. Lynn, *The Classic of Changes,* p. 80.

76. "Xici zhuan," A7, *Zhou yi zhengyi,* in *SSJZ,* vol. 1, p. 79; trans. Lynn, *The Classic of Changes,* pp. 56–57.

77. The brackets are mine.

78. "Xici zhuan," A11, *Zhou yi zhengyi,* in *SSJZ,* vol. 1, p. 82; trans. Lynn, *The Classic of Changes,* p. 65.

79. Hellmut Wilhelm, *Heaven, Earth, and Man in the Book of Changes* (Seattle: Univ. of Washington Press, 1977), p. 52.

80. Ibid., p. 32.

81. "Xici zhuan," A11, *Zhou yi zhengyi,* in *SSJZ,* vol. 1, p. 82; trans. Lynn, *The Classic of Changes,* p. 66.

82. "Xici zhuan," B12, *Zhou yi zhengyi,* in *SSJZ,* vol. 1, p. 91; trans. Lynn, *The Classic of Changes,* pp. 94–95.

83. "Xici zhuan," A12, *Zhou yi zhengyi,* in *SSJZ,* vol. 1, p. 82; trans. Lynn, *The Classic of Changes,* p. 67.

84. "Xici zhuan," B6, *Zhou yi zhengyi,* in *SSJZ,* vol. 1, p. 89; describes the symbolic mode of signification used by the attached phrases.

85. Hellmut Wilhelm, *Change: Eight Lectures on the I Ching,* in Hellmut Wilhelm and Richard Wilhelm, *Understanding the I Ching: The Wilhelm Lectures on the Book of Changes.* pp. 64–65.

86. Schwartz, *World of Thought,* p. 396.

87. "Xici zhuan," A4, *Zhou yi zhengyi,* in *SSJZ,* vol. 1, p. 77; trans. Lynn, *The Classic of Changes,* p. 51.

88. Peterson, "Making Connections," p. 112.
89. "Xici zhuan," A8, *Zhou yi zhengyi,* in *SSJZ,* vol. 1, p. 79; trans. Lynn, *The Classic of Changes,* p. 57.
90. *Lunyu yinde,* 3/14; trans. Waley, p. 97. The brackets are mine.
91. Ibid., 9/5; trans. Waley, p. 139.
92. "Xici zhuan," A11, *Zhou yi zhengyi,* in *SSJZ,* vol. 1, p. 82.
93. "Xici zhuan," B11, *Zhou yi zhengyi,* in *SSJZ,* vol. 1, p. 90.
94. "Xici zhuan," A11, *Zhou yi zhengyi,* in *SSJZ,* vol. 1, p. 82.
95. "Xici zhuan," A10, *Zhou yi zhengyi,* in *SSJZ,* vol. 1, p. 81; trans. Lynn, *The Classic of Changes,* p. 63.
96. On the influence of *Yizhuan* in the *Literary Mind,* see Hayashida Shin-nosuke 林田慎元助, *Chūgoku chōseibungaku kyōronshi* 中國中世文學評論史 (A History of Literary Criticism in Medieval China) (Tokyo: Sobunsha, 1979), pp. 329–335; Ma Bai 馬白, "Cong fangfalun kan *Zhou yi* dui *Wenxin diaolong* di yingxiang" 從方法論看周易對文心雕龍的影響 (The Influence of the *Changes* in *Wenxin diaolong* as Observed in the Way of Methodology), *Zhongguo wenyi sixiang shi luncong* 中國文藝思想史論叢 (Discussions on the History of Chinese Ideas of Art), vol. 1 (1985), pp. 136–158, and Wang Yunxi 王運熙, "*Wenxin diaolong* Yuandao he xuanxue sixiang de guanxi" 文心雕龍原道和玄學思想的關係 (The Relationship between Neo-Daoist Thought and the "Yuan Dao" chapter of *Wenxin diaolong*). *Wenxin diaolong yanjiu lunwenji* 文心雕龍研究論文集, ed. Zhongguo *Wenxin diaolong* xuehui 中國文心雕龍學會. Beijing: Renmin wenxue chubanshe, 1990, pp. 374–378.
97. For a succinct summary of the ongoing debates on the Dao in *Wenxin diaolong,* see He Yi 何懿, "Yuan Dao" 原道, in *Wenxin diaolong xue zonglan,* pp. 137–147.
98. These remarks are applied, respectively, to Cao Pi's "Discourse on Literature" ("Lun wen" 論文), Ying Chang's 應瑒 (?–217) "Discourse on Literature" ("Wen lun" 文論), and Li Chong's 李充 (Eastern Jin Dynasty) "The Grove of Writing Brushes" ("Hanlin" 翰林). See *WXDL* 50/72–97.
99. As Victor H. Mair has convincingly shown in his article, "Buddhism in *The Literary Mind and Ornate Rhetoric,*" Liu Xie is most likely to have also used Buddhist texts as an organizational model even though he does not openly acknowledge them as he does the *Book of Changes.* Mair also provides an extensive survey of the long-standing debate on the influence of Buddhism in the *Literary Mind.* See Victor H. Mair, "Buddhism in *The Literary Mind and Ornate Rhetoric,*" in *A Chinese Literary Mind: Culture, Creativity, and Rhetoric in Wenxin diaolong,* ed. Zong-qi Cai (Stanford: Stanford Univ. Press, 2000), pp. 63–81.
100. See *Zhou yi zhengyi, juan 7,* in *SSJZ.* vol. 1, p. 80.
101. On the "organismic" totality of literary experience presented in *Wenxin diaolong,* Pauline Yu, *The Poetry of Wang Wei: New Translations and Com-*

mentary (Bloomington: Indiana Univ. Press, 1980), pp. 4–5: "the notion of correspondences pervades Liu Xie's entire work, whose 'anatomy' of literature posits a number of organic relationships among the universe, writer, language, and literary work, and within the work as well."

102. Tracing the origins of this holistic mode of thinking, Hellmut Wilhelm writes, "The antithesis of 'above and below,' however, implies more than just the definition of their relative places. From the outset a relationship between the two positions is indicated: the relationship of correspondence. Above and below are not isolated powers; they are interrelated, and each influences the other. This is clear from the inscriptions on the oracle bones and from ancient songs that reveal their early origin in the fact that what is below precedes what is above. In these testimonials we often find added to the concepts of above and below a third word which characterizes this interrelatedness. 'Above and below stand in harmony,' it is said, or 'Above and below succeed each other.' Thus we have documentary proof that this concept existed in the Shang period, and doubtless it is of still greater antiquity." (Hellmut Wilhelm, *Change: Eight Lectures on the I Ching*, in Hellmut Wilhelm and Richard Wilhelm, *Understanding the I Ching: The Wilhelm Lectures on the Book of Changes*, p. 34).

103. Tu, *Way, Learning, and Politics*, p. 8.

CHAPTER 4: THE SYSTEMATICS
OF WESTERN AND CHINESE POETICS

1. Reading through the four volumes of *ZGLD*, I can find only one instance of a critic openly contesting the concept of literature put forward by a competing critical school. See Wang Bai 王柏 (1197–1274), "Ti Bixia shan ren Wang wen gong wenji hou" 題碧霞山人王公文集後 (A Postface to *Collected Writings of Mr. Wang of the Bixia Mountain*), *ZGLD*, vol. 2, p. 287.

2. On the features of Chinese cosmological thinking, see Andrew H. Plaks, "Complementary Bipolarity and Multiple Periodicity," in his *Archetype and Allegory in the Dream of the Red Chamber* (Princeton: Princeton Univ. Press, 1976), pp. 43–53; and Franklin M. Doeringer, "Unto the Mountain: Toward a Paradigm for Early Chinese Thought," *Journal of Chinese Philosophy* 17 (1990): 135–156.

3. For studies on the relationship between Chinese cosmological paradigms and poetics, see Andrew H. Plaks, "Conceptual Models in Chinese Narrative Theory," *Journal of Chinese Philosophy* 4 (1977): 25–47; Eugene Eoyang, "Polar Paradigms in Poetics: Chinese and Western Literary Premises," in *Comparative Literature East and West: Traditions and Trends: Selected Conference Papers*, eds. Cornelia N. Moore and Raymond A. Moody (Honolulu: College of Languages, Linguistics, and Literature, Univ. of Hawai'i and the East-West Center, 1989), pp. 11–21; and Liang Shi, "The Leopardskin of Dao and the Icon of Truth: Natural Birth Versus

Mimesis in Chinese and Western Literary Theories," *Comparative Literature Studies* 31.2 (1994):148–164.

4. Qian Zhonglian 錢 仲 聯, "Shi 'qi'" '釋 氣' (An Explanation of *Qi* or Vital Breath), *Gudai wenxue lilun yanjiu* 古 代 文 學 理 論 研 究 (Research on Classical Chinese Literary Theory) 5 (1981): 129–150, lists and discusses twenty-three *qi*-related terms. Peng Huizi 彭 會 資, *Zhongguo wenlun da cidian* 中 國 文 論 大 辭 典 (Comprehensive Dictionary of Chinese Literary Criticism) (Guangxi: Baihua wenyi chubanshe, 1990), pp. 286–334, lists as many as 103 *qi*-related terms.

5. It is important to stress that these five categories are interdependent and hence are often used interchangeably. For instance, *guqi* 骨 氣 and *xueqi* 血 氣, while literally belonging to the physiological category, are often used on the moral level. In addition to these five categories, there are terms such as *qidiao* 氣 調, *qiyun* 氣 韻, *qixiang* 氣 象, and *qihou* 氣 候, which may very well be taken as descriptions of the generalized conditions arising from the interplay of external and internal processes.

6. Hou Naihui 侯 逎 慧 attempts to examine the interaction of internal and external processes during literary creation within the framework of the all-embracing *qi* in her article "Cong 'qi' di yiyi yu liucheng kan *Wenxin diaolong* di chuangzuo lilun" 由 氣 的 意 義 與 流 程 看 文 心 雕 龍 的 創 作 理 論 (Theory of Literary Creation in *Wenxin diaolong:* A View from the Perspective of the Idea of *Qi* as Process), in *Wenxin diaolong zonglun* 文 心 雕 龍 綜 論 (Comprehensive Discussions of *Wenxin diaolong*), ed. Zhongguo gudian wenxue yanjiuhui (Taipei: Taiwan xuesheng shuju, 1988), pp. 241–283. For an English-language study of *qi* in Chinese poetics, see David Pollard, "*Ch'i* in Chinese Literary Theory," in *Chinese Approaches to Literature from Confucius to L'iang Ch'i-ch'ao,* ed. Adele Rickett (Princeton: Princeton Univ. Press, 1978), pp. 43–66.

CHAPTER 5: POETICS OF HARMONY

1. See for instance, Schwartz, *World of Thought,* and David L. Hall and Roger T. Ames, *Thinking through Confucius* (Albany: State Univ. of New York Press, 1987). The entry "Plato" in the indexes of both books gives an idea of the broad range of Plato's ideas being compared with Confucius'.

2. On the different ontological implications of Platonic and Chinese concepts of poetry, see Owen, *Readings in Chinese Literary Thought,* pp. 26–29. In the last section of this study, I will comment briefly on the different ontological implications of Plato's and Confucius' concepts of poetry. An in-depth exploration of those ontological implications requires more space than allowed here, and I have to leave it to a future occasion.

3. Even if Confucius' general observations on *wen* 文 (culture), *wenxue* 文 學 (culture and learning), and *yi* 藝 (arts) are included, his discussion is not of a scope comparable to that of Plato's.

4. There are good philological and aesthetic reasons for making this identi-

fication. Before and during Confucius' time, *shi* was already used alternately for the *Poetry* and poetry in general. The latter use abounds in early texts, including the *Poetry* itself. An excellent example is *"shi yan zhi"* 詩 言 志 ("Poetry expresses the heart's intent"), the earliest statement on poetry attributed to pre-Confucian times (see my discussion on this statement and early poetry in chapter 2). After the Han, this use of *shi* becomes dominant as the writing of poetry emerges as the primary belletristic pursuit among the literati. In addition to the philological reason, there is also an aesthetic reason for post-Han critics to identify the *Poetry* with poetry. After all, in discussing the *Poetry,* Confucius pays close attention to the issue of aesthetics as he seldom did with dealing with other subjects of learning. So it is quite justifiable for critics to draw out broad aesthetic implications from Confucius' remarks for poetry in general. Following this established interpretive tradition, I will present Confucius' remarks as comments on both the ancient anthology and poetry in general. For a general survey on the Confucian traditions in Chinese poetics, see Aoki Masaru 青 木 正 兒, *Shina bungaku shisōshi* 支 那 文 學 思 想 史 (A History of Chinese Literary Thought) (Tokyo, 1943), included in *Aoki Masaru zenshū* 青 木 正 兒 全 集 (Complete Works of Aoki Masaru) (Tokyo: Shunjūsha, 1969), vol. 1, pp. 19–39 and 153–158; and Guo Shaoyu 郭 紹 虞 (1893–1984), "Xian Qin Rujia zhi wenxueguan" 先 秦 儒 家 之 文 學 觀 (The Pre-Qin Confucian Concepts of Literature), in his *Zhaoyushi gudian wenxue lunji,* (Shanghai: Shanghai guji chubanshe, 1983), vol. 1, pt. 2, pp. 149–157.

5. Plato identifies aristocracy as "the government of the best" and compares it favorably with three other forms of government (timocracy, democracy, and tyranny) in Plato, *Republic,* bk. 8, 545–569; see Plato, *The Dialogues of Plato,* trans. and ed. Benjamin Jowett, (New York: Random House, 1937), vol. 1, pp. 803–828. On Plato's and Confucius' similar ideals of the government of the best and different proposed ways of producing the "best men," see Schwartz, *World of Thought,* pp. 96–97.

6. *Republic,* bk. 3, 404; *Dialogues,* vol. 1, p. 669.
7. *Republic,* bk. 3, 406–407; *Dialogues,* vol. 1, pp. 670–671.
8. *Republic,* bk. 3, 410; *Dialogues,* vol. 1, p. 675.
9. *Republic,* bk. 6, 486; *Dialogues,* vol. 1, p. 747.
10. *Republic,* bk. 7, 525; *Dialogues,* vol. 1, p. 785.
11. *Republic,* bk. 7, 526; *Dialogues,* vol. 1, p. 786.
12. *Republic,* bk. 7, 531; *Dialogues,* vol. 1, p. 790.
13. *Republic,* bk. 7, 531, 537; *Dialogues,* vol. 1, pp. 791, 797.
14. *Republic,* bk. 7, 537; *Dialogues,* vol. 1, p. 797.
15. *Republic,* bk. 7, 539; *Dialogues,* vol. 1, p. 799.
16. *Republic,* bk. 7, 540; *Dialogues,* vol. 1, p. 799.
17. *Republic,* bk. 7, 540; *Dialogues,* vol. 1, p. 799.

18. *Republic,* bk. 7, 540; *Dialogues,* vol. 1, pp. 799–800.

19. To understand how many different meanings the term *ren* encompasses, one only needs to take a look at the list of its different English translations given in Wing-tsit Chan, ed., *A Source Book in Chinese Philosophy* (Princeton: Princeton Univ. Press, 1963), p. 789. On the interpretations of *ren,* see Wing-tsit Chan, "Chinese and Western Interpretations of *jen* (humanity)," *Journal of Chinese Philosophy* 2 (1975): 107–129, and Tu Wei-ming, "*Jen* as a Living Metaphor in the Confucian *Analects,*" *Philosophy East and West* 31 (1981): 45–54.

20. *Lunyu yinde,* 8/4; trans. Waley, *The Analects of Confucius* (New York: Random House, 1938) VIII; 4, p. 133. See also *Lunyu yinde,* 2/14, 4/10, 7/37; trans. Waley, *Analects,* II, 14, p. 91; IV, 10, p. 104; VI, 16, p. 119; and VII, 36, p. 131.

21. *Lunyu yinde,* 7/38; trans. Waley, *Analects,* VII, 37, p. 131.

22. *Lunyu yinde,* 15/21, 13/23; trans. Waley, *Analects,* XV, 21, p. 197 and XIII, 23, p. 177. For another description of the harmonious character of a gentleman, see *Lunyu yinde,* 20/2; trans. Waley, *Analects,* XX, 2, p. 232.

23. See *Lunyu yinde,* 5/16; trans. Waley, *Analects,* V, 15, pp. 110–111.

24. *Lunyu yinde,* 16/8; trans. Waley, *Analects,* XVI, 8, p. 206.

25. *Lunyu yinde,* 12/5; trans. Waley, *Analects,* XII, 5, pp. 163–164.

26. *Lunyu yinde,* 2/4; trans. Waley, *Analects,* II, 4, p. 88.

27. *Republic,* bk. 3, 401–402; trans. Francis MacDonald Cornford, *The Republic of Plato* (New York and London: Oxford Univ. Press, 1941), p. 90. Here I use Cornford's translation instead of Jowett's because its more explicit mention of poetry and music suits the present discussion.

28. *Republic,* bk. 3, 401; *Dialogues,* vol. 1, p. 665.

29. *Republic,* bk. 3, 399; *Dialogues,* vol. 1, p. 662.

30. *Republic,* bk. 10, 597; *Dialogues,* vol. 1, p. 854.

31. Richard Kannicht, *The Ancient Quarrel Between Philosophy and Poetry* (Christchurch, New Zealand: Univ. of Canterbury, 1988), p. 30.

32. *Republic,* bk. 10, 605; *Dialogues,* vol. 1, p. 863.

33. Of the copious citations from Plato in Allan H. Gilbert, *Literary Criticism: Plato to Dryden* (Detroit: Wayne State Univ. Press, 1940), pp. 3–62, there are very few passages in which Plato does not subject poetry to criticism. W. J. Bate, ed., *Criticism: the Major Texts* (New York: Harcourt, Brace & World, 1952), pp. 39–49, selects only Plato's negative comments on poetry in *Ion* and book 10 of *Republic.* In more recent critical anthologies, we generally find a more balanced presentation of Plato's views of poetry. See, for instance, Alex Preminger, O. B. Hardison, Jr., and Kevin Kerrane, eds., *Classical and Medieval Literary Criticism: Translations and Interpretations* (New York: Frederick Ungar, 1974), pp. 21–96; and Robert Con Davis and Laurie Finke, eds., *Literary Criticism and Theory: The Greeks to the Present* (New York: Longman, 1989), pp. 44–59.

34. See Gerald F. Else, *Plato and Aristotle on Poetry*, ed. Peter Burian (Chapel Hill: Univ. of North Carolina Press, 1986), p. 4: "The shock that Sokrates then administered to his [Plato's] soul brought about a violent reaction against his earlier idolatry, denying and challenging everything that poetry had meant to him up to that time. He found himself faced by a choice between two worlds, two incompatible ways of life, and he chose 'philosophy.' But the choice necessarily brought with it the banishment of the poets, for they belonged irredeemably to the other world, the one he had rejected."

35. For Plato's poetic description of this double journey, see *Republic*, bk. 7, 514–520; *Dialogues*, vol. 1, pp. 773–779.

36. *Timaeus*, 47; *Dialogues*, vol. 2, p. 28.

37. William C. Greene, "Plato's View of Poetry," *Harvard Studies in Classical Philology* 29 (1918): 65. See also E. E. Sikes, *The Greek View of Poetry* (New York: Barnes & Noble, 1931), pp. 83–90.

38. *Laws*, 654; *Dialogues*, vol. 2, p. 432.

39. *Laws*, 660, 668, and 700–701; *Dialogues*, vol. 2, p. 438, 445–446, 474–476.

40. *Laws*, 817; *Dialogues*, vol. 2, p. 571.

41. *Lunyu yinde*, 17/8; my translation. Cf. Waley, trans., *Analects*, XVII, 9, p. 212.

42. Zhu Xi 朱熹 (1130–1200), ed. *Lunyu jizhu* 論語集注 (Collected Commentaries to *Analects*) (*SBBY* edn.), 9.3b.

43. For instance, when Zi Xia 子夏 relates the description of a woman's beautiful appearances to the issue of rituals, Confucius endorses his moralistic mode of interpretation and considers him a disciple fit to discuss the *Poetry* with. See *Lunyu yinde*, 3/8; trans. Waley, *Analects*, III, 8, pp. 95–96.

44. On Confucius' view of the *Poetry*'s transforming effects, Tu, *Way, Learning, and Politics*, p. 5: "The poetic vision, which emphasizes the internal resonance of the human community, involves the language of the heart. It speaks to the commonality of human feelings and to the mutuality of human concerns without resorting to the art of argumentation. A society harmonized by poetry possesses a synchronized rhythm. The interaction among people in such a society is like the natural flow of sympathetic responses to familiar musical tunes and dance forms."

45. Quoted in He Yan 何晏 (190–249), *Lunyu jijie* 論語集解 (Collected Explanations to *Analects*) (*SBBY* edn.), 17.4b.

46. *Lunyu jizhu*, 9.13b.

47. Huang Kan 皇侃 (488–545), ed. *Lunyu jijie yishu* 論語集解義疏 (Subcommentary to the *Collected Explanations to Analects*) (Nihon Ashikaga kan bon 日本足利刊本 edn.), 9.10b.

48. Wang Fuzhi, *Lunyu xunyi* 論語訓義 (Textual Interpretations of *Analects*) (Taiping yang shuju Chuanshan yishu edn.), 21.10.

49. *Lunyu jijie*, 17.4b.

50. Ibid., 9.13b.
51. *Lunyu yinde,* 15/17; my translation. Cf. Waley, trans., *Analects,* XV, 16, pp. 196–197.
52. Confucius cautions people against accusing heaven or laying blame on man and disapproves of complaints against family members or fellow men. See *Lunyu yinde,* 12/2; trans. Waley, *Analects,* XII, 2, p. 162.
53. *Lunyu zhijie* 論語直解 (Straightforward Interpretations of *Analects*), (Zhizhong xue jianyi edn.), 17.6b.
54. For studies on these four terms, see Guo Shaoyu 郭紹虞, "Xing guan qun yuan shuo pouxi" 興觀群怨說剖析 (An Analysis of the Statement "The *Poetry* may help to inspire, to observe, to keep company, and to express grievances"), in his *Zhaoyushi gudian wenxue lunji* (Shanghai: Shanghai guji chubanshe, 1983), vol. 2, part 1, pp. 390–411; and Lü Yi 呂藝, "Kongzi xing guan qun yuan benyi zaitan" 孔子與觀群怨本義再探 (Another Investigation: Confucius and the Statement "The *Poetry* may help to inspire, to observe, to keep company and to express grievances"), *Wenxue yichan* 文學遺產 (Literary Heritage), 1985.4, pp. 1–11.
55. *Lunyu,* 8/8; my own translation. Cf. Confucius, *Analects,* VIII, 8, p. 134.
56. Liu Baonan 劉寶楠 (1791–1855), ed. *Lunyu zhengyi* 論語正義 (Correct Meanings of *Analects*), *SBBY* edn., 20.9–10.
57. *Lunyu yinde,* 7/25; trans. Waley, *Analects,* VI, 24, p. 128.
58. *Lunyu yinde,* 6/27; trans. Waley, *Analects,* VI, 25, p. 121.
59. *Lunyu yinde,* 7/6; my own translation. Cf. Waley, trans., *Analects,* VII, 6, pp. 123–124.
60. The six Confucian arts (*liuyi* 六藝) are ritual, music, archery, charioteering, calligraphy, and arithmetic.
61. For a comprehensive study of the development of Plato's views of poetry through his early dialogues, the *Republic,* and later dialogues, see Else, *Plato and Aristotle on Poetry,* chapters 1–3. For English language studies on Confucius' views of poetry, see Donald Holzman, "Confucius and Ancient Chinese Literary Criticism," in Adele Austin Rickett, ed., *Chinese Approaches to Literature from Confucius to Liang Ch'i-ch'ao* (Princeton: Princeton Univ. Press, 1978), pp. 21–41, and Yau-woon Ma, "Confucius as a Literary Critic: A Comparison with the Early Greeks," collected in *Essays in Chinese Studies Dedicated to Professor Jao Tsung-i,* ed. Jao Tsung-i jiaoshou nanyou zengbie lunwenji bianji weiyuanhui (Hong Kong: Jao Tsung-i jiaoshou nanyou zengbie lunwenji bianji weiyuanhui, 1970), pp. 13–45.
62. *Dialogues,* vol. 1, p. 281.
63. Ibid., p. 330.
64. *Symposium,* 211; *Dialogues,* vol. 1, p. 335.
65. *Symposium,* 196; *Dialogues,* vol. 1, p. 322.
66. Thomas Gould, *The Ancient Quarrel between Poetry and Philosophy* (Princeton: Princeton Univ. Press, 1990), p. 222. In tracing the Greek ori-

gins of the concept of the poet as the Maker or the Creator, S. K. Heninger, Jr., singles out Plato's *Timaeus* as the most important source: "The *locus classicus* for the concept of the poet as maker occurs early in Plato's *Timaeus*, the one dialogue that enjoyed a continuing reputation throughout the middle ages and renaissance. . . . When Timaeus first mentions the creating deity in this cosmogony, he refers to him with two epithets: 'the poet and the father of this all'" (*Touches of Sweet Harmony: Pythagorean Cosmology and Renaissance Poetics* [San Marino, California: The Huntington Library, 1974], pp. 291–292).

67. See *Phaedrus*, 248; *Dialogues*, vol. 1, pp. 252–253. Cf. Else, *Plato and Aristotle on Poetry*, pp. 54–55: "[*Phaedrus*] 245e did *not* bring a rehabilitation of all poetry but a carefully nuanced appraisal of the true Muses' inspiration, which is equivalent to philosophy. . . . The merely mimetic poet, then, is left without any claim to real inspiration by gods *or* Muses. There is no reason for surprise at this harsh verdict. Most readers of the *Phaidros* have been seduced by Plato's mellow mood and the expansive tone of 245a into thinking that he has now forgiven the poets and renewed their old accreditation as inspired creatures. Not a bit of it. The mimetic poet— and that term still embraces all the major poets, especially Homer—is as far from 'the king and the truth' (*Republic*, 10.597e) as ever. Nothing that he is or knows or does can lift him out of the sixth circle to equal rank with the lover or the philosopher—unless someday he should begin to learn, and then gradually to climb the ladder of incarnations. But that climb would have to be made with the burgeoning 'wing' of Philosophy, warmed and guided by Love. There is no literary road to the top."

68. Gould, *The Ancient Quarrel*, p. 222.

69. On Plato's influence on the English Romantics, see E. Douka Kabitoglou, *Plato and the English Romantics* (London: Routledge, 1990).

70. William C. Greene, "Plato's View of Poetry," p. 75.

71. *Lunyu yinde*, 7/14; my translation. Confucius, *Analects*, VII, 13, p. 125. The *Shao* is a piece of music allegedly from the time of the legendary Emperor Shun.

72. *Lunyu yinde*, 3/25; my translation. Cf. Confucius, *Analects*, III, 25, p. 101.

73. *Lunyu yinde*, 8/19; my translation. Cf. Confucius, *Analects*, VIII, 19, p. 136.

74. On the fusion of spontaneous moral consciousness and aesthetic experience in this and other passages of *Analects*, see Xu Fuguan 徐復觀, *Zhongguo yishu jingshen* 中國藝術精神 (The Spirit of Chinese Art) (Taizhong: Sili Donghai daxue, 1966), pp. 1–44.

75. *Lunyu yinde*, 11/24; trans. Waley, *Analects*, XI, 25, p. 160. I have replaced the Wade-Giles romanizations with their *pinyin* equivalents.

76. Chan, *Source Book in Chinese Philosophy*, p. 38. I have replaced the Wade-Giles romanizations with their *pinyin* equivalents.

77. *Republic*, bk. 7, 521; *Dialogues*, vol. 1, 780.

78. Compare Plato's and Confucius' descriptions of their ideal governments by a philosopher-king and by a sage-king. Plato says, "Whereas the truth is that the State in which the rulers are most reluctant to rule is always the best and the most quietly governed, and the state in which they are most eager, the worst" (*Republic,* VII, 520; *Dialogues,* vol. 1, 779). Confucius says, "Among those that 'ruled by inactivity' surely Shun may be counted. For what action did he take? He merely placed himself gravely and reverently with his face due south; that was all" (*Lunyu yinde,* 15/5; trans. Waley, *Analects,* XV, 4, p. 193).

79. Xu Fuguan, *Zhongguo yishu jingshen,* pp. 18–19.

80. *Republic,* II, 377; *Dialogues,* vol. 1, p. 641.

81. Mihail I. Spariosu, *God of Many Names: Play, Poetry, and Power in Hellenic Thought from Homer to Aristotle* (Durham, N. C.: Duke Univ. Press, 1991), p. 150.

82. *Republic,* bk. 3, 400; *Dialogues,* vol. 1, p. 664.

83. *Republic,* bk. 3, 664; *Dialogues,* vol. 1, p. 665.

84. *Republic,* bk. 3, 395; *Dialogues,* vol. 1, p. 658.

85. *Republic,* bk. 3, 395; *Dialogues,* vol. 1, p. 658.

86. *Republic,* bk. 3, 398; *Dialogues,* vol. 1, p. 661.

87. *Republic,* bk. 3, 399; *Dialogues,* vol. 1, p. 663.

88. *Republic,* bk. 3, 399; *Dialogues,* vol. 1, p. 663.

89. *Republic,* bk. 3, 399–400; *Dialogues,* vol. 1, p. 663. See Else, *Plato and Aristotle on Poetry,* p. 32: "He [Plato] is not merely trying to limit mimesis to worthy objects, he is trying to limit it altogether, because it means variousness and multiplicity, and variousness and multiplicity are bad. He is out to breed and train a uniform, simple kind of men and is excluding anything that might defeat that purpose."

90. Another name of *The Book of Poetry,* derived from the rounding off of its three hundred and five poems to the whole number of three hundred.

91. *Lunyu yinde,* 2/2; my translation. Cf. Waley, trans., *Analects,* II, 2, p. 88.

92. *Lunyu yinde,* 3/20; trans. Waley, *Analects,* III, 20, p. 99.

93. See this criticism of formal excessiveness in music: "When the Master went to the town of Wu, he heard the sound of stringed instruments and singing. The Master said with a subtle smile, ('To kill a chicken does require the use (of) an ox-knife.'" *Lunyu yinde* 17/3; my translation. Cf. Waley, trans., *Analects,* XVII, 4, pp. 209–210).

94. *Lunyu yinde,* 3/25; my translation. Cf. Waley, trans., *Analects,* III, 25, p. 101.

95. *Lunyu yinde,* 15/11; my translation. Cf. Waley, trans., *Analects,* XV, 10, pp. 195–196.

96. *Lunyu yinde,* 17/16; my translation. Cf. Waley, trans., *Analects,* XVII, 18, p. 214.

97. *Lunyu yinde,* 9/15; my translation. Cf. Waley, trans., *Analects,* IX, 14, pp. 141–142.

98. *Lunyu yinde,* 13/3; trans. Waley, *Analects,* XIII, 3, pp. 171–172.
99. In his *Name and Actuality in Early Chinese Thought* (Albany: State Univ. of New York Press, 1994), pp. 35–95, John Makeham discusses Confucius' view on the language-reality relationship and reviews other Confucian and non-Confucian theories of naming.
100. *Lunyu yinde,* 14/27; trans. Waley, *Analects,* XIV, 29, p. 187.
101. *Lunyu yinde,* 15/41; trans. Waley, *Analects,* XV, 40, p. 201.
102. *Lunyu yinde,* 1/3; my translation. Cf. Waley, trans., *Analects,* I, 3, p. 84.
103. *Lunyu yinde,* 5/5; trans. Waley, *Analects,* V, 4, p. 107.
104. *Lunyu yinde,* 12/8; my translation. Cf. Waley, trans., *Analects,* XII, 8, p. 164–165.
105. See *Lunyu yinde,* 14/8; trans. Waley, *Analects,* XIV, 9, pp. 181–182.
106. Schwartz, *World of Thought,* p. 94.
107. In his dialogues, Plato repeatedly describes this quest of transcendental truth as an upward movement of the soul. See, for instance, his famous Fable of the Cave in the *Republic,* bk. 7, 514–523; *Dialogues,* vol. 1, pp. 773–782. On the ontological and epistemological implications of this vertical ascent, see Paul Friedlander, *Plato: An Introduction* (Princeton: Princeton Univ. Press, 1958), p. 227: "Plato's allegory of the cave is characterized by the dual meaning of the hierarchical ascent: the ascent of being and the ascent of knowledge, both exactly related to each other."

     On the influence of this epistemological tendency on Western philosophical thinking, Arthur Lovejoy, *The Great Chain of Being: A Study of the History of Ideas* (Cambridge, Mass.: Harvard Univ. Press, 1936), p. 59, writes: "Down to the late eighteenth century, most educated men were to accept without question the conception of the universe as a 'Great Chain of Being,' composed of an immense, or . . . infinite, number of links ranging in hierarchical order from the meagerest kind of *existents* . . . through 'every possible' grade up to the *ens perfectissimum.*" The title of this classic book is a fitting acknowledgment of the enduring influence of the "vertical" structure of Plato's epistemology. For a cross-cultural study of the notion of truth, see Smith, Huston, "Western and Comparative Perspectives on Truth," *Philosophy East and West* 30 (1980): 425–437.
108. Here I describe this axis as horizontal in comparison with Plato's unambiguously vertical axis, and do not mean to ignore Confucius' concerns with the vertical sociopolitical hierarchy. For sure, the Confucian axis of harmony is not exclusively horizontal just as the Platonic one is not exclusively vertical. These two axes are undoubtedly concomitant to the "immanent" thrust of Confucian thought and the transcendental thrust of Platonic thought. Here I must emphasize the word "thrust," because I do not want my contrast of the overall tendencies of these two thought systems to be mistaken as an oversimplified application of the Western conceptual labels "transcendental" (or "other-worldly") and "immanent" (or "this-worldly") in a cross-cultural context. While the term

"immanent" is useful for describing the overall tendency of the Confucian and some other Chinese thought systems, it necessarily contains philosophical and theological implications, such as the indwelling intelligent principle or pantheistic divinity, that are alien to the Chinese traditions. So, I have put the term inside quotation marks when using it in reference to the Chinese traditions.

109. *Daxue* (*SBBY* edn.), 2a; trans. James Legge, *The Great Learning*, in *The Four Books* (rpt. Taipei: Chengwen, 1971), chapter 3, pp. 358–359.

110. *Daxue*, 2a; trans. James Legge, *The Four Books*, chapter 3, p. 360.

111. Spariosu, *God of Many Names*, p. 172.

112. Hall and Ames, *Thinking Through Confucius*, p. 132.

113. *Republic*, bk. 7, 540–542; *Dialogues*, vol. 1, pp. 799–800.

114. The term "existential" is used here to denote that which pertains to existence or the act of living, and has nothing to do with the Western existentialism.

115. This existential quest of Confucius is by no means devoid of profound "transcendental" significance. His view of the merging of aesthetic experience and the ultimate good discussed earlier is an excellent example of the "transcendental" dimension in Confucius' thought. Explaining why Confucius and his followers choose to emphasize existential concerns and work through them toward his "transcendental" moral vision, Tu Weiming, *Way, Learning, and Politics*, p. 9, writes, "Confucius' existential decision to retrieve the deep meaning of human civilization as a way of rethinking the human project made it impossible for the Confucians to detach themselves totally from the world. They had to work through the world because their faith in the perfectability of human nature through self-effort demanded that they do so. . . . However, even though they were in the world, they could not identify themselves with the status quo. To be sure, they did not appeal exclusively to a transcendent referent as a source for symbolic action. Nor did they develop a realm of values totally independent of the political culture of which they were a part. Nevertheless, they had a rich reservoir of symbolic resources at their disposal in which the transcendent referent featured significantly."

116. For a discussion on Confucius' view of knowledge, see Roger T. Ames, "Meaning as Imaging: Prolegomena to a Confucian Epistemology," in *Culture and Modernity: East-West Philosophic Perspectives*, ed. Eliot Deutsch (Honolulu: Univ. of Hawai'i Press, 1991), pp. 226–244.

117. Christoph Harbsmeier, "Concepts of Knowledge in Ancient China," in *Epistemological Issues in Classical Chinese Philosophy*, eds. Hans Lenk and Gregor Paul (Albany: State Univ. of New York Press, 1993), p. 14, writes, "There is little room in traditional Chinese culture for knowledge for its own sake. There was little enthusiasm for 'academic knowledge' as cultivated by philosophers such as Plato and Aristotle, who continued the heritage of Socrates. For the ancient Chinese it was action that was

primary, personal action and political action. Insight was valued insofar as it led to successful action."

118. Harbsmeier gives a summary account of ancient Chinese epistemology in his article, "Concepts of Knowledge in Ancient China," in *Epistemological Issues in Classical Chinese Philosophy,* eds. Lenk and Paul, pp. 11–30. On Zhu Xi's theory of knowledge, see Tang Junyi 唐君毅, *Zhongguo zhexue yuanlun* 中國哲學原論 (On the Fundamentals of Chinese Philosophy), 2 vols. (Kowlong: Rensheng chubanshe, 1966), vol. 1, pp. 278–347.

CHAPTER 6: POETICS OF IMAGINATION

1. On this paradigmatic significance of imagination in Wordsworth's and other Romantics' views of literary creation, see Thomas MacFarland, *Coleridge and the Pantheist Tradition* (Oxford: Clarendon Press, 1969); James Engell, *The Creative Imagination* (Cambridge, Mass.: Harvard Univ. Press, 1981); Mark Kipperman, *Beyond Enchantment: German Idealism and English Romantic Poetry* (Philadelphia: Univ. of Pennsylvania Press, 1986); Geoffrey H. Hartman, *Wordsworth's Poetry: 1787–1814* (Cambridge, Mass.: Harvard Univ. Press, 1987); Alan Liu, *Wordsworth: The Sense of History* (Stanford: Stanford Univ. Press, 1989); and J. Robert Barth and John. L. Mahoney, eds., *Coleridge, Keats, and the Imagination: Romanticism and Adam's Dream: Essays in Honor of Walter Jackson Bate* (Columbia: Univ. of Missouri Press, 1990).

2. For studies on Liu Xie's theory of literary creation, see Ronald Egan, "Poet, Mind, and World: A Reconsideration of the 'Shen si' Chapter of *Wenxin diaolong,*" and Shuen-fu Lin, "Liu Xie on Imagination," collected in *A Chinese Literary Mind: Culture, Creativity, and Rhetoric in Wenxin diaolong,* ed. Zong-qi Cai (Stanford: Stanford University Press, 2001), pp. 101–126, 127–160. See also Huang Chungui 黃春貴, *Wenxin diaolung zhi chuangzuolun* 文心雕龍之創作論 (The Theory of Literary Creation in *Wenxin diaolong*) (Taipei: Wenshizhe chubanshe, 1978); Wang Yuanhua 王元化, *Wenxin diaolong chuangzuolun* 文心雕龍創作論 (The Theory of Literary Creation in *Wenxin diaolong*) (Shanghai: Shanghai guji chubanshe, 1979); and Shao Yaocheng (Paul Y. Shao) 邵耀成, "Shilun Liu Xie er cengci de 'chuangzuolun'" 試論劉勰二層次的 " 創作論 " (The Dual Nature of Liu Xie's Concept of the Creative Act: Monism and Organicism [author's own translation]), *Gudai wenxue lilun yanjiu* 古代文學理論研究 (Studies on Classical [Chinese] Literary Theory) 5 (1981), pp. 256–280.

3. William Wordsworth, *The Prose Works of William Wordsworth,* ed. W. J. B. Owen and Jane Worthington Smyser, 3 vols. (Oxford: Clarendon, 1974), vol. 1, p. 148. All subsequent citations of Wordsworth's prose works are from this edition.

4. Wordsworth, *Prose Works,* vol. 1, p. 122.

5. Ibid., p. 124.

6. Ibid.
7. Ibid., p. 148.
8. Ibid.
9. In the 1850 preface, Wordsworth changes "similar to that which . . ." to "kindred to that which . . ." perhaps to emphasize the difference between these two kinds of emotion. See *Prose Works,* vol. 1, p. 149.
10. Wordsworth, *Prose Works,* vol. 1, p. 126.
11. Ibid., p. 124.
12. Ibid., pp. 148 and 150.
13. Abrams, *The Mirror and the Lamp,* p. 104.
14. M. H. Abrams praises Wordsworth's linear arrangement of diverse and often opposing eighteenth century ideas into a coherent theory of literary creation: "It is the strength of Wordsworth's expressive theory, therefore, that he brings into its purview elements of the older conception that poetry is a deliberate art; it is its peculiarity that these elements are carefully relegated to a temporal position before or after the actual coming-into-being of the poem" (*The Mirror and the Lamp,* p. 113).
15. Owen, *Readings in Chinese Literary Thought,* p. 211.
16. Ibid., p. 278.
17. Ibid., p. 205, n. 77.
18. "Preface to *Lyrical Ballads* (1800)," *Prose Works,* vol. 1, p. 123.
19. Ibid., p. 138.
20. Abrams, *The Mirror and the Lamp,* pp. 103–104.
21. *The Prelude or Growth of a Poet's Mind,* ed. Ernest de Selincourt and a new edition corrected by Stephen Gill (Oxford: Oxford Univ. Press, 1970), XII, 1–14, p. 218. All references to *The Prelude* are to this edition. See a similar argument in *The Recluse,* vol. 11, 292–296.
22. On this intertwining of emotive and epistemological processes, Lilian R. Furst, *Romanticism in Perspective* (New York: Humanities Press, 1970), p. 220: "On the whole the Romantics envisaged the heart not only, or even primarily, as the fountain-head of happiness and sorrow, but particularly as an organ of knowledge. As a corollary to the rejection of rationalism, the mind was demoted from its controlling position and replaced by the heart as the means of perception: 'The feelings will set up the standard against the understanding, whenever the understanding has renounced its allegiance to the reason,' to use Coleridge's words. 'Only what we feel, we know' could well have been the motto of the Romantics."
23. *The Poetical Works of William Wordsworth,* eds. Ernest de Selincourt and Helen Darbishire, 5 vols. (Oxford: Clarendon, 1940–1949), vol. 4, p. 56. All references to Wordsworth's poems other than *The Prelude* are to this edition.
24. *Romanticism in Perspective,* p. 230.
25. Wordsworth, *Prelude,* II, 272–275, p. 27.
26. Wordsworth, "Tintern Abbey," ll. 76–83, *Poetical Works,* vol. 2, p. 261.

27. Wordsworth, *Prelude,* I, ll. 609–624, p. 18.
28. Wordsworth, "Tintern Abbey," ll. 23–48, *Poetical Works,* vol. 2, p. 260.
29. Wordsworth, *Prelude,* II, ll. 263–264, p. 27.
30. Wordsworth, *Prelude,* I, ll. 427–441, pp. 12–13.
31. Coleridge, *Biographia Literaria,* eds. James Engell and W. Jackson Bate (Princeton: Princeton Univ. Press, 1983), XIII, p. 304.
32. On the symbiotic relationship between Coleridge and Wordsworth, see Paul Magnuson, *Coleridge and Wordsworth: A Lyrical Dialogue* (Princeton: Princeton Univ. Press, 1988).
33. Cf. E. D. Hirsch, Jr., *Wordsworth and Schelling: A Typological Study of Romanticism* (New Haven: Yale Univ. Press, 1960), p. 136: "The idea, 'emotion recollected in tranquility,' implies emotion which is mediated by consciousness and self-awareness. In tranquility, one remembers the emotion, that which caused it, the man who had it, and one perceives the relations of all these to the life of things. This theme is common to Wordsworth and Schelling and to Hegel as well. Apperception is the 'truth' of perception, but it does not exclude perception."
34. Wordsworth, *Prelude,* II, ll. 381–392, pp. 30–31.
35. See Wordsworth, "Preface to the Edition of 1815," *Prose Works,* vol. 3, pp. 32–35.
36. See ibid., pp. 32–35.
37. Coleridge, *Biographia Literaria,* XIII, p. 304.
38. Nigel Leask, *The Politics of Imagination in Coleridge's Critical Thought* (London: Macmillan, 1988), p. 137.
39. Wordsworth, "Preface to the Edition of 1815," *Prose Works,* vol. 3, p. 37. On Wordsworth and Coleridge's debate on the difference between fancy and imagination, see Abrams, *The Mirror and the Lamp,* pp. 177–183.
40. Wordsworth, "'Prospectus' of '*The Excursion,*'" ll. 48–56, *Poetical Works,* vol. 5, p. 339.
41. Hirsch, *Wordsworth and Schelling,* p. 21.
42. Wordsworth, *Prelude,* II, ll. 321–330, p. 29.
43. Wordsworth, *Prelude,* XIII, ll. 84–95, p. 231.
44. Phillip du Plessis Mornay, *The Trewnesse of the Christian Religion,* translated from French by Phillip Sidney, collected in *Complete Works of Sir Phillip Sidney,* ed. Albert Feuillerat, 4 vols. (Cambridge, England: Cambridge Univ. Press, 1912–1926), vol. 3, p. 328.
45. Heninger, *Touches of Sweet Harmony,* p. 293.
46. W. J. B. Owen, *Wordsworth as Critic* (Toronto: Univ. of Toronto Press, 1969), n. 17, pp. 84–85.
47. This neglect of the stage of compositional execution is common to most Romantic critics. Edward S. Casey, *Imagining: A Phenomenological Study* (Bloomington: Indiana Univ. Press, 1976), p. 185, explains the reason for it: "According to the Romantic credo—and as predelineated in part by its Neoplatonic precursors—all authentic imagining (as opposed to the

spurious imagining of mere fancy) is creative: to imagine authentically is to *be* creative, whether or not this creativity is embodied in a work of art or any other tangible product. At the limit—a limit most closely approached in the aesthetic doctrines of Croce and Collingwood, who bring the Romantic doctrine of imagination to its logical conclusion—one need not concern oneself with the concrete expressions of creative imagination. Such expressions are merely a matter of 'techniques,' of 'externalization,' and are of secondary importance compared with the activity of pure imagination, which alone is truly expressive."

48. Yu Yuan 郁沅, Yang Lierong 羊列榮, and Xie Xin 謝昕, "*Wenxin diaolong* shenmei ganying lun tanwei" 文心雕龍審美感應論探微 (An Exploration of the Subtle Meanings of the View of Aesthetic Responses in *Wenxin diaolong*) in *Wenxin diaolong guoji xueshu yantaohui lunwenji* 文心雕龍國際學術研討會論文集 (Collected Essays from the International Symposium on *Wenxindiao long*), ed. Riben jiuzhou daxue zhongguo wenxuehui (Taipei: Wenshizhe chubanshe, 1992), pp. 99–115, take note of these two distinctive types of experience and call them, respectively, "outward responses" (*wai ganying* 外感應) and "inward responses" (*nei ganying* 內感應).

49. Owen, *Readings in Chinese Literary Thought*, p. 286. Slightly modified.

50. *A Midsummer Night's Dream*, V.i.12–17, *Shakespeare: The Complete Works*, ed. G. B. Harrison (New York: Harcourt, Brace & World, 1968), p. 536.

51. See *Wen fu* 文賦 (A Rhapsody on Literature), collected in *ZGLD*, vol. 1, p. 170.

52. Ibid; Owen, *Readings in Chinese Literary Thought*, pp. 173–174.

53. I have discussed the broader theoretical significance of Liu Xie's notion of *yixiang* in my essay "Yixiang, yijing shuo yu Liu Xie de chuangzuo lun" 意象、意境說與劉勰的創作論 (Theories of Yixiang [Idea-Image], Yijing [Idea-scape] and Liu Xie's Theory of Literary Creation), in *Wenxin diaolong guoji xueshu yantaohui lunwenji* 文心雕龍國際學術研討會論文集, ed. Taiwan Shifan Daxue guowen xi (Taipei: Wenshizhe chubanshe, 2000), pp. 375–388.

54. For comprehensive studies on Liu Xie's theory of rhetoric, see Xu Fuguan 徐復觀, "*Wenxin diaolong* de wentilun" 文心雕龍的文體論 (The Theory of Styles in *Wenxin diaolong*), in his *Zhongguo wenxue lunji* 中國文學論集 (Collected Writings on Chinese Literature) (Taipei: Minzhu pinglun she, 1966), pp. 1–83; and Wang Gengsheng 王更生, *Wenxin diaolong xinlun* 文心雕龍新論 (New Perspectives on *Wenxin diaolong*) (Taipei: Wenshizhe chubanshe, 1991), pp. 45–621.

55. Zhang Shaokang 張少康 distinguishes these two theories and discusses them separately in his *Wenxin diaolong chuangzuo lun* 中國古代文學創作論 (Theories of Literary Creation in Ancient China) (Taipei: Wenshizhe chubanshe, 1991), pp. 5–19 and 34–47. See also Zhu Liangzhi 朱良志, "Lun Zhongguo gudai meixue zhong di 'xujing' shuo" 論中國古代美學

中的虛靜說 (On the Theory of "Emptiness and Stillness" in Traditional Chinese Aesthetics) *Gudai wenxue lilun yanjiu* 古代文學理論研究 (Studies on Classical [Chinese] Literary Theory) 15 (1991), pp. 30–50.

56. Hirsch, *Wordsworth and Schelling,* p. 135.

57. *Republic,* VII, 515; *Dialogues,* vol. 1, p. 774.

58. Else, *Plato and Aristotle on Poetry,* p. 41.

59. *Timaeus,* 45b–c; *Plato's Timaeus,* p. 42.

60. Edward S. Casey, *Imagining,* pp. 1–20, summarizes different views of the interplay of the sensory and suprasensory in creative imagination held by major Western critics since Plato.

61. Emerson, *Nature,* in *The Collected Works of Ralph Waldo Emerson,* ed. Alfred R. Ferguson (Cambridge, Mass.: Harvard Belnap Press, 1971), vol. 1, p. 10. On the philosophical significance of Emerson's notion of seeing, see Leon Chai, *The Romantic Foundations of the American Renaissance* (Ithaca: Cornell Univ. Press, 1987), pp. 331–342.

62. "Vision of the Last Judgment," in *Complete Poetry and Prose of William Blake,* ed. David V. Erdman (Berkeley: Univ. of California Press, 1982), pp. 565–566. The punctuation of this paragraph is the one used in *The Poetry and Prose of William Blake,* ed. David V. Erdman and Harold Bloom (Garden City, N.Y.: Doubleday, 1965).

63. Fragments (1798–1799) from a notebook containing the first extant manuscript of "Christabel," vi, 1–15, *Poetical Works,* vol. 5, pp. 343–344.

64. On Wordsworth's descriptions of the eye's complex relationship with the transcendental reality, see Frederick A. Pottle, "The Eye and the Object in the Poetry of Wordsworth," in *Romanticism and Consciousness: Essays in Criticism,* ed. Harold Bloom (New York: Norton, 1970), pp. 273–287. Carlos Baker discusses how Wordsworth's poetical art is shaped by his view of the eye and suprasensory experience in "Sensation and Vision in Wordsworth," in *English Romantic Poets: Modern Essays in Criticism,* ed. M. H. Abrams (New York: Galaxy, 1960), pp. 95–109.

65. For the Chinese text, see *Zhuang Zi jishi* 莊子集釋 (The Book of Zhuang Zi, with Collected Annotations), ed. Guo Qingfan 郭慶藩, 4 vols. (Beijing: Zhonghua shuju, 1961), 1/2/117–119; trans. Burton Watson, *The Complete Works of Chuang Tzu* (New York: Columbia Univ. Press, 1968), p. 50–51. I have changed the style of romanization from the Wade-Giles to the *pinyin* system in this passage.

   For English-language studies on Zhuang Zi, see Victor H. Mair, ed., *Experimental Essays on Chuang-tzu* (Honolulu: Univ. of Hawai'i Press, 1983) and Paul Kjellberg and Philip J. Ivanhoe, eds., *Essays on Skepticism, Relativism, and Ethics in the Zhuangzi* (Albany: State Univ. of New York Press, 1996).

66. See Zhang Shaokang, *Wenxin diaolong chuangzuo lun,* pp. 8–15.

67. See *Zhuang Zi jijie,* 2/13/491.

68. See ibid., 4/24/843.

69. Unlike Zhuang Zi and other Daoist thinkers, Chinese Buddhists of later times, especially those in the Chan schools, do not stress the closing of eyes as an important requisite for a suprasensory union with the ultimate reality. Quite the contrary, they tend to believe that an open-eye contemplation of objects or scenes of nature can directly yield sudden enlightenment, a blessed moment in which one's attachment to both phenomenal and mental worlds is cut off and one is rendered into the state of Nirvāṇa. I shall wait for a future occasion to discuss the influence of this Buddhist view of sensory perception on the Tang and post-Tang theories of literary creation.

70. On Wordsworth's revelation of the transcendental essence through such a union, see Hirsch, *Wordsworth and Schelling*, pp. 22–23: "Unity with the object is a kind of unity with the beyond, for the reciprocal process itself evokes a sense of 'something far more deeply interfused' which dwells in all things, in

> the round ocean, and the living air
> And the blue sky, and in the mind of man.

The beyond is something that subsists within the subject and his object and also beyond them both. Subject and object are unified because of an essence which 'rolls through all things.' They are akin because they both belong to a greater totality. This totality is apprehended in the object, but it is never fully given in experience; it always reaches beyond, always stretches out toward the 'light of setting suns.'"

CHAPTER 7: POETICS OF DYNAMIC FORCE

1. Among numerous studies of Fenollosa and Pound's theory of the Chinese written character, see Archilles Fang, "Fenollosa and Pound," *Harvard Journal of Asiatic Studies* 20 (1957): 213–238; Hugh Kenner, "Poetics of Error," *Tamkang Review* 6–7 (1975–1976):89–97; William Tay, "Fragmentary Negation: A Reappraisal of Ezra Pound's Ideogrammic Method," in *Chinese-Western Comparative Literature: Theory and Strategy*, ed. John J. Deeney (Hong Kong: Chinese Univ. Press, 1980), pp. 129–153; Huang Guiyou, "Ezra Pound: (Mis)Translation and (Re) Creation," *Paideuma: A Journal Devoted to Ezra Pound Scholarship* 22, no. 1–2 (1993): 99–114; Jin Songping, "Fenollosa and 'Hsiao Hsueh' Tradition," *Paideuma* 22, no. 1–2 (1993): 71–97; Richard Londraville, "Fenollosa and the Legacy of Stone Cottage," *Paideuma* 22, no. 3 (1993): 100–08; Zhaoming Qian, *Orientalism and Modernism: The Legacy of China in Pound and Williams* (Durham and London: Duke Univ. Press, 1995), pp. 56–64; and Haun Saussy, "The Prestige of Writing: 文, Letter, Picture, Image, Ideography," *Sino-Platonic Papers* 75 (1997): 1–41. For a comprehensive study of Pound's translation of Chinese poetry, see Wai-lim Yip's *Ezra Pound's Cathay* (Princeton: Princeton Univ. Press, 1969).

2. Andrew Welsh, *Roots of Lyric: Primitive Poetry and Modern Poetics* (Princeton: Princeton Univ. Press, 1978), p. 101.

3. James J.Y. Liu, *The Art of Chinese Poetry* (Chicago: Univ. of Chicago Press, 1962), pp. 3–7.

4. For a typical harsh Sinological criticism of the essay, see George Kennedy, "Fenollosa, Pound and Chinese Characters," *Yale Literary Magazine* 36 (1958): 24–36.

5. For a linguist's critique of the ideographic myth, see John DeFrancis, *The Chinese Language: Fact and Fantasy* (Honolulu: Univ. of Hawai'i Press, 1984), pp. 132–148. DeFrancis focuses on criticizing the ideographic myth promoted by Sinologists and makes no mention of Fenollosa or Pound.

6. Ernest Fenollosa, "*The Chinese Written Character as a Medium for Poetry,*" ed. Ezra Pound (1936; rpt. San Francisco: City Lights, 1983), p. 8.

7. Ibid., p. 9.

8. D. D. Paige, ed., *The Letters of Ezra Pound, 1907–1941* (New York: Haskell, 1974), p. 131.

9. Fenollosa, *Chinese Written Character*, p. 7.

10. Ibid., p. 17.

11. Ibid., p. 10.

12. Ibid., p. 19.

13. Ibid., p. 20.

14. Ibid., pp. 20–21.

15. Ibid., p. 9.

16. Ibid., p. 10.

17. For a brief outline of the evolution of Chinese characters, see Zhu Renfu, 朱仁夫, *Zhongguo gudai shufa shi* 中國古代書法史 (History of Ancient Chinese Calligraphy) (Beijing: Beijing daxue chubanshe, 1992), pp. 1–77; and Chiang Yee, *Chinese Calligraphy: An Introduction to Its Aesthetic and Technique* (Cambridge: Harvard Univ. Press, 1966) pp. 18–40. For plates and discussions of the aforementioned scripts, see Tseng Yu-ho Ecke, *Chinese Calligraphy* (Philadelphia: Philadelphia Museum of Art and Boston Book & Art, 1971), plates 1–5.

18. The Oracle Bone Script (*jiaguwen* 甲骨文) is the earliest known form of Chinese writing, engraved on tortoise shells or animal bones and widely used from around the eighteenth century B.C. to the ninth century B.C. The Bronze Script (*jinwen* 金文) is the form of writing engraved on bronze vessels or stone drums and widely used from the ninth century B.C. to the third century B.C. The Small Seal Script (*xiaozhuan* 小篆) refers to the simplified script introduced by Li Si 李斯 (d. 208 B.C.), prime minister of the Qin, and widely used during the Qin Dynasty. In contrast to the Small Seal Script, many scholars apply the name "Large Seal Script" (*dazhuan* 大篆) to the scripts used before the Qin. To further differentiate the pre-Qin scripts, some scholars prefer to limit the reference of the Large Seal Script to the Zhou Script (籀文), allegedly developed by an Imperial Recorder named Zhou 籀 around the ninth century B.C. and widely used until the Warring States, and to give the name "An-

cient Script" (*guwen* 古文) to the predominant script used during the War-
ring States. "Seal Script" (*zhuanti* 篆體) is a general term for all scripts
used before and during the Qin, as opposed to the "Clerical-Style Script"
(*liti* 隸體) widely used during and after the Han. Modern script is de-
veloped from the "Clerical-Style Script" and therefore the two look very
much alike. The dates given here are meant to indicate when certain scripts
were widely used, without suggesting that they were used only in those
periods.

19. Fenollosa, *Chinese Written Character,* p. 8. However, his argument that
    these characters produce a visual semblance of an ongoing action (man-
    see-horse) in the mind of the Chinese is very tenuous.
20. Ibid., p. 10.
21. Yee, *Chinese Calligraphy,* p. 109.
22. To compare Fenollosa's analysis with a similar account of the evolution
    of Chinese characters, see Zong Baihua 宗白華, "Zhongguo shufa li di
    meixue sixiang" 中國書法里的美學思想 (Aesthetic Ideas in Chinese
    Calligraphy), *Meixue sanbu* 美學散步 (A Promenade in Aesthetics)
    (Shanghai: Shanghai renmin chubanshe, 1981), pp. 135–160.
23. Fenollosa, *Chinese Written Character,* p. 6.
24. For a discussion of the Six Methods, see Gao Ming 高明, *Zhongguo gu
    wenzi xue tonglun* 中國古文字學通論 (A Comprehensive Survey of the
    Studies on Chinese Ancient Characters) (Beijing: Beijing Univ. Press,
    1996), pp. 45–57.
25. On the profound influence of *shuowen jiezi* on the subsequent studies of
    Chinese characters, see Gao, *Zhongguo gu wenzi xue tonglun,* pp. 9–10,
    12–16, and 18–21.
26. Fenollosa, *Chinese Written Character,* p. 30.
27. Xu, *Shuowen jiezi zhu,* p. 1.
28. Ibid., p. 9. Cf. Dong Zhongshu 董仲舒, *Chunqiu fanlu yizheng* 春秋繁
    露義證 (Investigating the Meanings of *Luxuriant Gems of the Spring and
    Autumn Annals*), ed. Su Yu 蘇輿 (Beijing: zhonghua shuju, 1992), pp.
    328–329.
29. Fenollosa, *Chinese Written Character,* p. 41.
30. Jin, "Fenollosa and 'Hsiao Hsueh' Tradition," p. 87.
31. As we shall see, Chinese calligraphers and calligraphy critics came to explore
    this characters-nature relationship much earlier than did lexicographers.
32. Wang Anshi, *Wang Wengong wenji* 王文公文集 (Collected Writings of
    Wang Wenggong [Anshi]), 2 vols. (Shanghai: Shanghai renmin chuban-
    she, 1974), vol. 1, p. 236.
33. Fenollosa, *Chinese Written Character,* p. 10.
34. Ibid., p. 25.
35. Owen, *Traditional Chinese Poetry and Poetics,* pp. 21–23.
36. For a study of this chapter, see Tu Guangshe 涂光社, "Hanzi yu gudai
    wenxue de minzu tese—*Wenxin diaolong* lian zi' suixiang" 漢字與古代

文學的民族特色—文心雕龍練字隨想(Chinese Characters and the Unique Features of Classical [Chinese] Literature—Random Notes on the *Lianzi* Chapter of *Wenxin diaolong*), *Gudai wenxue lilun yanjiu* 古代文學理論研究(Studies on Classical [Chinese] Literary Theory) 14 (1989), pp. 261–280.

37. Shih, *Literary Mind,* p. 163.

38. Ibid., p. 163.

39. For a study of ideogram-based riddles, see Yu Yongben 愚庸笨, *Zhongguo wenzi de chuangyi yu quwei* 中國文字的創意與趣味 (The Creativity and Flavors of Chinese Characters) (Taipei: Daotian chuban youxian gongsi, 1995), pp. 56–99.

40. For the influence of Fenollosa and Pound on modern Chinese poetry, see Archilles Fang, "From Imagism to Whitmanism in Recent Chinese Poetry: A Search for Poetics That Failed," in *Indiana University Conference on Oriental-Western Literary Relations,* eds. Horst Frenz and G. L. Anderson (Chapel Hill: Univ. of North Carolina Press, 1955).

41. Fenollosa, *Chinese Written Character,* p. 9.

42. Michael Sullivan, *The Three Perfections: Chinese Painting, Poetry, and Calligraphy* (London: Thames & Hudson, 1974).

43. Han Yu 韓愈, *Han Changli shi xinian jishi* 韓昌黎詩繫年集釋 (A Chronological and Variorum Edition of the Poems of Han Changli [Han Yu]), annotated by Qian Zhonglian 錢仲聯, 2 vols (Shanghai: Shanghai guji chubanshe, 1984), vol. 1, pp. 794–885. Translation is taken with modifications from Wytter Binner and Kiang Kang-hu, *The Jade Mountain* (New York: Alfred A. Knopf, 1930), p. 167. (I have retranslated the first two lines to correctly convey the meaning of the original.)

44. Fenollosa, *Chinese Written Character,* p. 25.

45. On the rise of these four calligraphic styles, see Zhu Renfu, *Zhongguo gudai shufa shi,* pp. 78–184.

46. For a discussion of writing instruments and materials in Chinese calligraphy and painting, see Jerome Silbergeld, *Chinese Painting Style* (Seattle: Univ. of Washington Press, 1982), pp. 5–30. For a brief survey of these four calligraphic styles, see Yee, *Chinese Calligraphy,* pp. 59–105.

47. On the superiority of the cursive style to the standard styles (clerical and regular styles), Zhang Huaiguan 張懷瓘 (fl. 8th century) writes, "In standard script, the meaning is completed when the character is completed; but in cursive script, the potency [of the kinetic force] will not finish, even at the end of a column." (*Zhongguo meixueshi ziliao xuanbian* 中國美術史資料選編 [Anthology of Documents in the History of Chinese Aesthetics], ed. Beijing Daxue zexuexi, 2 vols. [Beijing: Zhonghua shuju, 1980], vol.1, p. 256); translation is taken from Yu-kung Kao, "Chinese Lyric Aesthetics" in *Words and Images: Chinese Poetry, Calligraphy and Painting,* eds. Wen Fong and Alfreda Murck [Princeton: Princeton Univ. Press, 1991], p. 79).

48. This is only a brief outline of the development of Chinese calligraphy as an art of dynamic movement. Yu-kung Kao discusses the aesthetic significance of the evolution of Chinese character from *wen* or pictograms (the earliest Oracle Bone Script) to *zi* or character (Seal Scripts) to *shu* or calligraphic styles in his "Chinese Lyric Aesthetics," pp. 74–80.

49. In Chinese calligraphy criticism, *shi* is used to denote the momentum of a dynamic force being released or the impregnation of a dynamic force in things. These two conditions seem to respond to what Fenollosa calls "things in motion" and "motion in things," and may be described as "momentum" and "propensity," respectively. For a study of *shi* in calligraphy and other realms of Chinese culture, see François Jullien, *The Propensity of Things: Toward a History of Efficacy in China,* translated from French by Janet Lloyd (New York: Zone Books, 1995).

50. Cited in Zhu Jia 祝嘉, *Shuxue shi* 書學史 (A History of the Studies of Calligraphy) (rpt. Chengdu: Sichuan guji shudian, 1984), p. 12; trans. Lucy Driscoll and Kenji Toda, *Chinese Calligraphy* (New York: Paragon, 1964), p. 27. Translation slightly modified.

51. Cited in Zhu, *Zhongguo gudai shufa shi,* p. 83.

52. Wei Shuo, "Bi zhen tu" 筆陣圖 ("The Diagram of the Battle Array of the Brush"), collected in *Zhongguo meixueshi ziliao xuanbian,* vol. 1, p. 160. Translation is taken with slight modifications from Driscoll and Toda, *Chinese Calligraphy,* p. 46.

53. Chen Si, *Shuyuan jinghua* 書苑菁華 (The Splendor of the Garden of Calligraphy) (Wang Ruli edn.), I; trans. Lucy Driscoll and Kenji Toda, *Chinese Calligraphy,* p. 35.

54. Quoted in Zong, *Meixue sanbu,* p. 135.

55. Quoted in Zong, *Meixue sanbu,* pp. 135–136.

56. Wang Xizhi, "Ti Wei Furen 'Bi zhen tu' hou" 題衛夫人筆陣圖後 (An Inscription on Lady Wei's "The Diagram of the Battle Array of the Brush"), collected in *Zhongguo meixueshi ziliao xuanbian,* vol. 1, p. 173. The translation is mine.

57. Welsh, *Roots of Lyric,* p. 101.

58. For the Three-Point Imagist Tenets, see F. S. Flint, "Imagisme," *Poetry* 1 (1913):199. Reed W. Dasenbrock examines Pound's assimilation of the Vorticist ideas for his revitalization of the Imagist movement in his *The Literary Vorticism of Ezra Pound and Wyndham Lewis* (Baltimore: John Hopkins Univ. Press, 1985), pp. 28–126.

59. Ezra Pound, *Gaudier-Brzeska* (New York: New Directions, 1970), p. 92.

60. Earl Miner examines Pound's indebtedness to Japanese haiku in his development of the "super-position" method in "Pound, *Haiku,* and the Image," *The Hudson Review* 9 (1956–1957): 570–584; reprinted in Walter Sutton, ed., *Ezra Pound: A Collection of Critical Essays* (Englewood Cliffs, N. J.: Prentice-Hall, 1963), p. 115–128. See also Miner's *The Japanese Tradi-*

tion in British and American Literature (Princeton: Princeton Univ. Press, 1958), pp. 108–155.

61. Fenollosa, *Chinese Written Character,* pp. 86–103.

62. The following account of Pound's contact with the Orientalists is based on information provided in Zhaoming Qian, *Orientalism and Modernism: The Legacy of China in Pound and Williams* (Durham and London: Duke Univ. Press, 1995), pp. 9–22.

63. Qian, *Orientalism and Modernism,* p. 14.

64. Ibid., p. 19.

65. Omar Pound and A. Walton Litz, eds., *Ezra Pound and Dorothy Shakespear: Their Letters, 1909–1914* (New York: New Directions, 1984), p. 256.

66. K. L. Goodwin, *The Influence of Ezra Pound* (London: Oxford Univ. Press, 1966), p. 4.

67. Paige, *Letters of Ezra Pound,* p. 59.

68. Lea Baechler and A. Walton Litz, eds., *Personae: The Shorter Poems* (New York: New Directions, 1990), p. 95

69. Qian, *Orientalism and Modernism,* pp. 51–52.

70. Ibid., pp. 54–55.

71. Ibid., p. 58. The brackets are mine.

72. Ibid., p. 71.

73. Ibid., p. 85.

74. Dasenbrock, *Literary Vorticism,* p. 108.

75. Fenollosa, *Chinese Written Character,* p. 3.

76. Ibid. The great esteem and admiration Pound had for Fenollosa are also aptly reflected in the fact that he later used the phrase "Ideogrammic Method" to characterize his Imagist-Vorticist poetics.

77. Fenollosa, *Chinese Written Character,* p. 9.

78. Ibid., p. 32.

79. Ibid., p. 22.

80. Welsh, *Roots of Lyric,* p. 52.

81. Fenollosa, *Chinese Written Character,* p. 21.

82. "Preface to *Lyrical Ballads,*" *Prose Works,* p. 126.

83. Samuel Taylor Coleridge, *The Statesman's Manual* (1816); Samuel Taylor Coleridge, *Complete Works of Samuel Taylor Coleridge* (New York: Harper & Brothers, 1854), vol. 1 pp. 437–438.

84. The emphasis is mine.

85. T. S. Eliot, ed., *Literary Essays of Ezra Pound* (Norfolk, Conn.: New Directions, 1954), p. 4.

86. Sanford Schwartz, *The Matrix of Modernism* (Princeton: Princeton Univ. Press, 1985), p. 93.

87. Jean François Billeter, *The Chinese Art of Writing* (Geneva: Skira, 1990), pp. 246–284, presents a similar view on this issue.

88. For studies on the origins of the Chinese written language, see He Jiu-

ying 何九盈, Hu Shuangbao 胡雙寶, and Zhang Meng 張猛, *Zhong-guo Hanzi wenhua daguan* 中國漢字文化大觀 (A Grand View of Chinese Characters and Culture) (Beijing: Beijing Univ. Press, 1995), pp. 3–14; Jonathan Chaves, "The Legacy of Ts'ang Chieh: The Written Word as Magic," *Oriental Art* 23, no. 2 (1977): 200–215; and William G. Boltz, *The Origins and Early Development of the Chinese Writing System,* American Oriental Society Series, no. 78 (New Haven, Conn: American Oriental Society, 1994), pp. 129–155.

89. Xu, *Shuowen jiezi,* p. 753. Translation is taken with slight modification from Boltz, *Origins and Early Development,* p. 135. Romanization has been changed from the Wade-Giles to the *pinyin* system.

90. Once written characters are traced to and identified with trigrams and hexagrams, they become entitled to all the claims made for the latter, not just the claims about their divine origin and efficacy. As shown in chapter 3, the Eight Trigrams are credited with having inspired all important civilizing inventions in the "Great Commentary" (*XCZ* B.2). Consequently, written characters, too, are long seen as the source of inspiration for developing various aspects of Chinese civilization. Even in our time, scholars continue to search in characters for clues to the defining features of Chinese literature and the arts as well as various branches of social science. For efforts to grasp the characteristics of Chinese aesthetics by examining the structural principles of characters, see, for instance, Lin Hengxun 林衡勛 "Zhongguo wenzi chuangzao di shenmei tezhi shitan 中國文字創造的審美特質試探" (An Inquiry into the Aesthetic Nature of the Creation of Chinese Characters), *Gu-dai wenxue lilun yanjiu* 古代文學理論研究 (Studies on Classical [Chinese] Literary Theory) 14 (1989), pp. 234–280; and Yu-kung Kao 高友工, "Zhongguo yuyan wenzi dui shige de yingxiang" 中國語言文字對詩歌的影響 (The Influence of Chinese Speech and Characters on Poetry-Writing), *Chung-wai wen-hsüeh* 中外文學 (*Chung-wai Literary Monthly*) 18.5 (1990), pp. 4–38. For an effort to discover in Oracle Bone and Bronze Scripts the prototypes and aesthetic principles of traditional Chinese architecture, see Sun Quanwen 孫全文 and Zeng Wenhong 曾文宏, *You Zhongguo wenzi tantao chuantong jianzhu* 由中國文字探討傳統建築 (Exploring Traditional [Chinese] Architecture through Chinese Characters) (Taipei: Zhan shi shuju, 1988). He Jiuying, et al., *Zhongguo Hanzi wenhua daguan,* pp. 3–14, provides a useful, comprehensive guide to the relationship of characters to numerous aspects of Chinese civilization.

91. Shih, *Literary Mind.* p. 337. I have changed his rendering of *shenli* 神理 from "Divine Reason," a Western philosophical and theological concept, to a more neutral phrase, "the spiritual principle." I have also changed "the piece 'Shao-hsia'" to " . . . pieces 'Shao' and 'Xia.'" These two pieces are the music of the times of Shun and Yu, respectively.

92. Pound discusses these three aspects of lyric in "How to Read Poetry," *Literary Essays of Ezra Pound,* pp. 25–27.

CHAPTER 8: POETICS OF DECONSTRUCTION

1. Jacques Derrida, *Of Grammatology,* trans. Gayatri Chakravorty Spivak (Baltimore: Johns Hopkins Univ. Press, 1974), p. 92.
2. Ibid., p. 90.
3. See Zhang Longxi, *The Tao and the Logos: Literary Hermeneutics, East and West* (Durham, N. C.: Duke Univ. Press, 1992), pp. 1–33; Zha Peide, "Logocentrism and Traditional Chinese Poetics," *Canadian Review of Comparative Literature / Revue Canadienne de Littérature Comparée* 19, no. 3, (1992): 377–394; and Cheng Jiewei, "Derrida and Ideographic Poetics," *British Journal of Aesthetics* 35, no. 2 (1995): 134–144.
4. See Michelle Yeh, "The Deconstructive Way: A Comparative Study of Derrida and Chuang Tzu," *Journal of Chinese Philosophy* 10, no. 2 (1983): 95–125; Chien Chi-Hui, 'Theft's Way': A Comparative Study of Chuang Tzu's Tao and Derridean Trace," *Journal of Chinese Philosophy* 17, no. 1 (1990): 31–49; Cheng Chung-Ying, "A Taoist Interpretation of 'différance' in Derrida," *Journal of Chinese Philosophy* 17, no. 1 (1990):19–30; Fu Hongchu, "Deconstruction and Taoism: Comparisons Reconsidered," *Comparative Literature Studies* 29, no. 3 (1992): 296–321; Xie Shaobo and John (Zhong) M. Chen, "Jacques Derrida and Chuang Tzu: Some Analogies in Their Deconstructionist Discourse on Language and Truth," *Canadian Review of Comparative Literature / Revue Canadienne de Littérature Comparée* 19, no. 3 (1992): 363–376; Wayne D. Ownes, "Tao and Différance: The Existential Implications," *Journal of Chinese Philosophy* 20, no. 3 (1993): 261–277; and Mark Berkson, "Language: The Guest of Reality—Zhuangzi and Derrida on Language, Reality, and Skillfulness," in *Essays on Skepticism, Relativism, and Ethics in the Zhuangzi,* eds. Paul Kjellberg and Philip J. Ivanhoe (Albany: State Univ. of New York Press, 1996), pp. 97–126.
5. For a succinct account of the origin, major scriptures, and leading figures of Mādhyamika Buddhism, see Hsüeh-li Cheng, *Empty Logic: Mādhyamika Buddhism from Chinese Sources* (New York: Philosophical Library, 1984), pp. 9–32; and C. W. Huntington and N. Wangchen Gesh, *The Emptiness of Emptiness: An Introduction to Early Indian Mādhyamika* (Honolulu: University of Hawai'i Press, 1989), pp. 25–67. Chr. Lindtner, *Nāgārjuna: Studies in the Writings and Philosophy of Nāgārjuna* (Copenhagen: Akademisk Forlag, 1982) provides useful synopses of Nāgārjuna's longer works and translations of his short ones. David Seyfort Ruegg, *The Literature of the Mādhyamika School of Philosophy in India* (Wiesbaden: Otto Harrassowitz, 1981) is a comprehensive survey of major literature of Mādhyamika Buddhism.
6. See Robert Magliola, *Derrida on the Mend* (West Lafayette, Ind.: Purdue Univ. Press, 1984), pp. 3–129; and David Loy, "The Clôsure of Decon-

struction: A Mahāyāna Critique of Derrida," *International Philosophical Quarterly* 37, no. 105 (1987); 59–80.

7. For a comparative study of Derrida and Indian Mādhyamika theories of language, see Harold Coward's *Derrida and Indian Philosophy* (Albany: State Univ. of New York Press, 1990). Coward also focuses his attention on the deconstructive philosophy of language in Derridean and Indian Mādhyamika Buddhism as well as other schools of Indian philosophy. He regards his study as an answer to the call by Professor T. R. V. Murti to rethink traditional schools of Indian philosophy from the perspective of language (p. 27).

8. These three words make up the subheading for the fifth section in Part I of "Dissemination" in Jacques Derrida, *Dissemination,* trans. Barbara Johnson (Chicago: Univ. of Chicago Press, 1981), p. vi.

9. When Derrida incorporated his early journal writings into *Of Grammatology,* he replaced the purely negative term "destruction" with the partially negative and partially positive term "deconstruction." He also considers "deconstruction" preferable to "desedimentation," another term he tried out before he settled upon "deconstruction."

10. *Dissemination,* pp. 7–15.

11. Derrida, *Of Grammatology,* p. 65.

12. Barbara Johnson, "Translator's Introduction," *Dissemination,* pp. xxiv–xxvi. Johnson's remarks on this essay provide, in her words, "a kind of roadmap that will detail some of its prominent routes and detours" (p. xxiv) for our understanding of Derrida's semantic investigations.

13. Cf. Jacques Derrida, *Writing and Difference,* trans. Alan Bass (Chicago: Univ. of Chicago Press, 1978), pp. xvi–xvii.

14. *Margins of Philosophy,* trans. Alan Bass (Chicago: Univ. of Chicago Press, 1982), p. 27.

15. Seng Zhao accepted, through his half-Indian and half-Kuchen teacher Kumārajīva 鳩摩羅什 (344–413), the Middle Doctrine of Nāgārjuna and laid the cornerstone for the Three Treatise School (*Sanlun zong* 三論宗), a truly systematic Buddhist philosophy in China. The Three Treatises are Nāgārjuna's *Mādhyamika śāstra* (Treatise on the Middle Doctrine), *Dvādaśanikaya śāstra* (Twelve Gates Treatise), and his disciple Aryadeva's *Sata śāstra* (One Hundred Verses Treatise). Seng Zhao's best-known works are "The Immutability of Things" ("Wu bu qian lun" 物不遷論), "The Emptiness of the Unreal" ("Bu zhen kong lun" 不真空論), and "On Prajñā not Cognizant" ("Banruo wuzhi lun" 般若無知論), collected in a book entitled *Zhao lun.* For an interpretive summary of these four essays as a philosophical system, see Fung Yu-lan, *A History of Chinese Philosophy,* 2 vols., trans. Derk Bodde (Princeton: Princeton Univ. Press, 1953), vol. 2, pp. 258–270. For recent book-length studies of Seng Zhao, see Li Runsheng 李潤生, *Seng Zhao* 僧肇 (Taipei: Dongda tushu gongsi, 1989; and Tu Yanqiu 涂艷秋, *Seng Zhao sixiang*

tanjiu 僧肇思想探究 (An Inquiry into the Thought of Seng Zhao) (Taipei: Dongchu chubanshe, 1995).

16. For a discussion of the ontotheological significance of this binome, see Willard Peterson, "Squares and Circles: Mapping the History of Chinese Thought," *Journal of History of Ideas*, vol. 49, no. 1 (1988): 47–60.

17. *You* and *wu* are normally translated as "existence" and "nonexistence". These two English words cannot suggest the *verbal* quality of these two characters. To bring out their verbal quality, I render them here as "exist" and "nonexist." I render *fei* as "not" rather than the prefix "non" in order to underline its status as an independent word and its verbal quality.

18. *Dissemination,* pp. 25–26.

19. Seng Zhao, "The Emptiness of the Unreal," collected in *A Source Book in Chinese Philosophy,* ed. W. T. Chan (Princeton: Princeton Univ. Press, 1963), p. 352. For different translations, see Walter Liebenthal, trans., *Chao Lun: The Treatise of Seng-chao,* 2nd rev. ed. (Hong Kong: Hong Kong Univ. Press, 1968), p. 56; *Three Theses of Seng Zhao,* trans. Xu Fangcheng, bilingual ed. (Beijing: Chinese Social Sciences Publishing House, 1985), pp. 26–27. Chan's anthology contains translations of only two of Seng Zhao's essays ("The Immutability of Things" and "The Emptiness of the Unreal"). Liebenthal's book is a complete translation of Seng Zhao's writings with copious annotations and citations from the Chinese texts. Despite its incompleteness, Chan's translation has the virtue of being faithful to the original and is adopted for citation in this article.

20. The Chinese text is cited from *Zhao Lun Zhongwu jijie* 肇論中吳集解 (The Zhongwu Collected Annotations to *Zhao Lun*), ed. Jing Yuan 淨源 (1011–1088), collected in *Luo Xuetang xiansheng quanji* 羅雪堂先生全集 (Complete Works of Mr. Luo Xuetang), first edition, vol. 19 (Taipei: Wenhua, 1968), 8241–8242. For a punctuated version of this passage, see *Taishō Shinshū Daizōkyō* 大正新脩大藏經 (The Newly Revised Edition of the Taishō Tripitaka), eds. Takakusu Junjirō 高楠順次郎 and Watanabe Kaigyoku 渡邊海旭 (Tokyo: Taishō Shinshu Daizōkyō Kanko Kai, 1927), no. 1858, vol. 45, p. 152.

21. *Zhuang Zi jijie,* 1/2/79; trans. Watson, *Complete Works of Chuang Tzu,* p. 43.

22. See, for instance, the discussion of *zheyu* by the Chan Master Huahai of the Baizhang (Mountain) 百丈懷海禪師 (720–814), in *Gu zunsu yulu* 古尊宿語錄 (Sayings of Ancient Eminent Monks), comp. Ze Zangzhu 賾藏主 (fl. 1131–1138), 2 vols. (Beijing: Zhonghua shuju, 1994), vol. 1, pp. 13–14.

23. In classical Chinese, particles function not only to establish syntax but also to indicate different kinds of pauses in lieu of punctuation.

24. Jacques Derrida, *Positions,* trans. Alan Bass (Chicago: Univ. of Chicago Press, 1972), p. 42.

25. Derrida, *Of Grammatology,* pp. 18–19.

26. John Sallis, *Deconstruction and Philosophy* (Chicago: Univ. of Chicago Press, 1987), p. xi.

27. *Phaedrus*, 274–275; trans. and ed. Benjamin Jowett, *The Dialogues of Plato*, vol. 1, p. 278.

28. Derrida, *Of Grammatology*, trans. Gayatri Chakravorty Spivak (Baltimore: John Hopkins Univ. Press, 1974), p. 34.

29. Derrida, paraphrasing Plato, in *Positions*, p. 12. See also Derrida's discussion of this issue in *Of Grammatology*, p. 39.

30. Derrida, *Of Grammatology*, p. 12.

31. Spivak, "Translator's Preface," *Of Grammatology*, p. xviii.

32. Derrida, "The Time of a Thesis: Punctuations," *Philosophy in France Today*, ed. Alan Montefiore (Cambridge: Cambridge Univ. Press, 1983), p. 45.

33. See Murray Krieger, "Poetics Reconstructed: The Presence and the Absence of the Word," *New Literary History* 7 (1976): 347–376.

34. Derrida, *Writing and Difference*, trans. Alan Bass (Chicago: Univ. of Chicago Press, 1978), pp. 279–280.

35. See G. C. Nayak, "The Mādhyamika Attack on Essentialism: A Critical Appraisal," *Philosophy East and West* 29, no. 4 (1979):467–490; Peter G. Fenner, "Candrakīrti's Refutation of Buddhist Idealism," *Philosophy East and West* 33, no. 3 (1983):251–256; and José Ignacio Cabezón, "Language and Ontology," *Buddhism and Language: A Study of Indo-Tibetan Scholasticism* (Albany: State Univ. of New York, 1994), pp. 153–170.

36. *Prasannapadā*, in *Bibliotheca Buddhica*, ed. Louis de la Vallée Pousin (St. Petersburg: Akad. Nauk-Izd. Vostochnoi Lit-ry, 1913), IV, p. 16.

37. Malcolm D. Eckel, "Bhāvaviveka and the Early Mādhyamika Theories of Language," *Philosophy East and West* 28, no. 3 (1978): 325.

38. On the influence of the early Mādhyamika on Dignāga's theory of *apoha*, see F. Th. Stcherbatsky, *Buddhist Logic*, 2 vols. (New York: Dover, 1962), vol. 1, pp. 27–31.

39. *Pramā a-samuccaya*, V. 1; trans. Stcherbatsky, *Buddhist Logic*, vol. 1, p. 459.

40. *Pramā a-samuccaya-v tti ad*, V. 11; trans. Stcherbatsky, *Buddhist Logic*, vol. 1, p. 463.

41. Dignāga, however, does not pursue his *apoha* to the point of a total denial of all ontotheological positions. It is probably for this reason that Stcherbatsky, *Buddhist Logic*, vol. 1, p. 14, puts Dignāga on the side of the idealists in his scheme of the three phases of Indian Buddhism. Dhirendra Sharma, *The Differentiation Theory of Meaning in Indian Logic* (The Hague: Mouton, 1969), pp. 19–46, discusses how Dignāga's followers pursue the *apoha* to different ontological conclusions. See also Bimal K. Matilal and Robert D. Evans, eds., *Buddhist Logic and Epistemology* (Bordrecht: Reidel, 1986), pp. 77–87, 185–191, 229–237.

42. Tang Yongtong 湯用彤 *Han Wei liang Jin Nan Bei chao Fojiao shi* 漢魏兩晉南北朝佛教史 (History of Chinese Buddhism from Han, Wei, Western and Eastern Jin, to Northern and Southern Dynasties) (Shang-

hai: Shangwu, 1938), pp. 330, 657, 670, raises doubt about the attribution of authorship of this essay to Seng Zhao on the grounds of its stylistic inconsistencies with his other writings.

43. *Taishō Shinshū Daizōkyō*, no. 1858, vol. 45, p. 157. My translation.

44. *Lao Zi jiaoshi* 老子校釋 (Collected Annotations to *Lao Zi*), ed. Zhu Xianzhi 朱謙之 (Beijing: Zhonghua shuju, 1984), p. 3; trans. D. C. Lau, *Lao Tzu: Tao Te Ching* (London: Penguin, 163), p. 57.

45. *Zhuang Zi jishi*, 3/17/572; trans. Watson, *Complete Works of Chuang Tzu*, p. 178.

46. Yuan Kang 元康 (Tang Dynasty) traces Seng Zhao's numerous allusions to *Lao* and *Zhuang* in his *Zhao lun shu* 肇論疏 (Annotation to *Zhao lun*), *Taishō Shinshū Daizōkyō*, no. 1859, vol. 45, pp. 161–200. Tu Yanqiu, *Seng Zhao sixiang tanjiu*, pp. 245–263, provides a list of twenty-one allusions to these two Daoist texts in Seng Zhao's works.

47. Hui Jiao, *Gao seng zhuan* (Beijing: Zhonghua shuju, 1992), p. 249.

48. See Seng Zhao, "Weimoji jing xu" 維摩詰經序 (Preface to *Virmalakīrtinirdeśa sūtra*), collected in Seng You 僧祐 (445–518), *Chu sanzang ji ji* 出三藏記集 (Collected Notes on the Production of the Buddhist Tripitaka) (Beijing: Zhonghua shuju, 1995), pp. 309–310.

49. Yuan Kang, *Zhao lun shu*, 肇論疏 (Annotation to *Zhao lun*), in *Taishō Shinshū Daizōkyō*, no. 1859, vol. 45, p. 163.

50. Yuan Kang, *Zhao lun shu*, in *Taishō Shinshū Daizōkyō*, no. 1859, vol. 45, p. 163.

51. For a study that focuses on the similarities between Zhuang Zi's and the Mādhyamikas' doctrines, see David Loy, "Zhuangzi and Nāgārjuna on the Truth of No Truth," in *Essays on Skepticism, Relativism, and Ethics in the Zhuangzi*, eds. Paul Kjellberg and Philip J. Ivanhoe, pp. 50–67.

52. *Lao Zi jiaoshi*, pp. 100–101; trans. Lau, *Lao Tzu*, p. 82. On the totalizing tendency of Lao Zi's cosmogony, see R. P. Peerenboom, "Cosmogony, the Taoist Way," *Journal of Chinese Philosophy* 17 (1990): 157–174. On the totalistic nature of the Dao, Russell D. Legge, "Chuang Tzu and the Free Man," *Philosophy East and West* 29, no. 1 (1979): 13–14: "*Tao* is the abstract category that embraces the totality of things. . . . *Tao* is *not* something *transcending* the world but just the all-inclusive whole of everything that exists at any given time."

53. See *Zhuang Zi jishi*, 4/26/944; trans. Watson, *Complete Works of Chuang Tzu*, p. 302: "The fish trap exists because of the fish; once you've gotten the fish, you can forget the trap. The rabbit snare exists because of the rabbit; once you've gotten the rabbit, you can forget the snare. Words exist because of meaning; once you've gotten the meaning, you can forget the words."

54. Commenting on the underlying totalizing tendency in the Daoist banishment of language, Wai-lim Yip writes, "In order to preserve things in their pristine wholeness, the Taoist evoke a deverbalized world that is be-

yond self, beyond consciousness beyond language where things can come freely to disclose before us as things" ("A New Line, A New Mind: Language and the Original Word," *Literary Theory Today*, eds. M. A. Abbas and T. W. Wong [Hong Kong: Hong Kong Univ. Press, 1981], p. 165).

55. *Taishō Shinshū Daizōkyō*, no. 1858, vol. 45, p. 157.
56. Ibid., no. 1859, vol. 45, p. 164.
57. Ibid., no. 1858, vol. 45, p. 152.
58. Ibid.; trans. Chan, *Source Book*, p. 356. Slightly modified.
59. Derrida, *Positions*, p. 13.
60. Ibid., pp. 64–65.
61. Cf. ibid., pp. 72, 74–76.
62. Derrida, *Positions*, pp. 42, 45, passim, 35.
63. Stcherbatsky, *Buddhist Logic*, vol. 1, p. 480.
64. For a brief introduction to these three Buddhist Essentialist schools before Seng Zhao, see chapter 20 of *Source Book*, pp. 336–342; and appendix 1 of Liebenthal, *Chao Lun*, pp. 133–150.
65. *Taishō Shinshū Daizōkyō*, no. 1858, vol. 45, p. 152.
66. Ibid., p. 152. "Material form" is perhaps a more accurate translation of 色 (*rūpa*) than "matter."
67. Ibid., p. 152.
68. See Tang Yongton 湯用彤 *Han Wei liang Jin Nan Bei chao Fojiao shi*, pp. 229–277.
69. See Lü Cheng 呂澂, *Zhongguo Foxue yuanliu luejiang* 中國佛學源流略講 (Brief Lectures on the Origins of Chinese Buddhism) (Beijing: Zhonghua shuju, 1979), pp. 32–34.
70. See Arthur E. Link, "The Taoist Antecedents of Tao-An's Prajñā Ontology," *History of Religions* 9, nos. 2–3 (1969–1970): 181–215; and Xu Kangsheng 許抗生 "Luelun liang Jin shiqi di Fojiao zhexue sixiang 略論兩晉時期的佛教哲學思想 (A Brief Discussion on the Buddhist Philosophical Thought of the Western and Eastern Jin Dynasties), *Zhongguo zhexue* 中國哲學 (Chinese Philosophy), 6 (1981), pp. 29–60.
71. Liebenthal, *Chao Lun*, 133.
72. For comments on the correspondences between Wang Bi's neo-Daoism and Dao-an's School of Original Nonexistence, between Guo Xiang's neo-Daoism and Zhi Daolin's School of Matter as It Is, see Tang Yongtong, *Han Wei liang Jin Nan Bei chao Fojiao shi*, p. 261.
73. Derrida, *Positions*, p. 43.
74. *Taishō Shinshū Daizōkyō*, no. 1858, vol. 45, p. 152; trans. Chan, *Source Book*, p. 356.
75. See *Zhuang Zi jishi*, 1/2/63–66; trans. Watson, *Complete Works of Chuang Tzu*, p. 40: "Where there is recognition of right there must be recognition of wrong; where there is recognition of wrong there must be recognition of right. Therefore the sage does not proceed in such a way, but illuminates all in the light of Heaven. He too recognizes a 'this,' but a 'this'

which is also 'that,' a 'that' which is also 'this.' His 'that' has both a right
and a wrong in it; his 'this' too has both a right and a wrong in it. So, in
fact, does he still have a 'this' and 'that'? Or does he in fact no longer have
'this' and 'that'? A state in which 'this' and 'that' no longer find their op-
posites is called the hinge of the Way. When the hinge is fitted into the
socket, it can respond endlessly. Its right then is a single endlessness and
its wrong too is a single endlessness."

76. Barbara Johnson, "Translator's Introduction," in Jacques Derrida, *Dis-
semination* (Chicago: Univ. of Chicago Press, 1981), p. xxxii.

77. Derrida, *Dissemination,* trans. Barbara Johnson (Chicago: Univ. of Chi-
cago Press, 1981), pp. 24–25.

78. For Derrida's critiques of these trinitarian concepts, see *Dissemination,* p.
20–25.

79. Derrida, *Dissemination,* p. 24.

80. Ibid., p. 25.

81. Ibid.

82. Ibid.

83. Ibid., p. 350.

84. Quoted without any documentation in *Dissemination,* p. 25.

85. Based on Nāgārjuna's *Mūlamādhyamakakārikā* (hereafter MK), XXVII,
21, 25, 28, R. D. Gunaratne presents this form of *catuṣkoṭi* in "Under-
standing Nāgārjuna's *catuṣkoṭi,*" *Philosophy* 36, no. 3 (1986): 219. Cf. David
J. Kalupahana, *Nāgārjuna: The Philosophy of the Middle Way* (Albany: State
Univ. of New York, 1986), pp. 387–391.

86. See also the important studies of *catuṣkoṭi* by R. D. Gunaratne: "The
Logical Form of *Catuṣkoṭi,*" *Philosophy East and West* 30, no. 2 (1980): 211–
240; Ives Waldo, "Nāgārjuna and Analytical Philosophy," *Philosophy East
and West* 25 no. 3 (1975): 281–290; "Nāgārjuna and Analytical Philoso-
phy, II" *Philosophy East and West* 28, no. 3 (1978): 287–298; Richard H.
Jones, "The Nature and Function of Nāgārjuna's Arguments," *Philosophy
East and West* 28, no. 4 (1978): 485–502; and Thomas E. Wood, *Nāgār-
junian Disputations: A Philosophical Journey through an Indian Looking-
Glass,* Monographs of the Society for Asian and Comparative Philoso-
phy, no. 11 (Honolulu: Univ. of Hawai'i Press, 1994).

87. Derrida, *Positions,* p. 40.

88. Ibid.

89. Ibid., p. 44–45.

90. Nāgārjuna, MK XXII, 11; trans. by Kalupahana, in his *Nāgārjuna,* p. 307.

91. Nāgārjuna, *Vigrahavyāvartanī,* 24, 23; trans. Frederick J. Streng, *Empti-
ness: A Study in Religious Meaning* (Nashville: Abingdon, 1967), p. 226.

92. Candrakīrti, *Prasannapadā,* 12; trans. Edward Conze, *Large Sutra on Per-
fect Wisdom* (Berkeley: Univ. of California Press, 1975), p. 144, n. 4.

93. *Taishō Shinshū Daizōkyō,* no. 1858, vol. 45, p. 156.

94. *Margins of Philosophy,* p. 25.
95. *Of Grammatology,* p. 65.
96. Spivak, "Translator's Preface," *Of Grammatology,* p. lxv.
97. *Taishō Shinshū Daizōkyō,* no. 1858, vol. 45, p. 150.
98. See a similar diagram drawn by Fung Yu-lan in his *A History of Chinese Philosophy,* trans. Derk Bodde, 2 vols. (Princeton: Princeton Univ. Press, 1973), vol. 2, p. 295.
99. Hsüeh-li Cheng, *Empty Logic,* p. 51.
100. *Taishō Shinshū Daizōkyō,* no. 1853, vol. 45, p. 15.
101. The diagram of Ji Zang's "Four Levels of Two Truths" is derived by adding these two lemmas to his teacher Fa Lang's "Three Levels of Two Truths." To be consistent with Ji Zang's wording, I have substituted "emptiness" for "nonexistence" in describing the seventh and eight lemmas.
102. See Ji Zang, *Sanlun xuanyi jiaoshi* 三論玄義校釋 (Collation and Annotation to *Profound Meanings of the Three Treatises*), annot. Han Tingjie 韓廷傑 (Beijing: Zhonghua shuju, 1897), p. 25.
103. See Fang Litian 方立天, *Fojiao zhexue* 佛教哲學 (Buddhist Philosophy), rev. ed. (Beijing: Zhongguo Remin Daxue chubanshe, 1991), pp. 356–358.
104. *Taishō Shinshū Daizōkyō,* no. 1852, vol. 46, p. 10; trans. Cheng, *Empty Logic,* pp. 51–52.
105. *Taishō Shinshū Daizōkyō,* no. 1853, vol. 46, p. 15.
106. Derrida, *Positions,* p. 14.
107. Ibid.
108. Ibid., p. 68.
109. Ibid., p. 14.
110. Coward, *Derrida and Indian Philosophy,* p. 140.
111. Ibid., p. 139.
112. Derrida, *Positions,* p. 6.
113. Taking note of this directional path, Robert Magliola writes, "I shall argue that Nāgārjuna's *śūnyata* ("devoidness") is Derrida's *différance,* and is the absolute negation which absolutely deconstitutes but which constitutes directional trace" (*Derrida on the Mend,* p. 89).
114. Hsüeh-li Cheng, *Empty Logic,* p. 55.
115. See Hsüeh-li Cheng's observations on the historical and doctrinal relationship of the Mādhyamika and the Chan (Zen) in his *Empty Logic,* chapter 3. For comparative studies of Derrida and Chinese Chan Buddhism, see Robert Magliola, "Differentialism in Chinese Ch'an and French Deconstruction. Some Test-Cases from the Wu-men-kuan," *Journal of Chinese Philosophy* 17, no. 1 (1990): 87–97; and Steve Odin, "Derrida and the Decentered Universe of Chan/Zen Buddhism," *Journal of Chinese Philosophy* 17, no. (1990): 61–86.
116. Francisco J. Varela, Evan Thompson, and Eleanor Rosch, *The Embodied*

Mind: Cognitive Science and Human Experience (Cambridge, Mass.: MIT Press, 1991), p. 229.

117. Varela, Thompson, and Rosch, *The Embodied Mind,* p. 218.

118. Gianni Vattimo, *The End of Modernity,* trans. J. Snyder (Baltimore: Johns Hopkins Univ. Press, 1989), p. 11.

119. Paraphrase of Vattimo's remarks in Varela, Thompson, and Rosch, *The Embodied Mind,* p. 229.

120. Varela, Thompson, and Rosch, *The Embodied Mind,* p. 230.

121. Ibid., p. 244.

122. Ibid., p. 254.

123. Ibid., p. 253.

124. See Yu, *Poetry of Wang Wei,* pp. 112–131.

125. See, for instance, Qui Shiyou 邱世友, "Liu Xie lun wenxue di boruo juejing" 劉勰論文學的般若絕境 (Liu Xie on the Incomparable Literary Realm of Prajñā), *Wenxin diaolong yanjiu* 文心雕龍研究 (Studies of *Wenxin diaolong*) 3 (1998), pp. 21–41. See also Qi Zhiang 祁志祥, *Fojiao meixue* 佛教美學 (Buddhist Aesthetics) (Shanghai: Shanghai renmin chubanshe, 1997), pp. 198–209.

126. See my article "*Wenxin diaolong* yu Ru Dao Fo jia di zhongdao siwei" 文心雕龍與儒、道、佛家的中道思維 (*Wenxin Diaolong* and the Confucian, Daoist, and Buddhist *Zhongdao* [Middle-Way] Modes of Thought), collected in *Lun Liu Xie jiqi Wenxin diaolong* 論劉勰及其文心雕龍 (On Liu Xie and *Wenxin diaolong*) (Beijing: Xueyuan chubanshe, 2000), p. 94–114.

EPILOGUE: REFLECTIONS

1. Michael Payne, ed., *A Dictionary of Cultural and Critical Theory* (Oxford: Blackwell, 1996), p. 392, defines Orientalism as follows: "A term for the European invention or idea of the Orient, associated with the thought of Edward Said. The Orient is not simply an originating place of European languages and CULTURE; it is also, in Said's view, an indispensable European image of the OTHER, which has made it possible for Europe to define itself. Furthermore, as a construct of European ideological DISCOURSE, orientalism has made it possible for the West to dominate, colonize, and restructure the Orient." Although the term "Orientalism" originally denotes the European construct of the Middle East, it is now commonly used to describe the derogatory portrayal of China, Japan, Korea, and other Asia countries in Western ideological discourses. This borrowed term in turns has inspired some scholars of Asia to invent the term "Occidentalism" to describe the equally derogatory depiction of the West in the anti-West discourses created and disseminated in these Asian countries. As I shall show below, cultural biases and racial stereotypes constitute the mainstay of both Orientalist and Occidentalist discourses.

2. In launching my criticism of various cultural biases and racial stereotypes, I have ventured into an important subject of investigation in the current postcolonial cultural studies. However, I do not have the least pretension that this book is a full engagement of this important subject. My discussion of Orientalist and Occidentalist discourses in West-China comparisons is conducted in general terms and does not include an extensive review of the current scholarship on the subject.

3. The crucial importance of such an "intracultural inquiry" has already been recognized by those working in West-China comparative philosophy. For instance, after completing their book *Thinking through Confucius*, David L. Hall and Roger T. Ames came to realize the importance of establishing broader intellectual and cultural contexts for their comparative studies and proceeded to write two successive volumes devoted to such an intracultural inquiry. "In the process of completing our *Thinking through Confucius*," Hall and Ames explain, "we realized the need for a sequel which would provide the broadest of contexts for the sorts of claims we were making there. Most of the comparative essays we have produced since 1987, both jointly and independently, have been written with that aim in mind. *Anticipating China*, and a second sequel which will follow soon after the publication of this work, are meant to realize that aim" ("Introduction," *Anticipating China*, p. xvi.). The "second sequel," or the third volume of the trilogy, mentioned here is their most recent book, *Thinking from the Han: Self, Truth, and Transcendence in Chinese and Western Culture* (Albany: State Univ. of New York Press, 1998). If they were to do their trilogy again, I would speculate that they might choose to begin with their intracultural inquiry (volumes 2 and 3) and then proceed to their comparative analyses now presented in the first volume.

4. Wai-lim Yip, *Diffusion of Distances: Dialogues between Chinese and Western Poetics* (Berkeley: Univ. of California Press, 1993), p. 20.

5. For a study on the Jesuits' appropriation of Confucianism, see Jacques Gernet, *China and the Christian Impact: A Conflict of Cultures*, trans. Janet Lloyd (Cambridge: Cambridge Univ. Press, 1985); and Lionel M. Jensen, "The Invention of 'Confucius' and His Chinese Other, 'Kong Fuzi,'" *Positions* 1.2 (1993): 414–449.

6. As early as in 1940–1941, Qian Zhongshu made an insightful and exhaustive study of such discourses on China in a series of three articles: Ch'ien Chung-shu (Qian Zhongshu), "China in the English Literature of the Seventeenth Century (I)," *Quarterly Bulletin of Chinese Bibliography* 1, no. 4 (1940): 351–384; "China in the English Literature of the Eighteenth Century (I)," *Quarterly Bulletin of Chinese Bibliography* 2, nos. 1–2 (1941): 7–48; and "China in the English Literature of the Eighteenth Century (II)," *Quarterly Bulletin of Chinese Bibliography* 2, nos. 3–4 (1941): 113–152. For a summary account of the Western perceptions of China since the late sixteenth century, see Jonathan Spence, "Western Perceptions from

the Late Sixteenth Century to the Present," in *Heritage of China: Contemporary Perspectives on Chinese Civilization,* ed. Paul S. Ropp (Berkeley: Univ. of California Press, 1990), pp. 1–14.

7. Qian Zhongshu 錢鍾書, *Guanzhui pian* 管錐篇 (Limited Views), 4 vols. (Beijing: Zhonghua shuju, 1979), vol. 3, pp. 969–971, gives a comprehensive and scathing account of this self-deceptive polemic widely used in Qing times.

8. See Liang Qichao 梁啓超, *Yinbing shi heji: Wenji* 飲冰室合集．文集 (Combined Collections of Writings from the Yinbing Studio: Essays) (Shanghai: Zhonghua shuju, 1936), vol. 1, 1.94–96; *Yinbing shi heji: Zhuanji* 飲冰室合集。專集 (Combined Collections of Writings from the Yinbing Studio: Specialized Essays) (Shanghai: Zhonghua shuju, 1936), vol. 2, 28.11–33; vol. 4, 50.29–40.

9. S. Wells Williams, *The Middle Kingdom* (New York: Scribner's, 1882; rev., 1907), 1:834.

10. Cited in Derk Bodde, *China's Cultural Tradition* (New York: Holt, Rinehart & Winston, 1963), p. 8. For a study on the Protestant missionaries' views of China, see S. W. Barnett and J. K. Fairbank, eds., *Christianity in China: Early Missionary Writings* (Cambridge: Harvard Univ. Press, 1984).

11. Pearl S. Buck, *Friend to Friend* (New York: John Day, 1958), pp. 121–122.

12. William Haas, *Destiny of the Mind in East and West* (New York: Columbia Univ. Press, 1946), pp. 127–128.

13. Cultural discrimination seems to outweigh racial discrimination in the minting of slurs against minorities. That slurs like *yi, hu, lu* are in the main culturally based is attested to by the fact the minorities often appropriated those slurs and applied them back to the Han Chinese. For instance, the rulers of the Northern Wei felt entirely comfortable with the term *yi* as they embraced it as a derogatory appellation for the Han Chinese. They had the confidence to ridicule the Han Chinese as *yi* or barbarians because they believed that they had taken over the Han Chinese as the legitimate heir to the Chinese culture. While the Chinese culture languished or even perished under the corrupt Han Chinese court, they contended, it regained its vitality and flourished thanks to their efforts to preserve traditional rituals and ethics. Later in Qing times, the Manchurian rulers adopted the same strategy to turn *yi* into a slur against the Han Chinese rulers by claiming themselves as the sole inheritors and protectors of the Chinese culture. In his essay "On the Distinction between 'the Chinese' and the 'Barbarians' (*yi*)" ("Hua Yi zhibian" 華夷之辨), *Guanzhui pian,* vol. 4, pp. 1486–1490, Qian Zhongshu examines numerous examples of *yi* and other similar slurs in official histories and concludes that those slurs, whether used by the Han Chinese or non-Han minorities, are intended to underscore an "inferiority" more in "ethos" than in "ethnos." Thanks to painstaking efforts by Ronald Egan, this and many other insightful and erudite essays by Qian are now available to Eng-

lish readers. For an English translation of this essay, see Qian Zhongshu, *Limited Views: Essays on Ideas and Letters,* selected and translated by Ronald Egan, Harvard-Yenching Institute Monograph Series, vol. 44 (Cambridge, Mass.: Harvard Univ. Asia Center, 1998), pp. 373–381.

14. See Wang Guowei 王國維, "Renjian cihua" 人間詞話 (Talks on *Ci* Poetry in the Human World) in *Wang Guowei wenji* 王國維文集 (Collected Works of Wang Guowei), eds. Yao Jianming 姚淦銘 and Wang Yan 王燕, 4 vols. (Beijing: Wenshi chubanshe, 1997), vol. 1, pp. 141–179; and "*Honglou meng* pinglun" 紅樓夢評論 (Critical Essay on the *Dream of the Red Chamber*) in *Wang Guowei wenji,* vol. 1, 1–23. I discussed Wang Guowei's adaptation of the traditional notion of *yijing* in my essay "Yixiang, yijing shuo yu Liu Xie de chuangzuo lun" in *Wenxin diaolong guoji xueshu yantaohui lunwen,* vol. 2, pp. 413–426.

15. See Zhu Guangqian 朱光潛, *Shilun* 詩論 (On Poetry) (Shanghai: Zhengzhong shuju, 1948).

16. I discussed Liang's and Lu's criticisms of traditional literary criticism in my article, "The Rethinking of Emotion: The Transformation of Traditional Chinese Literary Criticism in the Late Qing Era," *Monumenta Serica* 45 (1997): 63–110.

17. Yip, *Diffusion of Distances,* p. 18.

18. Ibid.

19. Ibid.

20. Ibid.

21. Chad Hansen, "Chinese Language, Chinese Philosophy, and 'Truth,'" *Journal of Asian Studies* 44 (1985): 492. Hansen also expounds this central thesis in his early work, *Language and Logic in China* (Ann Arbor: Univ. of Michigan Press, 1983) and answers the critiques of it in his later article, "Classical Chinese Philosophy as Linguistic Analysis," *Journal of Chinese Philosophy* 14 (1987): 309–330.

22. Hansen, "Chinese Language, Chinese Philosophy, and 'Truth,'" p. 492.

23. Ibid., p. 494. This characterization of Chinese intellectual activity is essentially a reiteration of "the notion that 'rationality' was not merely abandoned but altogether absent in China" (Jack Goody, *The East in the West* [Cambridge: Cambridge Univ. Press, 1996], p. 30). As shown by Goody (pp. 30–48), this notion undergirds the entrenched Eurocentric belief about the alleged intellectual deficiency of the Chinese, a deficiency that renders them incapable of embracing scientific, economic, and social changes needed for the rise of modern capitalism.

24. Hansen, "Chinese Language, Chinese Philosophy, and 'Truth,'" p. 514.

25. Ibid.

26. Ibid., p. 515.

27. Ibid.

28. Among numerous critical reviews of Hansen's thesis, see Cheng Chung-ying, "Kung-sun Lung: White Horses and Other Issues," *Philosophy East*

and West 33, no. 4 (1983): 341–353; A. C. Graham, "Review of 'Chad Hansen, *Language and Logic in Ancient China,*'" *Harvard Journal of Asiatic Studies* 45, no. 2 (1985): 692–703; Christoph Harbsmeier, "Review of 'Chad Hansen, *Language and Logic in Ancient China,*'" *Early China* 9–10 (1983–1985): 250–257; and Heiner Roetz, "Validity in Chou Thought: On Chad Hansen and the Pragmatic Turn in Sinology," in *Epistemological Issues in Classical Chinese Philosophy*, eds. Lenk and Paul, pp. 69–112.

29. Carine Defoort, "'The Transcendence' of *Tian*, a Review of *Law and Morality in Ancient China: The Silk Manuscripts of Huang-Lao* by Randall Peerenboom," *Philosophy East and West* 44.2 (1994): 347–368.

30. Randall P. Peerenboom, "The Rational American and the Inscrutable Oriental as Seen From the Perspective of a Puzzled European: A Review (and Response) in Three Stereotypes—A Reply to Carine Defoort," *Philosophy East and West* 44.2 (1994): 368–379.

31. Peerenboom, "The Rational American and the Inscrutable Oriental," p. 373.

32. Ibid.

Works Cited

WORKS IN WESTERN LANGUAGES

Abrams, M. H. *The Mirror and the Lamp: Romantic Theory and the Critical Tradition.* London: Oxford, 1953.

————, ed. *English Romantic Poets: Modern Essays in Criticism.* New York: Galaxy, 1960.

Albrecht, W. P. *Hazlitt and the Creative Imagination.* Lawrence: Univ. of Kansas Press, 1965.

Ames, Roger T. "Meaning as Imaging: Prolegomena to a Confucian Epistemology." In *Culture and Modernity: East-West Philosophic Perspectives,* ed. Eliot Deutsch, pp. 226–244. Honolulu: Univ. of Hawai'i Press, 1991.

Aristotle. *Aristotle: Poetics.* Trans. Stephen Halliwell. Cambridge, Mass.: Harvard Univ. Press, 1995.

Arnold, Matthew. *The Complete Prose Works of Matthew Arnold.* Ed. R. H. Super. 11 vols. Ann Arbor: Univ. of Michigan Press, 1962.

Babbitt, Irving. *Rousseau and Romanticism.* Boston: Houghton Mifflin, 1919.

Baechler, Lea, and A. Walton Litz, eds. *Personae: The Shorter Poems.* New York: New Directions, 1990.

Baker, Carlos. "Sensation and Vision in Wordsworth." In *English Romantic Poets: Modern Essays in Criticism,* ed. M. H. Abrams, pp. 95–109. New York: Galaxy, 1960.

Barnett, S. W., and J. K. Fairbank, eds. *Christianity in China: Early Missionary Writings.* Cambridge, Mass.: Harvard Univ. Press, 1984.

Barth, Robert, and John. L. Mahoney, eds. *Coleridge, Keats, and the Imagination: Romanticism and Adam's Dream: Essays in Honor of Walter Jackson Bate.* Columbia: Univ. of Missouri Press, 1990.

Barthes, Roland. *Critical Essays.* Trans. Richard Howard. Evanston, Ill.: Northwestern Univ. Press, 1972.

————. "The Structuralist Activity." In *Critical Essays,* trans. Richard Howard, pp. 213–220. Evanston, Ill.: Northwestern Univ. Press, 1972.

Bate, Walter Jackson, ed. *Criticism: The Major Texts.* New York: Harcourt, Brace & World, 1952.

Behler, Ernst. *German Romantic Literary Theory.* Cambridge: Cambridge Univ. Press, 1993.

Berkson, Mark. "Language: The Guest of Reality—Zhuangzi and Derrida on Language, Reality, and Skillfulness." In *Essays on Skepticism, Relativism, and Ethics in the Zhuangzi,* eds. Paul Kjellberg and Philip J. Ivanhoe, pp. 97–126. Albany: State Univ. of New York Press, 1996.

Billeter, Jean François. *The Chinese Art of Writing.* Geneva: Skira, 1990.

Binner, Wytter and Kiang Kang-hu. *The Jade Mountain.* New York: Alfred A. Knopf, 1930.

Birch, Cyril, ed. *Studies in Chinese Literary Genres.* Berkeley: Univ. of California Press, 1974.

Blake, William. *The Poetry and Prose of William Blake.* Eds. David V. Erdman and Harold Bloom. Garden City, N.Y.: Doubleday, 1965.

————. *Complete Poetry and Prose of William Blake.* Ed. David V. Erdman. Berkeley: Univ. of California Press, 1982.

Bloom, Harold, ed. *Romanticism and Consciousness: Essays in Criticism.* New York: Norton, 1970.

Bodde, Derk. *China's Cultural Tradition.* New York: Holt, Rinehart & Winston, 1963.

Boltz, William G. *The Origin and Early Development of the Chinese Writing System,* American Oriental Society Series, no. 78. New Haven, Conn.: American Oriental Society, 1994.

Bromwich, David. *Hazlitt, the Mind of a Critic.* Oxford: Oxford Univ. Press, 1985.

Brooks, Cleanth. *The Well-Wrought Urn: Studies in the Structure of Poetry.* New York: Renal, 1947.

Brooks, Cleanth, J. T. Purser, and R. P. Warren. *An Approach to Literature: A Collection of Prose and Verse with Analyses and Discussions.* Baton Rouge: Louisiana State Univ. Press, 1936.

Buck, Pearl. *Friend to Friend.* New York: John Day, 1958.

Bush, Susan, and Christian Murck, eds. *Theories of the Arts in China.* Princeton: Princeton Univ. Press, 1983.

Cabezón, José Ignacio. *Buddhism and Language: A Study of Indo-Tibetan Scholasticism.* Albany: State Univ. of New York, 1994.

Cai, Zong-qi. "The Rethinking of Emotion: The Transformation of Traditional Chinese Literary Criticism in the Late Qing Era." *Monumenta Serica* 45 (1997): 63–110.

———. "The Making of a Critical System: Concepts of Literature in *Wenxin diaolong* and earlier texts." *A Chinese Literary Mind: Culture, Creativity, and Rhetoric in Wenxin diaolong*, ed. Zong-qi Cai, pp. 33–59. Stanford: Stanford Univ. Press, 2001.

———. "*Wen* and the Construction of a Critical System in *Wenxin Diaolong*." *Chinese Literature: Essays, Articles and Reviews* 22 (2000): 1–29.

———, ed. *A Chinese Literary Mind: Culture, Creativity, and Rhetoric in Wenxin diaolong.* Stanford: Stanford Univ. Press, 2001.

Candrakīrti. *Prasannapadā* (Large Sutra on Perfect Wisdom). Trans. Edward Conze. Berkeley: Univ. of California Press, 1975.

Carlyle, Thomas. *On Heroes, Hero-Worship, & the Heroic in History.* Notes and introduction by Michael K. Goldberg. Berkeley: Univ. of California Press, 1993.

Cascardi, Anthony J., ed. *Literature and the Question of Philosophy.* Baltimore: Johns Hopkins Univ. Press, 1987.

Casey, Edward S. *Imagining: A Phenomenological Study.* Bloomington: Indiana Univ. Press, 1976.

Chai, Leon. *The Romantic Foundation of the American Renaissance.* Ithaca: Cornell Univ. Press, 1987.

Chan, Wing-tsit, "Chinese and Western Interpretations of *Jen* (Humanity)." *Journal of Chinese Philosophy* 2 (1975): 107–129.

———, ed. *A Source Book in Chinese Philosophy.* Princeton: Princeton Univ. Press, 1963.

Chang, Kwang-chih. *Early Chinese Civilization: Anthropological Perspectives.* Cambridge, Mass.: Harvard Univ. Press, 1976.

Chaves, Jonathan. "The Legacy of Ts'ang Chieh: the Written Word as Magic." *Oriental Art* 23, no. 2 (1977): 200–215.

Ch'en, Shih-hsiang. "In Search of the Beginning of Chinese Literary Criticism." In *Semitic and Oriental Studies.* Berkeley: Univ. of California Publications in Semitic Philology, vol. 11 (1951): 45–64.

———. "The *Shih Ching:* Its Generic Significance in Chinese Literary Theory and Poetics." *Bulletin of the Institute of History and Philology (Academia Sinica)* 39, no. 1 (1968): 371–413. Rpt. in *Studies in Chinese Literary Genres*, ed. Cyril Birch, pp. 8–41. Berkeley: Univ. of California Press, 1974.

Cheng, Chung-ying. "Kung-sun Lung: White Horses and Other Issues." *Philosophy East and West* 33, no. 4 (1983): 341–353.

———. "A Taoist Interpretation of 'Différance' in Derrida." *Journal of Chinese Philosophy* 17, no. 1 (1990): 19–30.

Cheng, Hsüeh-li. *Empty Logic: Mādhyamika Buddhism from Chinese Sources.* New York: Philosophical Library, 1984.

Cheng, Jiewei. "Derrida and Ideographic Poetics." *British Journal of Aesthetics* 35, no. 2 (1995): 134–144.

Chien, Chi-Hui. "'Theft's Way': A Comparative Study of Chuang Tzu's Tao and Derridean Trace." *Journal of Chinese Philosophy* 17, no. 1 (1990): 31–49.

Ch'ien Chung-shu (Qian Zhongshu). "China in the English Literature of the Seventeenth Century (I)." *Quarterly Bulletin of Chinese Bibliography* 1, no. 4 (1940): 351–384.

———. "China in the English Literature of the Eighteenth Century (I)." *Quarterly Bulletin of Chinese Bibliography* 2, nos. 1–2 (1941): 7–48.

———. "China in the English Literature of the Eighteenth Century (II)." *Quarterly Bulletin of Chinese Bibliography* 2, nos. 3–4 (1941): 113–152.

Chow, Tse-tsung. "Ancient Chinese Views of Literature, the Tao, and Their Relationship." *Chinese Literature: Essays, Articles, Reviews,* 1, 1 (1979): 3–29.

———, ed. *Wenlin: Studies in the Chinese Humanities.* Madison: Univ. of Wisconsin Press, 1968.

Coleridge, Samuel Taylor. *Complete Works of Samuel Taylor Coleridge.* New York: Harper & Brothers, 1854.

———. *Biographia Literaria.* Eds. James Engell and W. Jackson Bate. Princeton: Princeton Univ. Press, 1983.

Conze, Edward, trans. *Large Sutra on Perfect Wisdom.* Berkeley: Univ. of California Press, 1975.

Coward, Harold. *Derrida and Indian Philosophy.* Albany: State Univ. of New York Press, 1990.

Crane, R. S. "Questions and Answers in Teaching of Literary Texts." In *The Idea of the Humanities.* 2 vols. Chicago: Univ. of Chicago Press, 1966.

Culler, Jonathan. *Structuralist Poetics: Structuralism, Linguistics, and the Study of Literature.* Ithaca, N.Y.: Cornell Univ. Press, 1975.

Dasenbrock, Reed W. *The Literary Vorticism of Ezra Pound and Wyndham Lewis.* Baltimore: Johns Hopkins Univ. Press, 1985.

Davis, Robert Con, and Laurie Finke, eds. *Literary Criticism and Theory: The Greeks to the Present.* New York: Longman, 1989.

Davis, Walter A. Davis. *The Act of Interpretation: A Critique of Literary Reason.* Chicago: Univ. of Chicago Press, 1978.

Defoort, Carine. "'The Transcendence' of Tian, a Review of *Law and Morality in Ancient China: The Silk Manuscripts of Huang-Lao* by Randall Peerenboom." *Philosophy East and West* 44, no. 2 (1994): 347–368.

DeFrancis, John. *The Chinese Language: Fact and Fantasy.* Honolulu: Univ. of Hawai'i Press, 1984.

de Man, Paul. *Allegories of Reading: Figural Language in Rousseau, Nietzsche, Rilke, and Proust.* New Haven: Yale Univ. Press, 1979.

Derrida, Jacques. *Positions.* Trans. Alan Bass. Chicago: Univ. of Chicago Press, 1972.

———. *Of Grammatology.* Trans. Gayatri Chakravorty Spivak. Baltimore: Johns Hopkins Univ. Press, 1974.

———. *Writing and Difference.* Trans. Alan Bass. Chicago: Univ. of Chicago Press, 1978.

———. *Dissemination.* Trans. Barbara Johnson. Chicago: Univ. of Chicago Press, 1981.

———. *Margins of Philosophy.* Trans. Alan Bass. Chicago: Univ. of Chicago Press, 1982.

———. "The Time of a Thesis: Punctuations." In *Philosophy in France Today,* ed. Alan Montefiore. Cambridge: Cambridge Univ. Press, 1983.

Deutsch, Eliot. *On Truth: An Ontological Theory.* Honolulu: Univ. of Hawai'i Press, 1979.

———, ed. *Culture and Modernity: East-West Philosophic Perspectives.* Honolulu: Univ. of Hawai'i Press, 1991.

DeWoskin, Kenneth J. *A Song for One or Two: Music and the Concepts of Art in Early China.* Ann Arbor: Center for Chinese Studies, Univ. of Michigan, 1982.

Doeringer, Franklin M. "Unto the Mountain: Toward a Paradigm for Early Chinese Thought." *Journal of Chinese Philosophy* 17 (1990): 135–156.

Driscoll, Lucy, and Kenji Toda. *Chinese Calligraphy.* New York: Paragon, 1964.

Eckel, Malcolm D. "Bhāvaviveka and the Early Mādhyamika Theories of Language." *Philosophy East & West* 28 (1978): 323–336.

Egan, Ronald. "Poet, Mind, and World: A Reconsideration of the 'Shen si' Chapter of *Wenxin diaolong.*" *A Chinese Literary Mind: Culture, Cre-*

ativity, and Rhetoric in Wenxin diaolong, ed. Zong-qi Cai, pp. 101–126. Stanford: Stanford Univ. Press, 2001.

Egan, Ronald. See under Qian Zhongshu.

Eliot, T. S. *Selected Essays.* New York: Harcourt and Brace, 1932.

———, ed. *Literary Essays of Ezra Pound.* Norfolk, Conn.: New Directions, 1954.

Else, Gerald F. *Plato and Aristotle on Poetry.* Ed. Peter Burian. Chapel Hill: Univ. of North Carolina Press, 1986.

Emerson, Ralph Waldo. *The Collected Works of Ralph Waldo Emerson.* Ed. Alfred R. Ferguson. 3 vols. to date. Cambridge, Mass.: Belnap Press of Harvard Univ. Press, 1971.

Engell, James. *The Creative Imagination: Enlightenment to Romanticism.* Cambridge, Mass.: Harvard Univ. Press, 1981.

Eoyang, Eugene. "Polar Paradigms in Poetics: Chinese and Western Literary Premises." In *Comparative Literature East and West: Traditions and Trends: Selected Conference Papers,* eds. Cornelia N. Moore and Raymond A. Moody, pp. 11–21. Honolulu: College of Languages, Linguistics, and Literature, the University of Hawai'i, and the East-West Center, 1989.

Falk, Eugene H. *The Poetics of Roman Ingarden.* Chapel Hill: Univ. of North Carolina Press, 1981.

Fang, Archilles. "From Imagism to Whitmanism in Recent Chinese Poetry: A Search for Poetics That Failed." In *Indiana University Conference on Oriental-Western Literary Relations,* eds. Horst Frenz and G. L. Anderson. Chapel Hill: Univ. of North Carolina Press, 1955.

———. "Fenollosa and Pound." *Harvard Journal of Asiatic Studies* 20 (1957): 213–238.

Fenner, Peter G. "Candrakrīti's Refutation of Buddhist Idealism." *Philosophy East & West* 33 (1983): 251–256.

Fenollosa, Ernest. *The Chinese Written Character as a Medium for Poetry,* ed. Ezra Pound. 1936. Rpt. San Francisco: City Lights, 1983.

Ferguson, Frances. *Wordsworth: Language as Counter-Spirit.* New Haven: Yale Univ. Press, 1977.

Fingarette, Herbert. *Confucius: The Secular as Sacred.* New York: Harper Torchbooks, 1972.

Fong, Wen, and Alfreda Murck, eds. *Words and Images: Chinese Poetry, Calligraphy and Painting.* Princeton: Princeton Univ. Press, 1991.

Friedlander, Paul. *Plato: An Introduction.* Princeton: Princeton Univ. Press, 1958.

Fu, Hongchu. "Deconstruction and Taoism: Comparisons Reconsidered." *Comparative Literature Studies* 29, no. 3 (1992): 296–321.

Fung, Yu-lan. *A History of Chinese Philosophy.* Trans. Derk Bodde. 2 vols. Princeton: Princeton Univ. Press, 1973.

Furst, Lilian R. *Romanticism in Perspective.* New York: Humanities Press, 1970.

Gernet, Jacques. *China and the Christian Impact: A Conflict of Cultures.* Trans. Janet Lloyd. Cambridge: Cambridge Univ. Press, 1985.

Gilbert, Allan H. *Literary Criticism: Plato to Dryden.* Detroit: Wayne State Univ. Press, 1940.

Goodwin, K. L. *The Influence of Ezra Pound.* London: Oxford Univ. Press, 1966.

Goody, Jack. *The East in the West.* Cambridge: Cambridge Univ. Press, 1996.

Gould, Thomas. *The Ancient Quarrel between Poetry and Philosophy.* Princeton: Princeton Univ. Press, 1990.

Graham, A. C. "Chuang Tzu's Essay on Seeing Things as Equal." *Journal of the History of Religion* 9 (1970): 137–159.

———. "Review of 'Chad Hansen, *Language and Logic in Ancient China.*'" *Harvard Journal of Asiatic Studies* 45, no. 2 (1985): 692–703.

Greene, William Chase. "Plato's View of Poetry." *Harvard Studies in Classical Philology* 29 (1918): 1–75.

———. "The Greek Criticism of Poetry: A Reconsideration." *Harvard Studies in Comparative Literature* 20 (1950): 19–53.

Gunaratne, R. D. "The Logical Form of *Catuṣkoṭi.*" *Philosophy East & West* 30 (1980): 211–240.

———. "Understanding Nāgārjuna's *Catuṣkoṭi.*" *Philosophy East & West* 36 (1986): 213–234.

Haas, William. *Destiny of the Mind in East and West.* New York: Columbia Univ. Press, 1946.

Hall, David L., and Roger T. Ames. *Thinking through Confucius.* Albany: State Univ. of New York Press, 1987.

———. *Anticipating China: Thinking through the Narratives of Chinese and Western Culture.* Albany: State Univ. of New York Press, 1995.

———. *Thinking from the Han: Self, Truth, and Transcendence in Chinese and Western Culture.* Albany: State Univ. of New York Press, 1998.

Hansen, Chad. *Language and Logic in Ancient China.* Ann Arbor: Univ. of Michigan Press, 1983.

———. "Chinese Language, Chinese Philosophy and 'Truth.'" *Journal of Asian Studies* 44 (1985): 491–517.

———. "Classical Chinese Philosophy as Linguistic Analysis," *Journal of Chinese Philosophy* 14 (1987): 309–330.

———. "Term-Belief in Action: Sentences and Terms in Early Chinese Philosophy." In *Epistemological Issues in Classical Chinese Philosophy,* eds. Hans Lenk and Gregor Paul, pp. 45–66. Albany: State Univ. of New York Press, 1993.

Harbsmeier, Christoph. "Review of 'Chad Hansen, *Language and Logic in Ancient China.'*" *Early China* 9–10 (1983–1985): 250–257.

———. "Concepts of Knowledge in Ancient China." In *Epistemological Issues in Classical Chinese Philosophy,* eds. Hans Lenk and Gregor Paul, pp. 11–30. Albany: State Univ. of New York Press, 1993.

Harriot, Rosemary. *Poetry and Criticism Before Plato.* London: Methuen, 1969.

Harrison, G. B., ed. *Shakespeare: The Complete Works.* New York: Harcourt, Brace & World, 1968.

Hart, James A. "The Speech of Prince Chin: A Study of Early Chinese Cosmology." In *Explorations in Early Chinese Cosmology,* ed. Henry Rosemont, pp. 35–65. Chico, California: Scholar Press, 1984. Published as volume L, number 2 of *Journal of the American Academy of Religion Studies.*

Hartman, Geoffrey H. *Wordsworth's Poetry: 1787–1814.* Cambridge, Mass.: Harvard Univ. Press, 1987.

Heidegger, Martin. *The Question of Being.* Trans. William Kluback and Jean T. Wilde. New Haven, Conn.: College and University Press, 1958.

Henderson, John B. *The Development and Decline of Chinese Cosmology.* New York: Columbia Univ. Press, 1984.

Heninger, S. K., Jr. *Touches of Sweet Harmony: Pythagorean Cosmology and Renaissance Poetics.* San Marino, Calif.: Huntington Library, 1974.

Herder, Johann G. "Shakespeare." Trans. J. P. Crick. In *German Aesthetic and Literary Criticism: Winckelmann, Lessing, Hamann, Herder, Schiller, Goethe,* ed. H. B. Nisbet. Cambridge: Cambridge Univ. Press, 1985.

———. *Sämtliche Werke,* ed. Bernhard Suphan, 33 vols. Rpt. New York: Olms-Weidmann, 1994.

Hernadi, Paul. "Literary Theory: A Compass for Critics." *Critical Inquiry* 3 (1976): 369–386.

Hirsch, E. D., Jr. *Wordsworth and Schelling: A Typological Study of Romanticism.* New Haven: Yale Univ. Press, 1960.

Holzman, Donald. "Confucius and Ancient Chinese Literary Criticism." In *Chinese Approaches to Literature from Confucius to Liang Ch'i-ch'ao,* ed. Adel Austin Rickett, pp. 21–41. Princeton: Princeton Univ. Press, 1978.

Huang, Guiyou. "Ezra Pound: (Mis)Translation and (Re)Creation." *Paideuma: A Journal Devoted to Ezra Pound Scholarship* 22, nos. 1–2 (1993): 99–114.

Huntington, C. W., and N. Wangchen Gesh. *The Emptiness of Emptiness: An Introduction to Early Indian Mādhyamika.* Honolulu: Univ. of Hawai'i Press, 1989.

Ingarden, Roman. *The Cognition of the Literary Work of Art.* Trans. Ruth Ann Crowley and Kenneth R. Olson. Evanston, Ill.: Northwestern Univ. Press, 1973.

———. *The Literary Work of Art: An Investigation on the Borderlines of Ontology, Logic, and Theory of Literature.* Trans. George G. Grabowicz. Evanston, Ill.: Northwestern Univ. Press, 1973.

Iser, Wolfgang. *The Implied Reader: Patterns of Communication in Prose Fiction from Bunyan to Beckett.* Baltimore: Johns Hopkins Univ. Press, 1974.

Jin, Songping. "Fenollosa and 'Hsiao Hsüeh' Tradition." *Paideuma: A Journal Devoted to Ezra Pound Scholarship* 22, no. 1–2 (1993): 71–97.

Jones, Richard H. "The Nature and Function of Nāgārjuna's Arguments." *Philosophy East & West* 28 (1978): 485–502.

Jullien, François. *The Propensity of Things: Toward a History of Efficacy in China.* Translated from French by Janet Lloyd. New York: Zone Books, 1995.

Kabitoglou, E. Douka. *Plato and the English Romantics.* London: Routledge, 1990.

Kalupahana, David J., trans. *Nāgārjuna: the Philosophy of the Middle Way.* Albany: State Univ. of New York, 1986.

Kannicht, Richard. *The Ancient Quarrel Between Philosophy and Poetry.* Christchurch, New Zealand: Univ. of Canterbury, 1988.

Kao, Yu-kung. "Chinese Lyric Aesthetics." In *Words and Images: Chinese Poetry, Calligraphy and Painting,* eds. Wen Fong and Alfreda Murck, pp. 47–90. Princeton: Princeton Univ. Press, 1991.

Kennedy, George. "Fenollosa, Pound and Chinese Characters." *Yale Literary Magazine* 36 (1958): 24–36.

Kenner, Hugh. "Poetics of Error." *Tamkang Review* 6–7 (1975–1976): 89–97.

Kipperman, Mark. *Beyond Enchantment: German Idealism and English Romantic Poetry.* Philadelphia: Univ. of Pennsylvania Press, 1986.

Kjellberg, Paul, and Philip J. Ivanhoe. *Essays on Skepticism, Relativism, and Ethics in the Zhuangzi.* Albany: State Univ. of New York Press, 1996.

Krieger, Murray. "Poetics Reconstructed: The Presence and the Absence of the Word." *New Literary History* 7 (1976): 347–376.

Lacoue-Labarthe, Philippe. *The Subject of Philosophy.* Translated from French by Thomas Treizise, et al. Minneapolis: Univ. of Minnesota Press, 1993.

Lacoue-Labarthe, Philippe, and Jean-Luc Nancy. *The Literary Absolute: The Theory of Literature in German Romanticism.* Translated from French by Philip Barnard and Cheryl Lester. Albany: State Univ. of New York Press, 1978.

Leask, Nigel. *The Politics of Imagination in Coleridge's Critical Thought.* London: Macmillan, 1988.

Legge, James, trans. *The Chinese Classics.* 5 vols. Rpt. Hong Kong: Hong Kong Univ. Press, 1960.

———. *The Ch'un Ts'ew with the Tso Chuen.* In *The Chinese Classics,* vol. 5.

———. *The Four Books: Confucian Analects, the Great Learning, the Doctrine of the Mean, the Works of Mencius.* Rpt. Chengwen chubanshe, 1971.

———. *The Shoo King.* In *The Chinese Classics,* vol. 3. Taipei: Wenxin, 1971.

Legge, Russell D. "Chuang Tzu and the Free Man." *Philosophy East and West* 29, no. 1 (1979): 11–20.

Lenk, Hans, and Gregor Paul, eds. *Epistemological Issues in Classical Chinese Philosophy.* Albany: State Univ. of New York Press, 1993.

Liebenthal, Walter, trans. *Chao Lun: The Treatise of Seng-chao.* Hong Kong: Hong Kong Univ. Press, 1968.

Lin, Shuen-fu. "Liu Xie on Imagination." In *A Chinese Literary Mind: Culture, Creativity, and Rhetoric in Wenxin diaolong,* ed. Zong-qi Cai, pp. 127–160. Stanford: Stanford University Press, 2001.

Lin, Shuen-fu, and Stephen Owen, eds. *The Vitality of the Lyric Voice.* Princeton: Princeton Univ. Press, 1986.

Lindtner, Chr. *Nāgārjuna: Studies in the Writings and Philosophy of Nāgārjuna.* Copenhagen: Akademisk Forlag, 1982.

Link, Arthur E. "The Taoist Antecedents of Tao-An's Prajñā Ontology." *History of Religions* 9, nos. 2–3 (1969–1970): 181–215.

Liu, Alan. *Wordsworth: The Sense of History.* Stanford: Stanford Univ. Press, 1989.

Liu, James J. Y. *The Art of Chinese Poetry.* Chicago: Univ. of Chicago Press, 1962.

———. *Chinese Theories of Literature.* Chicago: Univ. of Chicago Press, 1975.

Londraville, Richard. "Fenollosa and the Legacy of Stone Cottage." *Paideuma: A Journal Devoted to Ezra Pound Scholarship* 22, no. 3 (1993): 100–108.

Lovejoy, Arthur. *The Great Chain of Being: A Study of the History of Ideas.* Cambridge, Mass.: Harvard Univ. Press, 1936.

Loy, David. "The Clôsure of Deconstruction: A Mādhyamika Critique of Derrida." *International Philosophical Quarterly* 27 (1987): 59–80.

———. "Zhuangzi and Nāgārjuna on the Truth of No Truth." In *Essays on Skepticism, Relativism, and Ethics in the Zhuangzi,* eds. Paul Kjellberg and Philip J. Ivanhoe, pp. 50–67. Albany: State Univ. of New York Press, 1996.

Lynn, Richard John, trans. *The Classics of Changes: A New Translation of the I Ching as Interpreted by Wang Bi.* New York: Columbia Univ. Press, 1994.

Ma, Yau-woon. "Confucius as a Literary Critic: A Comparison with the Early Greeks." Collected in *Essays in Chinese Studies Dedicated to Professor Jao Tsung-i.* Ed. Jao Tsung-i jiaoshou nanyou zengbie lunwenji bianji weiyuanhui, pp. 13–45. Hong Kong: Jao Tsung-i jiaoshou nanyou zengbie lunwenji bianji weiyuanhui, 1970.

MacFarland, Thomas. *Coleridge and the Pantheist Tradition.* Oxford: Clarendon Press, 1969.

Magliola, Robert. *Derrida on the Mend.* West Lafayette, Ind.: Purdue Univ. Press, 1984.

———. "Differentialism in Chinese Ch'an and French Deconstruction: Some Test-Cases from the Wu-men-kuan." *Journal of Chinese Philosophy* 17, no. 1 (1990): 87–97.

Magnuson, Paul. *Coleridge and Wordsworth: A Lyrical Dialogue.* Princeton: Princeton Univ. Press, 1988.

Mair, Victor H. "Old Sinitic *Myag, Old Persian Maguš, and English 'Magician.'" *Early China* 15 (1990): 27–47.

———. "Buddhism in *The Literary Mind and Ornate Rhetoric.*" In *A

Chinese Literary Mind: Culture, Creativity, and Rhetoric in Wenxin diao-long, ed. Zong-qi Cai, pp. 63–81. Stanford: Stanford Univ. Press, 2000.

———, ed. *Experimental Essays on Chuang-tzu*. Honolulu: Univ. of Hawai'i Press, 1983.

Makeham, John. *Name and Actuality in Early Chinese Thought*. Albany: State Univ. of New York Press, 1994.

Marks, Emerson R. *Coleridge on the Language of Verse*. Princeton: Princeton Univ. Press, 1981.

Matilal, Bimal K., and Robert D. Evans, eds. *Vigrahavyāvartan* (Emptiness: A Study in Religious Meaning). Trans. Frederick J. Streng. Nashville: Abingdon, 1967.

———. *Buddhist Logic and Epistemology*. Dordrecht: D. Reidel, 1986.

McCormick, Peter J. *Fictions, Philosophies, and the Problems of Poetics*. Ithaca: Cornell Univ. Press, 1988.

———. "Literary Truths." In *Fictions, Philosophies, and the Problems of Poetics*. Ithaca: Cornell Univ. Press, 1988.

McKeon, Richard. *Thought, Action and Passion*. Chicago: Univ. of Chicago Press, 1954.

Merleau-Ponty, M. *Phenomenology of Perception*. Trans. Colin Smith. London: Routledge & Kegan Paul, 1962.

Miner, Earl. *The Japanese Tradition in British and American Literature*. Princeton: Princeton Univ. Press, 1958.

———. "'Super-position' method in Pound, Haiku, and the Image." *The Hudson Review* 9 (1956–1957): 570–584. Reprinted in Walter Sutton, ed., *Ezra Pound: A Collection of Critical Essays*, pp. 115–128. Englewood Cliffs, N.J.: Prentice-Hall, 1963.

———. *Comparative Poetics: An Intercultural Essay on Theories of Literature*. Princeton: Princeton Univ. Press, 1990.

Moore, Cornelia N., and Raymond A. Moody. *Comparative Literature East and West: Traditions and Trends: Selected Conference Papers*. Honolulu: College of Languages, Linguistics, and Literature, the University of Hawai'i and the East-West Center, 1989.

Munro, Donald J. *The Concept of Man in Ancient China*. Stanford: Stanford Univ. Press, 1969.

Nayak, G. C. "The Mādhyamika Attack on Essentialism: A Critical Appraisal." *Philosophy East & West* 29 (1979): 467–490.

Nisbet, H. B. *German Aesthetic and Literary Criticism: Winckelmann, Lessing, Hammann, Herder, Schiller, Goethe*. Cambridge: Cambridge Univ. Press, 1985.

Odin, Steve. "Derrida and the Decentered Universe of Chan / Zen Buddhism." *Journal of Chinese Philosophy* 17, no. 1 (1990): 61–86.

Owen, Stephen. *Traditional Chinese Poetry and Poetics: Omen of the World.* Madison: Univ. of Wisconsin Press, 1985.

———. *Readings in Chinese Literary Thought.* Cambridge, Mass.: Harvard University Press, 1992.

Owen, W. J. B. *Wordsworth as Critic.* Toronto: Univ. of Toronto Press, 1969.

Ownes, Wayne D. "Tao and Differance: The Existential Implications." *Journal of Chinese Philosophy* 20, no. 3 (1993): 261–277.

Paige, D. D., ed. *The Letters of Ezra Pound 1907–1941.* New York: Haskell, 1974.

Payne, Michael, ed. *A Dictionary of Cultural and Critical Theory.* Oxford: Blackwell, 1996.

Peerenboom, Randall P. "Cosmogony, the Taoist Way." *Journal of Chinese Philosophy* 17 (1990): 157–174.

———. *Law and Morality in Ancient China: The Silk Manuscripts of Huang-Lao.* New York: State Univ. of New York Press, 1993.

———. "The Rational American and the Inscrutable Oriental as Seen from the Perspective of a Puzzled European: A Review (and Response) in Three Stereotypes—A Reply to Carine Defoort." *Philosophy East and West* 44.2 (1994): 368–379.

Peterson, Willard J. "Making Connections: 'Commentary on the Attached Verbalizations' of the *Book of Changes.*" *Harvard Journal of Asiatic Studies* 42.1 (1982): 67–116.

———. "Squares and Circles: Mapping the History of Chinese Thought." *Journal of History of Ideas* 49, no. 1 (1988): 47–60.

Plaks, Andrew H. *Archetype and Allegory in the Dream of the Red Chamber.* Princeton: Princeton Univ. Press, 1976.

———. "Conceptual Models in Chinese Narrative Theory." *Journal of Chinese Philosophy* 4 (1977): 25–47.

Plato. *The Dialogues of Plato.* 2 vols. Trans. and ed. Benjamin Jowett. New York: Random House, 1937.

———. *The Republic of Plato.* Trans. and ed. Francis M. Cornford. New York and London: Oxford Univ. Press, 1941.

———. *Plato's Timaeus.* Trans. and ed. Francis M. Cornford. Indianapolis, Ind.: Bobbs-Merrill, 1959.

Pollard, David. "*Ch'i* in Chinese Literary Theory." In *Chinese Approaches to Literature,* ed. Adele Rickett, pp. 43–66.

Pottle, Frederick A. "The Eye and the Object in the Poetry of Wordsworth." In *Romanticism and Consciousness: Essays in Criticism*, ed. Harold Bloom, pp. 273–287. New York: Norton, 1970.

Poulet, Georges. "Phenomenology of Reading." *New Literary History* 1 (1969): 53–68.

———. "Criticism and the Experience of Interiority." In *The Structuralist Controversy*, ed. Richard Macksey and Eugenio Donato. Baltimore: Johns Hopkins Univ. Press, 1970.

Pound, Ezra. *Gaudier-Brzeska*. New York: New Directions, 1970.

Pound, Omar, and A. Walton Litz, eds. *Ezra Pound and Dorothy Shakespear: Their Letters, 1909–1914*. New York: New Directions, 1984.

Pousin, Louis de la Vallée, ed. *Bibliotheca Buddhica*. St. Petersburg: Akad. Nauk-Izd. Vostochnoi Lit-ry, 1913.

Preminger, Alex, O. B. Hardison, Jr., and Kevin Kerrane, eds. *Classical and Medieval Literary Criticism: Translations and Interpretations*. New York: Frederick Ungar, 1974.

Qian, Zhaoming. *Orientalism and Modernism: The Legacy of China in Pound and Williams*. Durham and London: Duke Univ. Press, 1995.

Qian Zhongshu. *Limited Views: Essays on Ideas and Letters*. Selected and translated by Ronald Egan. Harvard-Yenching Institute Monograph Series, vol. 44. Cambridge, Mass.: Harvard Univ. Asia Center, 1998.

Qian Zhongshu. See Ch'ien Chung-shu (Qian Zhongshu).

Ransom, J. C. *The World's Body*. New York: Charles Scribner's Sons, 1938.

Richter, David P. *The Critical Tradition*. New York: St. Martin, 1989.

Rickett, Adele, ed. *Chinese Approaches to Literature from Confucius to L'iang Ch'i-ch'ao*. Princeton: Princeton Univ. Press, 1978.

Roetz, Heiner. "Validity in Chou Thought: On Chad Hansen and the Pragmatic Turn in Sinology." In *Epistemological Issues in Classical Chinese Philosophy*, eds. Hans Lenk and Gregor Paul, pp. 69–112. Albany: State Univ. of New York Press, 1993.

Ropp, Paul S., ed. *Heritage of China: Contemporary Perspectives on Chinese Civilization*. Berkeley: Univ. of California Press, 1990.

Rosement, Henry, Jr. "Explorations in Early Chinese Cosmology." *Journal of the American Academy of Religion Studies*, vol. 50, no. 2. Chico, Calif.: Scholar Press, 1984.

Rosen, Stanley. *The Quarrel Between Philosophy and Poetry: Studies in Ancient Thought*. New York: Routledge, 1988.

Ross, W. D., ed. *The Works of Aristotle Translated into English.* 12 vols. London: Oxford Univ. Press, 1908–1952.

Ruegg, David Seyfort. *The Literature of the Mādhyamika School of Philosophy in India.* Wiesbaden: Otto Harrassowitz, 1981.

Russell, Bertrand. *A History of Western Philosophy: And Its Connection with Political and Social Circumstances from the Earliest Times to the Present Day.* New York: Simon & Schuster, 1945.

Sallis, John. *Deconstruction and Philosophy.* Chicago: Univ. of Chicago Press, 1987.

Saussure, Ferdinand de. *Course in General Linguistics.* Trans. Roy Harris. London: Gerald Duckworth, 1983.

Saussy, Haun. *The Problem of a Chinese Aesthetic.* Stanford: Stanford Univ. Press, 1993.

———. "The Prestige of Writing: 文, Letter, Picture, Image, Ideography." *Sino-Platonic Papers* 75 (1997): 1–41.

Schwartz, Benjamin I. *The World of Thought in Ancient China.* Cambridge, Mass.: Harvard Belnap Press, 1985.

Schwartz, Sanford. *The Matrix of Modernism.* Princeton: Princeton Univ. Press, 1985.

Selden, Raman, ed. *The Theory of Criticism from Plato to the Present: A Reader.* London: Longman, 1988.

Sharma, Dhirendra. *The Differentiation Theory of Meaning in Indian Logic.* The Hague: Mouton, 1969.

Shelley, Percy Bysshe. *Shelley's Poetry and Prose: Authoritative Texts and Criticism.* Eds. Donald H. Reiman and Sharon B. Powers. New York: Norton, 1977.

Shi, Liang. "The Leopardskin of Dao and the Icon of Truth: Natural Birth Versus Mimesis in Chinese and Western Literary Theories." *Comparative Literature Studies* 31.2 (1994): 148–164.

Shih, Vincent Yu-chung. *The Literary Mind and the Carving of Dragons.* Hong Kong: Chinese Univ. Press, 1983.

Sidney, Phillip. *Complete Works of Sir Phillip Sidney.* Ed. Albert Feuillerat, 4 vols. Cambridge: Cambridge Univ. Press, 1912–1926.

Sikes, E. E. *The Greek View of Poetry.* New York: Barnes & Noble, 1931.

Silbergeld, Jerome. *Chinese Painting Style.* Seattle: Univ. of Washington Press, 1982.

Smith, Huston. "Western and Comparative Perspectives on Truth." *Philosophy East and West* 30 (1980): 425–437.

Spariosu, Mihail I. *God of Many Names: Play, Poetry, and Power in Hellenic Thought from Homer to Aristotle.* Durham, N.C.: Duke Univ. Press, 1991.

Spence, Jonathan. "Western Perceptions from the Late Sixteenth Century to the Present." In *Heritage of China: Contemporary Perspectives on Chinese Civilization,* ed. Paul S. Ropp, pp. 1–14. Berkeley: Univ. of California Press, 1990.

Stcherbatsky, F. Th. *Buddhist Logic.* New York: Dover, 1962.

Streng, Frederick J., trans. *Emptiness: A Study in Religious Meaning.* Nashville: Abingdon, 1967.

Sullivan, Michael. *The Three Perfections: Chinese Painting, Poetry, and Calligraphy.* London: Thames & Hudson, 1974.

Tay, William. "Fragmentary Negation: A Reappraisal of Ezra Pound's Ideogrammic Method." In *Chinese-Western Comparative Literature: Theory and Strategy,* ed. John J. Deeney, pp. 129–153. Hong Kong: Chinese Univ. Press, 1980.

Tseng, Yu-ho Ecke. *Chinese Calligraphy.* Philadelphia: Philadelphia Museum of Art and Boston Book & Art, 1971.

Tu, Wei-ming. *Way, Learning, and Politics: Essays on the Confucian Intellectual.* Albany: State Univ. of New York, 1993.

Van der Leeuw, Gerald. *Sacred and Profane Beauty: The Holy in Art.* Trans. David E. Green. New York: Holt, Rinehart & Winston, 1963.

Van Zoeren, Steven. *Poetry and Personality: Reading, Exegesis, and Hermeneutics in Traditional China.* Stanford: Stanford Univ. Press, 1991.

Varela, Francisco J., Evan Thompson, and Eleanor Rosch. *The Embodied Mind: Cognitive Science and Human Experience.* Cambridge, Mass.: MIT Press, 1991.

Vattimo, Gianni. *The End of Modernity.* Trans. J. Snyder. Baltimore: Johns Hopkins Univ. Press, 1989.

Waldo, Ives. "Nāgārjuna and Analytical Philosophy." *Philosophy East & West* 25 (1975): 281–290.

———. "Nāgārjuna and Analytical Philosophy, II." *Philosophy East & West* 28 (1978): 287–298.

Waley, Arthur, trans. *The Analects of Confucius.* New York: Random House, 1938.

Watson, Burton, trans. *The Complete Works of Chuang Tzu.* New York: Columbia Univ. Press, 1968.

Wellek, René, and Austin Warren. *Theory of Literature.* Third edition. New York: Harcourt Brace Jovanovich, 1975.

Welsh, Andrew. *Roots of Lyric: Primitive Poetry and Modern Poetics.* Princeton: Princeton Univ. Press, 1978.

Whitehead, Alfred North. *Modes of Thought.* New York: Free Press, 1968.

Wilhelm, Hellmut. *Heaven, Earth, and Man in the Book of Changes.* Seattle: Univ. of Washington Press, 1977.

―――. *Change: Eight Lectures on the I Ching.* Translated from German by Cary F. Baynes. Collected in Hellmut Wilhelm and Richard Wilhelm, *Understanding the I Ching: The Wilhelm Lectures on the Book of Changes.* Princeton: Princeton Univ. Press, 1995.

Wilhelm, Hellmut, and Richard Wilhelm. *Understanding the I Ching: The Wilhelm Lectures on the Book of Changes.* Princeton: Princeton Univ. Press, 1995.

Wilhelm, Richard. *Lectures on the I Ching: Constancy and Change.* Translated from German by Irene Eber. Princeton: Princeton Univ. Press, 1979.

―――, trans. *The I Ching or Book of Changes.* Translated from German into English by Cary F. Baynes. Princeton: Princeton Univ. Press, 1950.

Williams, S. Wells. *The Middle Kingdom.* New York: Scribner's, 1882; revised edition, 1907.

Wimsatt, W. K. *The Verbal Icon: Studies in the Meaning of Poetry.* Lexington: Univ. of Kentucky Press, 1954.

Wong, Siu-kit. *Early Chinese Literary Criticism.* Hong Kong: Joint Publishing Company, 1983.

Wood, Thomas E. *Nāgārjunian Disputations: A Philosophical Journey through an Indian Looking-Glass.* Monographs of the Society for Asian and Comparative Philosophy, no. 11. Honolulu: Univ. of Hawai'i Press, 1994.

Wordsworth, William. *The Complete Poetical Works of Wordsworth.* Ed. Andrew J. George. Boston: Houghton Mifflin, 1932.

―――. *The Poetical Works of William Wordsworth.* Eds. Ernest de Selincourt and Helen Darbishire. 5 vols. Oxford: Clarendon, 1940–1949.

―――. *The Prelude or Growth of a Poet's Mind.* Ed. Ernest de Selincourt. Corrected by Stephen Gill. Oxford: Oxford Univ. Press, 1970.

―――. *The Prose Works of William Wordsworth.* Ed. W. J. B. Owen and Jane Worthington Smyser. 3 vols. Oxford: Clarendon, 1974.

Xie, Shaobo, and John (Zhong) M. Chen. "Jacques Derrida and Chuang

Tzu: Some Analogies in Their Deconstructionist Discourse on Language and Truth." *Canadian Review of Comparative Literature / Revue Canadienne de Littérature Comparée* 19, no. 3, (1992): 363–376.

Xu, Fangcheng, trans. *Three Theses of Seng Zhao*. Beijing: Chinese Social Sciences Publishing House, 1985.

Yee, Chiang. *Chinese Calligraphy: An Introduction to Its Aesthetic and Technique*. Cambridge: Harvard Univ. Press, 1966.

Yeh, Michelle. "The Deconstructive Way: A Comparative Study of Derrida and Chuang Tzu." *Journal of Chinese Philosophy* 10, no. 2 (1983): 95–125.

Yip, Wai-lim. *Ezra Pound's Cathay*. Princeton: Princeton Univ. Press, 1969.

———. *Diffusion of Distances: Dialogues between Chinese and Western Poetics*. Berkeley: Univ. of California Press, 1993.

Yu, Pauline. *The Poetry of Wang Wei: New Translations and Commentary*. Bloomington: Indiana Univ. Press, 1980.

———. *The Readings of Imagery in the Chinese Tradition*. Princeton: Princeton Univ. Press, 1987.

Zha, Peide. "Logocentrism and Traditional Chinese Poetics." (*Canadian Review of Comparative Literature / Revue Canadienne de Littérature Comparée*) 19, no. 3, (1992): 377–394.

Zhang, Longxi. *The Tao and the Logos: Literary Hermeneutics, East and West*. Durham, N.C.: Duke Univ. Press, 1992.

WORKS IN CHINESE AND JAPANESE

Aoki Masaru 青木正兒. *Shina bungaku shisoshi* 支那文學思想史 (A History of Chinese Literary Thought). Tokyo, 1943. Included in *Aoki Masaru zenshū* 青木正兒全集 (Complete Works of Aoki Masaru). Tokyo: Shunjūsha, 1969, vol. 1.

Ban Gu 班固 (32–92), comp. *Han shu* 漢書 (History of the Han). Beijing: Zhonghua shuju, 1962.

Cai Zong-qi 蔡宗齊. "Yixiang, yijing shuo yu Liu Xie di chuangzuo lun" 意象、意境說與劉勰的創作論 (Theories of Yixiang [Idea-Image], Yijing [Idea-scape] and Liu Xie's Theory of Literary Creation). In *Wenxin diaolong guoji xueshu yantaohui lunwenji* 文心雕龍國際學術研討會論文集. (Collected Essays from an International Symposium on *Wenxin diaolong*), ed. Taiwan Shifan Daxue guowen xi. 2 vols. Taipei: Wenshizhe chubanshe, 1999, vol. 2, pp. 375–388.

———. "*Wenxin diaolong* yu Ru Dao Fo jia di zhongdao siwei" 文心雕龍與儒、道、佛家的中道思維 (*Wenxin Diaolong* and the Confucian, Daoist, and Buddhist *Zhongdao* [Middle-Way] Modes of Thought).

Collected in *Lun Liu Xie jiqi Wenxin diaolong* 論劉勰及其文心雕龍 (On Liu Xie and *Wenxin diaolong*), pp. 94–114. Beijing: Xueyuan chubanshe, 2000.

Chen Guying 陳鼓應. *Yi zhuan yu Daojia sixiang* 易傳與道家思想 (*Commentaries to the Book of Changes* and Daoist Thought). Beijing: Sanlian shudian, 1996.

Chen Mengjia 陳夢家. "Shangdai shenhua yu wushu" 商代神話與巫術 (Myths and Shamanistic Arts in the Shang Dynasty). *Yanjing xuebao* 燕京學報 (The Yanjing Journal) 20 (1936), pp. 484–576.

Chen Shou 陳壽 (233–297), comp. *Sanguo zhi* 三國志 (Memoirs of the Three Kingdoms). Beijing: Zhonghua shuju, 1959.

Chen Si 陳思 (Song Dynasty). *Shuyuan jinghua* 書苑菁華 (The Splendor of the Garden of Calligraphy). Wang Ruli edn.

Chow Tse-tsung 周策縱. *Gu wuyi yu liushi kao* 古巫醫與六詩攷 (Study of Ancient Shaman-Doctors and the Six Poetic Genres and Modes). Taipei: Jinglian chubanshe, 1986.

Chunqiu Zuo zhuan zhengyi 春秋左傳正義 (Correct Meanings of *the Zuo Commentary to Spring and Autumn Annals*). Commentary by Kong Yingda 孔穎達. In *SSJZ*.

Dong Zhi'an 董治安. *Xian Qin wenxuan yu xian Qin wenxue* 先秦文獻與先秦文學 (Pre-Qin Texts and Pre-Qin Literature). Jinan: Qi Lu shushe, 1994.

Dong Zhongshu 董仲舒 (ca. 179–ca. 104 B.C.). *Chunqiu fanlu yizheng* 春秋繁露義證 (Investigating the Meanings of Luxuriant Gems of *Spring and Autumn Annals*). Annot. Su Yu 蘇輿. Beijing: Zhonghua shuju, 1992.

Fan Wenlan 范文瀾 (1893–1969). *Wenxin diaolong zhu* 文心雕龍注 (Commentaries on *Wenxin diaolong*). Beijing: Renmin wenxue chubanshe, 1958.

Fan Ye 范曄 (398–466), comp. *Hou Han shu* 後漢書 (History of the Later Han). Beijing: Zhonghua shuju, 1965.

Fang Litian 方立天. *Wei Jin Nanbeichao Fojiao luncong* 魏晉南北朝佛教論叢 (Discussions on the Buddhism during the Wei-Jin Period and Northern and Southern Dynasties). Beijing: Zhonghua shuju, 1982.

———. *Fojiao zhexue* 佛教哲學 (Buddhist Philosophy). Beijing: Zhongguo Remin Daxue chubanshe, 1991.

Gao Heng 高亨, ed. *Shijing jinzhu* 詩經今注 (The *Book of Poetry*, with Modern Annotations). Shanghai: Shanghai Guji chubanshe, 1979.

Gao Ming 高明. *Zhongguo gu wenzi xue tonglun* 中國古文字學通論 (A

Comprehensive Survey of the Studies on Chinese Ancient Characters). Beijing: Beijing Univ. Press, 1996.

Gu Jiegang 顧頡剛 (1893–1980). *Gushi bian* 古史辨 (Analysis of Ancient History). 7 vols. Rpt. Hong Kong: Taiping shuju, 1962.

———. "Lun jinwen *Shangshu* zhuzuo shidai shu" 論今文尚書著作時代書" (A Letter on the Date of the Composition of *Shang shu*).

Guo Qingfan 郭慶藩, comp. *Zhuang Zi jishi* 莊子集釋 (The Book of Zhuang Zi, with Collected Annotations). 4 vols. Beijing: Zhonghua shuju, 1961.

Guo Shaoyu 郭紹虞 (1893–1984). "Xian Qin Rujia zhi wenxueguan" 先秦儒家之文學觀 (The Pre-Qin Confucian Concepts of Literature). In *Zhaoyushi gudian wenxue lunji.* Shanghai: Shanghai guji chubanshe, 1983, vol. 1, pt. 2, pp. 149–157.

———. "Xing guan qun yuan shuo pouxi" 興觀群怨說剖析 (An Analysis of the Statement "The *Poetry* may help to inspire, to observe, to keep company and to express grievances"). In *Zhaoyushi gudian wenxue lunji.* Shanghai: Shanghai guji chubanshe, 1983, vol. 2, pt. 1, pp. 390–411.

———. *Zhaoyushi gudian wenxue lunji* 照隅室古典文學論集 (Collected Writings on Classical Chinese Literature from the Zhaoyu Studio). 2 vols. Shanghai: Shanghai guji chubanshe, 1983.

———. "Zhongguo wenxue piping lilun zhong 'Dao' di wenti" 中國文學批評理論中道的問題 (The Issue of the "Dao" in Chinese Theories of Literary Criticism). In *Zhaoyushi gudian wenxue,* vol. 2, pp. 34–65.

Guo Shaoyu, and Wang Wenshen 王文生, eds. *Zhongguo lidai wenlun xuan* 中國歷代文論選 (An Anthology of Writings on Literature through the Ages), 4 vols., Shanghai: Shanghai guji chubanshe, 1979.

Guo yu 國語 (Speeches of the States). Annot. Wei Zhao 韋昭 (204–273). 2 vols. Shanghai: Shanghai guji chubanshe, 1978.

Han shu 漢書. See under Ban Gu 班固.

Han Yu 韓愈 (768–824). *Han Changli shi xinian jishi* 韓昌黎詩繫年集釋 (A Chronological and Variorum Edition of the Poems of Han Changli [Han Yu]). Annotated by Qian Zhonglian 錢仲聯. 2 vols. Shanghai: Shanghai guji chubanshe, 1984.

Hayashida Shinnosuke 林田慎元助. *Chūgoku chōseibungaku kyōronshi* 中國中世文學評論史 (A History of Literary Criticism in Medieval China). Tokyo: Sobunsha, 1979.

He Jiuying 何九盈, Hu Shuangbao 胡雙寶, and Zhang Meng 張猛. *Zhongguo Hanzi wenhu daguan* 中國漢字文化大觀 (A Grand View of Chinese Characters and Culture). Beijing: Beijing Univ. Press, 1995.

He Yan 何晏 (190–249), annot. *Lunyu jijie* 論語集解 (Collected Explanations to *Analects*). *SBBY* edn.

Hou Han shu 後漢書. See under Fan Ye 范曄.

Hou Naihui 侯迺慧. "Cong 'qi' di yiyi yu liucheng kan *Wenxin diaolong* di chuangzuo lilun" 由氣的意義與流程看文心雕龍的創作理論 (Theory of Literary Creation in *Wenxin diaolong:* A View from the Perspective of the Idea of *Qi* as Process). In *Wenxin diaolong zonglun* 文心雕龍綜論 (Comprehensive Discussions on *Wenxin diaolong*). Ed. Zhongguo gudian wenxue yanjiuhui. Taipei: Taiwan xuesheng shuju, 1988, pp. 241–283.

Hu Shi 胡適 (1891–1962). Zhongguo zhexueshi dagang 中國哲學史大綱 (A General Outline of the History of Chinese Philosophy). Beijing: Dongfang chubanshe, 1996.

Huang Chungui 黃春貴. *Wenxin diaolung zhi chuangzuolun* 文心雕龍之創作論 (The Theory of Literary Creation in *Wenxin diaolong*). Taipei: Wenshizhe chubanshe, 1978.

Huang Kan 皇侃 (488–545), ed. *Lunyu jijie yishu* 論語集解義疏 (Sub-commentary to the *Collected Commentaries on Analects*). Nihon Ashikaga kan bon 日本足利刊本 edn.

Huang Kan 黃侃 (1886–1935). *Wenxin diaolong zhaji* 文心雕龍札記 (Notes on *Wenxin diaolong*). Shanghai, 1962. Rpt. Taipei: Wenshizhe chubanshe, 1973.

Hui Jiao 慧皎 (497–554). *Gao seng zhuan* 高僧傳. (Biographies of Eminent Monks). Beijing: Zhonghua shuju, 1992.

Ji Zang 吉藏 (549–623). *Sanlun Xuanyi Jiaoshi* 三論玄義校釋 (Collation and Annotation to *Profound Meanings of the Tree Treatises*). Annot. Han Tingjie 韓廷傑. Beijing: Zhonghua shuju, 1987.

Jin Yuan 淨源 (1011–1088), ed. *Zhao Lun Zhongwu jijie* 肇論中吳集解 (The Zhongwu Collected Annotations to *Zhao Lun*). In *Lou Xuetang xiansheng quanji* 羅雪堂先生全集 (Complete Works of Mr. Luo Xuetang), vol. 19. Taipei: Wenhua, 1968.

Kao Yu-kung 高友工. "Zhongguo yuyan wenzi dui shige de yingxiang" 中國語言文字對詩歌的影響 (The Influence of Chinese Speech and Characters on Poetry-Writing). *Chung-wai wen hsüeh* 中外文學 (*Chung-wai Literary Monthly*) 18.5 (1990), pp. 4–38.

Lao Zi jiaoshi 老子校釋 (Collations and Explanations of *Lao Zi*). Annot. Zhu Qianzhi 朱謙之. Beijing: Zhonghua shuju, 1984.

Li Runsheng 李潤生. *Seng Zhao* 僧肇 (Seng Zhao). Taipei: Dongda tushu gongsi, 1989.

Liang Qichao 梁啓超. *Yinbing shi heji: Wenji* 飲冰室合集・專集 (Combined Collections of Writings from the Yinbing Studio: Specialized Essays). Shanghai: Zhonghua shuju, 1936.

———. *Yinbing shi heji: Zhuanji* 飲冰室合集・文集 (Combined Collections of Writings from the Yinbing Studio: Essays). Shanghai: Zhonghua shuju, 1936.

Lidai shufa zihui 歷代書法字彙 (Dictionary of Chinese Calligraphic Styles in Successive Dynasties). Ed. Datong shuju. Taipei: Datong shuju, 1981.

Liji zhengyi 禮記正義 (Correct Meanings of the *Book of Rites*). Annot. Kong Yingda 孔穎達 (574–648). In *SSJZ*.

Lin Hengxun 林衡勛. "Zhongguo wenzi chuangzao di shenmei tezhi shitan 中國文字創造的審美特質試探" (An Inquiry into the Aesthetic Nature of the Creation of Chinese Characters). *Gudai wenxue lilun yanjiu* 古代文學理論研究 (Studies on Classical [Chinese] Literary Theory) 14 (1989), pp. 234–280.

Liu Baonan 劉寶楠 (1791–1855), ed. *Lunyu zhengyi* 論語正義 (Correct Meanings of *Analects*). *SBBY* edn.

Liu Dajie 劉大杰 (1904–1977). *Zhongguo wenxue fazhan shi* 中國文學發展史 (A History of the Development of Chinese Literature). Revised edition. 3 vols. Shanghai: Gudian wenxue chubanshe, 1957–1958.

Liu Shipei 劉師培, "Wenxue chuyu wuzhu zhi guan shuo" 文學出于巫祝之官説 (An Explanation: Literature Came from the Officials in Charge of Shamanistic Incantations). *Zuo An waiji* 左盦外集 (Supplementary Collection of Zuo An) *Juan* 8. Collected in *Liu Shenshu yishu* 劉申叔遺書 (Posthumous Publications of Liu Shenshu). 4 vols. Taipei: Huashi, 1975.

Lu Kanru 陸侃如 and Feng Yuanjun 馮沅君, eds. *Wenxin diaolong yizhu* 文心雕龍譯注 (Translation and Commentaries on *Wenxin diaolong*). 2 vols. Jinan: Qi Lu shushe, 1981.

Lü Buwei 呂不韋 (?–235 B.C.). *Lü shi chunqiu* 呂氏春秋 (Spring and Autumn Annals of Mister Lü). Annot. Chen Qiyou 陳奇猷. Shanghai: Xuelin chubanshe, 1984.

Lü Cheng 呂澂. *Zhongguo Foxue yuanliu luejiang* 中國佛學源流略講 (Brief Lectures on the Origins and Development of Chinese Buddhism). Beijing: Zhonghua shuju, 1979.

Lü Yi 呂藝. "Kongzi xing guan qun yuan benyi zaitan" 孔子與觀群怨本義再探 (Another Investigation: Confucius and the Statement "The *Poetry* may help to inspire, to observe, to keep company and to express grievances"). *Wenxue yichan* 文學遺產 (Literary Heritage), 1985.4, pp. 1–11.

Lunyu yinde 論語引得 (Concordance to *Analects*). Harvard-Yenching Institute Sinological Index Series, supp. 16. Rpt. Shanghai: Shanghai guji chubanshe, 1986.

Luo Genze 羅根澤. *Zhongguo wenxue piping shi* 中國文學批評史 (A History of Chinese Literary Criticism). 3 vols. Shanghai: Gudian wenxue chubanshe, 1957–1961.

Ma Bai 馬白. "Cong fangfalun kan *Zhou yi* dui *Wenxin diaolong* di yingxiang" 從方法論看周易對文心雕龍的影響 (The Influence of the *Changes* in *Wenxin diaolong* as Observed in the Way of Methodology). In *Zhongguo wenyi sixiang shi luncong* 中國文藝思想史論叢 (Discussions on the History of Chinese Ideas of Art) 1 (1985), pp. 136–158.

Mao Shi yinde 毛詩引得 (Concordance to the Mao Text of the *Book of Poetry*). Harvard-Yenching Institute Sinological Index Series, supp. 9. Tokyo: the Japanese Council for East Asian Studies, 1962.

Mao Shi zhengyi 毛詩正義 (Correct Meanings of the Mao Text of the *Book of Poetry*). Annot. Kong Yingda 孔穎達. In *SSJZ*.

Min Ze 敏澤. "Woguo gu wenlun zhong de qinggan lun" 我國古文論中的情感論 (Theories of Emotion in our Country's Ancient Writings on Literature). *Gudai wenxue lilun yanjiu* 古代文學理論研究 (Studies on Classical [Chinese] Literary Theory) 4 (1981), pp. 284–308.

Peng Huizi 彭會資, comp. *Zhongguo wenlun da cidian* 中國文論大辭典 (Comprehensive Dictionary of Chinese Literary Criticism). Guangxi: Baihua wenyi chubanshe, 1990.

Qi Zhixiang 祁志祥. *Fojiao meixue* 佛教美學 (Buddhist Aesthetics). Shanghai: Shanghai renmin chubanshe, 1997.

Qian Zhonglian 錢仲聯. "Shi 'qi'" 釋"氣" (An Explanation of *Qi* or Vital Breath). *Gudai wenxue lilun yanjiu* 古代文學理論研究 (Studies on Classical [Chinese] Literary Theory) 5 (1981), pp. 129–150.

Qian Zhongshu 錢鍾書. *Guanzhui pian* 管錐篇 (Limited Views). 4 vols. Beijing: Zhonghua shuju, 1979.

Qiu Shiyou 邱世友. "Liu Xie lun wenxue di boruo juejing" 劉勰論文學的般若絕境 (Liu Xie on the Incomparable Literary Realm of Prajñā). In *Wenxin diaolong yanjiu* 文心雕龍研究 (Studies on *Wenxin diaolong*) 3 (1998), pp. 21–41.

Qu Wanli 屈萬里. "*Shang shu* bu ke jin xin di cailiao 尚書不可盡信的材料" (Material in *Shang shu* that is not Fully Trustworthy). *Xin shidai* 新時代 (New Era) 1.3 (1964), pp. 23–25.

Rong Geng 容庚 (1894–1983), comp. *Jinwen bian jinwen xubian* 金文編

金文續編 (A Collection of Bronze Inscriptions and an Addendum). Taipei: Hongshi chubanshe, 1974.

―――. *Jinwen bian* 金文編 (A Collection of Bronze Inscriptions). Beijing: Zhonghua shuju, 1985.

Ruan Yuan 阮元 (1764–1849), comp. *Shisanjing zhushu* 十三經注疏 (Commentary and Subcommentary on the Thirteen Classics). 2 vols. Beijing: 1977.

―――. "Shi song" 釋頌 (An Explanation of *Song*). *Yanjingshi yiji* 擘經室一集 (A Collection from the Yanjing Studio). *SBCK* edn.

Sanguo zhi 三國志. See under Chen Shou 陳壽.

Seng You 僧祐 (445–518), comp. *Chu sanzang ji ji* 出三藏記集 (Collected Notes on the Production of the Buddhist Tripitaka). Beijing: Zhonghua shuju, 1995.

Seng Zhao 僧肇. "Weimoji jing xu" 維摩詰經序 (Preface to *Virmalakīrtinirdeśa sūtra*). Collected in *Chu sanzang ji ji* 出三藏記集 (Collected Notes on the Production of the Buddhist Tripitaka), ed., Seng You 僧祐 (445–518) pp. 309–310. Beijing: Zhonghua shuju, 1995.

Shang shu zhengyi 尚書正義 (Correct Meanings of *Shang shu*). Commentary by Kong Yinda 孔穎達. In *SSJZ*.

Shao Yaocheng (Paul Y. Shao) 邵耀成. "Shilun Liu Xie er cengci de 'chuangzuolun'" 試論劉勰二層次的 "創作論" (The Dual Nature of Liu Xie's Concept of the Creative Act: Monism and Organicism [author's own translation]), *Gudai wenxue lilun yanjiu* 古代文學理論研究 (Studies on Classical [Chinese] Literary Theory) 5 (1981), pp. 256–280.

Shen Yue 沈約 (441–513), comp. *Shong shu* 宋書 (History of [Liu] Song). Peking: Zhonghua shuju, 1974.

Sima Qian 司馬遷 (ca. 145–86 B.C.), comp. *Shi ji* 史記 (Records of the Historian). 10 vols. Beijing: Zhonghua shuju, 1982.

Song shu 宋書. See under Shen Yue 沈約.

Sui shu 隋書. See under Wei Zheng 魏徵.

Sun Quanwen 孫全文 and Zeng Wenhong 曾文宏. *You Zhongguo wenzi tantao chuantong jianzhu* 由中國文字探討傳統建築 (Exploring Traditional [Chinese] Architecture through Chinese Characters). Taipei: Zhan shi shuju, 1988.

Taishō Shinshū Daizōkyō 大正新脩大藏經 (The Newly Revised Edition of the Taishō Tripitaka). Eds. Takakusu Junjirō 高楠順次郎 and Watanabe Kaigyoku 渡邊海旭. Tokyo: *Taishō Shinshū Daizōkyō* Kanko Kai, 1927.

Tang Junyi 唐君毅. *Zhongguo zhexue yuanlun* 中國哲學原論 (On the Fundamentals of Chinese Philosophy). 2 vols. Kowlong: Rensheng chubanshe, 1966.

Tang Yongtong 湯用彤 (1893–1964). *Han Wei liang Jin Nanbeichao Fuojiaoshi* 漢魏兩晉南北朝佛教史 (History of Chinese Buddhism from Han, Wei, Western and Eastern Jin, to Northern and Southern Dynasties). Shanghai: Shanghai shudian, 1991.

Tu Guangshe 涂光社. "Hanzi yu gudai wenxue de minzu tese—*Wenxin diaolong* lian zi suixiang" 漢字與古代文學的民族特色—文心雕龍練字隨想 (Chinese Characters and the Unique Features of Classical [Chinese] Literature—Random Notes on the "Lianzi" Chapter of *Wenxin diaolong*). *Gudai wenxue lilun yanjiu* 古代文學理論研究 (Studies on Classical [Chinese] Literary Theory) 14 (1989), pp. 261–280.

Tu Yanqiu 涂艷秋. *Seng Zhao sixiang tanjiu* 僧肇思想探究 (An Inquiry into the Thought of Seng Zhao). Taipei: Dongchu chubanshe, 1995.

Wang Anshi 王安石 (1021–1086). *Wang Wengong wenji* 王文公文集 (Collected Writings of Wang Wenggong [Anshi]). 2 vols. Shanghai: Shanghai renmin chubanshe, 1974.

Wang Fuzhi 王夫之 (1619–1692), annot. *Lunyu xunyi* 論語訓義 (Textual Interpretations of *Analects*). Taiping yang shuju Chuanshan yishu edn.

Wang Gengsheng 王更生. *Wenxin diaolong xinlun* 文心雕龍新論 (New Perspectives on *Wenxin diaolong*). Taipei: Wenshizhe chubanshe, 1991.

Wang Guowei 王國維 (1877–1927). "*Honglou meng* Pinglun" 紅樓夢評論 (Critical Essay on the *Dream of the Red Chamber*) in *Wang Guowei wenji*, vol. 1, 1–23.

———. "Renjian cihua" 人間詞話 (Talks on *Ci* Poetry in the Human World). In *Wang Guowei wenji*, vol. 1, pp. 141–179.

———. *Wang Guowei wenji* 王國維文集 (Collected Works of Wang Guowei). Eds. Yao Jianming 姚淦銘 and Wang Yan 王燕. 4 vols. Beijing: Wenshi chubanshe, 1997.

Wang Yi 王逸 (the Later Han Dynasty), ed. *Chu ci buzhu* 楚辭補注 (The *Songs of the Chu*, with Supplements and Annotations). *SPPY* edn.

Wang Yuanhua 王元化. *Wenxin diaolong chuangzuolun* 文心雕龍創作論 (The Theory of Literary Creation in *Wenxin diaolong*). Shanghai: Shanghai guji chubanshe, 1979.

Wang Yunxi 王運熙. "*Wenxin diaolong* Yuandao he xuanxue sixiang de guanxi" 文心雕龍原道和玄學思想的關係 (The Relationship between Neo-Daoist Thought and the "Yuan Dao" Chapter of *Wenxin diaolong*). *Wenxin diaolong yanjiu lunwenji* 文心雕龍研究論文集

(Collected Essays on *Wenxin diaolong*). Ed. Zhongguo *Wenxin diao-long* xuehui 中國文心雕龍學會, pp. 374–378. Beijing: Renmin wen-xue chubanshe, 1990.

Wei Zheng 魏徵 (580–643), et al., eds. *Sui shu* 隋書 (History of the Sui). Beijing: Zhonghua shuju, 1973.

Wen Yiduo 聞一多 (1899–1946). *Wen Yiduo quanji* 聞一多全集 (Complete Works of Wen Yiduo). Shanghai: Kaiming shudian, 1948.

Wenxin diaolong guoji xueshu yantaohui lunwenji 文心雕龍國際學術研討會論文集 (Collected Essays from an International Symposium on *Wenxin diaolong*). Ed. Riben jiuzhou daxue Zhongguo wenxuehui. Taipei: Wenshizhe chubanshe, 1992.

———. Ed. Taiwan Shifan Daxue guowen xi. Taipei: Wenshizhe chuban-she, 2000.

Wenxin diaolong xue zonglan 文心雕龍學綜覽 (A Comprehensive Survey of Studies on *Wenxin diaolong*). Ed. *Wenxin diaolong* xue zonglan bianweihui. Shanghai: Shanghai shudian chubanshe, 1995.

Wenxin diaolong zonglun 文心雕龍綜論 (Comprehensive Discussions of *Wenxin diaolong*). Ed. Zhongguo gudian wenxue yanjiuhui. Taipei: Taiwan xuesheng shuju, 1988.

Xia Chengtao 夏承燾, "'Caishi' yu 'fushi'" 采詩與賦詩, (On Collected Poetry and Presented Poetry). *Zhonghua wenshi luncong* 中華文史論叢 (Forum on Chinese Literature and History) 1 (1962), pp. 171–182.

Xiao Huarong 蕭華榮. "*Chunqiu* cheng shi yu Kongzi lun shi" 春秋稱詩與孔子論詩 (The Recitation of the *Poetry* in the *Spring and Autumn Annals* and Confucius' Discussion of the *Poetry*). *Gudai wenxue lilun yanjiu* 古代文學理論研究 (Studies on Classical [Chinese] Literary Theory) 5 (1981), pp. 192–209.

Xiao Tong 蕭統 (501–531), ed. *Wenxuan* 文選 (Anthology of Refined Literature). Commentary by Li Shan 李善 (d. 689). Beijing: Zhonghua shuju, 1977.

Xu Fuguan 徐復觀 (1903–1982). *Zhongguo renxinglun shi: xian Qin pian* 中國人性論史。先秦篇 (A History of Chinese Theories of Human Nature: The Pre-Qin Volume). Taizhong: Sili Donghai Daxue, 1963.

———. *Zhongguo wenxue lunji* 中國文學論集 (Collected Writings on Chinese Literature). Taizhong: Minzhu pinglun she, 1966.

———. *Zhongguo yishu jingshen* 中國藝術精神 (The Spirit of Chinese Art). Taizhong: Sili Donghai daxue, 1966.

———. *Zhongguo sixiangshi lunji xupian* 中國思想史論集續篇 (Collected Works on Chinese Intellectual History: A Sequel). Taipei: Shibo wenhua chuban shiye youxian gongsi, 1982.

Xu Kangsheng 許抗生. "Luelun liang Jin shiqi di Fojiao zhexue sixiang 略論兩晉時期的佛教哲學思想" (A Brief Discussion on the Buddhist Philosophical Thought of the Western and Eastern Jin Dynasties). *Zhongguo zhexue* 中國哲學 (Chinese Philosophy) 6 (1981), pp. 29–60.

Xu Shen 許慎 (30–124). *Shuowen jiezi zhu* 說文解字注 (Explanations of Simple and Compound Characters, with Annotations). Annot. Duan Yucai 段玉裁 (1735–1815). Rpt. Yangzhou: Jiangsu Guangling guji keyinshe, 1997.

Xu Zhongshu 徐中舒, ed. *Jiaguwen zidian* 甲骨文字典 (A Dictionary of Oracle Bone Graphs). Chengdu: Sichuan cishu chubanshe, 1990.

Yang Mingzhao 楊明照. *Wenxin diaolong jiaozhu shiyi* 文心雕龍校注拾遺. (Supplements to the Collations and Commentaries on *Wenxin diaolong*). Shanghai: Shanghai guji chubanshe, 1982.

Yang Shuda 揚樹達 (1884–1956). "Shi 'shi'" 釋詩 (Explaining the Word "Poetry"). In his *Jiweiju xiaoxue jinshi luncong* 積微居小學金石論叢 (Discussions on Philology and Bronze and Stone Drum Graphs from the Jiweiju Studio). Beijing: Kexue chubanshe, 1955, pp. 25–26.

Ye Shuxian 葉舒憲. *Shi jing di wenhua quanshi: Zhongguo shige di fasheng yanjiu* 詩經的文化闡述—中國詩歌的發生研究 (A Cultural Exegesis of *Shi jing:* Studies on the Genesis of Chinese Poetry). Wuhan: Hubei renmin chubanshe, 1994.

Yong Rong 永瑢 (Qing Dynasty), et al., eds. *Siku quanshu zongmu* 四庫全書總目. (General Catalogue of the Imperial Library). 2 vols. Rpt. Beijing: Zhonghua shuju, 1965.

Yu Yongben 愚庸笨. *Zhongguo wenzi de chuangyi yu quwei* 中國文字的創意與趣味 (The Creativity and Flavors of Chinese Characters). Taipei: Daotian chuban youxian gongsi, 1995.

Yu Yuan 郁沅. "Lun 'Yueji' meixue sixiang di liang pai" 論樂記美學思想的兩派 (On the Two Schools of Aesthetics in the "Records of Music"). *Zhongguo wenyi sixiangshi luncong* 中國文藝思想史論叢 (Discussions on the History of Chinese Ideas of Art) 1 (1984), pp. 44–78.

Yu Yuan 郁沅, Yang Lierong 羊列榮, and Xie Xin 謝昕. "*Wenxin diaolong* shenmei ganying lun tanwei" 文心雕龍審美感應論探微 (An Exploration of the Subtle Meanings of the View of Aesthetic Responses in *Wenxin diaolong*). In *Wenxin diaolong guoji xueshu yantaohui lunwenji*

文心雕龍國際學術研討會論文集(Collected Essays from an International Symposium on *Wenxin diaolong*), ed. Riben jiuzhou daxue Zhongguo wenxuehui. Taipei: Wenshizhe chubanshe, 1992.

Yuan Kang 元康 (Tang Dynasty). *Zhao lun shu* 肇論疏 (Annotation to *Zhao lun*). *Taishō Shinshū Daizōkyō,* no. 1859, vol. 45, pp. 161–200.

Ze Zangzhu 賾藏主 (fl. 1131–1138), comp. *Gu zunsu yulu* 古尊宿語錄 (Sayings of Ancient Eminent Monks), 2 vols. Beijing: Zhonghua shuju, 1994.

Zhan Ying 詹鍈, ed. *Wenxin diaolong yizheng* 文心雕龍義證 (Investigation of the Meanings of *Wenxin diaolong*). 3 vols. Shanghai: Shanghai guji chubanshe, 1989.

Zhang Binglin 章炳麟(Zhang Taiyan 章太炎, 1868–1936). *Wenshi* 文始 (Genesis of *Wen*). Taipei: Taiwan Zhonghua shuju, 1970.

Zhang Dainian 張岱年. *Zhongguo zhexue dagang* 中國哲學大綱 (A General Outline of Chinese Philosophy). Beijing: Zhongguo shehui kexue chubanshe, 1982.

Zhang Juzheng 張居正 (1525–1593), ed. *Lunyu zhijie* 論語直解 (Straightforward Interpretations of *Analects*). Zhizhong xue jianyi edn.

Zhang Shaokang 張少康. *Zhongguo gudai wenxue chuangzuo lun* 中國古代文學創作論 (Theories of Literary Creation in Ancient China). Taipei: Wenshizhe chubanshe, 1991.

Zhang Taiyan 章太炎. See under Zhang Binglin 章炳麟.

Zhong Hong 鐘嶸 (469–518). *Shi pin zhu* 詩品注 (*Grading of Poets,* with Annotations). Ed. Chen Yanjie 陳延傑. Beijing: Renmin wenxue chubanshe, 1980.

Zhongguo meixueshi ziliao xuanbian 中國美學史資料選編 (Anthology of Documents in the History of Chinese Aesthetics). Ed. Beijing Daxue zhexuexi. 2 vols. Beijing: Zhonghua shuju, 1980.

Zhou li zhushu 周禮注疏 (Commentary on the *Rituals of Zhou*). Annot. Zheng Xuan 鄭玄 (127–200). In *SSJZ.*

Zhou yi yinde 周易引得 (A Concordance to *Yi Ching* [*Yi jing*]). Harvard-Yenching Insitute Sinological Index Series, supplement no. 10. Rpt. Taipei: Chinese Materials and Research Aids Service Center, 1966.

Zhou yi zhengyi 周易正義. Commentary by Wang Bi 王弼 (226–249) and annotation by Kong Yingda. In *SSJZ.*

Zhou Zhenfu 周振甫. *Wenxin diaolong zhushi* 文心雕龍注釋 (Commentaries and Explanations of *Wenxin diaolong*). Beijing: Remin wenxue chubanshe, 1981.

Zhu Guangqian 朱光潛 (1897–1986). *Shilun* 詩論 (On Poetry). Shanghai: Zhengzhong shuju, 1948.

Zhu Jia 祝嘉. *Shuxue shi* 書學史 (A History of the Studies of Calligraphy). Rpt. Chengdu: Sichuan guji shudian, 1984.

Zhu Liangzhi 朱良志. "Lun Zhongguo gudai meixue zhong di 'xujing' shuo" 論中國古美學中的虛靜說 (On the Theory of "Emptiness and Stillness" in Traditional Chinese Aesthetics). *Gudai wenxue lilun yanjiu* 古代文學理論研究 (Studies on Classical [Chinese] Literary Theory) 15 (1991), pp. 30–50.

Zhu Renfu 朱仁夫. *Zhongguo gudai shufa shi* 中國古代書法史 (History of Ancient Chinese Calligraphy). Beijing: Beijing daxue chubanshe, 1992.

Zhu Rongzhi 朱榮智. *Wenqi yu wenzhang chuangzuo guanxi yanjiu* 文氣與文章創作關係研究 (Studies on Literary *Qi* and the Process of Literary Composition). Taipei: Shida shuyuan, 1988.

Zhu Xi 朱熹 (1130–1200), ed. *Lunyu jizhu* 論語集注 (Collected Commentaries to *Analects*). *SSBY* edn.

Zhu Yingping 朱迎平, ed. *Wenxin diaolong suoyin* 文心雕龍索引 (Indexes to *Wenxin diaolong*). Shanghai: Shanghai guji chubanshe, 1987.

Zhu Ziqing 朱自清 (1898–1948). *Shi yan zhi bian* 詩言志辨 (An Analysis of "Poetry Expresses the Intent"). Beijing: Guji chubanshe, 1956.

Zhuang Zi 莊子 (fl. 369 B.C.). See under Guo Qingfan 郭慶藩.

Zong Baihua 宗白華. *Meixue sanbu* 美學散步 (A Promenade in Aesthetics). Shanghai: Shanghai renmin chubanshe, 1981.

———. "Zhongguo shufa li di meixue sixiang" 中國書法里的美學思想 (Aesthetic Ideas in Chinese Calligraphy). In his *Meixue sanbu,* pp. 135–160.

Index

"Great Plan" ("Hong fan"), 86
"Great Preface to the *Book of Poetry*"
("Shi daxu"), 2, 69, 85, 98, 105;
compared with earlier statements
on poetry, 49; four functions of
poetry, 47–49; and "Record of
Music," 45–46, 269n. 49, 277n. 41;
and *Wenxin diaolong*, 49–50. *See
also* Confucian moral harmony;
Confucius' concept of literature
Greene, William C., 11
Guan Dao advocates. See *"Wen yi
guan Dao"*
Guan Zi, 243
Guo Xiang, 224
Guo yu. See *Speeches of the States*
Guwen yundong (Ancient Prose
movement), 61

Hass, William, 244
Hall, David L., 139
Han Tingjie, 232
Han Yu, 60, 130, 183
Hanfei Zi, 65
Hartman, Geoffrey, 28
He Jingming, 64
heart's intent (*zhi*), 39; English
translation of, 264n. 6
Hegel, Georg Wilhelm Friedrich, 106,
226
Heidegger, Martin, 212, 235
Herbert, George, 191
Hesiod, 11
"Hongfan." *See* "Great Plan"
Horace, 9
Huang Di (Yellow Emperor), 198
Huang Kan, 123, 130
Hui Jiao, 216
Husserl, Edmund, 20–21, 25
hymns (*song*), 48

idea-image (*yixiang*), 56
idea-scape (*yijing*), 246
Images (*xiang*), 91–92, 219; relation-

ship with ideas (*yi*) and words
(yan), 93–94. *See also* "Great
Commentary"
Ingarden, Roman: compared with
Wellek and Warren's views, 23–24;
stratified literary structure, 21–22;
Wellek and Warren's insufficient
acknowledgment of their debt
to, 23. *See also* phenomenological
criticism
intracultural perspective, 3, 239–241,
313n. 3
Iser, Wolfgang, 25–26
investigate things (*gewu*), 139

Ji Zang, 204
Ji Zha: comments on the *Book of
Poetry*, 40–42
Jiao Hong, 64
Jiao Xun, 65
"Jin *Zishuo* biao." *See* "Memorial
on the Submission of *Discourse
on Characters*"
Jinendrabuddhi, 216
Jise zong (School of Matter as It Is), 223
junzi (gentleman), 114; Confucius'
ideal of, 116–117

Kant, Immanuel, 106, 226
King Jing, 43
King Li, 78
King You, 78
Kong Anguo, 123
Kong Yingda, 36, 39
Kui, 35

Lady Wei Shuo, 189, 200
langue / parole dichotomy: as basis
of structuralist binarisms, 23; and
deconstruction, 28; and Saussure,
26. *See also* deconstructive criti-
cism; structuralist criticism
Lao Zi. See *Classic of the Way and its
Power, The (Dao de jing)*

About the Author

Zong-qi Cai is associate professor of Chinese and comparative literature at the University of Illinois, Urbana-Champaign. He is the author of *The Matrix of Lyric Transformation: Poetic Modes and Self-Presentation in Early Chinese Pentasyllabic Poetry* (Michigan, 1996) and the editor of *A Chinese Literary Mind: Culture, Creativity, and Rhetoric in Wenxin diaolong* (Stanford, 2001).